Broken Bonds

Broken Bonds

What Family Fragmentation Means for America's Future

Mitch Pearlstein

ROWMAN & LITTLEFIELD
Lanham • Boulder • New York • London

Published by Rowman & Littlefield
A wholly owned subsidiary of The Rowman & Littlefield Publishing Group, Inc.
4501 Forbes Boulevard, Suite 200, Lanham, Maryland 20706
www.rowman.com

16 Carlisle Street, London W1D 3BT, United Kingdom

British Library Cataloguing in Publication Information Available

Library of Congress Cataloging-in-Publication Data

Pearlstein, Mitchell B., 1948-
Broken bonds : what family fragmentation means for America's future / Mitch Pearlstein.
pages cm
Includes bibliographical references and index.
ISBN 978-1-4422-3663-9 (cloth : alk. paper) -- ISBN 978-1-4422-3664-6 (electronic)
1. Families--United States--History--21st century. 2. Interpersonal relations--United States. I. Title.
HQ536.P3787 2014
306.850973--dc23
2014008096

™ The paper used in this publication meets the minimum requirements of American National Standard for Information Sciences Permanence of Paper for Printed Library Materials, ANSI/NISO Z39.48-1992.

Printed in the United States of America

For children who arrive in this world on the wrong side of Lottery Roads.

Contents

Acknowledgments

When a person writes about the biggest domestic problem facing his country, his gratitude for the people aiding his efforts ought to be big, too. They are. I start with profound thanks to one of the most talented groups of men and women I've ever worked with, the book's forty respondents, who were uniformly generous with their insights and time when I came calling, from California to northeast of the New York island, with questions such as: "At the risk of melodrama, what do you think the United States might come to look like when you take your last breath?" And there were hard questions, too.

As I note in the introduction, the respondents did not represent a scientific sample, only a brilliant one. They were a perfect group for what I might describe as a qualitative exercise in academically informed journalism. It was a pleasure visiting with every one of them face to face, coast to coast, and home in Minnesota.

Toward the end of the interviews in late 2013, I had the good fortune of visiting the staff and nationally drawn Research Advisory Group of the Oklahoma Marriage Initiative in Oklahoma City. The OMI is regularly recognized as the best such program in the nation, and while I was there for just a few days, it was easy to see why, starting with their hospitality. Much obliged.

Lugging two pocket-sized recorders around the country may not be physically challenging, but I can say without question this project would have been fiscally impossible without the support of the Lynde and Harry Bradley Foundation, the Chiaroscuro Foundation, the LML & FTL Lanners Foundation, Karen and Mahlon Schneider, and others. Thank you for your faith.

This is not the first book of mine for which Beverly Hermes has transcribed interviews, upward of four thousand pages and counting. Simply put, I can't imagine anyone better at her craft or more enjoyable to work with. On further thought, make that I can't imagine anyone *as* terrific at her craft. I extend my ongoing thanks to her.

My American Experiment colleague Peter Nelson turned the digitally recorded interviews into CDs and then sent them off to Beverly, once again never losing a word along the way. I readily concede I wouldn't have had a clue how to do it myself. My appreciation to him as well as to Britt Drake, another American Experiment colleague, who, in addition to once again leading the way with formatting, electronically carved out and sent hundreds of separate excerpts to the respondents so that they might review how I had quoted and paraphrased them.

Great thanks as well to another American Experiment colleague, Peter Zeller, for getting me from city to city as cheaply as possible, driven as he is at playing Orbitz against Travelocity against Expedia against Priceline against Kayak and who knows what else. My debt to old friend and Senior Fellow Kent Kaiser for constructing an especially helpful index for the book, and to Anne Mason for leading the way in promoting it every which way across the continent.

As for the rest of the staff and our board of directors, everyone contributed if only by doggedly *not* barking, "Aren't you done yet?"

This is the second book of mine that Rowman & Littlefield has published; the third, actually, if we include an anthology about the fatherhood movement that I coedited sixteen years ago along with Wade Horn and David Blankenhorn. I've been proud to be associated with R & L and its imprints each time, and I'm particularly thankful this time around to Jon Sisk, Ben Verdi, Laura Reiter, Gene Margaritondo, and Sarah Stanton.

This likewise is at least the third book in which I've gratefully noted that I do much of my writing at my neighborhood Caribou Coffee. Yes, I have an office at Center of the American Experiment and another one at home, but something about the Caribou at Forty-Sixth and Nicollet in south Minneapolis strings out the best words in me. In addition to the better-than-Starbucks coffee, it must be all the hospitable human beans there.

And then there is my wife, the Rev. Diane Darby McGowan, who, in a book such as this, is implicitly the North Star, as how could I ever have the nerve to write about the importance and joys of marriage if I weren't in a very good one myself? I couldn't and wouldn't.

I'm writing these last paragraphs in our kitchen, as the two of us have just finished dinner. She went upstairs to rest, as she's had a taxing day, having visited a doctor who had drawn blood, albeit not much but not on purpose either. Somewhere between the chicken and broccoli, I was struck by the sequence of the previous half-dozen hours. We had seen the doctor together (don't worry; she'll live). We had driven home together. She had watched a recorded episode of *Downton Abbey* as I worked elsewhere in the house. And then we reconnected for dinner—no television this time but certainly wine.

The term "quality time" is more frequently used in talking about parents and children than it is used in talking about husbands and wives. Either way, I've never liked it very much, as it can suggest a need to seek orchestrated and "meaningful" moments rather than simpler daily kinds. Excitements and extravaganzas have their place, but a really good time for me—being the measured but ultimately romantic guy I am—is simple and warm time together.

A loving thank you to Diane and the rest of our family and friends for simple and warm times together. In ways you don't know, you've given life to this book. And to me.

Minneapolis
March 2014

Introduction

> They talked about slow declines, not fast ones. They saw a future America suffering the kinds of troubles we currently have, only more so. A place where have-nots have a harder time becoming haves. They imagined the United States as still the world's leader, but perhaps not. Still an economically successful nation, but a less innovative one. They assumed a less-unified America with whiffs of unraveling.
>
> —Selected views of respondents in *Broken Bonds*

Whatever one might think about the state of mobility or economic inequality in the United States, however one might gauge their harm or benignity, I assume very few people would relish participating in the current job market weighed down by poor academic and occupational skills. For present purposes, I trust that's all the agreement we need to adequately appreciate the nature and size of the problem we confront: the lastingly hard and angering grind facing millions of men and women as long as their marketable skills remain weak. But as decades of empirical research continue to show, weak skills and other shortcomings are precisely what very large numbers of young people growing up in fragmenting families are disproportionately entering the job market with, if they enter it at all.[1]

Or, if you will, in order to adequately recognize the giant problem before us, one need not argue over arcane statistical questions about exactly how much mobility has slowed or if it has, in fact, done so in deep or dangerous ways. We need not fight over the extent to which we've become increasingly unequal economically; nor debate whether our nation's fundamental decency has been corrupted by the superrich's exploitation of amenable tax policies; nor hunker down in ideological bunkers; nor mix it up over anything similarly contentious. Rather, all one need do is recognize how rampant family fragmentation is leading to huge numbers of boys and girls growing up in single-parent homes, where they learn less and are shortchanged in other ways when compared to fellow young citizens who are fortunate enough to grow up with both their biological parents under the same roof.

So that we may all at least start off on the same page, I presume that, whatever philosophical or methodological disagreements various scholars, columnists, and other opinion leaders might have regarding what's going on with quartiles and quintiles, just about everyone agrees this is one of the most difficult times in our country's history to support oneself, much less one's family, without strong and relevant job skills—skills increasingly born of a good education.

This book is a follow-up to one I wrote three years ago, *From Family Collapse to America 's Decline : The Educational , Economic , and Social Costs of Family Fragmentation,* whose core argument is that huge family-breakdown rates in the United States—possibly the highest in the industrial world[2] —are leading to weakened educational and job skills among growing numbers of young and not-so-young people, which in turn are leading, and can *only* lead, to deepening class divisions in a nation that has never viewed or understood itself in such splintered ways. As to what such a more-demarcated America might come to look like, I suggested in that book that it wouldn't be pretty, but I didn't go much beyond that, as I never attempted to paint any future national portrait. Doing that—at least sketching with some rigor what we might come to look like and *be*—is the not-modest aim of this new effort. At this current book's heart are interviews with forty accomplished and well-informed men and women who live in areas stretching from Boston, New York, and Washington in the East to Olympia, Palo Alto, and San Francisco in the West.

Fear of offending politically correct, as well as more-legitimate, sensibilities is what has kept many observers from adequately acknowledging the scope and costs of family fragmentation. Most people, unsurprisingly, are loath to risk being called dirty names, especially "sexist" and most especially "racist," with "homophobe" having risen rapidly as a slander of choice. ("Classist" has fallen to a distant fourth, as it has never taken hold as anything fearsome.) When it comes to considering the ways in which fragmentation, in particular, will continue contributing to harder class demarcations, most observers over the last two generations have kept determinedly quiet, surely for similar reasons. But in this instance, an additional factor is a lack of pertinent imagination on the part of most men and women, as speculating seriously about the future is intellectual heavy lifting of an elusively airy sort. If academics, for instance, are usually not inclined to say anything publicly about something in a field or subfield other than their narrow own, expecting sizable numbers of them (or others) to say anything out loud about the very nature of the United States years ahead is asking quite a bit. This is another way of saying that I'm indebted to interviewees for boldly sharing their thoughts and insights about the contours of American maps, both current and decades from now.

A core assumption of the book is the centrality of marriage. Charles Murray is right when he writes, "Over the last half century, marriage has become the fault line dividing American classes."[3] And if marriage doesn't rebound, also likely accurate is Kay Hymowitz's nightmarish vision of a "self-perpetuating single-mother proletariat on the one hand, and a self-perpetuating, comfortable middle class on the other. Not exactly," she writes, "what America should look like, is it?"[4] Hymowitz later came to be one of our forty respondents.

A related assumption of the book is that Americans, historically and generally speaking, have not spent exorbitant time or energy understanding the United States in the class-bound ways now developing. Needless to say, the United States has always had distinct social classes and all sensate citizens have known it. This has been reality even without taking into account imprisoned lives on plantations and many millions growing up on the other sides of thousands of tracks. But in a spirit of Tocqueville, from our country's very start we have downplayed class differences while accentuating the permeability of classes above. This has been wonderfully advantageous, but changes in family structure are undercutting this signature brand of American optimism and progress.

If the centrality of marriage is the book's main lens, its core challenge is viewing our nation's future measurably through it. This is another way of saying that yes, of course, many factors are implicit in every step of America's way forward. But when seeking to comprehend what's leading to hardening distances between and among classes, our interest is in focusing specifically on barely rivaled rates of family fragmentation as a principal cause. This is the book's assignment, again, since so many other observers have been so adamantly opposed to taking into account "family breakdown" when sizing up equal and unequal opportunities.

Admittedly, or I should say satisfyingly, there has been an increase in the amount written about inequality and mobility in the approximately twenty months from the time I began writing this introduction to the time I finished the conclusion. The same is true, although to a much lesser extent, in regard to how marriage, or its absence, figures in it all.[5] But these connections, between inequality and mobility on the one hand, and families and fragmentation on the other, have not been examined from nearly as many angles, by nearly as many acute observers, as is the case here.

For a perfect example of how matters of marriage have been side-stepped, consider "The Broken Contract" by George Packer, a passionate essay on growing income inequality in *Foreign Affairs*.[6] Shortly after declaring inequality "the ill that underlies all others," as it's like an "odorless gas" pervading "every corner of the United States," sapping the strength of our democracy along the way, Packer concludes the piece by itemizing how inequality will "continue to mock the American premise of opportunity for all." Here's an excerpt:

> Inequality divides us from one another in schools, in neighborhoods, at work, on airplanes, in hospitals, in what we eat, in the condition of our bodies, in what we think, in our children's future, in how we die. Inequality makes it harder to imagine the lives of others—which is one reason why the fate of over 14 million or so permanently unemployed Americans leaves so little impression on the country's political and media capitals. Inequality erodes trust among fellow citizens, making it seem as if the game is rigged.

This represents only about a third of Packer's detailed recitation of the possible costs of growing differences in income and wealth. Yet, how many times in the essay does Packer cite the unprecedented fragmentation of American families as a cause, no matter how partial or small? Zero—he doesn't mention it once.[7]

Or consider an Associated Press story (in the Minneapolis *Star Tribune*) with the headline "Demographic Changes Are Amplifying Racial Inequities."[8] It cites that, in 2010 in the United States, 13.5 percent of Asian children, 18 percent of non-Hispanic white children, 34 percent of Hispanic children, 38 percent of Native American children, and 39.4 percent of black children were living in poverty. How many times was family fragmentation noted in this recitation as any factor whatsoever? Zero once more.

Or consider President Barack Obama's major speech on inequality in December 2013.[9] Here is the lone passage dealing with "single-parent households" or "absent fathers":

> The decades-long shifts in the economy have hurt all groups: poor and middle class; inner-city and rural folks; men and women; Americans of all races. And as a consequence, some of the social patterns that contribute to declining mobility that were once attributed to the urban poor—that's a particular problem for the inner-city: single-parent households or drug abuse—it turns out we're seeing that pop up everywhere. A new study shows that disparities in education, mental health, obesity, absent fathers, isolation from church, isolation from community groups—these gaps are now as much about growing up rich or poor as they are about anything else.

As a former speechwriter myself, I know an enticing speech (with interesting punctuation) when I hear or read one, and this was an enticing speech. For our purposes, however, most telling and disappointing in the way Obama viewed single parenthood and absent fathers is the way he saw them solely as consequences of growing inequality and tougher mobility rather than also as causes. Causation in his text goes one way only, and words such as "marriage" and "married," once again, never show up.

The same dynamic, as one might imagine, applies to widespread reluctance in journalistic and other circles when it comes to acknowledging the connection between the fall of marriage and the failure of academic achievement to rise. As I've noted before,[10] Richard Rothstein is one of the most important writers in the country arguing that significant progress in reducing achievement gaps is impossible so as long as "lower-class" (his term) students face so many social and cultural obstacles, starting with poverty. This is a fair and on-target point, and in real ways, a variation on what I've long argued. But there is also a huge difference. Hardly ever, for example, in his influential book *Class and Schools*[11] does he begin to consider the fact that the connection between epidemic family breakdown and incomes (among other shortcomings) is powerful. Never does he begin to acknowledge that rates of family fragmentation in the United States are higher than just about anyplace else. It's a remarkable omission, not that his blind spot is the least bit rare.

For example, the highest profile education book in 2013 probably was Diane Ravitch's *Reign of Error : The Hoax of the Privatization Movement and the Danger to America 's Public Schools*. Is there anything in it about how family fragmentation has been known to affect students' academics? No.[12]

For contrast, compare Packer's, Obama's, Rothstein's, and Ravitch's incomplete approaches with this more candid and accurate one, in a 2013 speech, by a first-term senator from Utah, Mike Lee: "The fact is, the problem of poverty in America is directly linked to family breakdown and the erosion of marriage among low-income families and communities. Implicit marriage penalties in our tax code and welfare programs surely need legislative remedies. But what we're really talking about is a question of culture, not policy incentives."[13]

Putting aside the hyperactive fears many have when it comes to possibly giving offense, it's hard to understand how so many writers are incapable of typing words such as "marriage" or "fathers." This is especially the case since eloquent and forceful ideas about families are by no means wholly owned by scholars and other thought leaders on the Right.[14] For example, take political philosopher Bill Galston, for decades one of the Democratic Party's intellectual guiding lights and one of President Clinton's most important advisers. "The weakening of families," he has written, is "fraught with danger for liberal societies."

> [S]trong families rest on specific virtues. Without fidelity, stable families cannot be maintained. Without a concern for children that extends well beyond the boundaries of adult self-regard, parents cannot effectively discharge their responsibility to help form secure, self-reliant young people. In short, the independence required for liberal social life rests on self-restraint and self-transcendence—the virtues of family solidarity.[15]

Or as the libertarian Charles Murray might vary the theme: "[F]amilies with children are the core around which American communities must be organized—must, because families with children have always been, and still are, the engine that makes American communities work."[16]

In rounded numbers, about 40 percent of American babies are currently born outside of marriage. This breaks down to almost 30 percent of non-Hispanic white girls and boys, more than 50 percent of Hispanic children, and more than 70 percent of African American children. All these numbers are substantially higher in inner cities and other low-income communities, as well as higher among women and men with less than four-year college degrees.[17]

As for divorce, calculating rates is harder than most people assume, if, indeed, anyone assumes anything about it at all. Nevertheless, we do know that divorce rates have been reasonably stable since the 1980s, after having exploded in the two decades prior. Even better, divorce rates have been decreasing among well-educated couples. But even with this good news, it's still estimated that between 40 percent and 50 percent of first-time married couples in the United States divorce.[18] Improvement or not, this is still a terribly high number. Moreover, there has been a stunning increase in cohabitation—relationships, which by virtual definition, especially in the United States, are shorter-lived than marriages—in recent decades.

And there are telling but frequently overlooked data pertaining to the percentage of American boys and girls living with only one (or none) of their parents in any particular year. In 2009, for example, 75 percent of white, non-Hispanic children and 86 percent of Asian children lived with two parents. This was in comparison to 67 percent of Hispanic children and only 37 percent of black children. But keep in mind that significant numbers of two-parent teams are actually composed of a biological parent and a stepparent, or a biological parent and an adoptive parent. For instance, in 2009 again, among black children living with two parents, only 79 percent lived with both their biological mother and biological father. Completing the point, stepfamilies can be hard on children. They can be hard on everyone involved, in fact.[19]

This is an apt spot to also note that among the nearly 60 percent of American men and women with high school degrees but not four-year college degrees, nonmarital birthrates, marriage rates, and divorce rates are increasingly resembling those of lower-income Americans rather than those of better-educated and more-affluent fellow citizens, as was more likely the case only a few decades ago.[20]

But yes, finally, there is (qualified) good news to be found. For instance, birthrates for girls and young women aged fifteen to nineteen have been going down for most of the last two decades, with the drop between 2007 and 2011 an amazing 25 percent. Overall, the teen birthrate in 2011 was at an all-time low of 31.1 per 1,000 teenagers.[21] By no means should this progress be gainsaid. Still, these good and encouraging numbers can't erase the fact that since marriage is close to absent in these situations, an enormously high proportion of children, born quite frequently to children themselves, will try to grow up minus one of their parents, usually their father.

Add up all the "churning" (as sociologist Andrew Cherlin aptly puts it), and it's dismayingly fair to say the United States just about leads the world in such bad news. This is the case despite our country's many virtues and advantages—paradoxically including unusually high levels of religious observance.

Also, before going on, I'd like to insert a quick note on the term "family fragmentation" itself. I'm not certain how it has come to be the favored term of art in academic and other quarters, over "family breakdown," although I've recently heard it may have been inspired by the invaluable cultural historian Barbara Dafoe Whitehead, though she demurs at the attribution. Whitehead is another one of our respondents. Granted, the term does a better job of alluding to families that never fully form in the first place. And humanely, it also connotes less personal failure than do references to "breakdown." On the other side of the semantic ledger, however, "fragmentation" inaccurately connotes less danger to society than does "breakdown," which is "unfortunate," as they say in diplomatic circles. Nevertheless, in keeping with current usage, I'll rely mostly on "family fragmentation" but will frequently use "family breakdown" for stylistic reasons. Effectively, they're synonymous.

A frequent and unsurprising criticism of my emphasis on family fragmentation is that, while it's doubtless contributing to growing income inequality and constrained mobility in the United States, it's only one of several reasons why large segments of Americans are increasingly living in separate worlds, and frankly (goes the charge), it's not as consequential a factor as I have long claimed. For causes and culprits bigger than fragmentation, goes the counterargument, think of those damn money manipulators on Wall Street. Or tax cuts disproportionately benefitting the rich. Or the weakening of private-sector labor unions. Or job-eating technological advances. Or cheap labor in Asia. Fine, if those are someone's preferences.

But nowhere in my argument is there blindness, willful or otherwise, to the many nonfamily disuniting factors at play not just in the United States but elsewhere in the world. In fact, I have no major disagreement with a brilliant analysis by George Friedman that claims that millions of workers started getting seriously hurt when American corporations, in order to regain efficiencies and remain afloat, started getting "re-engineered" in the vicinity of the 1980s. Such restructurings succeeded in creating substantial value, though, obviously, not for those who had been laid off. While some new value flowed to the remaining workers, "much of it went to the engineers who restructured the companies and the investors they represented."[22]

I also agree with this hard-to-argue-against excerpt regarding Tea Partiers and Occupiers from journalist E. J. Dionne's *Our Divided Political Heart : The Battle for the American Idea in an Age of Discontent*: "In the broadest sense," he writes, both centrifugal movements "were the products of anger unleashed by the country's economic troubles and the anxiety created by fears of American decline. Both spoke in angry tones. In quite different ways, both condemned the bailouts of bankers and financiers." With even protest movements "subject to cultural sorting: the Tea Party expressed its rage by reaching back to older right-wing views. Occupy Wall Streeters to some of the protest traditions of the left."[23]

Also hard to argue with are many of the observations of another journalist, Bill Bishop, whose book, *The Big Sort*, Dionne cites several times. "Political divisions today," Bishop writes, "are as much a result of values and lifestyles as they are of income and occupation. And with those divisions has come a pervasive and growing separation. Americans segregate themselves into their own political worlds, blocking out discordant voices and surrounding themselves with reassuring news and companions."[24]

Notwithstanding the various and powerful ways in which family makeup reflects as well as shapes the "values and lifestyles" Bishop writes about, both he and Dionne are right in detailing the many political, economic, media, and other factors not tied to marriage in any significant way that are putting miles between and among classes and other groups. But then, in a metaphoric and telling next breath, Bishop writes of how one of his interviewees, who grew up in a small town near Dallas, had been "shocked by a rape and a rash of pregnancies at his high school" and had "blamed Dallas," which he saw as "reaching out to touch his hometown." Bishop's interviewee then spoke of how, when he later moved north for work, "he decided to distance himself from all things citified." The obvious implication was that "citified" entailed "race" among other things.

This anecdote aligns with a passage in a book by Elijah Anderson, another respondent and one of our nation's most perceptive ethnographers in matters of race. In a study of on-the-ground life in Philadelphia, and immediately after describing how strangers tend to keep their distance from young African American males, Anderson writes this about young African American females: "The young black woman with children in tow triggers another set of stereotypes. This figure is simultaneously pitied and despised, rather than simply feared; she is imagined simultaneously as downtrodden and overly assertive, burdened by motherhood yet hypersexualized. Respectable she is not."[25] This is another example of how the disintegration of marriage in many places is contributing to our country's fracturing.

Our analytic starting point is the serious degree to which family fragmentation diminishes educational achievement (what kids actually learn) and educational attainment (at a minimum, whether they graduate high school). This, in turn, has great bearing on where they later wind up on income ladders: Do they land on a low rung early on but remain there only temporarily as they work their way up, as young people usually do? Or do they start on a low rung and pretty much stay bolted there for the rest of their working lives?

Such connections between family fragmentation on the one hand and how children do educationally and years later in life on the other hand can be summed up concisely if harshly: I know of no aspect of life in which children who grow up in broken or never-formed two-parent families do as well, on average, as boys and girls who grow up with both their parents. By "no aspect of life," I mean to encompass a roster of bad things that can happen to young people, as well as the many bad things they often inflict on themselves (and others), making their lives poorer and tougher: drug abuse, criminal behavior, mental illness, physical illness, early sexual initiation, and more, all in addition to and often emanating from educational shortcomings.

The book of mine mentioned earlier, *From Family Collapse to America 's Decline*, deals at length with family fragmentation's effects on learning, so I'll refrain from retracing that evidence here.[26] But to give a sense of how the dynamic continues to play out for many African American girls and boys in particular, a 2010 report by the Educational Testing Service, *The Black-White Achievement Gap : When Progress Stopped*, provides one of the most judicious analyses I know. The two authors, Paul E. Barton and

Richard J. Coley, take proper pains in talking about the full gamut of reasons why disproportionate numbers of black boys and girls do so poorly academically, citing, among other things, very high incarceration rates among African Americans; continuing reverberations from the explosion of crack use several decades ago; immense differences between African Americans and others not just in income but also in wealth; "poisonous music"; students' fears of being accused of "acting white" if they work hard and do well in school; too much crime; too few strong and stabilizing churches; and not-very-good schools, often with not-very-good teachers. But Barton and Coley are also compelled to write, "It's very hard to imagine progress resuming in reducing the educational attainment and achievement gap without turning these family trends around," by which they mean progress likely won't resume in this area without "increasing marriage rates and getting fathers back into the business of nurturing children." The very idea, they argue, of a "substitute for the institution of marriage for raising children is almost unthinkable," although in fairness they do add that "stronger support for the family is not."[27] I trust I need not point out that problems such as immense incarceration rates, immense differences in both income and wealth, and being forced to raise children in terrible neighborhoods are, themselves, the products, at least partially, of the demise of marriage especially in inner cities across the country.

The next dots to be connected are between matters of marriage and education on the one hand and economic mobility on the other. Isabel Sawhill has long been one of my preferred economists in regard to such issues for a variety of reasons, which very much include her leadership in creating the National Campaign to Prevent Teen and Unplanned Pregnancies. Here are three points she made in 2010: (1) income in the United States is less equally distributed than it was several years ago; (2) income is more correlated with education than it had been; and (3) it's also more correlated with family structure than it had been. Even if parental income were not tied to children's success (she acknowledges that it is, of course), Sawhill writes we would still have "good reasons to believe that the particular form of income inequality we have experienced in the U.S. has set the stage for the greater persistence of class in the future."[28]

To complete this portion of sequencing, let's turn to one of the more important books in recent years on mobility's slowdown, Timothy

Noah's *The Great Divergence : America 's Growing Inequality Crisis and What We Can Do about It.*

Noah's basic argument is that the United States is increasingly becoming a nation of haves and have-nots, with the top 1 percent now collecting about 21 percent of all income, which is more than double its share in the late 1970s. Another way of grasping this growing "divergence" is coming to uncomfortable grip, for example, with how rising from poverty here, Noah contends, has come to be harder than in almost any comparable nation, with income distribution, moreover, now more unequal in the United States than in various places sometimes slurred as "oligopolistic Banana Republics."

While I have no interest in getting into an economic "he said/he said," please note that Scott Winship of the Brookings Institution points out that the "median household in the U.S. is twice as rich as it was in 1960, at the peak of the supposed 'Golden Age' of the American middle class." Yet then again, he also writes, "[T]he degree of income inequality we have in the U.S. is truly mind boggling." This is the case even though "that fact tells us nothing about whether inequality is problematic."[29]

Please also note that in determining who has what, many of the reports showing up in newspapers do not factor in the kinds of cash, food, medical, rent, energy, and other supports low-income people receive from government. As statistical oversights go, this is not a small one. Also, economist Thomas Sowell writes that mobility studies usually ignore immigrants, who are indeed moving up.[30]

Noah, who is a very good and prolific journalist, argues that single parenthood's "contribution to the Great Divergence must be judged minimal because it increased mostly before 1980, when the Great Divergence was just getting under way."[31] Nonetheless, he rightly acknowledges that 40 percent of single-parent families have incomes below the poverty line as compared to only 8 percent of two-income households. (The proportion is a full 50 percent of single-parent homes if those "near poverty" are included.) And he cites two respected economists, Claudia Goldin and Jane Katz, who "calculate that the increase in economic return to education is responsible for about 60 percent of the increase in wage inequality between 1973 and 2005."[32] I would just note once more the connections between family structure and educational performance.

Adding it all up, while Noah obviously isn't oblivious to family fragmentation's reach, he doesn't focus on it nearly as much as I do in regard to the further splintering of Americans from one another. Though, for the sake of argument, let's assume he's right and I'm overstating. Key, though, from my perspective is not only how fragmentation leads to quintile and quartile changes of one kind or another but also how it's hurting in-the-flesh boys and girls who disproportionately do poorly in school and in other ways—and who then wind up, short years later, doing commensurately poorly occupationally.

Or, if you will, I'm less interested in how family breakdown is responsible for an "x" or "y" fraction of mobility loss. Rather, my emphasis is on how family breakdown is inherently shortchanging millions of kids, making it extra hard for them to eventually succeed economically and in other spheres of life, such as becoming marriageable in the loving, but realistically demanding, eyes of possible spouses.

With all that said, I return to the book's fundamental question: what might the United States come to look like with starker class divisions, provoked in consequential part by high rates of family fragmentation compounded by an increasingly unforgiving economic environment (a worldwide jobs market, more to the point, where, unless Americans bring reasonably decent educations and demonstrably strong skills to the table, their chances of success, measured not just in paystubs, are weaker than ever before)?

The heart of *Broken Bonds* is a detailed analysis of what a sizable group of men and women said in interviews, with interplay between their views and my own. "Interplay" means that readers should not have a hard time figuring out what I believe about most matters, though clear-cut emphasis is on respondents and their opinions: forty Americans who made their respective cases in thirty-five interviews, averaging somewhat more than an hour each and conducted between November 2012 and November 2013. (Four of the five interviews with two people involved husbands and wives.) These interviewees definitely don't constitute a scientific sample, and to the extent they're representative of any particular demographic, it's of unusually well-educated and thoughtful citizens who, frankly put, are better suited and practiced than are most in addressing the kinds of complex and conceptual societal, familial, and policy matters dissected here.

More specifically, twenty-five are men and fifteen are women (see appendix 1). Seven are African American, Hispanic, or Native American.

Most hold graduate or professional degrees, with their mean age north of fifty. A majority reside somewhere between Massachusetts and Virginia on the East Coast, or somewhere between Washington State, California, and Arizona on the West Coast.[33] While a case can be made that the group leans mildly right, it also contains celebrated feminist scholars such as Stephanie Coontz and Elaine Tyler May, economists Glenn Loury and Isabel Sawhill, ethnography and social work professors Elijah Anderson and Ron Mincy, and esteemed Democratic public servants Judge Bruce Peterson and Don and Arvonne Fraser. National Public Radio's Krista Tippett is also in the mix, as is family psychologist William Doherty, as is C. Peter Magrath, who has served as president of four universities. The plan was to interview some of the smartest people I know (or hoped to know), and to my good fortune, I succeeded even better than I thought I might.

Instead of using a conventional questionnaire in which everyone is asked the same question in the same order, I used what sociologist John Lofland has described as "intensive interviewing with an interview guide."[34] Or what I describe as "going with the flow of semi-structured interviews bordering on conversations." With variations, this is the fourth time I've used this method, the first time with my dissertation at the University of Minnesota thirty-four years ago and with two other books more recently. In each previous instance, sessions were audio recorded and then transcribed resulting in anywhere from about 850 pages to about 1,400 pages of double-spaced transcripts. The number this time around was again about 1,400 pages. As for what one does with so much information, the answer is to ferret out, as meticulously as possible, insights, agreements, disagreements, ironies, and various other patterns and intriguing findings by—more figuratively than literally, but not by much—taking up residence in the data.

By actively recruiting some of the most impressive and influential public intellectuals, policy leaders, and other leading players across the country, I knew I would have great and quotable grist with which to work. What I did not anticipate was just how good and quotable much of that grist would be. Starting about halfway through the interviews, I increasingly realized I was "sitting on gold," to borrow a cliché, and that I was intellectually obliged to make the very best use of it. I think I've come really close to doing so.

A central point needs to be made about approach. As I noted above, to expect people to imagine in any detail what the United States might come to look like decades from now is to expect quite a bit, as speculating can be hard work and accurately predicting many times harder. Interviews in which people are asked, right at the top, what they think the United States will come to look like years hence might routinely end very early, as many, maybe most, men and women likely would quickly run out of things to say. Or they simply would not have enough confidence to share what they thought, especially if the interviewer used a recorder. (I actually used two to be on the safe side.)

Key to sidestepping this limitation is a fundamental assumption of the book: current societal problems that are cited by respondents and that are at least partially caused by family fragmentation are much more likely to get worse than better. This is the case because problems resulting from fragmentation tend to reinforce themselves. Or as respondent Barbara Dafoe Whitehead put it, "Not only are there growing divisions as to who marries, leading to wildly diverging family lives for kids, but advantage replicates advantage and disadvantage is replicated generationally. That's why I'm worried."

Consider, for example, academic performance. Children born outside of marriage to poorly educated girls and young women disproportionately wind up poorly educated themselves. The same degenerative dynamic applies to crime, early sexual initiation, and many other areas, including poverty itself. So when I asked questions, for example, about whether respondents thought Americans in the main currently have an adequate sense of the actual lives lived by the children of incarcerated parents, and those respondents emphatically answered "no," it's not an ungrounded leap to conclude that Americans in the main likely still won't have an adequate sense of the actual lives of such children anytime in the foreseeable future, especially since it's hard to see what might intervene to cause them to sufficiently reduce their fears and expand their hearts. Bad things of all sorts are more likely to spiral down than up.

Or at the core of the conceptual matter, given who respondents are and what they know—exceptionally accomplished men and women who know a lot about a lot—chances are much better than even that their evaluations of current circumstances are reasonably on target.

Did I also ask less roundabout questions about what the United States might come to look like? Of course, as in this direct one posed at the end of conversations: "In sum, considering all we've been talking about as well as at the risk of melodrama, what do you think the United States might come to look like in the days of your last breath?" But such questions notwithstanding, it's certainly fair to say that much of the book builds on extrapolation.

Here's another example of the kind of reinforcing dynamic I'm talking about, this time as discussed by Professor Ron Mincy of Columbia University, one of the book's respondents. In answering the "last breath" question right above, he reported anticipating "really substantial levels of inequality, such that the income and other economic prospects of children who grow up with the support of both of their parents, and those who don't, will look very different." This is the case, he said, "because these are the kinds of things that get reinforced at many stages in human development: in terms of the quality of schooling they experience; in terms of their school readiness; and in terms of the ability of their parents to expose them to a variety of experiences that's going to get them into a good college."

The rest of the introduction quickly notes three essential caveats and introduces several main themes expressed by the more than three dozen respondents.[35]

The first caveat is the fact that millions of American kids currently growing up with only one parent are doing great, while millions of kids growing up under the best of circumstances are doing lousy. This is a big country, and family makeup is by no means certain destiny. Still, in a nation of well more than three hundred million people, "on average" can mean powerful troubles and sadness for many people.

The second caveat is that it's surely not my aim to be unfair or unkind to single mothers, or single fathers, or any noncustodial parents, though I recognize some people will have a hard time not interpreting my intentions and the book itself in those ways. My apologies in advance, though trust me when I say I appreciate how "stuff" often happens. Speaking geometrically, I'm often struck by how nonlinear, how dramatically roundabout most family sagas are.

And third, it's right and proper to note that I'm in my second marriage, as is my wife of twenty-two years, who was a single mother for a long time after her own divorce. I used to say that I was in my second and last marriage, but as I've said or written on every apt occasion since Diane corrected me, I'm in my second and *ultimate* marriage.

CHAPTER 1: "HOW BIG OF A PROBLEM?"

A good starting point is gauging the severity with which respondents view family fragmentation, making the following question usually the first thing I asked after exchanging pleasantries: "Getting to the core question, how big a problem would you rate family fragmentation in the United States as a whole?" While a relative few interviewees rated it as no more than a "six or seven on a scale of 10," or only *sometimes* a big problem, or sometimes not a problem at all, most men and women used terms such as "huge," "massive," or a "15 on a scale of 10."

What's most informative here is not any tallying of middling or extreme adjectives or big or small numbers, but rather the reasoning behind such evaluations, as succinctly captured, for instance, in a metaphor by writer Kay Hymowitz: "Family breakdown is the shadow behind all sorts of other problems that people are much more easily conversant about." Or as another writer, David Blankenhorn, put it, "It's the problem that drives so many other problems." Ron Mincy noted that "male fertility rates are much higher among men who have no capacity to support their kids." Political scientist Lawrence Mead calls fragmentation the "largest or second largest social problem in America." The only one he puts on the same level is declining levels of work, particularly among men. And Robert Woodson, founder of the Center for Neighborhood Enterprise, ranked fragmentation as "*the* most crucial issue in the United States today" and tied it directly to extraordinary increases in African American incarceration rates.

Stephanie Coontz, author of books such as *Marriage, A History* and *The Way We Never Were,* was one of the respondents who, without being blasé in the least, argued that gauging family fragmentation's severity nevertheless needs to be viewed in contingent terms, as in: "It depends how you define fragmentation and to what extent it's a symptom or a cause. I do see it as part of larger social problems, but not the most fundamental cause of those problems." As for myself, I've long said that extraordinarily high rates of family fragmentation in the United States constitute the "overwhelming social disaster of our time."

CHAPTER 2: "WHY ARE FAMILY FRAGMENTATION RATES SO HIGH?"

Respondents were not skimpy in giving reasons for why churning is so rampant in our country. Starting with the most conceptual and philosophical explanations, some interviewees talked about a weakening of the Judeo-Christian ethic as well as a rise in "hyper-individualism." Some decried what they saw as related declines in personal responsibility or simply a culture from which children need protection. Likewise, Peter Bell, chairperson of the American Refugee Committee, talked about how certain intellectuals "often provide intellectual cover for bad behavior." And many respondents criticized a widespread reluctance to be "judgmental."

In relation to this last point about people's unease in passing judgment, National Public Radio's Krista Tippett added this about her own divorce: "Everyone was incredibly supportive. I don't think everyone *should* have been so unquestionably supportive. Religious communities could have stepped in and said, 'What can we do?' 'How can we help?' 'You need to think about this.' Religious communities could do this in loving but honest ways."

Some respondents, generally on the right side of the aisle, focused on tax and other public policies, especially those pertaining to welfare, which, they claimed work as disincentives to marrying. Respondents on the left side of the aisle were more likely to cite fundamental economic changes that make it more difficult for men and women, but especially men, to support families. Think here of sociologist William Julius Wilson's argument about good paying jobs for low-skilled men leaving core cities—but applied continent-wide. A dotted line away, historian Elaine Tyler May argued that what would change the lives of a majority of Americans is a "political culture that valued the common good; one where society in the form of the government was understood to ensure the common good." Questions of race and racism also weaved through conversations such as these. And then there were arguments about how unsuccessful educational policies continue to be a very large part of many problems.

CHAPTER 3: "HOW WELL DO WE KNOW AND FEEL FOR EACH OTHER?"

This chapter draws mostly on questions about the extent to which respondents think that Americans in the main have a decent sense of the actual lives lived by poor people as well as the actual lives lived by adults who have been or who are currently incarcerated, and their children in each instance. As much as any set of questions, this one starts from the premise that whatever social conditions and perceptions are now the case, chances are strong they will worsen because the ills of family fragmentation, once again, often reinforce each other generationally.

So, for example, if one is of the mind that Americans, generally speaking, don't currently have a decent sense of the actual lives lived by adults and children who are disproportionately caught up in family troubles, it's hard to imagine Americans, generally speaking, having higher empathy quotients in the future. And strong doubt about the ability of more fortunate Americans to feel the pain of less-fortunate Americans is exactly what respondents reported nearly unanimously.

Bruce Peterson is a Hennepin County (Minneapolis) district judge. In response to a question about the degree to which average Americans have an adequate sense of what children of incarcerated parents contend with, he said this: "You know, I'm not sure *I* do and I see their parents all the time. I get secondhand reports from *Guardians ad Litem* and others, but I don't feel I have a sense of it."

Brown University's Glenn Loury spoke of sociologists and ethnographers "who go in communities and chronicle the random violence that populates the lives of people living in certain quarters of our society. The violent acts, including homicides. The amount of violence that goes on inside families. The amount of partner abuse and child abuse. I'm not sure," he completed the point, "people understand how chaotic, how stress-laden, how impoverished, in every sense of that word the lives of some of these people—who are our fellow citizens—are."

Another respondent talked of a "growing lack of solidarity and sense of awareness of what's going on between folks on the higher end of the economic ladder and those at the lower end whatever their race may be." And instead of speaking of Americans feeling empathy, other interviewees spoke of disdain, pity, and guilt.

CHAPTER 4: "STUCK IN PLACE?"

On one side of the ledger, a respondent said, "I sure see a lot of people pouring coffee," and another more starkly described current income disparities in the United States as "grotesque and unethical."

On the other side of the inequality ledger, historian Stephan Thernstrom argued that much of what is written about it in the United States is simply wrong, insofar as most studies look only at pretax income, when in fact our tax system is really quite progressive. So much so, he claims, that we look more like Germany, Norway, and Sweden than most people imagine. Another respondent, Lee McGrath of the Institute for Justice, rhetorically asked: "What do the wealthy do with their money? It's not sitting idly in bank accounts. In fact it's not in bank accounts at all. It's in investments and those investments are building things. Building factories. . . . They are employing people."

Economist Isabel Sawhill framed matters less sunnily: "Growing class divisions in America are not just divisions of income. It's not just income inequality. It's also gaps in family formation patterns and it's a matter of gaps in educational achievement. When you put all those things together, it seems to me we have a bifurcating society in which the children of very advantaged parents who are raised in stable families, who get good schooling, and who go on to be successful have very different life prospects than children who are born to single-parent families; usually to parents without much education, who don't do well in school, and who go on to have lot less success in life."

The aforementioned David Blankenhorn, a founder of both the fatherhood and marriage movements, generalized about lower-middle-class and working-class Americans in even dimmer terms: "They're not doing well. They're not doing well any way you want to measure it. Marriage is disintegrating for them. Their world is too much of one-parent homes, serial relationships, chaotic lives, educational failure, and shrinking horizons. And a sense that life on television, and life downtown, are doing one thing, while the American middle is increasingly resembling the poor when it comes to family formation patterns, which is contributing to this class divide."

But then there were comments like this by education scholar and prolific writer Chester E. (Checker) Finn Jr.: "There's still a welcome degree of social mobility for people who get educated and work hard. It's possible to get ahead. It's possible to get your kids ahead."

CHAPTER 5: "HOW WILL WE GOVERN?"

Moving to more explicit discussions about the future, I usually asked a series of questions toward the end of interviews about what respondents saw as government's future role as well as what they wanted that role to be. I also read them a short passage speculating about the possibility of some kind of "illiberal" movement (read "authoritarian," "fascist," "Marxist," or some other type) taking hold in the United States, provoked by the perhaps growing frustrations "out there" we had been talking about. What did interviewees think of its likelihood? No one expected anything of the kind any time soon, but that doesn't mean many respondents were pleased about the route they saw our nation taking.

Of the possible rise of an ugly order, Checker Finn said, "I don't know if what you're talking about leads then to a sort of fascistic or authoritarian outcome. It may just lead to Western Europe where everything is tolerated. Everything is permitted. There's not much economic growth. There's not much ambition. There's not much vigor or dynamism in society. But there is, God knows, tolerance of everybody doing everything, and the welfare system keeps you from suffering the consequences of your own folly."

It's fair to say most respondents were not enthused about government expanding its job description in the ways implied by one interviewee who lamented the "absolute refusal of Americans to make long-term investments" and who "despairs" when thinking about our "political paralysis and intransigence." Likewise, most were not in agreement with the few who argued for higher taxes.

Of government's reach, one respondent predicted we'll "just keep trying to spend more money to fix things that we cannot fix without addressing cultural questions." Another said, "At some point you'd think somebody will realize there's nothing more government can do, as no amount of transfer payments can compensate for a lack of social capital." And someone else argued and hoped that "government gets out of the way," as "today's poverty is mostly a problem of the soul, and government, for various reasons including the Establishment Clause, is incapable of addressing problems of the soul." Framing matters internationally, Stanford economist Eric Hanushek noted that "while other countries are trying to emulate the old United States, the United States is trying to emulate the old Sweden and Scandinavia in terms of redistribution."

CHAPTER 6: "WHAT WILL AMERICA LOOK LIKE AND BE?"

Near the end of just about every interview, I asked: "In sum, considering all we've been talking about as well as at the risk of melodrama, what do you think the United States might come to look like in the days of your last breath?" Not everyone answered this question with fear or resignation. There was at least one prediction, for example, of Americans rediscovering a sense of collective mutual aid as funneled through government and made possible by higher taxes. There also was at least one exclamation of optimism propelled by confidence in American dynamism, made possible by less government and lower taxes. And one participant saw an "America of the future which, in many ways, was the America of the past," with safer and stronger urban communities."

But most respondents, in regard to family fragmentation, made prognoses such as these: "A wasting disease, not a heart attack." "A slow decline, nothing apocalyptic." "We'll manage problems, not resolve them." "Maybe we'll muddle along."

A number of respondents anticipated an even-less-encouraging future, as in this passage by political scientist Lawrence Mead: "The functioning population may come to be overwhelmed by the burdens of the nonfunctioning population, leading the former to withdraw. Rather than take responsibility, better-equipped Americans will say, 'We cannot keep helping the way we have. This is too much for us. We are exhausted. We have compassion fatigue or the equivalent.'"

Geographer John Adams's dark vision went this way: "America's future is going to have enclaves of people protecting what they have while the population of the country changes its composition in terms of age, background, and subculture. The ability of people to take advantage of the system is going to magnify for those who know how to do it, along with their kids, and those left behind are going to be a larger fraction of the total, and they're going to be mystified and politically inert, and that won't be healthy."

Harvard political scientist Paul Peterson said the United States likely would grow at the "European rate" if we "don't address the underlying family and educational quality issues" we had been talking about. If we don't adequately deal with them, he contended, "we are likely to be eclipsed by the growth of China and probably India," and the "centers of power are going to move to other parts of the world."

CHAPTER 7: "WHAT TO DO?"

The most interesting idea in regard to saving troubled marriages was Professor William Doherty's grassroots conception of "Marital First Responders," which he described as training people who already are confidantes to "up their game" in "responding helpfully" to people having marital problems and who come to them. "We know from a big body of research," the University of Minnesota family social scientist said, "that people who are in relationship struggles turn to their families and friends before turning to any professionals, including clergy."

In regard to helping fathers and husbands who are being released from prison, Larry Mead, in keeping with growing conservative interest in mitigating the severe collateral consequences of incarceration, argued: "We have to make it quite clear to any man who comes out of prison, whatever his previous life, that we are going to make it possible for him to live a civilized life going forward."

As one might expect, other suggestions included making divorce more difficult (at least for couples with children) and reviving something approaching the stigma once associated with out-of-wedlock births. Also as expected, respondents called for improvement in grades K–12 so that young people might better succeed at marriage and parenthood later on, and they likewise talked about the necessity of cleaning up "the culture." Entrepreneur Todd Peterson said, "We need to show that partnerships of all kinds"—by which he meant professional and business partnerships, not just romantic and marital ones—"are success strategies, not nuisances."

Inspired by something I once heard the late columnist Bill Raspberry say, my own starting point, in recent years, for reducing family fragmentation has focused on boys, as they regularly become the men that women don't want to marry, and for very good reasons. Like Mead, I've also been thinking about how to safely help ex-offenders cleanse their names and get on with their lives so they can be better husbands and fathers.

Capturing, in sum, the supreme difficulty of all this, particularly when it comes to reducing out-of-wedlock births, Kay Hymowitz concludes with modesty: "This is something I've been thinking about for over a decade now and I don't have an answer. The only thing I know how to do is push for a consensus that it's, in fact, a problem. We're so far away from actually effecting any change. We have to get to the point where people actually believe nonmarital births are a problem."

CHAPTER 8: "CONCLUSION"

A brief concluding chapter will note key points already made as well as a couple of new ones.

NOTES

1. Here are four places where information, as well as leads to other research, on the effects of family fragmentation on children can be found: National Fatherhood Initiative, www.fatherhood.org; Fragile Families and Child Wellbeing Study, www.fragilefamilies.princeton.edu; Institute for American Values, www.americanvalues.org; and the Marriage Project at the University of Virginia, www.nationalmarriageproject.org.

2. Scott M. Stanley and Galena K. Rhoades, "Marriages at Risk: Relationship Formation and Opportunities for Relationship Education," in *What Works in Relationship Education : Lessons from Academics and Service Deliverers in the United States and Europe*, edited by H. Benson and S. Callan (Doha, Qatar: Doha International Institute for Family Studies and Development, 2009), 21–44.

3. Charles Murray, *Coming Apart : The State of White America , 1960–2010* (New York: Crown Forum, 2013), 149.

4. Kay Hymowitz, *Marriage and Caste in America : Separate and Unequal Families in a Post -Marital Age* (Chicago: Ivan R. Dee, 2006), 5.

5. Three of the more remarked upon are Jason deParle, "Two Classes, Divided by 'I Do,'" *New York Times*, July 14, 2012; Ari Fleisher, "How to Fight Income Inequality: Get Married," *Wall Street Journal*, January 12, 2014; and of course, Charles Murray, *Losing Ground: American Social Policy, 1950–1980* (New York: Crown, 2012). Also see Raj Chetty, Nathaniel Hendren, et al., "Where Is the Land of Opportunity? The Geography of Intergenerational Mobility in the United States," Working Paper 19843, National Bureau of Economic Research, Cambridge, MA, January 2014.

6. George Packer, "The Broken Contract," *Foreign Affairs*, November–December 2011, 20–31.

7. Two years later, George Packer followed up with an award-winning, four-hundred-plus-page book on these themes, *The Unwinding: The Inner History of the New America* (New York: Farrar, Straus and Giroux, 2013). I frankly did not have time to read it, but I hoped to learn from its index if it dealt in any reasonable way with questions of marriage or family fragmentation—but it doesn't have an index. Jason

DeParle, however, in the title alone of his July 15, 2012, *New York Times* article makes this focus clear: "Two Classes, Divided by 'I Do.'"

8. Minneapolis *Star Tribune*, July 15, 2013.

9. December 4, 2013, http://www.politico.com/story/2013/12/obama-income-inequality-100662.html.

10. Mitch Pearlstein, *From Family Collapse to America's Decline: The Educational, Economic, and Social Costs of Family Fragmentation* (Lanham, MD: Rowman & Littlefield, 2011), 64–65.

11. Richard Rothstein, *Class and Schools: Using Social, Economic, and Educational Reform to Close the Black-White Achievement Gap* (Washington, DC: Economic Policy Institute, 2004).

12. Diane Ravitch, *Reign of Error: The Hoax of Privatization and the Danger to America's Public Schools* (New York: Alfred A. Knopf, 2013).

13. Senator Mike Lee, "Bring Them In," (remarks to the Heritage Foundation's Anti-Poverty Forum), Washington, DC, November 13, 2013.

14. Such eloquent and forceful ideas about marriage are just *mostly* owned by conservatives and Republicans, especially when it comes to articulating them in public.

15. William Galston, "Liberal Virtues," *American Political Science Review* 82, no. 4 (December 1988), 1282. Galston has been writing brave things about two-parent families since at least the 1980s. See, for example, William A. Galston, "A Liberal-Democratic Case for the Two-Parent Family," *The Responsive Community*, Winter 1990–1991, 14.

16. Murray, *Coming Apart*. To the question of how my argument differs from Murray's, the answer is "fundamentally, not much," as he has again written a brilliant book. Three differences that do exist between his book and this one are my seeking forty voices other than just my own; my addressing the lives of all Americans, not just white citizens; as well as my spending significantly more time focusing on what we might do to improve matters.

17. *National Vital Statistics Reports* 62, no. 1 (June 28, 2013), tables 13 and 14.

18. http://www.apa.org/topics.divorce. The 40–50 percent divorce rates generally refer to first marriages, with divorce rates for subsequent marriages regularly reported as higher.

19. U.S. Census Bureau, "Living Arrangements of Children: 2009," Household Economic Studies, June 2011.

20. W. Bradford Wilcox and Elizabeth Marquardt, "When Marriage Disappears: The Retreat from Marriage in Middle America," The National Marriage Project and the Institute for American Values, December 2010.

21. Alexandra Sifferlin, "What's behind the Drop in U.S. Teen Birth Rates?," http://healthland.time.com/2013/05/24/whats-behind-the-drop-in-u-s-teen-birth-rates/.

22. George Friedman, "The Crisis of the Middle Class and American Power," *Geopolitical Weekly*, January 2013.

23. E. J. Dionne, *Our Divided Political Heart: The Battle for the American Idea in an Age of Discontent* (New York: Bloomsbury, 2012), 45–46.

24. Bill Bishop, *The Big Sort: Why the Clustering of Like-Minded America Is Tearing Us Apart* (Boston: Mariner, 2008), 36.

25. Elijah Anderson, *The Cosmopolitan Canopy: Race and Civility in Everyday Life* (New York: W. W. Norton, 2011), 99.

26. Pearlstein, *From Family Collapse to America's Decline*. In particular, see chapters 3 and 5.

27. Paul E. Barton and Richard J. Coley, *The Black White Achievement Gap : When Progress Stopped*, Policy Information Report, Educational Testing Service, July 2010, 35.

28. Isabel Sawhill, "Do We Face a Permanently Divided Society?," (paper for Tobin Project conference on Democracy & Markets: Understanding the Effects of America's Economic Stratification), April 1, 2010.

29. Scott Winship, "Myths of Inequality and Stagnation," Brookings Institution, March 27, 2013. The article originally appeared in *National Review*.

30. Thomas Sowell, "A Tiger of a Book," March 18, 2014, http://townhall.com/columnists/thomassowell/2014/03/18/a-tiger-of-a-book-n1810354/print.

31. Timothy Noah, *The Great Divergence: America's Growing Inequality Crisis and What We Can Do about It* (New York: Bloomsbury, 2012), 57.

32. Noah, *The Great Divergence*, 92.

33. Twenty-one respondents are from outside Minnesota. Among the nineteen who live amid ten thousand lakes, several clearly are also national leaders, not just state players. I'm thinking here, for instance, of scholars John Adams, William J. Doherty, and Elaine Tyler May, all of the University of Minnesota; Krista Tippett of National Public Radio; feminist activist Arvonne Fraser; and former congressman and progressive reformer (as well as Arvonne's husband) Don Fraser.

34. John Lofland et al., *Analyzing Social Settings : A Guide to Qualitative Observation and Analysis*, 4th ed. (Belmont, CA: Wadsworth, 2006).

35. A number of the quotes and paraphrases by respondents in the summary of seven of the chapters of this book do not appear in the main text. In order to squeeze as many insightful and provocative comments into the book as possible, several quotes and paraphrases appear in these summaries only.

ONE

How Big of a Problem?

How big of an American problem is family fragmentation? If I didn't think it was immense, I wouldn't have written this book. But what might the three-dozen-plus men and women I interviewed for it think about the question? And since many current adverse conditions—be they economic, political, social, educational, or otherwise—are more likely to deteriorate rather than improve, given how problems associated with fragmentation tend to fuel each other, what might present-day observations by uncommonly insightful and practiced observers portend for our country's future? Here are a-half-dozen voices to start.

Historian Stephanie Coontz has written important and high-profile books such as *The Way We Never Were* and *Marriage, A History*. I don't know if she considers herself a "feminist historian," or even if she finds anything accurate or friendly about the term, though many people, in both friendly and unfriendly camps, view her as one. I'll stay away from such labels as much as possible throughout and simply report I thoroughly enjoyed my conversation with her on her family's longtime farm outside of Olympia, Washington. I also wound up agreeing with her more than once or twice.

I obviously concurred, for instance, when she said that "one of the worst things for kids is sexualized households where you have a lot of people going in and out," as well as when she lamented the ghastly high out-of-wedlock birthrates and divorce rates discussed in the introduction. And I resonated when she spoke of the painful situations often faced by single mothers who, because they are "so close to the bone" financially, can't keep promises they've made to their children.

Citing a study by sociologist Allison Pugh, Coontz talked about how such women often say, '"Next week, I'll take you to a movie,' but somebody steals their wallet, or they lose it, or they have a flat tire, if they have a car at all, and then they simply can't keep their promises." Yet if and when she has some extra cash, "she will just sort of drop it on her children." Pugh calls this "windfall childrearing," and Coontz acknowledged it's not the soundest way of raising kids. "On the other hand," she was fast to point out, "how do you tell a single mother who has had to break five promises in a row that she shouldn't buy a new Transformer game for her child when she gets a comparative windfall?" (Don't worry. I don't know what a "Transformer" game is either.)

I personally took extra note here because I recalled how, about thirty-five years earlier when, as an impoverished graduate student, I made a $100 down payment on a car for which I had no earthly way of making monthly payments. It was a nonrational, bordering on irrational, move, but I had just grown too tired of being in my early thirties and poor to be particularly prudent. I almost immediately backed out of the deal, and as self-imposed penance, I told the sales manager to keep the down payment, not that he seemed inclined to return it.

Still, I parted company with Coontz, albeit more by degree than kind, when she said fragmentation's severity depends on how you define it "and to what extent it's a symptom or a cause. I don't think there's anything in and of itself that necessarily disqualifies single parents, or divorced parents, or cohabitating parents from doing a good job raising their kids. Yet I do see America's exceptionally high family fragmentation as a part of a larger problem." I likewise see fragmentation as a result of problems and forces, and I realize that single parents successfully raise their children under tough circumstances every day. I would argue, though, it's more instructive to turn the equation around, with fragmentation more accurately understood as causing big problems rather than resulting from them.

The next views about family fragmentation are tougher. They also more closely resemble the emphases and tone of respondents in general.

Ron Haskins, a developmental psychologist by training, focuses on matters of families and inequality, among other topics, at the Brookings Institution. Almost two decades ago, he was the key Republican staffer in the U.S. House of Representatives when Republicans in that chamber led the way in winning major welfare reform in 1996. The new law, known by its acronym TANF (Temporary Assistance for Needy Families), could be said to have two main goals: significantly increasing the number of single mothers in the paid workforce and increasing their marriage rates. The first goal was achieved more substantially and rapidly than many people thought possible, while realizing the second goal remains just as distant as it was back then. It was in this context that I asked Haskins how he rated family fragmentation as a problem facing the nation.

> On a scale of one to ten, probably a fifteen; it's the biggest problem we have. It's having a tremendous impact on children. We already have trouble in competition with other countries. Our academic achievement is in the pits. Until the last thirty years or so, we led the world in education, now we're way down the list. We have so many studies regarding fragmentation's effects on children with so many techniques, including longitudinal studies with very good data, controlling everything we can control for, and over and over again we get the same results.

Referring specifically to the chaos in many single-parent households, with mothers and fathers moving on to new relationships, Haskins said: "So imagine these households. Anybody who has ever suffered through the breakup of a serious relationship knows of the consternation and drama involved. This is the environment in which many single mothers are trying to raise their children, but pretty soon they have kids from two fathers or even more in the same household. It's a tragedy and it's going to have real impacts on the country."

Ron Mincy teaches in Columbia University's School of Social Work and, with colleagues Irv Garfinkel and Princeton's Sara McLanahan among others, has led the invaluable "Fragile Families Study," which continues to track thousands of children born in large cities and their parents. His answer to the same question I posed to Haskins four months earlier about fragmentation's size as a problem dealt with similar themes.

"Oh, I think it's huge. It has dimensions that policymakers and others are just getting their minds wrapped around, especially when it comes to what I call 'multiple partner fertility.' We've historically focused on what might be considered 'first families.' But we're increasingly focusing on subsequent childbearing with subsequent partners. These behaviors are creating family complexities which we haven't figured out yet."

For an example of such complexities, Mincy cited child support payments, an area in which he has done a lot of work. "How should we think about establishing child support payments? It gets really, really complex when you recognize that the nonresident father of a child actually has *another* family, and *another* family, and *another* family. How should he be made to divide up a portion of his income across his multiple children?" This presumes, of course, he has any income to begin with.

"Then there are all the children," Mincy continued, "growing up with half-siblings. What's the nature of those relationships? How are parents dividing up their parenting resources across all the children in the same household, and not just when it comes to money?"

Drawing on simple multiplication, Brown University economist Glenn Loury noted, "Forty-eight hours of adult supervision per family per day is twice as many as twenty-four hours; two incomes are bigger than one; and two temperaments are better than one when dealing with the difficulties of raising children."

Political scientist Lawrence Mead calls family fragmentation the "largest or second-largest problem in America," with declining work levels, particularly among men, its only rival. As for numbers associated with fragmentation, including more than a 40 percent nonmarital birthrate for the country as a whole and more than a 70 percent rate for African Americans, Mead called them "catastrophic."

Writer Kay Hymowitz's succinct metaphor was that family breakdown is the "shadow behind all sorts of other problems that people are much more easily conversant about." The second half of her comment pertained not just to a reluctance to discuss fragmentation head-on because of politically incorrect intimidations but also to an inability of many people to grasp marriage as a critical *institution*. "When you talk about institutions failing people, that's something the Left understands. They'll understand, for example, that banks fail people. But they do not comprehend that marriage is also an institution." Or as another writer, Katherine Kersten, put it, "The family is the most fundamental of social institutions, as it's the most important in shaping next generations, which is critical if democracies hope to continue as democracies."

Or as another two institutions, the University of Virginia-based National Marriage Project and the New York-based Institute for American Values have argued: "Marriage is not merely a private arrangement; it's also a complex social institution. Marriage fosters small cooperative unions—also known as stable families—that enable children to thrive, shore up communities, and help family members succeed during good times and to weather the bad times."[1]

A reminder: In going forward, please keep in mind a fundamental dynamic at play in this first chapter, as framed well by journalist Reihan Salam. "[A]s skills, resources, and networks are passed from one generation to the next, the damage accumulates, and the gap between adults who come from a history of stable families and those who come from a history of unstable ones grows. Viewed through this lens, the fact that the children of affluent families are far more likely to be affluent than the children of poor families . . . is hardly surprising."[2]

And a preview: My first inclination at this juncture was to arrange responses in ascending order of calamity, but I quickly realized that gradations of fear about fragmentation are barely discernible more often than not. Still, some respondents challenged my premises more than others did, while other interviewees held forth from distinctive angles, including religiously contoured ones. Those two groups are up next. From there, we'll consider several comments that connect issues of fragmentation and educational performance particularly well. And from there, we'll conclude the chapter with more fleshed-out comments by three respondents who have spent professional lifetimes pondering and writing about families, poverty, and related subjects: William Doherty, Heather Mac Donald, and David Blankenhorn.

As did Evergreen State College historian Stephanie Coontz, University of Minnesota historian Elaine Tyler May conceived family fragmentation as more symptom than cause. "I see it," May argued, "in some ways as a result of other changes taking place socially, politically, economically, culturally. So that in and of itself, family fragmentation may or may not be a problem, depending on the particulars of the specific family involved. But I do see it in some cases as a serious problem." Later in our conversation May put it: "In a classic way, you respond as a conservative and I respond as a liberal; which is to say I see fragmentation as a symptom of economic hardship, oppression, and lack of opportunity." I had been stressing matters of culture at the time, including what is sometimes called a "culture of poverty," a concept May doesn't believe to be real.

Arvonne Fraser, since the 1960s one of Minnesota's most important feminist public servants and activists, rated family fragmentation as "not so great," albeit a problem in need of addressing, one reason being "too many low-income men are not marriageable." She prefaced her comment by saying "I think I will disagree with the two of you," the two of us being me and her husband Don Fraser, now ninety, who represented Minneapolis in Congress for sixteen years and then served fourteen years as mayor of the city. Of brave note, Don might have been the first major Democratic politician in Minnesota, in the mid-1980s when he was mayor, to talk repeatedly about family fragmentation, or what he more carefully called "unsupported women."

This is a good juncture to note that when talking and writing about the causes, effects, and everything else about family fragmentation, particularly in urban cores, "all of the above" is a weasel answer only if one intends it to be. "Institutional discrimination," for example, can be real—albeit routinely exaggerated as an impediment. "Personal responsibility" is necessary—albeit routinely downplayed as essential. I was advised a long time ago not to envision chickens and eggs, but marble cakes. Likewise swirling its way through just about everything we're talking about is a lot of history, much of it very bad history when it comes to race.

Less metaphorically, here's how ethnographer Elijah Anderson, one of our respondents, opens an anthology he edited, *Against the Wall: Poor, Young, Black, and Male*: "Living in areas of concentrated ghetto poverty, still shadowed by the legacy of slavery and second-class citizenship, too many young black men are trapped in a horrific cycle that includes active discrimination, unemployment, poverty, crime, prison, and early death."[3]

A dozen pages later, Anderson adds this about young black males in inner cities:

> Typically his home life is female-centric; he lives with his mother, perhaps along with his grandmother or an aunt, but not with a father. The men in his life are his brothers and cousins, occasionally an uncle or a grandfather. Seldom does he have the direct influence of a father who lives nearby and stays in touch. When a father figure is present, he is rarely an effective role model. The man may be compromised by poverty to the point where he is involved in crime and hustling. He might take or sell drugs. He is unlikely to be a strong, upstanding man with a job and a sense of connection with mainstream society and the wider culture.[4]

One might not concur with every point Anderson makes or how he makes it, but it's impossible to deny the complexity he describes. Similarly, one can disagree with what's possibly interpretable as a downplaying of personal responsibility, both in this and similar analyses, and still appreciate how terribly hard life can be for many young black males growing up in neighborhoods that not too many people reading this would be inclined to visit without a police escort. When it comes to family fragmentation, especially in communities where it's most severe, it's not an evasion to say that a great number of things can make critical differences.

We'll hear more from Professor Anderson, who was a respondent, when he takes different but reinforcing tacks.

Stanford political scientist Terry Moe's caveats are methodological. It's not that he doesn't describe nonmarital birth data and divorce data as "horrifying," as he does. His problem, instead, has to do with "disentangling all the different factors involved." Or, as he puts it: "OK, so families have been breaking down and we know that is not a good thing. But there are all kinds of other things going on in society that lead to inequality and other problems."

These are more than fair points, but, as you recall from the top of the introduction, my argument is not dependent on determining the statistically precise extent to which family fragmentation affects mobility under this or that circumstance. Rather, it's grounded in simply acknowledging that widespread fragmentation is leading many millions of young and not-so-young people—indisputably to *some* consequential degree—to do less well on average than they otherwise would, first academically and then vocationally, in comparison to other Americans lucky enough to grow up with both their biological mother and father in the same home.

Economist Isabel Sawhill is a former senior official in the Clinton administration and, as a senior fellow at the Brookings Institution, works closely with Ron Haskins. At the Brookings Institution, they codirect the Center on Children and Families and have written about many of the issues considered here. She also is the founder and still president of the board of directors of the National Campaign to Prevent Teen and Unplanned Pregnancy. She did, in fact, describe family fragmentation as "definitely a problem." But Sawhill also said it's not the biggest one facing the nation, which she contended are global warming and nuclear terrorism. When I said that another respondent had described fragmentation as a "fifteen on a scale of ten" (I didn't say it was Haskins, who said it just ninety minutes earlier), she said: "It's very difficult to say how important it is because it's intertwined with so many other trends," just as Coontz, May, and Moe argued in their own ways. "But, no, I don't think it's a ten or fifteen. I think it's more like a six or a seven, perhaps."

Bruce Peterson is a Hennepin County (Minneapolis) district judge. A self-described "progressive," I met him about a half-dozen years ago when we both participated on a panel, the specific topic of which I no longer recall. But as is my habit, I talked at least in part about family fragmentation (family "breakdown" back then), as did Bruce, and it immediately became clear we agreed much more than disagreed on the subject. Which makes it unsurprising that he answered "huge" and "nothing bigger" when I asked: "How big of a problem do you see family fragmentation in the United States?" He also said:

> I have two calendars right now where I see large numbers of people mostly unrepresented by counsel so I interact with them personally. One calendar is for our "Co-Parent Court Project" where we're working with lower-income unmarried parents. The other is the Brookdale calendar, which I handle one week a month and which deals with domestic violence, DWIs, and the like. [The Brookdale court is in Brooklyn Center, an inner-ring suburb north of Minneapolis.] Out at Brookdale I've come to just assume the people I'm seeing who are in trouble a lot come from some kind of fragmented family. The number of people I see in that kind of trouble and who come from stable, married families is very small. I've come to just assume that family fragmentation goes with chaotic and difficult lifestyles.

Twenty minutes later I asked how much lighter his workload as a judge might be if far fewer children were born outside of marriage. "Oh, I think significantly less. I've stopped even asking 'Where's the father,' when kids come before me. Juvenile court, family court, criminal court, they're all the same people." The following Monday evening Judge Peterson sent me this thematically identical postscript:

> Monday at Brookdale court is busy because people unfortunate enough to get locked up on Friday or on the weekend don't make it to court until today. Before me today appeared a young woman—a girl—who had just turned 18. She had a 10-month-old son. She lived with her grandmother because she and her mother don't get along. The charge was stealing baby formula from a supermarket although she said she had enough food for the baby and that she "just did it." *She had been in jail for three days and did not know where the baby was.* [Italics in the

original.] To be fair, she said she believed some relative had him but didn't know which one. Neither her own father nor the father of the baby was ever mentioned as possibilities.

As one might expect as well as appreciate, Krista Tippett, host of National Public Radio's *On Being*, approached the book's questions in religiously, culturally, and personally animated ways. As for classifying fragmentation's magnitude, she said: "I don't know the statistics, so I'll answer as a mother. It's a big problem. It's often a tragedy on a personal level. I don't think there's much support for marriages and families to stick together in this culture."

Tippett, who makes no secret of her own divorce, went on to say:

> I have this sense that in previous generations people were just more organically surrounded by communities, by extended families, by neighbors who were in each other's business, by church or other religious communities, which were really webs of relationships. I grew up in a church in Oklahoma where we were three times a week and at dinner one night a week. It was an entire social web. There were certainly downsides to these inherited webs. They weren't all idyllic. But I think that this idea of a nuclear family in which a father, mother, and babies are supposed to figure all this out by themselves is pretty new in human history. I knew this even when my children were born. It was completely uncharted territory and I understood that in previous eras I would have had a mother or grandmother around. I had a sense of the loneliness of families and the loneliness of marriages.

To which I intruded: "And the loneliness of non-marriage?"

"And the loneliness of non-marriage. Sure. Absolutely."

What Lisa Graham Keegan had to say flows from what Krista Tippett said and then flows into what Kristin Robbins and Robert Woodson will say in a moment.

For Keegan, who has served as superintendent of public instruction in Arizona, the "essence of family is taking care of each other. We promote each other for what each of us is created to do, and we are with each other for the long haul. Two people together in the miraculous institution of marriage is a lovely poetry for how we should approach life in general." Then she said, a little less poetically: "The way we talk about marriage in such constipated terms horrifies me."

Kristin Robbins, executive director of the Economic Club of Minnesota, has been a longtime volunteer and advocate for policies that empower families, particularly in regard to school choice and chronic homelessness. We'll return to her work with an innovative community development organization, but for now please note that while she said family fragmentation is "one of our biggest problems," she also correspondingly argued that "cultural shifts in America are making it very difficult to say some lifestyle choices are better or worse." The resulting silence is "allowing fragmentation to continue, hurting not just one segment of the population, but increasingly all of us."

My guess is Robert Woodson, a seventy-five-year-old former social worker and founder of the Center for Neighborhood Enterprise in 1981, has walked alongside more low-income Americans than anyone else whose office is anywhere close to K Street or Connecticut Avenue in Washington. As with Robbins, we'll return in a later chapter to what Woodson sees as the role of faith-imbued activism in reconstructing marriage in communities where its collapse has been most violent.

But for now, Woodson, who's African American and continues to lead CNE, called fragmentation "*the* most crucial issue facing the United States, as the family is where people are socialized." And that "a lot of the violence and family dissolution I'm seeing in the black community are only forty years old." These two developments have indeed been linked at the hip and holster over these decades, a span not far off from Daniel Patrick Moynihan's warning in 1965 about the combustibility of single-parenthood and crime, among other very bad problems.

Stanford's Eric ("Rick") Hanushek has been a leader for years in econometrically demonstrating the connection between a nation's economic growth and its students' academic achievement (or shortage thereof), particularly when it comes to science and math. This led him in our conversation to describe family fragmentation as "a huge problem that really affects where kids end up." Most of his work, he says, is "not about the family but rather what we can do through schools and society to overcome problems many families deed over to schools. From all the evidence we have," he went on, "it's clear the human capital achievement skills people have at the end of school are very dependent on what their families looked like."

I've frequently cited Hanushek, as when he has argued that while the relationship between cognitive skills on the one hand and individual productivity and incomes on the other hand are strong, the relationship between labor force quality and economic growth for a nation as a whole is perhaps even stronger. This is the case insofar as a "more skilled society" may lead to higher rates of invention, enable companies to introduce improved production methods, and lead to faster introduction of new technologies.[5]

Along with her historian husband, Stephan Thernstrom, political scientist Abigail Thernstrom, who is a former vice chair of the U.S. Commission on Civil Rights, has written books such as *No Excuses: Closing the Racial Gap in Learning* and *America in Black and White: One Nation, Indivisible.*[6] In describing family fragmentation as a "huge" problem, she made a point about educationally enriched homes, and their opposites, I had not heard put that way before. "I'm particularly concerned about children who have so little going for them. When we look at high-performing kids, like our own grandchildren, where do they get educated? They get educated at home, even though they go to school a certain number of hours a day. I always think of our now-adult children as having been homeschooled in effect. The dinner table was a school."

Speaking of dinner tables, John and Judith Adams spent a lot of time around theirs with their four (now-adult) children as they were growing up. Anything but random gatherings, such family times together were concretely carved into everyday routines. John, who is a (partially) retired geography professor at the Hubert H. Humphrey School of Public Affairs at the University of Minnesota, would make sure to make it home for dinner every evening, even if he had to return to his campus office afterward.

Judith described herself as a community volunteer who has worked for many years in Catholic schools with low-income children. At a full two hours, my conversation with the two of them was the longest of any session for this project, as I kept asking questions, struck as I was by their faith-filled and purposeful successes as a family, now extended with nine grandchildren and literally scores of cousins and other relatives. This is the way Judith answered my first question about the severity of family fragmentation:

> I think it's massive. The kids I tutor in some of the schools I work in don't have an understanding of what "family" means anything at all like mine. Kids come to school hungry because their mom put the breakfast cereal on the top of the refrigerator and they can't reach it, but she has already gone to work. Grandma is there, but grandma has to take care of the baby their mom just had with her recent boyfriend.

I first met University of Minnesota family social scientist William Doherty about a dozen years ago, which also was around the time I read his *Soul Searching: Why Psychotherapy Must Promote Moral Responsibility,*[7] a wonderful book that argues that family therapists should not be agnostic to the point of indifference concerning the fate of their clients' endangered marriages. Instead, if there is a reasonable chance of reconciliation, therapists should help husbands and wives explore the possibility of staying together. More recently, he has collaborated with the aforementioned Judge Bruce Peterson in investigating new ways of helping Twin Cities couples going through the divorce process to step back from the brink.[8] This is novel work since judges, lawyers, and others in the legal portion of the "divorce industry" may be even less interested in saving troubled marriages than therapists have been—at least therapists who haven't read anything by Bill. As was the norm, I opened my conversation with Doherty by asking about fragmentation's seriousness.

"I see it as a massive problem that, more than anything else, jeopardizes the next generation. It's huge. I worry deeply about the have-nots. I've been used to high divorce rates for some time and have taken some comfort in their leveling off and going down a bit. The shock for me, however, continues with nonmarital birth rates. That's the one with linear increases and no leveling off yet. How high can they go? Those are the kids who are the worst off."

Doherty made an important distinction between children of divorce and children whose parents never marry at all. No other interviewee made the comparison as explicitly.

> The kids of divorce look like they're privileged in comparison with kids born outside of marriage, again on average. The kids born to not-married parents are truly the fatherless generation. Men who do marry but then divorce are increasingly investing in their kids and staying invested in them. This good news actually has created new challenges for those of us who work with families, as there is more shared parenting going on—and, therefore, more potential for conflict. But what it also has done has been to increase a fathering gap between men who haven't married and those who have but later divorced. Marriage links fathers to their children in a way that nothing else does. So if a marriage ends, the man is more apt to be linked to his children. Children of never-married parents, however, are in high-risk family situations right from the beginning. They are babies.

I don't remember when I first read anything by Heather Mac Donald, but I know of no writer more fearless when it comes to not just the most difficult issues facing our nation but also the most verboten ones. The intersection of family fragmentation and race, of course, is the politically correct epicenter of where most scholars, politicians, and other leaders refuse to tread. Mac Donald, however, goes there regularly with intelligence and fairness, and sometimes, when I read something of hers that I think is particularly strong, I'll drop her a congratulatory e-mail. I had assumed I was one of many admirers who routinely do so, but as she had told me previously, during our interview, she again said that was not the case.

> Well, I get some feedback, but generally, Americans are oblivious to how serious a problem fragmentation is. I think there's a real naiveté about the importance of traditional family structures and the fact that atomized individuals are just not able to carry on the socializing functions that families can. Among the more libertarian conservatives, there's the idea that choice is the highest good, the paramount good. So nobody should criticize anybody's choices in regard to family structure. Then, of course, there's the whole feminist celebration of strong women and its resulting devaluation of men because it would be heresy to say that strong women can't do it all. Yes, I get some positive feedback, but I don't think that even readers, say, of *National Review* get it.

By "get it," Mac Donald, who is a contributing editor with the Manhattan Institute's *City Journal*, was referring back to an opening comment of hers that despite entitlement spending and debt, family fragmentation is our "biggest," problem, as "the family unit is the absolute basis of society. It is responsible for civilizing human beings and creating adults who are capable of engaging in the economy. With families breaking down at the rates they are, our chance of being able to take care of other large economic problems recedes. Single mothers are the frequent fliers in government assistance problems. Other problems pale in comparison."

David Blankenhorn, the founder and president of the previously mentioned Institute for American Values and author of the path-breaking *Fatherless America* in 1995,[9] is another writer as well as respondent I've been lucky to work with for a long time in both the fatherhood and marriage movements. A native of Jackson, Mississippi, who saw the civil rights movement up close and personal as a child, Blankenhorn, it's fair to say, is instinctively a progressive. But because few on the left side of the aisle have been nearly as inclined or practiced at speaking out forcefully on the importance of marriage, he tends to be identified as a man of the right. While there isn't anything untoward about being a man of the right, for the record, he's not. This is how he started our conversation:

"Foreign policy and global issues aside, family fragmentation is our biggest domestic crisis. It's our most urgent challenge because it's the problem that drives so many other problems, whether it's crime, educational failure, mental distress among young people, failed potential, sharpening class divides, or just unhappy and bruised lives." Referring to Ron Mincy, who I coincidentally interviewed later that afternoon at Columbia, Blankenhorn continued:

> I remember when Ron was an officer at the Ford Foundation and he helped me and you and others better understand problems of fatherhood. Whatever the exact percentage of out-of-wedlock births among African Americans was at the time, he said that number was what motivated him to do his work. I remember him saying how upset and angry and heartbroken he was by that number. And that's my feeling, too. I look at the more than 70 percent of children in the African American community born outside marriage as well as the more than 40 percent for America as a whole and all the damage and suffering of children they imply, and I say if I could change just two numbers in America it would be those. It would not be unemployment rates, or new business starts, or people with health care coverage, or people with adequate incomes. As important as all those things are, if I could only change two numbers, it would be 70 percent and 40 percent.

Summing up what we've read and heard so far, most interviewees rate family fragmentation as a terrible problem, with "huge" the favored term of ugly art. On those occasions when fragmentation is described in less-severe terms—closer, for example, to a "six" than a "fifteen" on a scale of ten—it's almost always understood as causing real trouble and pain for millions of children and adults. As for matters of mobility, suffice it to say that among the approximately twenty respondents quoted above no one is of the mind that fragmentation doesn't retard upward climbs for millions of young and older people, especially African Americans, to one extent or another. Neither does anyone deny that it hurts our country as an economic whole. And if one accepts one of the principal premises of the book—namely, that problems associated with family fragmentation tend to grow worse insofar as they reinforce each other—it's hard to see how similarly experienced panelists in foreseeable years ahead might have more optimistic things to say.

Among questions begged by all of this is why rates of family fragmentation in the United States are so destructively high. It's to this mystery—if it's mysterious at all—to which we turn in chapter 2.

NOTES

1. *The State of Our Unions : Marriage in America 2012,* National Marriage Project at the University of Virginia and the Center for Marriage and Families at the Institute for American Values, Charlottesville, Virginia, 2012, xii.

2. Reihan Salam, "Modern Family," *National Review,* April 22, 2013, 20–21.

3. Elijah Anderson, *Against the Wall: Poor, Young, Black, and Male* (Philadelphia: University of Pennsylvania, 2008), 3.

4. Anderson, *Against the Wall,* 15–16.

5. Eric A. Hanushek, "The Economic Value of Education and Cognitive Skills," in *Handbook of Education Policy Research,* edited by Gary Sykes, Barbara Schneider, and David N. Plank (New York: Routledge, 2009), 42.

6. Stephan Thernstrom and Abigail Thernstrom, *America in Black and White: One Nation, Indivisible* (New York: Touchstone, 1997); *No Excuses : Closing the Racial Gap in Learning* (New York: Simon & Schuster, 2003).

7. William J. Doherty, *Soul Searching: Why Psychotherapy Must Promote Moral Responsibility* (New York: Basic Books, 1995).

8. William J. Doherty, Melissa Froehle, Bruce Peterson, "Back from the Brink: New Hope for Both Marriage and Divorce," (roundtable moderated by Mitch Pearlstein, Center of the American Experiment, April 2011).

9. David Blankenhorn, *Fatherless America: Confronting Our Most Urgent Social Problem* (New York: Basic Books, 1995).

TWO

Why Are Family Fragmentation Rates So High?

All the sobering news so far makes a body politic wonder how in the world the United States gets out of bed every morning, much less continues leading the planet in the ways we do. Excluding glorious legacies, a relatively free economy, and the possibility of providence, one explanation might be that all other nations also have problems, routinely nasty ones. But why is it that Americans do so poorly, both comparatively and absolutely, when it comes to the big and consequential matter of holding our families together?

One basic answer is that in order to adequately alleviate a problem, it's essential to first talk freely about it. Suffice it to say that's not the case with family fragmentation. An easy route here would be to simply cite political correctness as the overriding culprit, offer a couple of rude examples of its silencing powers, and call it a case-closing day. But P.C. is not the only potential silencer; sometimes it's a tendency a lot more honorable, such as humility. And sometimes it's a single mother crying in the pews.

Several months before writing this chapter I spoke at a Unitarian church in the Twin Cities. One might imagine that Unitarian churches might not be inclined to hear from someone who talks about family matters the way I do, but that, happily, has not been the case. I've been invited to speak to a number of them in Minnesota over the years, and I'm always grateful for the opportunity. I don't recall ever being treated ungraciously, but on this specific Sunday morning, I was struck by how many people in the congregation seemed to be agreeing with me. Not only didn't I see any rolling eyes, but when I saw heads move, they went up and down in concurrence instead of side to side in dismissal.

Much the same was the case in the hour-plus conversation after the service. But in-between the two sessions, as I was talking with four or five people, we were joined by a woman, perhaps in her early thirties, who, it was clear, wasn't the least bit happy with me. It also was clear she had been crying, not that I had noticed this from the lectern. With a voice still quivering, she said she was a single mother of two children who were doing great despite what I had been saying moments before about how many kids are hurt by out-of-wedlock births and divorce, and that she was livid, claiming I had essentially blamed her for the "demise of the nation."

With the people around us now obviously uncomfortable, I said something about how I was sorry she had been hurt by what I had said, but that I had not accused her of somehow personally causing the country's fall. I went on to say—repeating what I had said during my remarks about my own now-adult and quite successful stepsons—how millions of kids growing up in tough circumstances are doing great, while millions of other kids growing up under great circumstances are doing badly, and that I was very pleased her children were doing well. But I then noted that there are hundreds of places across the country where one can go for blocks without finding more than handfuls of two-parent families. Did she think that single-parenting in those situations was good for the children involved? No answer.

Moving on to the Twin Cities Episcopal church where my wife is a deacon, its rector (and one of my respondents), Paul Allick, assured me he has thought about saying from the pulpit the kinds of things I've occasionally suggested clergy should say about fragmentation, but that he prefers talking about such matters in smaller groups such as Bible studies and adult education classes. "Questions come up all the time about how we live in this culture as Christians. I find that when I open the door to discussing out-of-wedlock births and divorce, people feel so relieved that we get to talk about them in a civilized and compassionate way and to just reflect on what it means for us."

While I might be strangely compelled to risk public fragging over fragmentation, relatively few people are so inclined. This reluctance is especially the case with many people in public life, and even more so now that we live in a YouTube world. One person, though, who is well-practiced is the Brookings Institution's Ron Haskins, who in our conversation, reported on having attended a conference a week or two earlier with about six hundred mostly liberal men and women, where he said: "Marriage is the biggest problem in the country and at the heart of the problem is that very few people are talking about it. We need a lot more people, especially elected officials and community leaders saying, 'This is the most crucial part of your life.'"

I asked him what kind of reaction he got.

> Nobody really said anything, but you could tell some were getting ready to fight while others seemed to agree with me, but they didn't want to say so. I think not wanting to be judgmental is a big part of it. There actually are humble people in America who don't want to go around saying, "I'm doing it right and you're not. You *should* be married." We're pretty good about being judgmental about gambling and crime and so forth, but people don't want to be when it comes to marriage.

Moments later he took an additional tack:

> But I think the biggest barrier is that most people don't really understand the situation we've put ourselves in. They don't understand the consequences. They can see on television and in the popular culture how things certainly have changed, but I don't think they realize the destructive effects family breakdown is going to have on future generations or the effects it's already having on crime rates, school dropouts, and so forth. It's like people not paying attention to federal deficits. If people had a better understanding of what the consequences are going to be in both cases—not *maybe* but in *fact*—they might be more venturesome.

Jason Adkins, who leads the Minnesota Catholic Conference, argued similarly: "We simply refuse to say that one family structure is better than another. We refuse to make normative judgments about what's good and what isn't. So while the social science has been clear for a long time about the effects of family fragmentation—'Dan Quayle was Right' and all that—a non-judgmentalism creeps in and we're unable to overcome it."

Peter Bell, a leader in several Minnesota spheres, including chairmanship of the American Refugee Committee, drew a connection with academia's penchant for "practicing sociology to an extreme." This proclivity, he argued "provides rationales and excuses for family fragmentation," which in turn "destigmatizes and normalizes it," with a "fear of being judgmental" driving it all. And with discussions about family structure having become even more complicated in recent years with the immersion of same-sex marriage into the P.C. mix, the *City Journal*'s Heather Mac Donald talked about how it has become even more difficult to "valorize the biologically two-parent family."

In conservative circles more than in liberal ones, explanations for why fragmentation rates in the United States are so high center on how governmental policies, especially since the mid-1960s and the War on Poverty, have spurred unwise sexual and family behavior by subsidizing it. While such policies and programs may not actually "cause" recipients and potential recipients to do imprudent and irresponsible things, they unquestionably "enable" such behavior by recipients and potential recipients. I'm sadly thinking here of a member of my own family who was never forced to seriously wonder how she could support a child she came to have as a young single mother, as well as support herself, as she implicitly knew that TANF and a roster of other welfare programs would be there simply for the applying. And if by very off chance, she didn't know about them, a slew of websites, including those operated by governmental agencies themselves, were eager to inform her. Harvard political scientist Paul Peterson (the first of four Petersons in this chapter) substantiated the point.

> I can see why many single women may decide they want to remain that way, or if they're married, why they want to become single again, even though they're raising children. It's not always pleasant living with somebody who isn't compatible with you for one reason or another. As society has become more tolerant of single-parenthood, it has become easier to make decisions like that. Government may not provide single parents with great resources, but it does provide health care. It does provide access to nutrition through what used to be called the Food Stamp program. It does provide some minimum maintenance. Housing is the biggest challenge people face, but they generally solve that. Single parents with children can manage—not well—but they can manage to live in situations that weren't conceivable seventy-five years ago. So we have a New World. Government policies, reinforced by social attitudes, creating conditions under which this is occurring.

Looking back those seventy-five years and more, Lee McGrath of the Institute for Justice argued that progressives of Woodrow Wilson's time and Franklin Roosevelt's time saw families just as conservatives of their times did—as the central institution in society. "More modern progressives, however, particularly starting with the War on Poverty, have been less concerned with the institution of the family and this has been incredibly detrimental. It was not unusual," McGrath asserted, "for our parents to have friends who were shamed by the idea of divorce, and my father, who was a high school teacher, spoke of girls in the 1950s and early '60s shamefully dropping out of school to have babies. But shame in these ways," he summed up, "no longer exists and has been replaced by public policies that are not only void of shame, but which tend to subsidize dysfunction."

Educator Chester E. ("Checker") Finn Jr. of the Thomas B. Fordham Foundation refers to public policies over a similar span of time. "Budget cliffs or not, we're not about to undo the compensating mechanisms we've created that make it easier and at lower cost for families to come apart. The fundamental provision of Social Security, for instance, means that parents are less dependent on their children to look after them in old age; which means they don't have to remain close to their children; which leads to thin to nonexistent relationships."

While Lee McGrath speaks of "shame," Heather Mac Donald speaks of "stigma." "You can say that a world that uses stigma to enforce social norms produces the kinds of possible injustices that literature has always seized on. The poor girl, for instance, who's seduced by the clergyman in her village and who is now a fallen woman. That was unfair and one sympathizes, of course. But the use of stigma resulted in far fewer people in such situations at a time when society couldn't afford its own upkeep, much less welfare programs."

Before continuing, another quick reminder about assumptions and approach is useful. What, after all, is the connection between understanding why family fragmentation rates in the United States are as high as they are and speculating about future family structure *and*, therefore, the country's class structure? The dynamic again is uncomplicated. Unless we understand the reasons fragmentation rates are as bad as they are, we will fail to measurably reduce them. And given the ways in which the often pathological effects of fragmentation make each other even worse, we also will fail in reversing the distancing of classes in America.

Returning to Ron Haskins, he had been talking enthusiastically about the contribution President Obama could make in strengthening marriage by talking—not lecturing—about its importance and joys, when he branched into talking about opportunity, which he suggested was the best characteristic of the "American Way." "By opportunity," Haskins said,

> I don't mean anything complex at all. I mean kids who by ten or eleven when they're in middle school can see a path on which they can really make it. They expect to go to college, and they can see great consequences. That's what America has always been based on: People seeing they have opportunity and going for it. But I've done research, I'm on boards, I've visited communities—especially black communities—and I just don't see that optimism and hope for the future there. If you ask the kids if they're going to college, they all say "Yes," but they can't believe it. I don't see how they could believe it because so many of their friends don't go. Actually, their friends are getting murdered.

Geographer John Adams also talked about the dispirited failure of many young and not-so-young people in taking advantage of very real opportunities. His specific reference is to African Americans and American Indians, two groups with very high nonmarital birthrates. "They often lack the focus of doing things on behalf of future plans that immigrant kids have in spades. I've always been struck by how quickly Somali men took over the taxi business in the Twin Cities. You wonder, what about the other folks who are chronically unemployed and underemployed. Why can't they get their act together? Of course they lack the attributes that make it possible."

One of the questions I asked many respondents was, "What's the glue holding the country together?" We'll get more fully to that discussion next chapter, but here's a bridge to it, again by John Adams. "Given that bad things happen to almost all people at some time in their lives, those who have the glue, those who are part of a family that has a common outlook about what a good life means, are in better shape. If bad things happen to individuals in such families, they have the tools to get beyond them instead of letting problems divert them from their chosen paths. Families without that structure or attitude about life don't have the tools. The critical piece missing in these disorganized families is the idea you have a future and you can act today in the interest of it."

It goes without saying that not all single-parent families are disorganized or bereft of "glue" and cohesion, but a disproportionate number are. And again, in regard to the chapter's main question about why fragmentation rates are so high, it also goes without saying that young people emerging from disproportionately disorganized families, as well as men and women not making good use of opportunities there for the taking, are less likely to marry successfully if they ever marry at all.

Many of what we might call "more-conceptual" conversations about why many men and women are not doing marriage very well these days dealt with themes of American individualism and questing. Starting with David Blankenhorn of the Institute for American Values, here are several theorized ties between large American ideas and large-scale family fragmentation.

"Fragmentation," Blankenhorn said,

> seems to be somehow connected with Anglo culture because other countries "competing" with us in this area also seem to be English speaking. I suspect it has something to do with traits that we like in other ways: a strong streak of individualism; a strong emphasis on individual rights; a kind of leave-me-alone type of freedom; not very communalistic; not very interested in conforming to the expectations of social institutions; a kind or irreverent, wide-open, pig-stomping, over-the-top attitude about life in general. All of that makes ours an endlessly interesting and endlessly dynamic country. But when you take some of those same values and introduce them into family relationships between parents and children and between husbands and wives it leads to a very fragile family system with a great deal of fragmentation and a great deal of suffering.

Checker Finn puts matters similarly but less harshly when he says, "We're a questing, moving, and often entrepreneurial people willing to strike out into new territory and try new things, start new things, invent new things, move to new places. We're less set in our ways. This has a lot of plusses for the economy and for other aspects of society. But just like I might move from Ohio to D.C., I might move from Sally to Susie to Max in the course of my life of relationships."

Bruce Peterson, the Hennepin County district judge we met last chapter, is more severe when he contends: "We don't have a communal society. We don't have a kind and gentle society. We have a rugged individualistic society where self-interested people strive for personal fulfillment. We have a throwaway culture: meet my needs, and if the product or person doesn't, I'll look elsewhere." Peterson's comment came right after his psychologist wife Lissa Peterson said, "We have a genetic pool of breakaway people. We're the blood of immigrants who left what was unsatisfying to them. They were intolerant of the status quo and ventured forth."

Jason Adkins again spoke of family fragmentation and right notions of individualism and trust that echo both Burke and Tocqueville.

> One of the biggest challenges I see with increasing fragmentation is the rise of a kind of individualism that makes it difficult to trust and work within an institutional framework. One of the things holding society together is a framework of nongovernmental institutions and associations, as they are the sources of solidarity, community, and support which are necessary for human flourishing. Burke called them "little platoons" and we often refer to them as comprising civil society. No man is an island and we all need these support structures to grow and develop whether they're schools, churches, voluntary associations, bowling clubs, or whatever you want to call them. But we're seeing how an unhealthy individualism is leading to declining trust in some of those institutions as well as diminishing levels of participation in them. There's an attitude that they don't matter. But as those institutions decline, something has to fill the gaps they leave, and oftentimes it's the state.

But what's the source of such separatist individualism? Adkins argued it's partially the product of the difficulty many fragmented families have in "modeling a community." Often such families "don't have a full-blown communitarian dimension; they don't have the kind of solidarity that shows people how to live with others, give to others, sacrifice for others, and work together as a team." Adkins acknowledged this is not always the case, of course, and that many parents make extraordinary sacrifices for their children. "But the self-serving individualism at the source of much family fragmentation is plainly taking its toll," he said, especially in his generation. (Adkins is thirty-six.)

"It is hard," he continued "to develop a sense of solidarity when one parent has walked out of the family, or your parents have decided they would be happier if they went their separate ways. Children are forced to embrace a distorted, but understandable, sense of independence just to survive emotionally. We cannot assume that the effects on individuals of a permissive divorce culture will not have broader social consequences."

Before going further, and with all due respect to the learned arguments above and below, permit me to interrupt and simply note that Americans make a lot of babies outside of marriage and get divorced a lot *because they can*. Compared, after all, to powerful and persuasive centrifugal forces everywhere, what, at the end of the evening, is dissuading, much less preventing, people from stepping out of marriages lasting lifetimes, or marriages of any kind? Or, as cited by a respondent paraphrasing a radio talk show host, "We are the victims of our own vast prosperity."

As much as I dislike the term, let's move on by spending some "quality time" with William Doherty of the University of Minnesota, as he discussed several previously mentioned themes albeit in different ways. "Aside from Native peoples and Africans brought here as slaves," he correctly pointed out, as did Lissa Peterson, "we are a nation of immigrants."

> We're less rooted, which is one of our strengths as well as one of our weaknesses. I suspect we have always had more family fragmentation than Europe. We led the way in the mid- to late-twentieth century and now the twenty-first century with individualism, doing one's own thing. It's a powerful norm, what I call the consumer culture of marriage and relationships. We have led the way in the decline of a duty ethic and more towards a how-is-this-working-for-me ethic. We have culturally relativized marriage so much. We've mostly lost our cultural voice on the topic.

Speaking about marriage as an institution in ways similar to how writer Kay Hymowitz did last chapter, Doherty argued, "Academics in the area are reluctant to talk about the benefits of marriage as an institution. Another way of saying this is that we don't think much in terms of institutions. We think more easily in terms of individuals and individual choice. So for me, cultural issues and how they shape values and behavior are really huge."

Doherty argued that clergy also haven't been saying much of a helpful sort. "Many churches and faith communities haven't found their voice on family fragmentation ever since the 1960s. The mainstream churches have emphasized freedom from oppressive family structures and individual self-determination, but they haven't found their voice when it comes to matters of personal well-being *and* family stability." Contributing to the problem is the way churchgoers "jump around and religion shop," causing clergy to be "very worried about offending their congregants." Or as Checker Finn summed up more bitingly, "The liberal faiths don't even try to tell people what their familial obligations are."

A further reason for institutionalized silence, one we haven't noted yet, is the fact that "a lot of family fragmentation," according to Doherty, "is part and parcel of women's choices, and that's why there's such a powerful pushback to this conversation. Women initiate about two-thirds of divorces. People are concerned that such talk is part of an agenda to put women back in the kitchen or keep them in dangerous relationships." For the record, that's not what the talk here is about or any other place I know.

The rest of this chapter looks at a variety of other arguments as to why family fragmentation often borders on the routine before finishing off with a few more points regarding religion.

Surprisingly or not, comparatively few respondents explicitly cited continuing racism or other bigotries as major contributors to fragmentation. Still, historian Elaine Tyler May used the word "oppression," as in: "I think of oppression as a heavy weight, as something pressing down. I think of poorer, especially nonwhite communities, where opportunities are so limited you almost cannot escape boxes of hardship." And Judge Peterson, when asked about the role race and ethnicity plays in everything we talked about, answered quickly and emphatically: "Race is the most significant factor in every sociological development in this country. It's all race related. You can't take several million people, enslave them for two hundred years, repress them for another hundred, and then expect them, even within another fifty years, to successfully join a prosperous, mainstream society. I was going to bring this up. As you're asking questions, I'm picturing people I see in court. Our Co-Parent Court is about 80 percent African American. It's a huge issue."

But it was Chris Stewart, who leads the African American Leadership Forum in the Twin Cities, who framed matters of race in historic and institutional terms more explicitly than did anyone else. Here's a portion of his argument, which we will return to in chapter 7 when we discuss ways of strengthening both marriage and mobility.

> I could design an experiment that puts today's white folks, for the next century, into the same exact opportunity structures that black folks have been in and then you and I can have this conversation a century from now and the numbers would look quite different, because families don't exist in vacuums. There was a 250-year history of tearing the black family apart by law, custom, commerce, and social policy. Then

> 100 years of severe racial and economic discrimination. Then another 50 years of poverty policy that favored dis-unification of families rather than nuclear families. Where in discussions about personal responsibilities and the superior social behaviors of white men does this history receive adequate assessment?

And:

> Having been an inner-city father working for millionaires, the right questions center on the availability of opportunities. What are the life-altering opportunities that come with your address? Let's look at what's available, not whether I'm a good parent or a bad parent, or whether I'm a good kid or a bad kid. My own education happened in a lot of very nice libraries and I'm a *big* supporter and consumer of them. But as someone who loves them and goes to every one I possibly can, I assure you they're very different. There are big possibilities in some libraries and much smaller possibilities in others. That, for me, is symbolic for the larger opportunity structure. What I found in libraries changed my life.

And then:

> You can't ignore the fact that there's a reason why I know not to live in certain areas if I want my family to thrive. It's not because I believe the mythology that says I'm such a great parent and have such a strong family that you can plop me anywhere and my kids are still going to do well. There are some neighborhoods I will not move to, not because of the other people, but because there's nothing there for a strong childhood.

Whether or not interviewees volunteered much about race during our sessions, none, assuredly, would disagree with Kay Hymowitz, who said, "Obviously, it's not like you just end discrimination and put Humpty Dumpty back together again."

Still, and without ignoring or gainsaying our nation's racial history, respondents focused more on the role of behavior than on the role of race, as when Heather Mac Donald argued: "If you have bourgeois values of discipline—showing up on time, not talking back to your boss, not buying more than you can afford—you're going to advance," regardless of race.

In a statement not unrelated to what she previously said about marriage as an institution, Kay Horowitz creatively talked about marriage as "software for the brain." "Imagine a guy," she said,

> who grows up in a world where there's no marriage. He has sex with a woman and she gets pregnant. Fine. They deal with it. But now imagine a guy who grows up in a world where there's marriage all around and he assumes he will, in fact, marry before having a child. So he gets involved with a woman and now in the back of his mind he's asking himself: "Is she really the one? Is she somebody I could marry?" In other words, many of the important questions people should ask about those they're involved with are housed in marriage-embedded "software for the brain." But the messages and signals of such software are lost on great numbers of Americans because they live in worlds virtually without marriage. In other words, when there's no marriage, it's much harder for people to formulate what they're looking for, thereby increasing their chances of making serious, lifelong mistakes; mistakes which can hurt children most of all.

Returning to Bill Doherty, he did some well-informed speculating that transitions nicely from Hymowitz's cranial software when he argued, "We haven't developed sufficient interpersonal competencies. Or, if you will, many people haven't developed the RQ, the relationship intelligence to pull these things off. So it's not surprising that the group pulling off marriage best is college-educated folks who somehow along the way have developed more relational skills and competencies."

I asked him to play with the idea that Barbara Dafoe Whitehead persuasively expands on in regard to non–college-educated men in chapter 7. This is how he put it:

> Again it's pretty speculative, but college at its best gives people a bit more cognitive flexibility to better understand how there are multiple perspectives. The kind of interpersonal competence now required for couple stability may be at a historic high: the ability to problem-solve together; the ability to see two people, not just one, on adult developmental trajectories in life; and the ability to work together without hierarchies as determined by gender. This kind of marriage isn't based on traditional moorings any longer. So it comes down to the ability of couples to work together in a larger culture that has devalued the stability of marriage. And in that environment, it makes sense that people with the strongest interpersonal skills and personal capacity—habits of mind and heart—are going to get married, in part, because they think they can succeed at it.

Minneapolis entrepreneur (and Ivy League alumnus) Todd Peterson might demur here, as he argued that "colleges and graduate schools are notably moot on the important topic of partnering as a success strategy, particularly marital partnerships."

Doherty offered an additional comment about how our "aspirations for marriage" are greater than ever before, which aligns with one by historian Stephanie Coontz, who talked about how family fragmentation is "ironically . . . exacerbated by our romanticizing marriage and coupling." That comment, in turn, aligns with an observation about very poor men and women—far from college-educated couples with high RQ's—by Harvard scholars Kathryn Edin and Timothy W. Nelson in their recent book about low-income fathers, *Doing the Best I Can*.

"It may not be surprising," they write, "that most fathers we spoke with are deeply cynical about marriage, yet it is striking how many still aspire to it nonetheless. The imagined bride, though, is not just someone to raise the kids and share the bills. Instead, these men say they long for, and must hold out for a 'soul mate' as a marital partner." This does not augur well, as such "high standards for marriage," Edin and Nelson write, cast the actual relationships a man may have with the mothers of his children in a "profoundly unflattering light."[1]

As was the case with explicit references to racism, not a great amount was said about how economic troubles facing the nation have had a great amount to do with the erosion of marriage. This, though, was not the case with urban ethnographer Elijah Anderson of Yale and, for a long time before that, the University of Pennsylvania, who drilled down on the economy and economic opportunities, employing a pool metaphor.

> The metaphor of the cue ball hitting the rack comes to mind. During the current economic downturn, the families of the working poor have been hit very hard. Increasingly, they've become scattered, dislocated, and broken down. They are faced with what I call "structural poverty"; poverty that occurs when jobs and opportunities have been eliminated through no fault of these people themselves, but by forces beyond their control. Among the survivors, despite the structural forces, there is often a strong belief in the work ethic and personal responsibility. And these lucky few, people who've been able to dodge the metaphorical cue ball, may be inclined to "blame the victim," and to prop themselves up by putting down the next person, and in a way that may be self-serving, ignoring the role of the wider structure. And in the wider society there appears to be similar tendency to blame the victim as well.
>
> In turn, overwhelming numbers of inner-city families struggle and many become desperate—they try to make a living anyway they can.

> I've observed ethnographically that what is left of the inner-city economy, really a default economy, rests essentially on three prongs: low wage jobs, or what is left of them, including jobs "off the books." Welfare payments, or TANF, and what is left of that. Or bartering, begging, and at times outright street crime. If any one of these prongs is unproductive, people rely on the other two, while many rely on all three simultaneously. The drug trade is the most lucrative element of the underground economy, and many young people will do what they can to survive, any way they can. But the drug trade, of course, has an utterly devastating effect on the local communities, which have become increasingly violent.

In an argument aligned with sociologist William Julius Wilson's, Anderson noted,

> All this is going on in a global economy where corporations are sending their jobs, first to nonmetropolitan America, and then to developing nations all over the world. If you take a trip around the country, and go from town to town, from Detroit to Cleveland to Dayton to Philadelphia—parts of these cities look as though they're economically strip-mined. Or ride the Amtrak from Philadelphia to New York and observe shuttered and disused factory after factory, workplaces that formerly employed those who are currently poor. These workers, in effect, are now competing with poor people all over the world. This means their standard of living declines, thereby negatively impacting the very structures of our lives, the family being the most deeply affected institution. Most importantly, what people need now are jobs with family sustaining wages.

Does all of this have at least a dotted-line connection to matters of race as raised above? Of course. And does it run nearly diametrically counter, or at least seemingly so, to what NYU's Lawrence Mead, for example, says in chapters 6 and 7 about low-income men looking for and finding work? Yes again. Stay tuned for his take on jobs and filling them.

One of the things I find fascinating about Anderson's approach is his accentuation—as an ethnographer and sociologist—of economic matters. In a similar way, I've long been fascinated by economists who focus, as appropriate, on social and cultural matters. I'm thinking, for example, of Glenn Loury and the late John Brandl, both superb economists who have keenly understood the shaping power of something called "culture" in general and religious faith in particular. This is not a profound insight on my part, but I've long viewed it as an intellectually intriguing one.

Let's begin closing the chapter by returning to how matters of religion weave through so much.

The temptation, of course, is to argue that if Americans only lived out their professed faiths more faithfully, if only they took standard-issue homilies more literally, and if only mainline churches in particular hadn't grown so understanding of human frailties, family fragmentation wouldn't pose nearly the constellation of problems it does. Maybe so, but respondents also touched other bases, starting with David Blankenhorn's recalling of Michael Harrington's comment about how the most important thing to know about Sweden is that it has Swedes. "The most important fact about American churches," Blankenhorn says, "is they have Americans in them." He also noted that "religious institutions are culture followers more than culture shapers of important things."

Jason Adkins admitted to possibly sounding like a "cranky conservative" when he talked about how "we're piggy-backing on the residue of Judeo-Christian civilization, and the principles, premises, and assumptions on which it's based are disintegrating." I asked what principles and assumptions he was talking about. To say he also sounded like the head of a Catholic organization (which he is) is not to slight his comments but is only to acknowledge that some number of other respondents would frame matters differently.

"The dignity of the human person," he started cataloging, "the sacredness of human life, the importance of the common good, the importance of equality properly understood, the reality of original sin in human affairs and the need to strive against it," all were being undermined by the "acceleration of what we might call 'relativist thinking' in schools and the media's influence on our culture." The 1990s, he contended, "now seem like years of peace and stability where the moral fiber of the country was relatively strong compared to what we've seen emerge since. I know it probably all sounds trite and cliché, but I think there's real truth in it."

I don't know if the Rev. Paul Allick agrees with Adkins, but he talked about how mainline churches have indeed gone a long way in accepting divorce—as he has done so himself—albeit largely out of "pastoral concerns." I interpreted this to mean that priests, ministers, and rabbis are counseling congregants who are in more pain than ever before in their lives, and that, almost regardless of a congregant's marital failures or transgressions, most clergy have come to implicitly understand that such moments of counseling are not the time—nor is it any longer the age—for throwing the Book at them. "We keep getting," Allick reported, "more and more freedom to express ourselves and think what we want to think. God is being taught more and more as a loving and forgiving God only. Pretty soon there's no ground to stand on anymore. There are no shared values about what's proper and what isn't. There's a price to the freedom, because if you give up your responsibility, then all you have is anarchy. I love myself. Look at me."

All of which is in keeping with Harvard's Paul Peterson's argument that "religion does not enforce the marriage contract." Rather, "religion in the United States is joining the group that meets your particular need. It's a voluntary religion. You don't have an authoritarian church that pervades the entire society and lays down the rules and lays down the stigma. We don't have the scarlet letter anymore. All religions have become very supportive and comforting of those who are poor and single."

The United States is regularly described as one of the most religious nations on earth. And while families that pray together—as well as do other things together, starting with eating dinner—presumably are more likely to stay together, that's not to say that divorce rates in some of the more religiously engaged parts of the country aren't higher than in other parts, because they are. Or, that African Americans, who are often said to be more religious than are white Americans, don't have higher out-of-wedlock birthrates, as they do and by a large margin. And it's surely not for me to gauge if anyone's faith is rooted in something other than a "true faith relationship with God," as one interviewee put it.

Even so, I have no trouble arguing that families in general would be better off if weekly church attendance in the United States was going up rather than down, which is where it's actually heading.[2] Yet in doing so, I'm forced also to acknowledge, as historian Steve Thernstrom made clear in one of our earliest interviews, that "churches in this country are very heavily female-dominated, and for them to play a major role in strengthening marriage, there would need to be a major shift in male attitudes about attending." This unfortunately dovetails with one of the more-sobering lessons learned from marriage enrichment programs aimed at low-income men and women initiated during the George W. Bush administration last decade: in simplest terms, men in particular don't like attending meetings.

Finishing off the chapter and moving to the next, we have reviewed factors contributing to very high family fragmentation rates in United

States, ranging from honorable to not-so-honorable explanations for not talking about it in the first place; superficially optimistic but really dispirited young people; governmental policies that aid and abet fragmentation; salutary and malignant versions of American individualism and questing; salutary and malignant conceptions of American culture more generally; race and racism; poorly distributed software of the brain; equally poorly distributed "RQ"; and fundamental matters of religion. It's impossible to see how family makeup and fragmentation numbers in the United States will improve as long as the perverse pressures within these remain as strong as they are.

In chapter 3, we'll continue moving closer to the core question—what might our country come to look like?—by considering the extent to which more-successful and more-fortunate Americans are thought to have a decent sense of the actual lives lived by less-successful or less-lucky ones. Included among the latter are men and women who are currently incarcerated or have been incarcerated in the past, as well as their children. The idea, once more, is that if respondents don't think more-affluent Americans have an adequate understanding and feel for the lives of much-poorer ones, and if respondents similarly don't think there's much empathy in circulation, it's hard to imagine how actual supplies of fellow-feeling might increase and how actual class divisions might blur unless fragmentation rates somehow significantly move in a healthier direction.

NOTES

1. Kathryn Edin and Timothy J. Nelson, *Doing the Best I Can: Fatherhood in the Inner City* (Berkeley: University of California, 2013), 205.

2. Weekly church attendance in the United States has declined steadily, if modestly, since 1970 (Robert D. Putnam and David E. Campbell, *American Grace: How Religion Divides and Unites Us* [New York: Simon & Schuster, 2010], 76).

THREE

How Well Do We Know and Feel for Each Other?

Another way of teasing out what the United States might come to look like begins by considering the degree to which Americans (as surmised by respondents) have a decent sense of the lives lived by low-income fellow citizens, a disproportionate portion of whom are single mothers and single fathers and their children. It's likewise helpful to consider the degree to which Americans in general have an adequate sense of the actual lives lived by presently or previously incarcerated men and women and the day-to-day lives of their children. Once again, of course, a decidedly disproportionate portion of such parents never married.

As we shall see, the ignorance that an enormous number of "average" Americans are assumed to have about the daily realities of poor Americans—a great many of whose lives are made even more difficult because of criminal records—is both cause and effect of class divisions that often are sharp already. But what might the United States come to look like when shared experiences and understandings—again, here is the critical dynamic—further shrink and common ground further erodes because of the reinforcing impediments and toxins of family fragmentation?

Early in most conversations, I asked at least a couple of questions from among these four:

"To what extent do you think Americans who have never been incarcerated have a reasonably accurate sense of the actual lives lived by Americans who have been incarcerated?"

"What about the children of those who are currently or have been incarcerated? To what extent do you think Americans who never have been incarcerated have a reasonably accurate sense of the lives lived by those girls and boys?"

I asked a similar question about poverty in general:

"To what extent to you think middle-class and upper-class Americans have a reasonably accurate sense of the actual lives lived by low-income men, women, and children?"

And I asked a question about national cohesion:

"If I were to ask you about the sources of 'glue' holding our society together, what would you say those sources are?"

We'll return to this last question about national glue. But overwhelmingly the most frequent answers to the first three questions are variations on the theme of "They don't have a clue," as when Peter Bell said, "My quick answer is I don't think Americans know the depth and breadth of America's really disorganized families, fragmented families, families where there are numbers of half-brothers and half-sisters and there's no men in their lives. They move frequently and there are financial challenges all the time. People are frequently leaving households to go to one institution or another—a group home, prison, or whatever—and then coming back. I don't think most Americans, across the political spectrum, have a clue about that kind of instability." Bell, who has held many senior posts in both private and public sectors in Minnesota, was the founder several decades ago of a chemical dependency program aimed at serving African Americans.

In regard to what Americans on upper rungs know about Americans on lower ones, Columbia University's Ron Mincy referred specifically to Washington leaders. "Where it gets really scary is when you're testifying before a congressional panel made up of men our age and older and they are *completely* clueless about the complexity of what's going on. That was one of the more frightening experiences I've ever had."

Writer Kay Hymowitz said it was her impression that "all that many upper-income people have to offer is better birth control. That's the only thing they'll talk about. They think that's the problem."

Latino media entrepreneur Alberto Monserrate said,

> It's true most people have never experienced and have never seen some of the things we've been talking about. I've always estimated that about 20 percent of the people in this country just have no interest in

> people of color. Whatever you say, they're not going to care. I think they feel superior. There's also real racism, with much of it concentrated in the South and directed at African Americans and immigrants of color. My sense is much of this was dormant for a time, but ever since Barack Obama has been president, it has been more vocal. I do a lot traveling for my businesses and I've heard people who were very supportive of Bill Clinton use the *n* word when talking about Obama. I don't believe these people are representative of most Americans, but they do exist in substantial numbers.

"I also believe," Monserrate added, "when it comes to immigration, there's a direct and positive connection between knowing immigrants and supporting immigration reform."

Brown University's Glenn Loury spoke of sociologists and ethnographers "who go in communities and chronicle the random violence that populates the lives of people living in certain quarters of our society. The violent acts, including homicides. The amount of violence that goes on inside of families. The amount of partner abuse and child abuse. I'm not sure . . ." he completed the point, "people understand how chaotic, how stress-laden, how impoverished, in every sense of that word, the lives of some of these people—who are our fellow citizens—are."

In response to my asking about whether average Americans have a decent sense of the lives of men who go back and forth to prison, Loury answered similarly: "I'm pretty sure they have no clue about the lives of these people. I haven't done any systematic interviewing on this, but I can tell you that when I lecture about these subjects around the country, people are invariably shocked by what I report."

I asked for an example.

After an audible sigh picked up by the transcriber, Loury said, "There are almost twice as many African American children with a parent who has served time in prison for a year or more before the kid reaches fourteen than white children with the same experience, even though there are six times as many white children as there are black children. So the experience of a parent who has been in prison, while it is not the majority experience among young African Americans, it is for a big number of kids." Historian and writer Barbara Dafoe Whitehead wondered how anyone could know about the lives of men who have been incarcerated unless he or she is a "good soul who's part of a prison ministry or something like that."

From prison, Loury moved to food insecurity.

> There's a sociologist at the University of Wisconsin named Alice Goffman, who spent perhaps a year living in inner-city Detroit trying to figure out how many calories a day do people there take in, where does their food come from, where does the money for their food come from and things like that. She writes of "Molly," who is basically pimping her daughter out to a fifty-something guy down the block who has a pretty good job and promises he will keep lights on in her place and keep some food in the refrigerator. He comes in with a bag of groceries and then goes out with the daughter. Goffman reports this.
>
> Or mothers laying down at eleven in the morning and trying to rest quietly so they can be strong enough to supervise the kids when they come home from school at four and then get something on the table for them to eat. Goffman estimates that the approximately sixty mothers she got to know pretty well were getting less than two thousand calories a day, with some as low as fourteen hundred. When I tell my kids here at Brown about things like that, they have not a clue. Their jaws just fall slack. They can't believe that in America—quote/unquote—people are living like that.

From food insecurity, Loury reported on similarly intriguing research by economist Sendhil Mullainathan at Harvard, who has written about how low-income people spend perhaps 20 percent of their money on (in Loury's words) "paying late fees, getting telephones lines reestablished after they've been cut off, and high interest on short-term loans they've taken out because they're in a debt cycle from which they never quite get out." Most people, Loury completed the point, "don't know how poverty becomes a self-reinforcing thing, because it carries with it a lot of other stuff."

Reaffirming Loury's point about reinforcing, historian Stephanie Coontz reminded me of my comment earlier in our interview about how I once bought a new car I couldn't afford when I was an economically distressed graduate student precisely because I had grown painfully tired of being an economically distressed graduate student. I wound up sacrificing the hundred dollars of earnest money because of my manifestly bad decision, but Coontz was right in noting that as someone approaching a doctorate, I wouldn't have to defer a new vehicle forever. "When you deferred gratification, you eventually got the gratification, but there have been a lot of studies showing that the ability of poor people to say 'no' one more time gets worn down. I think that's what people don't get about poverty in America. The extent to which it wears down people's ability to make the kinds of decisions they start out wanting to make."

Lisa Graham Keegan spoke of her husband, who had been a justice of the peace (akin to a lower court judge) in Arizona, and how he used to say, "'The decision making is horrific.' Women staying with men who are dangerous to themselves and their children. All my husband could say to them was, 'I feel compelled to tell you, this ends with you dying.' Life comes at them so raw. We don't empathize with the lack of options in so many lives."

Family therapist Bill Doherty agreed that most Americans have very little sense of the "churning" (as sociologist Andrew Cherlin notably puts it) in lower-income and nonmarital families. But he went on to say that Americans in general have a better sense of the lives of men, women, and children caught up in divorce and its aftermath, as more people have one kind of experience with it or another. Still, he argued, too many people are being led to believe in idealistic possibilities of a "good divorce" with husbands and wives being reasonable and having a "good working business relationship."

> That's the term mediators and others use: "a good working business relationship." So you've had an intimate relationship and now you have a business relationship. And if you have a good working business relationship, goes the thinking, your kids will be fine because divorce itself doesn't hurt kids. Rather, it's conflict during the divorce and after. There are people all over this town and country telling people that right now. But research in the last decade has put the lie to that, particularly in terms of the instability that occurs in kids in the years after the divorce. This conception of divorce creates an idealized picture instead of the more common experience of two people who were once deeply in love with each other, who marry, build up a life together, then become alienated and demoralized, at which point one of them pulls the plug on their dreams for lifelong union.

But to the rescue comes the "good divorce," which, according to Doherty, assumes a "high level of rationality and emotional self-management" and a belief that "while we couldn't do marriage well, we'll nonetheless do divorce well." Or "good luck," as both he and I might curtly put it. While Americans, Doherty argued, know more about the results of divorce than the results of out-of-wedlock births, that doesn't mean they know terribly much about either.

Doherty made certain to stress that, of course, divorced people have obligations to be as constructive as possible, especially for their children.

His complaint is the "idealization" message by divorce professionals who whitewash the harm of divorce.

But "knowing" or "not knowing" about people who might be hurting is one thing. What about actually having empathy for them and their predicaments? Recall what historian Elaine Tyler May said in the introduction about how Americans are more likely to be disdainful than empathetic in such matters. As summary judgments go, hers seems overly severe. Then again, here is what Yale's Elijah Anderson had to say when I asked if he thought Americans in the main had an adequate sense of lives lived by the children of incarcerated men or poor kids in general:

"Generally, Americans don't have a clear idea of the plight of children, and many others just don't care. In today's incredibly competitive environment, many simply find it easy to blame the victim and turn a blind eye to the struggles of others. Many of these very people increasingly have their own financial challenges, and when money and opportunities become scarce, they simply 'go for themselves' or simply may do what they can do to help their own and not others, whom they sometimes rationalize as 'undeserving.'"

I respect what May and Anderson have to say, but I would like to think that closer to our true state of affairs and affinities, but still far from encouraging, is C. Peter Magrath's take on the matter.

Respondent Magrath, for whom I worked at both Binghamton University and the University of Minnesota in the 1970s, has served as president of those two institutions as well as West Virginia University and the University of Missouri. "You can know something intellectually and theoretically," he says, "as I think I do about a lot of things. But that doesn't mean you can really feel it emotionally or know what it's like to *be* in their situations; to be a girl or a boy who's six or seven, from a broken family with nothing that's stable in their lives. To know how it really feels? I don't think so. But maybe that's normal human behavior."

Barbara Dafoe Whitehead, when asked if most Americans, especially upper-income ones, at least had empathy for those whose low-income lives they didn't know much about, said they might if, for example, they had contact with them in their churches, or mosques, or synagogues or if they got to know something about their family circumstances through hiring them as yardmen or nannies, or if the "stories" of low-income men, women, and children "were well told." But the days of regular daily contact, she said, were mostly over.

Was this the kind of interaction, I asked, she had on College Avenue in Appleton, Wisconsin, where she grew up in the 1940s, 1950s and 1960s?

"Exactly. And shopping at the same supermarket instead of one group going to Whole Foods and the other group going to a food pantry. Or going to the YMCA instead of some people now going to private health clubs. Or kids now playing video games at home. All these local institutions that brought people together—lower-middle class, middle class, and upper-middle class—have sorted themselves into separate categories. It's just harder."

In similar spirit, Kristin Robbins, who, along with her husband and three daughters, is a very active and engaged volunteer both locally and abroad, said the only way to be "three dimensional about a person's life and appreciate their struggles and heroism" is by actually interacting and getting to know them. "The secret to success is simple but costly—entering into long-term relationships with kids and families and guiding them as a true friend. It works, but investing the time and energy requires something most people in our fast-paced society can't or don't want to give: time."

But not much interacting, intense or otherwise, is taking place at increasingly iconic Whole Foods stores, even when they're located on a corner in Atlanta where men wait for day jobs. "So as you're driving into this Whole Foods in your BMW," as told by a respondent who assured me he drives lesser vehicles, "you go past fifteen guys who are pretty tough looking, looking for a day's work. There's that kind of jarring juxtaposition." He and his wife, he continued, had been "walking down a fancy street in New York the other day, and several people stopped us looking for money. Then we got on the subway and several more people came through the cars looking for money. So you brush up against it. But that's obviously not to say we have a very good picture of what day-to-day life is like for poor people."

A common refrain among interviewees is not only did they think *Americans* don't know much about the tough and impoverished lives of many fellow citizens, but, they conceded, *they* don't know much either.

Also showing up in the conversations was the energy, and sometimes passion, with which some respondents decried the huge numbers of Americans, especially minority men, in jails and prisons and otherwise caught up in the criminal justice system. Most frequently cited crimes in these instances were those involving drugs, which often led to interviewees indicting what they saw as the life-ruining excesses of the War on Drugs. Here, for instance, is Elaine Tyler May.

> Well, let's look at the most beleaguered demographic, young black men. The War on Drugs has created situations where drug infractions that used to be misdemeanors are now felonies. They go to prison. They come out of prison. They can't vote. They can't get a legitimate job because they have felony convictions. So what does that allow them to do? It allows them to sell drugs or do something else illegal if they can't get jobs otherwise. And then the next thing you know they're back in prison. This is the kind of thing I'm talking about when I use the word "oppression." People not being given a chance.

At the core of criticisms such as these is the belief that by incarcerating a higher proportion of people than just about any other nation on earth, the United States stands morally stained. Here, this time, is David Blankenhorn, responding initially to a question about whether Americans have an adequate sense of the actual lives lived by children whose parents have been incarcerated.

> I'm absolutely convinced the answer is no. We—and when I say "we" I include me—do not know what it's like. This is a problem that's the *other*. For people in elite positions, that's the *them*. This is the dark people. This is the people we don't know except as we might run across them, but that's it. Many Americans for many good and understandable reasons, as well as many bad reasons, think that locking up an entire generation of our young people is a good thing because it's putting dangerous guys in jail and keeping us safe. What I've come to believe, however, is that it's a bad thing. It's a mark of shame. We should be in a national discussion about how and why we have failed young people in this way. I understand the importance of locking up criminals in the interest of trying to keep us safe. But I completely reject the idea that somehow we should be happy about incarcerating a whole generation of young people, especially minorities.

My own view is that while America's being home to huge numbers of offenders and ex-offenders does not speak well of American culture and society, it's not as if our government sends people to prison for the heck of it. It sends people away because they do bad and often violent things, seriously hurting many innocent people in the process. But none of these caveats subtracts from the fact that unless crime rates in the United States decrease significantly, which blissfully would lead to a decrease in the number of men rendered unmarriageable because of rap sheets blocking their way to decent jobs, marriage in many communities across the country will remain a mostly emptied institution.

Returning to Glenn Loury, he, too, raises important questions about the wisdom of various crime-fighting policies as well as essential questions about the often prohibitive difficulties faced by offenders in starting over, as when he asks: "Must a record last forever? Is there no way out? Couldn't we have a regime in which we said, 'Purge after seven years,' or whatever the number may be so that a person can reenter civil society? Because what we've now got is a kind of excommunication of people." In similarly redemptive spirit, I'll accentuate the importance of aiding reentry in chapter 7. But for now, here is Loury, who for a long time has been one of our nation's most interesting and challenging scholars in matters of inequality and race, acknowledging what commands acknowledging regarding the connections between fragmentation and criminal behavior.

> What we've got are poorly socialized men who are acting in socially inappropriate and sometimes dangerous ways, who then come into the protectorate of society's laws and enforcement apparatus. They haven't learned impulse control. They haven't learned to delay gratification. They don't know how to deal with their anger. Their legitimate employment opportunities may be de minimis because of underdeveloped cognitive abilities and useful skills. They may not have seen anyone around them modeling right ways of dealing with various situations: this is how life is and what a "quote/unquote" man does. I don't want to put this just on men, but if we're talking about incarceration, there are ten men in prison for every woman. They haven't been socially developed to live as responsible adults among other people. All this directly connects in my mind to their home environments during their formative years.

Or as I put it, fathers matter, and it's impossible to see how fragmented families won't continue producing radically disproportionate numbers of offenders who live, if not constantly on the run, then perpetually at the margins. This is the case no matter how strategically or technologically sophisticated law enforcement agencies become—"Broken Window Theory" and all—in reducing crime rates overall.

To finish off this section, here are two other points in regard to how children, especially, may be affected by incarcerated parents, starting with Ron Haskins talking about a program in Oklahoma City that works with men coming out of prison.

> The guy who runs it is a former prisoner. I consider myself fairly well-informed about these kinds of things, but listening to him describe his own life and those of the people he works with and what they confront, I realized on a ten-point scale I had about a two or three in understanding what it's really like, especially emotionally. Just think of the things that happen. If they're incarcerated for any length of time the women in their lives often will move on to other men. This happens even if they're married and even if their wives don't abandon or end their marriages. News, however, about these things trickles through, and the men find out about them. Then they have a hell of a time finding employment. Their children, moreover, may be alienated. The kids still love them, but there are big problems. A year is a century to kids. They have developed all kinds of other relationships and now, suddenly, the main authority figures in their lives are back. There are so many concrete consequences of being away that, yes, Americans have only a modest idea of how difficult incarceration is for children and all others concerned.

But what if children are better served by *not* maintaining ties with their father? Several respondents were of the same mind as one who asked: Suppose a kid is living with a drug-dealing father. Is it really necessarily worse for the boy or girl if he winds up in prison? No.

The most basic connection between *family* cohesion and *national* cohesion has to do with how shortages of the former lead to shortages of the latter.

Or, if you will, if American families come to be readily characterized by disorder, America will come to be less firmly rooted in ordered liberty.

Or if you prefer, think of national epoxy as a proxy for fellow-feeling.

As noted above, in order to dig deeper into divisions, I asked most respondents a question about unity: "If I were to ask you about the sources of 'glue' holding our society together, what would you say those sources are?" Thinking closer to home than I anticipated but, at the same time, insightfully, Checker Finn started off by saying, "My wife and I are part of the glue in a variety of extended relationships involving kids, grandkids, grandparents, sisters-in-law, older relatives, and on. Families are not defunct; they're just in trouble." (My apologies to Dr. Finn and his distinguished physician wife, but before reading another word, consider the perhaps halving, or more, of these intricate relationships if the two were no longer married.)

As one of the country's most acute and alert education scholars for five decades, Finn naturally also spoke of how "many communities think their school is part of the glue. Just try to close one in a neighborhood or a small town, even if it makes economic and policy sense to do so. People rise up and say, 'That would be the end of our community.'"

"Churches," Finn went on, "also are a form of glue. And we still have a surprisingly Tocquevillian collection of civic institutions that we've always had. An awful lot of people turn up at those Monday Rotary Club meetings around the country, though I'm not personally sure why. My sister belongs to a knitting club, which makes it easier for her—she's single—to see the world, because she travels with members of the club. There's a bit of glue there. Some people are glued to their favorite radio station or rock band, but I'm wandering now."

Finn's comment about churches reminded me of an idea I had been playing with for several months. People often talk about their "church home." But the more time I'm around houses of worship because of my wife's ministry, the more I've come to believe the idea can be usefully expanded by conceiving churches straight out as being people's "home," not just their "church home." This is more than just a word game and it doesn't ignore the fact that most people have other places to bunk at night. But the enormous meaning, not to mention time and money, many people invest in their church—or temple or mosque, as it may be—has led me to increasingly conceive of churches, for a sizable number of Americans, as their home, *period*.

The most succinct answer, however, to the question of what's holding society together was Abby Thernstrom's, who bluntly said, "I didn't know our society *is* being held together." The best I can tell, she didn't say this simply for satirical or sarcastic effect.

More expansively, let's return to writer Katherine Kersten, from whom we last heard in chapter 1. Her immediate answer to the question of what's holding our society together was, "Throughout the history of this country, it's been the American Creed," which I asked her to define.

> It's a certain set of convictions, attitudes, and beliefs about the value of the individual, about the nature of the good life, and about rights and responsibilities. It's about forms of government, majority rule, minority rights, and the principles embodied in the Constitution and Declaration of Independence. It's about an aspirational vision of what's possible for average human beings to accomplish. In Catholic parlance, it's about

> subsidiarity and local control. We solve our own problems. Central to all of that, of course, has been the family, the place of the family, and the notion that everything radiates from the family. Obviously, this whole set of assumptions is changing quite rapidly.

She added a few moments later:

> We share in the precious heritage of the West, which requires a certain kind of mind for it to continue. I very roughly recall a quote that if Lincoln didn't say it he should have: "Not one generation can pass where these ideas are not transmitted from father to son without disaster in the country resulting from the failure to pass on our heritage and the principles by which we live."[1] That's why the family is so critically important, as it's where qualities of character, love, generosity, hard work, thrift, and gratitude—all so critical to self-government—are shaped. No institution but the family is capable of molding a democratic character. That's the connection.

It's not unrelated to note here that one of Kathy's four children is a police officer in Texas. He's in his mid-twenties but just about every day deals with domestic disputes involving usually older, drug- and alcohol-fueled men and women. The fact that it's routinely left to him to be the grownup in such encounters speaks to the sorry state of a great number of marital, cohabitating, and other intimate relationships. Suffice it to say there are subpopulations in the United States—drunken abusers being just one—for whom the lofty ideas and demanding behaviors Kathy talks about when it comes to family life in the United States are of a different universe.

The thoughtful and quotable David Blankenhorn began answering the question about American glue by saying what it *isn't*. "It isn't race. It isn't language. It isn't religion. It isn't the fact that your ancestors were from here. None of those things is true, which makes the United States fairly distinctive in the history of societies." As for what the national adhesive might be, he started by referring to his conception of the American Creed: a free society, the idea of living together in freedom, and ordered liberty. From there he moved on to religion, albeit in a more inclusive sense than how he did so immediately above. As Blankenhorn suggested, think of sociologist Peter Berger's "sacred canopy."

"For most of our country's history," he argued, "we lived under a kind of moral and religious umbrella that said we had a responsibility to Jewish and Christian religious teachings. We were 'One Nation Under

God.' Boys Town might put it, 'Every boy can pray to God in his own way, but every boy must pray.' That way of thinking doesn't hold us together nearly as much as it used to. Some of the breakdown in civility and decency in public life is due to the fraying of that kind of moral umbrella."

Blankenhorn then took off in a way that no one else did, and only a minority of respondents likely would conceive of doing, focusing on what he saw as a benign strain of "multiculturalism" as up-to-date glue.

> I resisted this for a long time, but if all you were doing was wandering around public schools in America, you would be absolutely convinced that the national civic religion was something called "multiculturalism." It's frequently taught in a very heavy-handed way, and a lot of people, especially older ones, mistrust it, including me in some ways still. But I have come to be friendlier to it as possibly another way of saying, "e pluribus unum," though sometimes we forget the "unum" part. Multiculturalism could be one way to say to kids: "Look, there are all different kinds of people in this country of ours and we've got to get along together." I would like to layer onto that some older themes of ordered liberty, the meaning of the Constitution, and the ideals of our other founding documents. And we need to make certain to remember we're more than just a beautiful mosaic of differences.

Completing his interpretation, Blankenhorn said, "Some of the language in all this is off-putting, and I wish it could all be done with a more historically minded recognition that interest in having a wide variety of people get along just didn't pop up ten or twenty years ago. But I'll tell you what. I'll take it over what I was taught growing up in Mississippi any day of the week. Here's what I was taught in Jackson: 'White Christians are just about the finest people there are and others aren't.' I'll take multiculturalism over that any day of the week." (Blankenhorn is white, Christian, and in his 50s.)

In a yesteryear excursion of my own, David's reference to how interest in everybody getting along is not a new thing got me thinking about an assembly program I participated in when I was in the third or fourth grade of an overwhelmingly Jewish elementary school in Queens—P.S. 215—more than fifty-five years ago.

We had an Easter program, with parents invited and the whole Brownie camera bit. There wasn't any religious music, but I still remember dressing up and strolling on stage as if we were parading on Fifth Avenue. Actually, the one song I do recall was Irving Berlin's "Easter

Parade." If any Jewish parents objected to their little kids celebrating Christianity's most sacred holiday, I don't recall anyone doing so, not that I remember very much from grammar school to begin with. Did any Christian parents object? Again, I don't know, though if I were to guess, I would say no. Suffice it to say I was not an insider in any of this, as I didn't spend much time in principals' offices until high school. But might such unifying non-reactions be likely now? No. Might the original decision to hold such a program—in a school with mostly Jewish students—be replicated now? Hard to imagine. Actually, it likely wouldn't be seen as kosher in too many public schools regardless of student body makeup.

Beyond the fact that "Easter Parade" was written by the Jewish Irving Berlin, what's to be learned from this long-ago school event, as it pertains to glue, both then and now? One lesson might be that "multiculturalism" as practiced a half-century ago under names such as "brotherhood" could be more inviting and less prickly than are some of the kinds practiced now.

I'm intrigued with Blankenhorn's contention and subscribe to a modest point. But sticking with the musical aside just a little longer, my wife and I attended a wonderful performance in Minneapolis by the Mormon Tabernacle Choir the very night before I wrote this part of the chapter. The immense ensemble from Salt Lake City was on a midwestern tour, and I counted a grand total of perhaps a half-dozen black faces in the three-hundred-plus, all Mormon singers and orchestra members; not a very impressive multicultural ratio. But here are some of the songs they performed:

Two Welsh hymns: "Guide Us, O Thou Great Jehovah" and "Awake and Arise."

Two African American spirituals: "I Want Jesus to Walk with Me" and "Rock-a-My Soul," both performed by a black soloist.

A Nigerian carol: "Betelehemu."

A Sephardic wedding song: "Ah, el novio no quere dinero!"

And, from the "American Songbook": "Sunrise, Sunset," from *Fiddler on the Roof*; "I've Got Rhythm," by George Gershwin via New York's old Lower East Side; and "Count Your Blessings Instead of Sheep," by Irving Berlin again.

My guess is most people leaving the concert that night felt closer to their fellow citizens than if they had spent those same two hours getting sensitivity trained.

How does all this talk about multiculturalism—good, bad, or innocuous—fit with concerns about family fragmentation? Most directly, if the diminution of marriage is already splitting families, neighborhoods, and nation, the last thing needed is additional sources of division, which overwrought conceptions of multiculturalism lead to.

An additional cause of national fracturing is disagreements over just how special—or not special at all—Americans think our country is. A few minutes after Abby Thernstrom's jab about the United States not being held together by glue or much of anything else, she also said, "I think there's a worrisome absence of American exceptionalism." Kathy Kersten (not knowing what Abby had offered) said, "I still think there's an underlying notion of American exceptionalism that draws us together." But seconds later, she also said, "It's perhaps declining because we hear so little about it, certainly not in our schools anymore—quite the opposite." A bitter tasting fruit of multiculturalism, do you think?

I interviewed the distinguished political scientist Abby Thernstrom in tandem with her distinguished historian husband Stephan Thernstrom. Here's one exchange between them. Keep in mind that this is not the only source of American glue Steve cited.

> ST: Let's not forget, we are a united people partly for the reason we have a written Constitution. We have a structure of national government and principles relating the powers of the states to the federal government. We have a very intricate system that helps give us some kind of consciousness that we are Americans.
>
> AT: I'm not convinced the fact we have a written Constitution and a legal framework within which people have to operate in the country constitutes glue. I don't know what the numbers are—surely someone has done some polling on this—regarding the percentage of Americans who actually know we have a written Constitution.
>
> ST: They don't need to know it. It has its effect. We've got a couple hundred years of history, including a great test in which close to a million people died. If you looked at polling data, there have been a lot of questions over the years, for example, on the sense of pride people around the world have for their countries. To questions like "Do you have pride in being an American?" the numbers are much higher in the United States than for comparable questions, for in-

> stance, in Germany and even France. We are a land of opportunity. That is why we are still the largest immigrant-receiving country in the world. I don't know if anybody has done this for China or India, but if the United States opened its doors wide enough, we could double our population in a year.

As if on cue, albeit six months later and across the continent, Sally Pipes, longtime head of the Pacific Research Institute in San Francisco and a naturalized American citizen from Canada, suggested that the glue keeping us reasonably one is immigrants. "People come to this country because it is the land of opportunity. People who see that and come here, they're the glue holding the country together and they will continue doing so."

A main antidote to not knowing about Americans of other stations is assuring that everybody has a good chance of boarding trains heading north. How does everything we've been talking about so far about family fragmentation play out when it comes to economic and social mobility? This is where we now go.

NOTE

1. Lincoln surely would have been proud to say it, though Google has no record of him doing so.

FOUR

Stuck in Place?

How will Americans who grow up with measurably less support than that of luckier fellow citizens fare in coming years? What are their chances of working their way up, first educationally and then occupationally? If their chances are abridged, how does that endanger the fluidity and dream of American mobility? Would the United States still stand as the world's iconic "Land of Opportunity"? For purposes of this chapter, "measurably less support" means living as a young child or adolescent only intermittently, if ever, with a married mother and father. "Luckier fellow citizens" in the above usage refers to men and women who reach eighteen with their parents having been married throughout.

Please keep in mind again that I'm not interested in arguing over the precise degree to which economic mobility has slowed in the United States because of family fragmentation or any other reason—if it has slowed significantly at all. This is the case for no other reason than I have neither the skills nor tools for such calculating. Rather, I'm interested in how men and women with weak educations and, therefore, quite likely, weak job skills might do in a job market that promises to grow (or *threatens* to grow) increasingly demanding because of persistently tougher domestic and international competition.

More to the point, I'm interested in how forty well-informed respondents size up the entropy of family fragmentation in terms of its educational and occupational reach in the lives of a great number of men and women. But before recalling what Brookings economist Isabel Sawhill had to say in the introduction about this bad mixture, it's important to get a sense of the methodological and other caveats Stanford political scientist Terry Moe (in tandem with economist Eric Hanushek) repeatedly challenged me with during our conversation in Palo Alto. It's also a good idea to get a clearer sense about what proportion of Americans we're principally talking about.

"Surely," Moe argued, "family fragmentation has something to do with inequality in our society. But any effort to explain growing inequality is much more complicated than that. I'm usually not a big fan of people who say, 'It's more complicated than that.' But there's a lot going on: globalization, changes in technology, those kinds of things. Somehow the decline of the family needs to be linked to that."

To which I responded each time he made a similar point, "Yes, right, absolutely, I agree with you." I implicitly do the same in the book's very first sentence: "Whatever one might think about the state of mobility or economic inequality in the United States, however one might gauge their harm or benignity, I assume very few people would relish participating in the current job market weighed down by poor academic and occupational skills." I'm interested in measurements that are very human, not particularly arcane. Or if you prefer, I'm not interested in statistical heavy lifting.

Still, one statistic we do need to concern ourselves with is the proportion of Americans, more or less, who are increasingly threatened by cramped opportunity. One division of labor has the split at one and ninety-nine, as in a royal 1 percent of wealthiest Americans doing a job on the plebeian rest. As rallying as this might be in some quarters, it's a largely meaningless breakdown given that the proportion of men and women doing extraordinary well in the United States is many times bigger than a lone percent.

In rounded terms, about 30 percent of adult Americans have at least a four-year college degree. A little less than 60 percent of adults have graduated high school but do not have a baccalaureate. This leaves about 10 to 12 percent who have neither graduated high school nor earned a GED later on. But given the way the marital and nonmarital patterns of the biggest cohort (the nearly 60 percent) are increasingly resembling those of lower-income men and women, concern is warranted for what can be described as a significant swath of us. This is certainly not to say that everyone without a B.A. is in trouble, as that would be nonsense. (Paid a plumber or your hair stylist recently?) But "significant swath," harsh though it may sound, is a fair description of the number of people who will be scrambling more than what might be thought of as an American norm for such things. This not pretty prospect will be reinforced by the fact that (according to one estimate) young couples marrying for the first time today have "only about a 50 percent chance of remaining together through life."[1] And as noted, more than 40 percent of American babies already come into this world outside of marriage. Or as David Blankenhorn put it, "I don't see how we can remain a majority middle-class society without a majority-married society."

Back to Isabel Sawhill, who said in our conversation,

> Growing class divisions are not just divisions of income. It's not just income inequality. It's also gaps in family formation patterns and it's a matter of gaps in educational achievement. When you put all those things together, it seems to me we have a bifurcating society in which the children of very advantaged parents, who are raised in stable families, who get good schooling, and who go on to be successful, have very different life prospects than children who are born to single-parent families, usually to parents without much education, who don't do well in school, and who go on to have a lot less success in life.

Let the record show, and needless to say, I agree with Sawhill, who has served in senior positions in Democratic administrations.

Let the record also show I agree with Ross Douthat, a conservative columnist for the *New York Times*, in his framing of matters, this time politically. "Yes, social issues like abortion help explain why [unmarried women] lean Democratic. But the more important explanation is that single life is generally more insecure and chaotic than married life, and single life with children—which is now commonplace for women under thirty—is almost impossible to navigate without the support the welfare state provides."[2] Douthat also writes that those who are "unchurched" are not only "bright young atheist[s] reading Richard Dawkins," but they're just as likely to be underemployed working-class men "whose secularism is less an intellectual choice than a symptom of [their] disconnection from community in general." Republicans, Douthat persuasively contends, often badly understand these men, casting them as "lazy moochers or spoiled children seeking 'gifts' rather than recognizing the reality of their economic troubles." Troubles that frequently tie directly back to family fragmentation, one way or another.

Flowing from Douthat's framing is this one by historian and interviewee Stephanie Coontz.

> People are nostalgic for the 1950s and '60s. There are some things I would be nostalgic for, too. That was a period when if you were a guy and a high school dropout, you could earn a wage to support a family. Wages for the bottom 50 percent were rising faster than for the top 20 percent and income inequality was decreasing. There were two things, one good and one bad. The good part was that it was really possible for a man to support a family. The bad part was that it was impossible for a woman to support herself without getting herself a guy. That meant that she often put up with relationships that you and I would consider absolutely unacceptable. It's one of those historical tradeoffs. Domestic violence has gone way down since the 1950s and '60s, clearly. When you combine a woman's new ability to live without marriage with a man's declining ability to provide, you get to this issue.

Coontz is right, of course, about the ability of women to now live without men, and not just by themselves but with their children as well. A possible implication in this passage, however, may be that most or nearly all such women are able to do so because of their participation in the paid workforce. But it has to be understood, not that Coontz would disagree, that millions of women are able to raise their children without the economic benefits of marriage only because of the dramatic expansion of the welfare state since the pivotal decades she mentions. Public benefits, while not *causing* women to have babies outside of marriage, and while not *causing* men to abandon their responsibilities, have been making it *possible* for many women and men to do exactly those things.

Respondents, obviously, are of assorted mind regarding all of the above. Here's Checker Finn, for example, on the power of education to overcome.

> It's incontrovertible that at the high end there's a greater gap between the ultra-rich and everybody else. At the same time, there's still a welcome degree of social mobility for people who get educated and work hard. It's possible to get ahead. It's possible to get your kids ahead. I keep seeing this especially in immigrant families, as they arrive with what might be called immigrant values of working hard, keeping the grocery store open eighteen hours a day, and saving enough money to send the kids to college.

Finn went on to tell a story about a cab ride he had taken while researching a book about selective public high schools.[3]

> I was being driven from Midtown Manhattan to Townsend Harris High School in Queens by an Indian immigrant taxi driver. I asked if he knew, by chance, where the school was. He said yes, as his son had just been admitted, and he was clearly pleased. I asked why he was sending his son there and he came back with two answers. The sad one, the bleak one, was that it was safer than any school in his part of town. "You don't have police there at the end of the day to keep gangs from fighting." But then he added (this could have been my grandparents speaking in 1900), "I want my son to have a better life in America than I have. I want him to go to college. I don't want him to be a taxi driver. I want him to be a success, and he will be if he goes to this high school." The man believed that, and he's probably right.

Katherine Kersten told of other cab rides, but similar stories, of immigrants and unacceptable neighborhood schools.

> The typical cab driver who comes to get me when I go to the airport is someone from Somalia or Ghana or some other place around the world. The drivers complain to me about what's happening to their kids in public schools. My heart just went out to one guy who said, "I live in Columbia Heights [an inner-ring Minneapolis suburb]. I came from Ghana ten years ago. I'm afraid for my kids at their schools here. Our children are well behaved. My wife and I want the best for them. They go to school and they see this kind of stuff. What can I do?" I talked to him about school choice and charter schools and I gave him my number. I told him to please call, that I could help him find a good and safe school for his children.

When I asked Lisa Graham Keegan a cluster of questions including whether she thought the country was simply not hospitable to poor people, she allowed, "I am impaired at all times by my optimism. I want to believe a lot of things that may or may not be true. I want to believe we are not afraid to allow poor people to succeed, and that we don't believe in a zero-sum game where if you win I lose. Although I have to say there has been more than one instance in my school-choice career of really nasty conversations with suburban families who don't want *those* kids in 'our neighborhoods.'"

What about kids growing up under tough circumstances, disproportionately in single-parent homes, who manage to graduate high school and go on to college? Once there, what are their prospects for success, broadly defined? Often, "broadly delimited" is one answer. Here again is Stephanie Coontz of Evergreen State College in Washington.

"If you come from a low-income neighborhood" Coontz said, "and go to a low-income school, chances are you're not prepared for college work. I will work for hours one-on-one with some of these kids every week. But, oh, my God! Many of them come in without any of the habits, skills, expectations, or the intellectual backgrounds they need. And if they drop out, they end up having to pay off student loans."

Compare Coontz's comments, especially about expectations and cultural backgrounds, with those of Columbia's Ron Mincy, who is African American. "I'm the first person in my extended family to go to college. There are a lot of unwritten rules. A broad swath of the population will continue not being exposed to a lot of things. Even if they have opportunities to go to college, there are lots of reasons why not having an earlier generation or two precede you means you're not going to max out on the experience."

Earlier in our conversation, when discussing what it takes to do superior graduate work at a place like Columbia, Mincy spoke about how there really are differences between students who do their undergraduate work at first-tier institutions and those who do their undergraduate work at weaker places. This shouldn't be a surprise, but it bears noting more often than is the case. "I'm thinking about the skills you want to acquire in order to perform really well as a professional. The big difference I see is in writing and communication skills along with social skills that enable people to make it in the workplace. I see significant differences between graduate students who receive their bachelor's degree from Ivy League–caliber universities as opposed, for example, to one of the city colleges in New York."

A few minutes before that Mincy spoke of an additional source of inequality I had never considered when it comes to college graduates. "When my son graduated from college, I was astounded by the number of other young men who were graduating with child support orders." Mincy acknowledged the tiny sample size, but he had been taken aback by how much of the new graduates' new earning power already had been spoken for.

After noting that more is being written now than has been in a long time about whether income inequality is growing and mobility is decreasing in the United States, I often asked questions such as these:

"Where do you come down regarding current claims and arguments about mobility and inequality?"

"Do you see current-day American society as simply not set up economically and in other ways for more than a relative few low-income people to succeed?"

"Or do you see avenues of opportunity as quite open?"

Here are several of the more interesting answers, starting with Harvard historian Stephan Thernstrom, who I interviewed along with his political scientist wife, Abigail Thernstrom.

Steve argued that "a lot of the concern about rising income inequality is terribly misplaced," as calculations, he said, are usually based on pretax incomes. While it's not generally believed by the academic establishment, he continued, "it is pretty well established that if you look at inequality on an *after*-tax basis, the United States has one of the most progressive tax structures in the world. We're very similar to Norway, Sweden, and Germany." He also argued that most people don't compare "the quality of their economic lives" to those of LeBron James or Bill Gates. Similarly, he contended that if offered a choice between a bigger slice of a nongrowing pie as opposed to a constant share of a briskly growing one, most citizens would pick the second option, as would he.

I agreed that most Americans had, in fact, been making that choice for a long time. But I added that one of the driving forces behind the book is that while Americans have not been particularly "envious," in coming years, because of the combination of huge family fragmentation rates and more demanding job markets, I see anger, frustration, and class divisions growing inevitably. To which, both Steve and Abby agreed.

NYU political scientist Lawrence Mead also challenged what might be called the prevailing narrative in academic and other circles when he argued:

> The inequality question is mostly—not entirely, but mostly—the creation of intellectuals. It's something that liberal economists worry about. It's not something that average Americans worry about. The average American is concerned about opportunity rather than equality. He and she want a chance to get ahead and believe that they have an opportunity to do so. They're not so concerned about rich people making a lot of money. The fact that inequality has grown is not a high-level public concern. The public is much more concerned about unemployment, because unemployment threatens their ability to get ahead and have a secure life. It's only when there are very extreme cases, or what looks like privilege on Wall Street, that the public starts seeing any connection between inequality and opportunity.

Mead allowed that the "liberal side of the spectrum" has succeeded in making a more-convincing case for inequality in recent years, even though that's not the nation's main problem. "What we should be worrying about much more is the breakdown of society at the bottom, and we should worry more about its social rather than the economic aspects." In fact, he argued, by addressing the social side of the equation, we could do a great deal to reduce inequality.

Larry Mead has written several of the most consequential books about poverty and welfare reform in the United States over the last four decades.[4] We'll get to some of his suggestions, especially in regard to getting more men to work in chapters 6 and 7.

Lee McGrath of the Institute for Justice extended Mead's dismissal of worries about economic inequality. His response was that such concerns "completely miss the mark. Markets are valuing talent. These are private organizations. They can employ who they want and they can reward who they want. The fact that income inequality is growing is much more a product of very talented and hard-working individuals being rewarded for extraordinary dedication to their work."

As I did with Steve and Abby Thernstrom, I told McGrath that his views may well be accurate or largely accurate on their merits, but they don't speak to rising fear—and, therefore, they don't speak to the political discontent—infusing the issue. The "Occupy" movement, I went on, was just an early warning shot. "Would you agree or disagree?" I asked. "I completely disagree," he answered, and we were off again.

"The Occupy Movement," McGrath said, "is just street-level theater and not reflective of anything other than a media-savvy response to the generally well-intentioned Tea Party Movement."

> What do the wealthy do with their money? It's not sitting idly in bank accounts. In fact, it's not in bank accounts at all. It's in investments, and those investments are building things. They're building factories. They are building service organizations. They are employing people. Their wealth is not stagnant and unproductive. Quite the contrary, as it's being reinvested in research, development, and philanthropy. It's dynamic and doing incredibly good things. The good things that come from prosperity are horribly underestimated by the Left. The return to consumers is far greater than the return to investors.

Differing, Stanford's Terry Moe argued that concerns about inequality are legitimate, as growing disparities in opportunity and income are "not good for society."

> But we may be in a transition period, and it's important in many respects to go with it and not try to clamp down and stifle. Innovation often leads to these kinds of inequities in the short term. Maybe a hundred years from now people will look back and say, "Wow. There was this huge shift and for a while everything was out of whack. There were a large number of people who weren't qualified to do the kinds of jobs available, and in some sense, we had a bifurcation of the labor market. A lot of people were not getting anywhere, and other people were thriving and getting paid a lot of money. But over time, people better understood where the money was, and they retooled." You can see it already with how competition to get into selective colleges is greater than it ever was. So, it may be in another twenty or thirty years, adjustments will have been made and there will be a new equilibrium.

Moe's Stanford colleague, economist Eric Hanushek, argued that there's still a lot of mobility in the United States, as measured over time and it's especially apparent in Silicon Valley. "When you ask some of the kids what they're going to do after graduation they say, 'I don't know yet. I'm just going to start a business.' There's this amazing willingness to take chances and maybe win—but then again maybe not. But around here, it's not a bad mark against you to fail. They just say, 'The last company I tried didn't work.'"

At another point in our conversation, focusing no longer on one of the world's great wellsprings of talent but rather on the economy as a whole, Hanushek argued that it will "deal with the labor force it has. If we have low-quality workers, we're going to have a low-quality solution to what the economy looks like. If we have high-quality workers, the economy will adapt and produce high-quality jobs and opportunities." Or, as he more succinctly and technically put it, "It's all endogenous."

In fairness in closing off this section, let's not forget renditions of economic and social landscapes stormier than those just pictured. Here, for example, is the University of Minnesota's Elaine Tyler May's stark answer to a novella-length question I had just posed about familial, economic, military, and other notions of security.

> Once you have a Third World economic reality in the United States, which is what we have, then people become desperate for the kind of security that puts food on the table. You're talking jobs. People can't

> live on minimum-wage jobs anymore. Jobs are being outsourced. I think it was Andrew Carnegie who said something about how corporate executives should never earn more than some large multiple of what their poorest-paid workers got. Whatever that number was, gaps between our best-paid and worst-paid workers are now much, much larger. They're grotesque and unethical. Our tax structure and wage structures are messed up, and they're tearing our country apart.

Fitting here is Stephanie Coontz gentle jibe at me, "Now, this might upset you, but one problem of course is the decline of unionization."

After I noted that she was not the first person to point this out, she added: "My dad had a high school degree but he was able to save enough to go back to school because he had a union job. Those are so rare now."

Also fitting is a statistical nugget reported by Ron Mincy: "The only category of American men who have earned more than their fathers since 1974 are those who have gone on to graduate school."[5]

All of the above in this chapter, and much in previous chapters, are best understood as inquiries about opportunity. What are the chances of making it in America in the second decade of the twenty-first century? What might it be in the future? What does it take to succeed? More to the point, what does it take for young people who haven't had the luckiest starts in life to succeed, particularly those growing up, perhaps exclusively, in single-parent homes? Let's start by spending extended time with Ron Haskins, who, along with Isabel Sawhill, directs the Brookings Institution's Center on Children and Families.

My appointment with Haskins wound up being just a couple of hours before he had a presentation to make at Brookings. Meaning he had only a short amount of time to talk with me. But the subjects at hand animated him so that he just kept on talking, faster and more passionately, as we went along, trying to fit everything in. Here are excerpts from what he had to say about matters of opportunity, starting with questions of college access.

> Something I try to think about as much as I can—not that I've reached any profound insights—is the impact of family fragmentation on opportunity. To me, opportunity is the single most important characteristic of the "American Way," and to the nation's credit, we have created a lot of opportunities to go to college. Part of it is governmental assistance. I regularly take a look at College Board reports on the costs of college as well as the sources of funds for attending. It's over $100

billion of public money between tax breaks, grants, and loans. Increasingly, good schools—Harvard does this already—pay for everything if you're poor and a good student. You can go to college virtually free. Places that don't have that have lots of scholarships. There's a lot of money available, not just Pell Grants, and there's privately sponsored help as well. I came to better realize just a few years ago that the biggest barrier to college is not "lack of access" as it's regularly put, but rather students not learning nearly enough in K–12. We offer a lot of remedial courses, but they don't work very well. It's amazing how so many problems go back to our K–12 system and preschools. They need to be so much better.

Haskins, one should know, has championed more effective early childhood programs for years. As for the way in which poor high school performances by low-income students are, in fact, the single greatest obstacle to college enrollment, research by Jay Greene backs him up. As Greene writes, "The number of students who enroll in [a four-year] college is very similar to the number of students who are college ready," and this holds true for African Americans, Hispanics, American Indians, and whites. "The similarity between the college-eligible and college-entering populations throws the College Access Myth into a considerable level of doubt. There is not a large pool of students who are academically prepared for college but are failing to gain admission because of inadequate affirmative action or financial aid policies."[6]

Haskins, who knows something about government, having served as the lead Republican staffer in the House of Representative during the passage of welfare reform in 1996, concluded:

The media are full of stories about how opportunity has gone to hell. They're greatly exaggerated. Between federal and state governments, we now spend a trillion dollars a years on means-tested programs. These programs have an enormous impact on poverty rates, and while it's harder to calculate their effects on opportunity, there certainly are some. With the partial exception of tax breaks, we have one of the most progressive income tax codes in the world with money going disproportionately to those at the bottom. So government does a lot. But many people, by the way they live their lives, are not cooperating. Too many kids are just not trying hard enough in school and they don't continue their education as they should. A lot of the things we do in government are lucky to tread water because of the lack of personal responsibility. What's the best path for kids? It's living with parents who love and guide them. That's their best opportunity.

Obviously again, some number of respondents would disagree with Haskins's more individualistic, as opposed to institutional, conception of obstacles faced by many young people as well as older people. Or, referring to the chapter's title, they would have a different take on the degree to which millions are stuck in socioeconomic place. They also would take doubly unkindly to his saying that one reason he's a Republican (albeit a self-described "moderate" one) is that Republicans are less likely to make excuses for people. "Liberals," Haskins charges, "just make so many excuses. It's society. It's government. OK, so do you just give up or do you do what Geoffrey Canada does and say there are no excuses—study hard and you're going to college, period."

In the language of real estate, Haskins's critics would be more inclined to cite the stunting power of *location, location, location,* as in bad neighborhoods and other dangerous and depleting environments, than Haskins does here, not that he's the least bit blind to their argument, disagreeing more in degree than in kind. Roughly in this vein (perhaps very roughly), I asked some respondents what they thought former Secretary of Labor Robert Reich meant when, in effect, he spoke of *distance, distance, distance.* The specific question went like this: "Robert Reich has written about the 'secession of the successful.' What do you think he meant by that?" Answers didn't vary much thematically, with this one by the Rev. Paul Allick being typical. "You tend to forget about who you left behind and you don't want to interact in that world anymore. That's what it would mean to me."

Judge Bruce Peterson said, "I suppose he means the successful are seceding from responsibility for bringing everybody along." He then added, "That's why I always like going to New York. In New York, everybody is falling all over everybody. There's no separation there."

Stephanie Coontz had the best rhyming answer when she quoted what her grandmother used to contemptuously call, "Get what you can. Can it. And then sit on the can."

And then there was Peter Bell, who said pointedly: "I think Reich means the successful are increasingly not interacting with what used to be more frequently called the 'underclass' and that they're in private schools, private clubs, and gated communities." (The term "gated communities" came up more than once or twice.)

> I suspect Reich also goes further and that he means more-successful people are less empathetic and less willing to help lower-income peo-

> ple by paying more in taxes and the like. It's in keeping with the argument, for example, that if the Twin Cities had just one school district instead of dozens, the fates of kids in both affluent and impoverished communities would be entwined, causing residents to more likely pay higher taxes for education. There's some truth to that, but it's ultimately shallow and would not come close to resolving our education problems. Issues with the poor rest mostly with the poor, not the wealthy.

My conversation with Kathy Kersten about what it now takes to succeed took a novel turn when she cited the complexity of Medicare. "Just think what it takes to help an elderly parent navigate the system. My mother lives in a wonderful residential care facility. She's got six kids who help her. We see the kind of stuff she receives, Medicare Part D and all the other parts with all kinds of complex requirements. We think, gee, if she didn't have us to help her get through the red tape and all those forms with small print, how would she do it? That was not the case in her parents' lives. Things weren't nearly as complicated."

The jump from there to starting a business was short. "The addition of layers and layers of regulations," she said, "as well as higher and higher taxes has made it increasingly difficult for ordinary people to succeed. If a person didn't have a college degree, he used to be able to start his own little store and make it on Main Street. But now the extraordinary amount of OSHA requirements, EEOC requirements, health care, and other rules are just overwhelming, making it difficult for small-business men and women to succeed."

At which point I recalled a small luncheonette my maternal grandparents owned in Brooklyn in the late 1940s and early 1950s. They ran it despite the fact that neither of them could read, having both immigrated from rotten situations in Eastern Europe decades earlier. Their two sons, who could read but who never graduated high school, certainly helped them. But the remarkable fact remains that my grandfather and grandmother were able to start and successfully run a small business in this country, as recently as my childhood, without having the most basic of educational skills.

Might anything close to this be possible now? Maybe for a tiny number of green grocers and other shop-keeping immigrants working eighteen hours a day, eight days a week, with a lot of family help. Suffice it to say, though, what it takes to succeed in business two generations after my grandparents did so in their small way is a lot more *education, education, education* than used to be the case. (Since you asked, my favorite as a five-year-old was a toasted Drake's pound cake with ice cream. And as someone who turned sixty-five while writing this book, let's just say Medicare's learning curve is steeper than anticipated.)

Given all that we have discussed about family fragmentation and associated issues, not just in this chapter but from the start, what might it all suggest for the long-term political and civic well-being of the United States? What might it suggest for government's future roles? What *should* it suggest about government's future roles? That's our next stop.

NOTES

1. R. Raley and L. Bumpass, "The Topography of the Divorce Plateau: Levels and Trends in Union Stability in the United States after 1980, *Demographic Research* 8 (2003): 245–60.

2. Ross Douthat, *New York Times*, November 17, 2012.

3. Chester E. Finn Jr. and Jessica A. Hockett, *Exam Schools: Inside America's Most Selective Public High Schools* (Princeton, NJ: Princeton University, 2012).

4. Here are four insightful books about poverty in the United States by Lawrence M. Mead: *Beyond Entitlement: The Social Obligations of Citizenship* (New York: Free Press, 1986); *The New Politics of Poverty: The Nonworking Poor in America* (New York: Basic Books, 1992); *Government Matters: Welfare Reform in Wisconsin* (Princeton, NJ: Princeton University, 2004); and *Expanding Work Programs for Poor Men* (Washington, DC: AEI, 2011).

5. Several respondents in this and other chapters cite various statistics. For the sake of the book's integrity, I hope they are all on target, though as a practical matter, I cannot so vouch.

6. Jay P. Greene, *Education Myths: What Special-Interest Groups Want You to Believe about Our Schools—And Why It Isn't So* (Lanham, MD: Rowman and Littlefield, 2005), 110–11.

FIVE

How Will We Govern?

It's safe to say Americans have resonated much more over the centuries, at least rhetorically, to guarantees of individual liberty over those of economic security. This is especially the current case when it comes to Republicans and conservatives, as it's hard to think of any word in their lexicon or any beam in their ideology that comes close to matching "freedom" in either frequency or muscle. But, if in coming years, precipitated in good measure by fragmentation, increasing numbers of citizens find it difficult to fend for themselves and provide for their families (if, in fact, they have families) might demands for minimal government lose appeal and power? Might family fragmentation, in fact, contribute to an American electorate that increasingly resembles those of government-heavy Western Europe instead (comparatively speaking) of government-light voters in this country? I've increasingly assumed "yes" in both instances, and respondents notably agreed more often than not.

A parallel dynamic at play when it comes to national, as opposed to economic, security is seen in most Americans' acceptance of often-long Transportation Security Administration (TSA) lines at airports. The same may be said of National Security Agency (NSA) interest in our phone calls. Consent to such intrusions in each instance (when, in fact, people do) is no better than grudging, and barely that. But also in each instance, it's ultimately understood by most that safeguarding the physical well-being of citizens in an age of mass terror trumps a portion of our historic and soul-deep allegiance to liberty, as in civil liberties.

But because of the persistence and severity of family fragmentation and its disruptions (here's the connecting tissue in all of this), might something akin wind up happening when it comes to additional governmental involvement in economic and various other parts of our lives? A great number of citizens hate and oppose such governmental reach. But might even greater numbers come to see further public subsidizing, despite its inevitable encroachments, as essential to their well-being, and if so, will such policies increasingly come to be, one contentious way or another?

Not to sensationalize matters, but what is the possibility of radical movements of one sort or another rising from all of these ruptures? Political philosopher Laurence Cooper, for example, argues that while such a movement has never succeeded in the United States in any mass way, that's not to say that the kinds of economic and other disruptions that might result from widespread family fragmentation couldn't lead to the "emergence of a powerful, organized, illiberal political movement." This is a possibility, he has written, however "remote" it may be.[1] But how remote is "remote" in this instance, and how might such an un-American development, on the chance it came to be, disfigure us?

We'll return to questions such as these shortly, but to start, what do respondents think government can do, or at least should try to do, when it comes to reducing, if not family fragmentation rates themselves, many social and other effects of those high rates?

Over a span of more than forty years, starting in the late 1960s, C. Peter Magrath led four public universities (one of them twice) as either president or chancellor and served as president of the most important association voice in Washington on behalf of land-grant and major state universities, the Association of Public and Land-Grant Universities. I worked for him during two of those assignments back in the 1970s, first at what is now Binghamton University and later at the University of Minnesota. Now in his early eighties, Magrath unsurprisingly has a fair amount of faith in what government can do. And as someone who began his academic life as a constitutional scholar, he's unsurprisingly fond of citing Justice Brandeis's famous description of states as "laboratories of democracy." He's of the mind that problems posed by family fragmentation are too severe for the federal government to ignore or for state governments to refrain from conducting time-limited—thereby more politically feasible—experiments aimed at easing difficulties.

He's also of the mind, speaking more broadly, that there's more agreement across the nation than is usually assumed when it comes to divisive issues, even abortion. "I could be wrong about this, but I think I'm right," he said. "I do not believe we are as fractured between extreme left and extreme right as it may appear." He said the way we gerrymander congressional districts causes much of the problem, making primaries the only thing that matters in many districts. "I don't know whether it is two-thirds or three-quarters, but I believe at least two-thirds of us are moderates. Some of us more liberal; I'm probably on that side. And others are more conservative. But that a majority of us are really centrists and we are still a nation of moderates, even idealists. With the right leadership at all levels, I like to think that we can get people to come together." He also suggested that "both Left and Right are prepared to use government to accomplish their objectives."

Let's say for the sake of argument Magrath (pronounced "Ma-Grah," by the way) is right on his proportions, not that I necessarily think he's wrong. What kinds of public policies could be adopted that would make actual and significant dents in the proportion of children growing up, either entirely or for long stretches, with only one parent at home? It's an elemental question, especially given that the list of potentially potent policies, I would argue, is a lot shorter than many people assume and hope for. But that's not to say it's an empty list, as witness ideas such as the following, several of which will be expanded on in chapter 7.

I had just asked education scholar Chester (Checker) E. Finn Jr. about what new responsibilities, if any, he saw government at all levels taking on in coming decades because of high rates of family fragmentation, and he noted how he had written on various occasions about how many kids (rough as it sounds) need "culture transplants." They need to be immersed, he has said, in a value system other than what they may experience at "home or in the hood," with the same imperative for change applying to the role models and adult relationships in their lives. Think here of unapologetically middle-class values, as celebrated and taught in what have been called "sweating the small stuff" schools.[2] But bigger (some might say "swollen") public sectors likely would be the result of enlarged conceptions and jobs for public schools. Especially given that he was a senior official in the U.S. Department of Education during the Reagan administration (where I worked for him, too), I asked what he thought of the public sector taking on such new responsibilities.

> I'm almost unable to pass judgment on that because I take it for granted there are a bunch of kids for whom there's no good alternative in the here and now. To the extent we can get more schools to take on more and do it well, it's better for the kids who need it. Is it a good thing long term, in the big picture? I honest to God don't know. But I tend not to subscribe to the view that making things better makes them worse. I prefer the view that if we can do something to improve the lot of innocent children who are being damaged by very bad circumstances, we should do it.

I followed up by asking more specifically about how he saw the assumption of greater governmental responsibilities fitting with "longstanding and broadly accepted ideas about the role of government in the United States?" He spoke of how vouchers could limit the ways in which government might insinuate itself in the lives of students and families. "Let government provide the resources, but let private organizations run the schools. Still in all," he conceded, "this does mean bigger government in terms of total budgets and the range of activities that it supports. I don't know what to do about it, though."

Eric (Rick) Hanushek is a Stanford economist who has econometrically investigated a wide range of key questions regarding education and who, along with Finn, is commonly identified as conservatively inclined. (As is the case throughout this chapter in particular, I'm trying hard not to misleadingly or unfairly overlabel.) I had just asked how he would rate family fragmentation as a problem in the United States.

As he's quoted as saying in chapter 1, Hanushek said that most of his work is not about families as such but rather about what we can do via schools and society to overcome problems "that some families deed over to schools." To which, I skeptically wondered about the very capacity of governmental policies to overcome the kinds of fragmentation numbers we've been talking about. To which, Hanushek perhaps surprisingly answered: "I'm actually optimistic where this is concerned. We have lots of evidence that good teachers can overcome bad family backgrounds." He reported, for example, on research he had done years earlier in Gary, Indiana, in which he found that students lucky to have "good" teachers regularly made year-and-a-half achievement gains in a year, whereas less-lucky students with "bad" teachers averaged only half-year gains. "In just one academic year, there was up to a full year of difference in what the two groups of students learned. Just compound a few of those and you can see how we can either make up for, or reinforce, achievement differentials that kids come to school with."

I again expressed doubts, this time about the feasibility of bringing exemplary schools to mass scale as well as the likelihood of ever winding up with great numbers of such great teachers in more than occasional places. After acknowledging that teacher unions, school boards, administrators, and others resist much of what both of us favor, Hanushek argued that "if we could replace the bottom 5 to 8 percent of teachers with just average teachers, we could jump dramatically in terms of international rankings. But more than that, it would have enormous impacts on the U.S. economy in the future."

Somewhere between 5 and 8 percent of American public-school teachers, I would contend, might not sound like a particularly large number (actually, it's a positively enormous number), but how, exactly, given union contracts and other employee protections, are they to be effectively let go or counseled out of the profession? Not that Hanushek ever suggested it, but might not government someday be called on to give at least a nudge and a poke (also known in some quarters as an intrusion) to get the deed done?

Not only is NYU political scientist Lawrence Mead routinely described and/or ridiculed as a conservative scholar, but that's exactly how he has described himself. As noted earlier, he has written incisively and prolifically about poverty in the United States and possible means of lessening it. We'll also examine some of his views more extensively, in chapters 6 and 7, when we focus most specifically on ways of reducing family fragmentation and its effects. But for now let me just tease his willingness to further involve government, this time in work programs. He had just described why so many men have such extraordinarily hard times finding and holding jobs, when I asked, not felicitously, "How do you get these guys to work?"

"I think you use the child-support system and the criminal justice system. You basically attach mandatory work programs to both of these systems by saying, for example, 'You must work as part of your child support arrangements, or we're going to put you in jail. We'll help you, but you must work. On the criminal justice side, ex-offender programs often involve work, and these programs are quite similar to those regarding child support. They entail mandatory assignments where a man has to work or go back to prison."

Programs of this sort, Mead continued, do in fact exist. "But they are at the state level and no one inside the Beltway knows about them. Evaluations so far are not as strong as we had for welfare reform, but enough to be encouraging. I advocate cautious expansion of these programs, as they should become a major dimension of social policy for low-income men. This would effectively be welfare reform for men."

I asked if such jobs would include any public sector ones created expressly for the purpose.

"Yes," he said. "I think we need to be ready to do that if required, though how far it might be required is unclear."

Respondents on the left side of the aisle, of course, were more full-throated in what they hoped government would do in ameliorating the effects of family fragmentation specifically and poverty more generally. Recall, for instance, historian Elaine Tyler May's enveloping call for a "political culture that valued the common good." One where "society in the form of government was understood to ensure the common good." And then there is this abridged exchange with historian Stephanie Coontz:

> MP: Do you see government taking on additional responsibilities in coming years given the data we've been talking about, the high rates of fragmentation?
>
> SC: I think our government is in some ways more intrusive than others already, because it's always running around and picking up what corporations and people are allowed to do. That's what worries me. We have too much after-the-fact government intervention now. But the answer is not to say, "No government at all. Starve the beast." Rather, it's to say, "What are the things we really need to do?" If we want public housing, let's build it instead of giving incentives to private developers to build it and then having to go in, with a lot bureaucracy and regulations, to keep them from cheating. Why don't we just build public housing?
>
> MP: Someone could come back—it's not an exact response to the point you're making—and say that government becomes intrusive in the lives of a lot of families because a lot of men and women have been making babies the way they are. If the family breaks down, that's when the government steps in.

SC: Well, if the government would step in earlier and provide a better education system instead of the fragmented, totally unequal one we've got now, and work to establish jobs in which people do well if they perform well, families would do better. A Chinese friend of mine said that we Americans have all these fancy things with which to rescue people or pull them up once they've gone over the cliff, but we never build the kinds of roads that prevent them from going over it. I thought it was a very good analogy.

MP: Someone could come back, though, and say, "That's exactly what we've been trying to do with the War on Poverty and similar programs since the mid-1960s."

SC: The War on Poverty had some problems, but it gets a bad rap. Under both Johnson and Nixon, the War on Poverty was actually quite effective, working hand in hand with a growing economy. Between 1965 and 1975, the poverty rate for elders was halved, child poverty fell from 22 to 15 percent, and hundreds of thousands of poor people got dental care and adequate nutrition for the first time. But after 1973, when real wages started to fall for the bottom 60 percent and the income gap increased, poverty gained ground again—and too many politicians jumped at the excuse to give up the fight.

Since my job was to draw out respondents and not debate them, I brought the exchange to a close by simply contending that the War on Poverty "had been put together in about twenty-two minutes of bureaucratic time."

Keeping an eye on what all this might portend for government's reach and efficacy in the future, Peter Bell's comments provide a good link between what government can do and what it cannot, especially when it comes to the most troubled among us.

Bell is one of my colleague cofounders of Center of the American Experiment, the conservative and free-market think tank we started with others in Minneapolis in 1990. He has had an unusually varied career, having served, for example, as a banker and as the longest-tenured chairman ever of the Twin Cities' seven-county metropolitan planning and service agency, as well as being the founder in the 1980s of what was originally called the Minneapolis Institute for Black Chemical Abuse. And as mentioned earlier and as I write, he's the chairperson of the

American Refugee Committee. A former addict himself, he recognizes that there are "always people who benefit significantly from this or that government program." But, particularly going back to his work in chemical dependency and in contrast to classic twelve-step programs, he discovered "very quickly" that if the goal is deep, wide, and fundamental change, there are "real limits to what government can do." Government, in other words, can help mitigate but not necessarily do much more.

Yet, while he is critical of those who assume government can do more than it's built to do, he said conservatives who claim government facilitates the breakup of families regularly "overstate their case." They're not fundamentally wrong, he suggested, only frequently overbroad in their strictures. I agree. Bell, in turn, agreed with me when I said there are a lot of conservatives who place far too much confidence in the ability of inherently secular institutions, meaning public schools in this instance, to deal with what are in many ways spiritual problems. Many of the consequences of fragmentation, he said, are just too "harsh" for this to be otherwise.

Refining what all this might portend for government's reach and efficacy, let's proceed from the assumption noted a few pages back—indeed, this is a central premise of the book—that regularly increasing hardship and discontent resulting from ceaselessly high family fragmentation rates will put relentless pressure on the public sector to do *more*. Assuming that federal, state, and local governments can somehow scratch together a sizable number of additional dollars—not a safe assumption whatsoever—is it realistic to assume they can effectively do what they seek to do, which millions of voters will be clamoring for? Will government be capable of measurably relieving pain caused, in part, by high rates of out-of-wedlock births and divorce? Will government somehow be capable of measurably reducing out-of-wedlock births and divorces to begin with?

Kristin Robbins argued in the negative because government "can't walk alongside." I agree. Interpret "alongside" as you choose, either in religious terms (as in instilling strength and hope of the most intrepid kind) or in very practical terms (as in helping immigrant parents fill out collegiate financial aid forms for their children). In whatever sense, I think it's fair to say government can't walk alongside because it's not allowed to adequately distinguish between people, which is to say truly recognize them as individuals, discern what they might need and what they're capable of, and then lovingly—sometimes tough lovingly—help them help themselves.

Importantly, it's not just a matter of government attempting to do more and succeeding in only middling ways. Rather, as has been the case since the Progressive Era a century ago and the Great Society starting a half-century ago, when government further immerses itself in matters of social welfare, it can wind up marginalizing and sometimes substituting for nongovernmental efforts in the area. This is to say the very kind of charities and other organizations best equipped, not to write conveyor-belt checks, but to help hand to hand, face to face, and heart to heart.

As I was gearing up to write this book, I invited a wide variety of friends and colleagues in Minnesota and across the country to write short essays, generally in the vicinity of a thousand words, for a Center of the American Experiment symposium titled *Fragmented Families and Splintered Classes: Why So Much Churning? What Can be Done? What Will America Come to Look Like?*[3] (Sound reasonably familiar?) Three dozen men and women wound up writing for the publication, one of whom was the aforementioned Lawrence Cooper, a political scientist at Carleton College and an American Experiment senior fellow. He made powerful points such as these:

"The success—and in the long run, even the survival—of self-government requires more than a wise constitution supplemented by prosperity. Self-government also requires a citizenry with certain dispositions and character traits. Some of these traits, or virtues, are private or domestic. These are the qualities necessary for success and satisfaction amid a modern, commercial society: moderation, self-control, the ability to defer gratification, and the like."

Still, these qualities, he continued, as important as they are, "are not enough to undergird successful self-government. In addition to the domestic virtues that make for peace and material well-being are public virtues, the qualities that make for spirited, intelligent, and responsible citizenship." These, he said, are the "vigorous virtues," qualities such as "respect for the rights of others, *protectiveness* toward others, patriotism, and the ability and inclination to engage in civic life."

If it is true, Cooper also said, that self-governance is dependent on a certain kind of family life, then "widespread family fragmentation might well threaten the stability and even the survival of our political order."

The point, he went on to say, is not that family fragmentation leads "directly to illiberal politics," but it does tend to lead to a "pervasive sense of frustration and grievance and therewith humiliation. These unhappy sentiments" he argued, "can create a fertile ground for illiberal politics. Think of the appeal of authoritarian ideologies to once prosperous people during the 1920s and '30s. . . . Could such a threat arise in America in a serious way?"

To further draw out respondents on how they thought family fragmentation might affect politics and governance in years ahead, I read most of them, not any of Cooper's excerpts above, but most of following passage from the opening of his essay:

> Continued high rates of family fragmentation would surely bring many unpleasant results—not only economic and social results, but political ones as well. I'd like to focus on one of the latter: The possibility, however remote, of the emergence of a powerful, organized, *illiberal* political movement. Such a thing [at least a triumphant one], is unprecedented in American history, but so are today's high rates of family fragmentation, let alone the even-higher rates projected for tomorrow. America may be exceptional, but Americans aren't exempt from the needs and tendencies of human nature.

What, I asked respondents, did they think Cooper was driving at? When many of them wanted to know what he meant by *illiberal,* I said I could guess, but I wanted them to speculate, occasionally adding something about "Dr. Rorschach" being curious, too. It's fair to say that while several respondents on the Right sometimes saw such tendencies inherent in the "Occupy Wall Street" movement, several respondents on the Left had similar worries about the "Tea Party" movement.

A few conservatives likewise expressed concerns about Tea Partiers, as in this comment by a right-leaning respondent who asked for anonymity on this one point: "I think the Occupy Movement has totalitarian and violent parts to it. But I think the Tea Party Movement does, too. There's this attitude in both instances that *we* have the truth and the answers, and by gosh, we're never going to compromise." Another right-leaning interviewee, not a fan of populism's edgier strains, criticized Tea Party enthusiasts on those grounds. I don't recall anyone on the Left worrying about Occupiers.

For the record, before going on, while the inflexibility of some Tea Partiers might be likened to the immovability of 350-pound nose guard in a goal-line stand, "totalitarian" and "violent" are epithets much too far. Stalin was a totalitarian. Mao was a totalitarian. Tea Partiers, even on their angriest or grumpiest days, are of an entirely different genus. Staying with football, think of them more as agitated football coaches fearing for their teams after losing nine in a row. Also for the record, some of my best friends are Tea Partiers.

In terms of the likelihood of Cooper's dark possibility actually coming to be, answers ranged from "I'm not so pessimistic" to "It can indeed happen here," with no one predicting it actually would. Here's a sampling of relative fears.

Writer Heather Mac Donald: "Who's going to be in the 'illiberal movement'? People who come from intact families and say, 'We're sick of supporting the underclass.' Or people in the underclass themselves?"

I said it was a good and fair question, adding that I had assumed Cooper was talking about people who were not doing well, who were not finding good-paying jobs because they had bad educations, which were caused in part by growing up in fragmented and chaotic situations—people, in other words, who are angry and frustrated and want "theirs." To which she argued:

> We're seeing that already. I don't want to be apocalyptic, and I'm not, but we do have increasingly strong class-warfare politics and rhetoric. It's clear that President Obama's raising taxes in the last budget was an end in itself, as there was a need to show all those "wealthy" people we're not going to take it any longer. I don't think the Occupy Wall Street movement was so trivial or marginal. I think it speaks to a pervasive belief that wealth is zero-sum and that somebody is wealthy at the expense of somebody else.

Completing the point, Mac Donald spoke of how she was decreasingly confident, not that she was ever hugely confident, that the American public is really as conservative as often advertised.

Judge Bruce Peterson: "I think that's always a great danger, as I've had some experiences in my life which taught me the fragility of institutions. A few hard knocks can crack something you think is quite stable. I've thought that if there had been a very significant attack again after 9/11, there would have been a lot of really bad repercussions. Our civil liberties just about cracked as it was, so I'm attuned to the possibility of disintegration."

Kristin Robbins, executive director of the Economic Club of Minnesota:

> Oh, I definitely think we could end up where Greece and Spain are down the road, with part of such problems driven by fragmentation, as it drives dependency on government. Given the coming demographic realities of an aging population, a smaller workforce, and greater dependence on government programs [Robbins continued] the more difficult it will be to fund these programs and pay interest on the debt. These programs will eventually have to be curtailed and taken away. But because so many people will have been dependent on the federal government, they won't be able to draw on the support of family and community and that could drive social and political unrest. I absolutely think that. If we had stronger families, both nuclear and extended, as well as stronger neighborhoods, that would be a hedge against the political unrest we see elsewhere in the world when government is forced to reduce public assistance due to economic realities.

Five-time university president C. Peter Magrath: "I'm thinking of European countries where underclasses are so economically disaffected and angry that people become neo-Nazi types. They don't have jobs or decent educations, and they murder and do all kinds of horrible things. So yes, this is potentially a serious problem in the United States."

Writer Kay Hymowitz: "I see the logic behind such expectations, but there are a couple of reasons I'm not quite willing to go there. Remember what Francis Fukuyama described in the *Great Disruption*?[4] There is something in human nature that needs order, and we'll look for ways to create it. I don't know what form a revival would take. I don't even know if it would be in the form of a revival of bourgeois marriage. It might be something else, but it won't necessarily be chaos or a popular uprising."

Hymowitz, in a useful reminder, also stressed the difficulty of predicting anything about marriage because of the "difficulty in presuming anything at this point." The economy, she said, will change, as will technology, as will other things.

Also by way of cautions, political scientist Terry Moe, who challenged me methodologically more than any interviewee, said in response to my reading the Cooper paragraph: "My first reaction is, why focus on family fragmentation? There are all kinds of people who are not getting good jobs and who don't have good opportunities. It can have something to do with globalization and competition. It can have something to do with technology, right?"

"All of the above," I said.

"Or," he continued, "it can have something to do with tax policies, or other public policies, and on and on."

"That's exactly correct," I agreed. But recall my clear recognition in the introduction that constraints on mobility in the United States have many causes; it's just that most politicians, scholars, and other players and observers routinely fail to acknowledge family fragmentation as one of the big ones, if they acknowledge it at all.

As for the more substantive portion of this part of our conversation, Moe said: "If those things create a bifurcation of the classes where you have gross inequities that divide American society, inequities far greater than anything this nation has yet experienced, then it's hard to tell exactly what would happen because we really haven't had that in modern times." But if such inequities came to be, might we wind up with the reactions Cooper says are at least possible? "Anything is possible," Moe concluded, "but I doubt that a truly illiberal movement would rise up and take hold of American politics and government."

No surprise given their earlier remarks, but historians Stephanie Coontz and Elaine Tyler May suggested Cooper and I had things upside down.

"I think," Coontz said, "he may have it reversed. The sorts of things that are creating family fragmentation are also creating an illiberal, totalitarian bent among people who are *not* living in fragmented families." She, too, cited Tea Party people for "taking it over the top."

From there, Coontz took aim on "just one more thing": the gun debate. "I'm not some namby-pamby liberal. I live off the land as much as possible, including deer meat last night for dinner. But when people talk about, 'Don't take my guns away because I need rapid-fire assault weapons in case the cops come for me,' it terrifies me. They're talking about self-defense against what they consider to be a totalitarian state, which might just mean, as far as I can see, a state that asks them to pay their taxes. That scares me."

May refrained from using "totalitarian" but still took shots at the Tea Party Movement, which she associates with "fringy" tendencies. "A lot of it is very scary with people promoting and voting for policies that aren't necessarily in keeping with their personal needs but with some kind of ideological fervor. I do think there is some class warfare going on, but it's not from the bottom up; it's in the other direction. The class warfare is against the poor. That scares me a lot more than family fragmentation."

And then there was historian Stephan Thernstrom who, in reference to Cooper and with a bit of academic humor, expressed surprise that a political scientist would write of "human nature in the first place."

While lots of Americans, as we've discussed, are doing great, perhaps larger numbers are closer to stuck. Or, just as important, they feel that way. It's hard not to believe, I would contend, that increasing numbers of men and women will feel marginalized—steamed too—by worldwide shifts that are supremely remunerative for some men and women but appreciably less so for many others. From there, it's a straight line to a growing number of people not only increasingly looking to government for assistance but also not taking kindly to tax and other policies they assume favor the "rich." Conservatives especially frequently talk about the "politics of envy" and how they don't work in the United States. As rhetorical shorthand goes, it has been a useful jab. The only problem is "envy" in political settings looks to be a growth stock.

Or if you will, do I believe the Occupy Movement, as nonrational and disorganized as it has been, portends something lasting, albeit not necessarily in its present form? Yes, I'm afraid I do. Referring back to the top of this chapter, I anticipate many voters decreasingly resonating to calls for economic liberty and increasingly favoring demands for economic security, as somehow assured by government. Ironically and unfortunately, this in turn will further stymie the very men and women most in need of the good-paying jobs that freer economies are most likely to create.

Everything we've discussed so far has been in the service of the book's fundamental question: What might our country look like if massive family fragmentation continues? That is where we now turn more fully in chapter 6, followed by ideas in chapter 7 for reducing enormous numbers of nonmarital births and divorces as well as their many shortchanging effects on millions.

NOTES

1. Laurence D. Cooper, "Aristotle and Locke Vindicated," in *Fragmented Families and Splintered Classes: Why So Much Churning? What Can be Done? What Will America Come to Look Like?*, a symposium of Center of the American Experiment, Minneapolis, MN, October 2012, 14–15.

2. See, for example, David Whitman, *Sweating the Small Stuff: Inner-City Schools and the New Paternalism* (Washington, DC: Thomas B. Fordham Institute, 2008).

3. *Fragmented Families and Splintered Classes: Why So Much Churning? What Can be Done? What Will America Come to Look Like?* Center of the American Experiment. Minneapolis, MN, October 2012.

4. Francis Fukuyama, The *Great Disruption: Human Nature and the Reconstitution of Social Order* (New York: Free Press, 1999).

SIX

What Will America Look Like and Be?

One of the final questions I asked almost all respondents went like this: "In sum, considering all we've been talking about as well as at the risk of melodrama, what do you think the United States might come to look like in the days of your last breath?" A radically reduced composite answer—which is not necessarily an "on-average" answer—might read something like this:

On the more optimistic, albeit much slimmer side of the ledger, some interviewees were confident their own middle-class and comparatively affluent children and grandchildren, along with their similarly situated friends, likely would have good lives and that their generation likely would well-serve the nation. A few interviewees placed faith in the overcoming power of free markets. Or in the generative power of immigration. Or in the ability of low-income neighborhoods to turn themselves around. Or in the emergence of new and better-suited family forms. Or they speculated about a possible religious awakening or simply cited the hope they already derive from religious belief. But such comments and spirit—and not just in response to the melodramatic question above—were decidedly in the minority, as much more numerous were worries and worse about our nation's future.

No respondents predicted anything apocalyptic with certainty; no one saw very high rates of family fragmentation necessarily doing us in completely or nearly so. To the extent they viewed such rates as an ailment, they used terms such as a "wasting disease" rather than a "heart attack." They talked about slow declines, not fast ones. They saw a future America suffering the kinds of troubles we currently have, only more so. A place where problems caused and exacerbated by family breakdown are managed, not fixed, and where have-nots have harder times becoming haves. A place, possibly, where children are raised to be older, not wiser or more purposeful.

They imagined the United States as still the world's leader, but perhaps not. Still an economically successful nation, but a less innovative one. They assumed a less unified America with whiffs or stronger scents of unraveling. When talking about disparities and divisions, several respondents spoke unusually starkly about matters of culture, values, behavior, and race. Some spoke of a commonweal with further eroding trust, especially between men and women (black men and black women even more so), with nonmarital birthrates and divorce rates perhaps even higher than are those today. A place in which millions of boys and girls are no better educated than they currently are and, consequently, no better prepared for marriage-hospitable careers. A nation where those incapable of cutting it might be further cut out, tranquilized figuratively, and sometimes literally, by latter-day bread, circuses, and legally prescribed drugs.

Writer Kay Hymowitz cited various possibilities like these in our conversation, as when she predicted "more nonmarital childbearing among educated classes." But, at the very end, after I asked if there was anything she'd like to add, she offered a useful caution.

> Ever since I've been in the business of pontificating and punditing, I've sometimes been overly pessimistic about the ways things were going. I mean *overly*. I remember reading back in the 1990s about the coming rise of "new predators" and believing such young people would in fact arrive in great numbers, but they never did. Logic and my belief system tell me that family breakdown can only lead to truly terrible consequences. But things, happily, somehow don't necessarily turn out that way in reality. What I suspect we're talking about is something closer to a slow decline, nothing apocalyptic.

Checker Finn spoke similarly.

> I can't be melodramatic. Assuming I live for twenty more years, say, to the age of eight-eight, more or less what my father did, I don't think we're going to do anything that's dramatically different from what we're doing today. This is all incremental stuff, and as with frogs in increasingly hot water, we'll barely be aware of rising temperatures.

> There will be a little more of everything we've been talking about. There will be a little more family fragmentation—maybe a lot more. There will be more people in prison. There will be more people dependent on various government agencies and private charities to make ends meet. I see it as a wasting disease, not a heart attack.

Peter Bell continued the incremental tack, although he preferred to see his demise as fifty years out. (To strengthen rapport during our conversation, I suggested sixty.) "I think we'll be in relative, not absolute decline. Everybody will be better off in America in fifty years, but our influence in the world will be significantly diminished. Divisions in our country will grow larger, not smaller. Many of the problems associated with our relative decline, including dysfunctional individuals and dysfunctional communities, will be managed, not resolved."

To the specific role played by family fragmentation in our nation's relative decline, Bell said, "It's at the core, as I can't think of a greater contributing factor."

As with many others, Harvard's Paul Peterson gave a freighted laugh when I asked what he thought our country would look like when he breathed his last. After assuring him no interviewee had yet come up with an exact date, and after he noted, "It could happen tomorrow," he said if what I was really asking about was the course of the twenty-first century, the United States likely would grow at the "European rate" if we "don't address the underlying family and educational quality issues" we had been talking about.

In addition to growing slowly, Peterson, contended, "We are likely to be eclipsed by the growth of China and probably India. The centers of power are going to move to other parts of the world, and we're going to be a place to visit the Washington Monument and Yosemite National Park."

After assuring him his answer was one of the more quotable so far Peterson continued, further darkening already dim visions.

> We presumably could have a pleasant existence, just as the Europeans, as long as we have a protector out there. We're going to be dependent on another country to protect what we value. We don't know, of course, what the impact of an ideologically oriented Islamic movement will be. We do know that centuries ago, a militant Islamic religious movement had a profound effect on the rest of the world. There's some of that same energy now, but the militants don't yet have the resources

> or technical capacity to challenge world powers, so we have to think it's more likely the Chinese or Indians will be the dominant force.

"I see the United States," Peterson concluded, "drifting quietly into some sort of dependent position in the world."

Not sufficiently comprehending what he was saying, I asked how our country would come to be dependent and require the protection of other nations. How would that play out?

> It would be up to them to decide. No longer would it be up to us. The Europeans, fortunately, have had the United States as their protector. If the Chinese decide they want to have a market economy and a liberal world culture, then that's just fine. If they have other plans, we may not be able to stop them. China and India are potential threats, absolutely.
>
> If a nation doesn't have the economic resources to secure its borders it's dependent on decisions made elsewhere in the world. So yes, I do believe these forces can undermine our prosperity. It's not going to happen overnight. Just as with the steady slide of European nations after World War I, from being dominant forces to highly dependent on their former colony, we may find something similar. It's not a serious problem that the Chinese and Indian economies are growing so long as we're maintaining our own economic strength. That just makes the whole world more prosperous, and that's good for all of us. We don't need to worry about the Chinese economy growing at 8 percent a year. We just have to worry about our economy growing at 1 or 2 percent a year.

Only a little less somber, and after acknowledging that "only God knows" what the United States might come to look like, David Blankenhorn, in ways akin to others, said, "Maybe like now, only more so." He then drew connections between civil society—of which marriage is a vital strut—and trust.

"One of the things that evaporates when civil society decays is trust. Can I trust you? If you tell me you're going to deliver bricks on Friday, are you really going to do that? If someone says, 'I want to start a business with you,' or 'I care for you,' or 'I want to marry you,' can they be believed? The answer in a diminished civil society increasingly will be 'no.' Or, 'Who knows?'" Neither answer is conducive to bridging distances, social and otherwise.

In a somewhat different context, economist Glenn Loury spoke of "how rapidly things can change." Since the 1970s, he went on, "we've seen a revolution in the structure of family relationships, in the role of women, in attitudes about sex and sexuality, in accepting homosexuality and so forth. These have been really radical changes in a relatively short period of time, and I don't see any reason to expect they won't continue. Some of this stuff looks like an unraveling to me. To be replaced by what, I don't know."

As with Blankenhorn, family psychologist Bill Doherty also spoke about deficits of trust, in his envisioning, severe ones between men and women.

> Here's what I'm afraid of. I'm afraid we're going to have epidemic proportions of gender mistrust. It's already the case in the African American community, and it's increasingly happening in low-income white communities. Fundamental gender mistrust: females to males and males to females. But at a gut visceral level, females to males.
>
> If men are not seen by women as reliable life partners—mates to have a child with, commit to, and marry—that's going to be a self-perpetuating cycle because men won't be present in the lives of children, with the image that children have of men often distorted through the eyes of their mother as well as by the men coming in and out of her life, frequently fleetingly. Both boys and girls are increasingly going to grow up with male-negative attitudes, which are prominent in lower social classes now. If that spreads, we're in real trouble.

In good academic fashion, these comments by Doherty came only after he encapsulated major opposing ideas. "The counter position is that family structures have been changing throughout history and that human beings are quite resilient and that we will find a way to live healthily in this new environment. Maybe fragmentation rates will diminish a bit, just like divorce rates have, and nonmarital births probably will level off. And if we emphasize more social equality through education and health care [goes the counter argument], we will be in a different place, though not necessarily a worse one."

To which I jumped in and said I certainly recognized that conceptions of marriage have changed radically over the centuries but that I didn't know of one instance in which the role of men as fathers—or simply their presence—has been so, let's just say, constrained. We've had different kinds of marriage, but we haven't had situations in which kids, in very large numbers, are growing up without their fathers. To which Doherty agreed and importantly added that even when fathers were off "fighting wars or fishing at sea, they were still *psychologically* present."

Given that parental death rates used to be so much higher because of epidemics, famines, and wars, the heart of the matter for Doherty is not simply families with missing adults, but rather the "alienation and break-up of two people who have brought children into the world and how that can *never* be good for kids—save, of course, for instances of violence, abuse, and the like." He pointed out that what he had just done was emphasize the *process* that leads to rearranged families. "We know that children who have a widow or widower parent do better than boys and girls whose parents come apart in other ways, as the deceased father or mother lives on psychologically." I agreed and reinforced his point by noting how a surviving parent can say to a child, if he or she has done well, "Your father would have been so proud of you," with Doherty adding how such a mother might also complimentarily say, "You're just like him."

An aside about an aside: During this portion of my conversation with Professor Doherty, he pointed out how we don't have nearly the number of orphans we used to, and that, oh, by the way, "the new operational definition of an orphan is a child whose mother has died. The first time I saw that was about a dozen years ago in an article in the *Journal of the American Medical Association*. These were low-income kids whose mother had died."

I asked how he interpreted the usage.

"The father is peripheral. Therapists and others, when talking about low-income children often say, 'The father is not in the picture,' and I always say, 'Whose picture?'"

Let's talk more specifically about mobility or its lack. In a few moments, let's also talk more specifically about how very difficult matters of race might factor in all of this. And importantly, as you read, please keep in mind once more that the focus of the book is not on the precise statistical degree to which mobility may or not be decreasing, or the exact degree to which inequality may be increasing. Those are critical empirical debates for better-equipped others to pursue, though quite obviously, these are not the best of times for people on lower rungs to climb their way up, much less sprint there. Rather, my interest pivots on personal and broader questions like these:

Regardless of what methodologically and ideologically diverse economists might claim, would you choose to compete in an increasingly competitive market place with weak skills?

More precisely, by "weak skills" I mean the kind of poorly remunerative academic and vocational skills and credentials that afflict disproportionate numbers of young people who grow up in single-parent households?

Thinking decades ahead, would you choose to have your children or your grandchildren attempt to make good lives for themselves and their families handicapped in such ways?

Do you think any of this—which is to say, the extent to which an enormous and perhaps growing number of citizens will perform less well than they otherwise might—will benefit the United States in any conceivable way, be it economically, socially, or in any other fashion?

One of the crispest comments about inequality in the thirty-five interviews with forty respondents was by National Public Radio's Krista Tippett: "This inequality of possibility is toxic. It flies in the face of our image of ourselves. I wouldn't want to romanticize the past, but I know that in my lifetime this has become a place of less possibility for many people. I'm deeply concerned about the United States."

I asked if she thought this was particularly the case for men. She said she didn't know, but that as a mother of a son, she worried it might be. "There is some kind of inborn chutzpah in men and boys, but for that to flourish, you still need to have the right ground beneath your feet. Right?" A moment later, she added, at the risk of overgeneralizing, that men and boys often have "hard surfaces" but "soft centers," and they're "more vulnerable than they look or like to pretend."

"The right ground beneath your feet" would seem to include having a good education housed about six feet up from one's shoes. But not a single interviewee ever said a single good thing about the kinds of education kids growing up in one-parent homes frequently get. "We've got an awful lot of kids," political scientist Abigail Thernstrom argued, "coming into adulthood without the necessary skills to do well, and that picture is not likely to change in the near future."

Abby, who has visited large numbers of inner-city and other schools, especially when she and her historian husband Stephan Thernstrom wrote *No Excuses: Closing the Racial Gap in Learning,*[1] went on: "With few exceptions, teachers are terrified of delivering messages that can be heard as dissing mom. Some public schools don't dare *not* having nursery schools in them. 'Oh, you're pregnant, Sally? Well, then, you don't have to do your schoolwork until you're on your feet, and then we'll take care of the baby.' These schools are just total disasters."

I noted at this point that Justice Sandra Day O'Connor, in a Supreme Court case a decade earlier dealing with affirmative action admissions at the University of Michigan Law School, argued that preferences wouldn't be necessary twenty-five years hence because K–12 achievement gaps largely would be erased by then.[2] Abby and I agreed there was no evidence whatsoever this would be the case, starting with the debilitating fact that nonmarital birthrates for African Americans remain hugely higher than for whites, and that kids scheduled to graduate high school twenty-five years subsequent to O'Connor's prediction already have been born.

A respondent's comment that might come across as arrogant when it wasn't is a good gateway to next pages. With emphasis, the interviewee said, "I'm certainly hopeful about *my* kids and I'm certainly hopeful about their friends. It's all the other people who didn't start their lives with the vision we were blessed to have who I fear for."

Two interviews in particular, involving three interviewees, focused especially frankly on woven questions of culture, values, and behavior. Which is to say, often inescapably on questions of nationality, ethnicity, and race as well. Obviously, this is tough, elusive, and sensitive stuff, and each of these two conversations deserves to be considered at some length.

John Adams is a geographer, and while he keeps his hand in, he's an emeritus professor at the University of Minnesota's Hubert H. Humphrey School of Public Affairs. When I asked his wife, Judith Adams, how she would describe herself, she said simply "Judith." For the record, along with John, she raised three sons and a daughter and has volunteered extensively over the years in churches, schools, and other settings. One might additionally say they are a religiously engaged couple who made certain to have dinner as a family almost every night when their accomplished adult children were growing up and that their home life in those earlier years is far from incidental to their current views. To the question concerning what the United States will look like when she takes her last breath, Judith said, "It's generally going to be browner than it is now. People like us are going to become dinosaurs even more."

I asked what she meant by "people like us."

"People like John and myself. Educated, upper-middle-class white people who have a certain idea about what a coherent life is."

To which John added, "I agree with that and what's going to happen is already happening. It's been happening since William Julius Wilson first wrote about how people of means are going to move away from trouble spots and they're going to create enclaves to protect what they believe is worth protecting. They're going to leave turmoil and leave people to fend for themselves." By "means," John referred not just to money but

> ideas about how to plan one's life and hold it together. How to look after one's kids and take care of things. How to maximize benefits and minimize risks.
>
> That's the future, I think. It's going to be enclaves protecting what they have while the population of the country changes composition in terms of age, background, ethnicities, and subcultures. The ability of people to take advantage of the system is going to increase for those who know how, and those left behind, who will comprise a larger fraction of the total, will be mystified. They're going to be politically inert because those on the other end will better know how to manipulate the system to get what they want out of it. That's not going to be healthy.

A moment later I asked what he thought former Labor Secretary Robert Reich meant by the term the "secession of the successful."

"The same thing," he said. And although there are many good people who live lives of generosity, most people "don't see any reason to turn around and walk back to such problems."

John at this point did talk about a very successful retired businessman in the Twin Cities, a mutual friend of ours in his early eighties who works with boys in trouble and who "knows how to befriend, help, and instruct." I can attest he's remarkable. "But, you know, that's largely water over the dam. Retrieving people who are already damaged when they're in their twenties is very different from investing in them when they're young. I'm not sure that what schools teach is a replacement for the cultural transmissions they need. We almost forbid schools from doing that kind of instruction. We can't replace what used to happen around the house when you were drying dishes with your mom and she was talking what happened during the day when she was talking to Mrs. So and So."

Earlier, when talking more broadly about schooling, John noted how "watching TV and exchanging texts is not the same as accompanying your mom and dad to the hardware store when you're seven and they need a new part for a machine that needs to be fixed. There's more than a knowledge gap here." The perhaps overly harsh way I usually put such matters is that if you need some kind of "program" to learn what people historically have learned naturally in families, you're dead. Not dissimilarly, later in the year, Barbara Dafoe Whitehead and I were talking about research concerning the many millions of more words generally spoken to middle-class children than are spoken to lower-income children, before reaching kindergarten.[3] "Those studies," she said, "about vocabulary and talking to children, all that really, really matters." After I described a potential situation in my family in which a child might not fare well in this regard, Whitehead continued: "To me, it's so interesting because I now have an eight-month-old grandson, and it's as natural as breathing to talk and sing to him. To think it isn't natural, that one has to learn to do them, is another example of the divide."

My conversation with John and Judith Adams then turned to immigration, and comparisons between many immigrants and many born-and-bred citizens were not terribly attractive to the latter.

For a number of years, Judith volunteered at a well-respected, largely minority Catholic school in St. Paul in which immigrant children from Africa had come to outnumber African American boys and girls. "The immigrant kids were totally different. They were focused in school. They already had good language skills. The differences were amazing. They're going to figure things out and bypass their African American counterparts. And they're not going to bring them along because they really don't identify with African Americans."

To illustrate the point, Judith spoke of an Eritrean refugee who had lived with her and John for a while and who worked at a local supermarket. African American girls would hang around wanting to talk to him after he got off, but he had no interest in them. "He would come home really disgusted, saying, 'Those are not nice girls. I will never marry one of those girls. I will go back to Eritrea and find a wife.'"

John followed up a few moments later by talking about how immigrants usually have been forward looking. "When they arrived, for the most part, they kept their heads down. They looked around to see how things were done in the host country, and they adjusted their behavior to fit what they had learned as well as what they needed to learn in order to get along." This, he went on, has been in contrast to many native born citizens, disproportionately of color, who consequently have been left behind.

Recall here how Sally Pipes (a naturalized citizen herself) had similarly enthusiastic things to say about the economic and other powers of immigration.

To finish this segment, also recall Bill Bishop and his book *The Big Sort* from the introduction. He wrote, for instance, "Americans segregate themselves into their own political worlds, blocking out discordant voices and surrounding themselves with reassuring news and companions."[4] Here's geographer John Adams in like fashion:

> There are people in this country moving to places where they think that what they believe, and how they think lives ought to be lived, will be reinforced. Many people migrate for economic opportunities, especially young people. At certain points, though, people tend to move to where they're going to feel supported, with better schools, better neighbors, better this, better that.
>
> Many of our relatives are homeschooling their kids as a device for insulating them from what they feel are pernicious influences in a culture they don't believe in. At holiday time, we get cards and letters from them, so we hear what they're up to. It's pretty interesting how some people, as Judith says, figure out how to cope. They're going to program their kids so that by the time they're seventeen or eighteen, they are going to be self-sufficient and confident in their beliefs and the way they want to live.

"They have a hundred percent family backing," Judith noted, "that's the thing. They have a family structure that supports them at every turn."

To which, John concluded, "In almost all cases—actually I can't think of an exception—where there is a healthy family in our extended family, they're part of a community, and that community is reinforced by participation in a religious community. Sometimes it's Catholic. Sometimes it's Mormon. Sometimes it's Baptist. Sometimes it's this or that. But they find a place where they can get the support they need to help their family be healthy."

I would bluntly reinforce the point by contending that communities are more likely to be *communities*—reasonably stable places that nourish rather than disorganized places that exacerbate—if two-parent married families significantly outnumber one-parent unmarried ones. Similarly, recall Charles Murray's description of communities and neighborhoods in which married families are sparse as "rudderless." They are much the same dynamics with much the same fallout in each instance.

The second interview warranting a fuller discussion was with NYU's Lawrence Mead, who spoke about how the "gist of America really isn't freedom. Freedom isn't our secret. Our real secret is obligation. It's internalized obligation. That's what makes freedom possible." In brush strokes too broad for some, he rooted much of his argument in contrasts between Western and non-Western societies. "The really distinctive thing about America is that we distribute the burdens of freedom very widely. We expect ordinary people to cope with a set of responsibilities they would not face in a more-protected society where the government does things for you and where society tells you how to behave. We, however, have chosen the burdens of freedom. Our whole system is dependent on people who can deal with internalized obligations and follow them most of the time."

A few minutes earlier, Mead had suggested that "much of the sensitivity" among upper-income men and women regarding marriage and divorce has to do with guilt.

> It's all about reconciling values they know they should honor with the way they actually live. Now, my sense is that there isn't much guilt involved among the groups where marriage is collapsing the greatest. There might be shame. There might be a sense that they've disappointed other people. But that's not the same thing as guilt.
>
> They're responding to necessity. They're engaging in survival. "So I have to split. I can't remain married. I can't avoid unwed pregnancies. Life happens to me." That's the strongest sense you get from studies of low-income Americans. They believe life happens to them. They are passive. The environment imposes things on them, so they're not responsible. That's the attitude that has to be turned around before the marriage problem, as well as the work problem, can be overcome.

And perhaps even more disconcertingly:

> I think we're likely to see a polarization between the competent and less competent. What I worry about most is that the groups that accept moral obligations as an internal requirement will become more and more burdened not only with various countries falling apart abroad but also burdened at home by taking care of those without an adequate sense of individual obligation and purpose. Maybe more than half of

> society will be trying simply to survive and dealing, consequently, with associated disorders.
>
> There's a saying in the government that work flows to the competent man until he submerges, and I think that's what's going to happen to mostly white, middle-class and upper-class men and women. They will be more and more burdened taking care of people who have given up or who never had a sufficient sense of personal responsibility; people who bear the burdens, not of freedom, but un-freedom.
>
> In earlier decades relatively few Americans chose the burdens of un-freedom. This was the case even though society and the economy were vastly more hostile than they are now. Historians emphasize how desperately poor Americans were in the 1930s, but they rarely gave up. Did they abandon the idea that they we're in charge of their lives at some individual level? No. But that is what's often missing now. We're vastly richer, vastly more secure. The chance of destitution is minimal in America today even among the very, very poor. But we're falling apart because people are abandoning the burdens of freedom.

How might all this play out? Perhaps, he said, by the more routinely married "functioning population" becoming overwhelmed and saying, "We cannot. This is too much for us. We are exhausted. We have to live our lives. We have compassion fatigue or the equivalent. And hence we must withdraw." Think "secession of the successful," only more severely.

Lisa Graham Keegan hadn't heard about Mead's particular fears, but her answer to the same question about our future was an exquisitely personal counterpoint of faith.

> I think we are so bound, Mitch, to do the work we're sent to do. It's a huge and emotional issue for me. You want to go as fast as you can and do as much as you can as the tool you are for a greater purpose. If and when I'm rocking on the porch, I'll worry that I hadn't been bold enough. Or I hadn't seen through somebody else's eyes well enough to know that whatever was in my pristine Episcopal brain wasn't going to work for somebody who had nothing. So what do I think our country and world will look like? My fear is that we will too often continue raising our children to be older rather than to do their service and be more purposeful.

As sobering as most of these projections are, and as noted at the top of the chapter, a number of respondents found grounds for optimism, or at least hopefulness. Here are a lucky seven comparatively attractive, if not always great, expectations.

I had just asked Lee McGrath, who leads the Minnesota outpost of the free market–animated Institute for Justice, the "last breath" question: "Oh, I'm incredibly optimistic. We are a country that fought a civil war because it couldn't compromise, but largely absent that one horrible event, we remain a nation that deals with its political issues through compromise, debate, and exchange. It may take a while, but we eventually get things right." He added that we're also a "dynamic" country in which recognition of family fragmentation as a major problem is "clearer than it has ever been."

After McGrath also added a few statistics demonstrating the financial wisdom of getting married and getting a good education, I noted that he might have been the first person to put such a sunny face on the future. What I also should have noted was my lack of confidence that freedom and free markets (even though I share McGrath's enthusiasm for them) could somehow lead millions of both young and older Americans to adequately change their most intimate behavior. This, for no other reason than freedom and free markets surely haven't done so yet.

Economist Eric Hanushek was at least partially optimistic when he predicted, "If we work toward better solutions to some of our current problems, the United States can look like it has over the last seventy-five years in terms of international leadership economically and politically. But if we don't solve them, we're not going to look the same. The American people," he argued, "still will be comfortable, but we might not be doing the jobs we want to do. We might not be the innovators. We may be back to manufacturing the things that innovators elsewhere produce." Earlier in our conversation, and in terms of educational progress, Professor Hanushek suggested a measure of optimism in that there's "lots of evidence that good teachers can overcome bad family backgrounds."

At the risk of leaving the impression of shooting down respondents' every encouraging utterance, I'm afraid I just don't see the United States graduating, hiring, and retaining nearly enough such teachers anytime in the foreseeable future. And as for Hanushek's first point about innovation, keep in mind that perhaps more prolifically than anyone else, he has done world-class work in demonstrating the connections between a population's math and science wherewithal and its economic strength. Completing the discouraging circle, no longer are there any doubts that (1) American students are doing poorly in math and science compared to immense numbers of students elsewhere in the world; (2) massive family fragmentation has something to do with this shortcoming; (3) connections between weakened math and science knowledge and depleted occupational productivity are strong; and (4) we're not close to escaping the whirlpool.

Historians Elaine Tyler May and Stephanie Coontz found optimism in notions of common good and youthful goodness.

"I'm an optimist by nature," May said, "and I would like to think that Americans will come to realize that once they turned their back on the common good everybody suffered. Everybody. And that it was fantasy for people to try and make it on their own and to hell with everybody else. So I would like to think that by the time I breathe my last breath, Americans will have regained a sense of the necessity, goodness, and value of supporting the common good."

When I then asked May if there was anything she would like to add or subtract, she added, "Going back to your original question about whether family fragmentation is a problem, again I would just say: 'It depends.'"

Coontz spoke in not dissimilar spirit. "Sometimes I look at the political paralysis and intransigence and I despair. I look at the absolute refusal of Americans to make long-term investments. We can't think ahead, for example, about climate change, repairing our infrastructure or anything like that. It scares me. On the other hand," she went on, "I look at some of the young people, including my son, and the *extraordinary* capacity they have to worry about other people, to have deep friendships with the other sex, even if their sexual habits are not mine. I think maybe they will do better than my generation did."

Some interviewees, as noted, spoke more of hopefulness than of optimism as such. Here's Kristin Robbins, who has worked as a volunteer with low-income families for a long time, especially in an unusually effective Twin Cities program known as "The Banyan Community."

> Kids who grow up in fragmented families don't want that for their own children later on. If we can show them a way out, whether it's the Banyan or some other group that comes alongside and shows them their lives can be different, they will choose that. They just don't know the way out. They're desperately looking for paths that will let them go in different ways than those in which they were raised. Contrary to persistent stereotypes, these kids are not lazy. They're not dumb. In fact, when they are given the necessary tools for success—high expectations, mentors, opportunities to leave their often isolated communities,

> and access to networks that middle-class families enjoy—these kids can outwork and outperform their middle-class peers. They want to do better for themselves and their children. I have a lot of hope for that.

Bob Woodson is the founder and legendary president of the Center for Neighborhood Enterprise, headquartered in Washington, D.C.

> I'm hopeful. I've had to practice revolutionary patience, but I think I've found answers in the people I serve. When I go to communities run by my grassroots leaders, it's the America I long to see, to live in. I can go into neighborhoods where it's peaceful. You can leave your camera someplace and someone will bring it to you. Where people are serving people and they're not trying to destroy each other. I have seen the America of the future that in many ways is the America of the past. So that has caused me to be hopeful, as I witness it every day.

Ten minutes later Woodson said, "I travel around this country. There is a thirst for restoration."

Returning more specifically to matters of family arrangements, Judge Bruce Peterson urged that I not allow pessimistic respondents to blind me. In condensed form, he also said things like this:

> I believe we're at a great turning point in our culture, in our consciousness. All sorts of systems of hierarchy, coercion, control, and competition are not serving people well. They're going to be dispensed with. Technology is a huge, leveling factor, as everybody has information. So I think there are going to be lots of changes, lots of different social forms available to people. Because of economic, energy, and other shortages, we're going to become more communal by necessity. So don't be pessimistic, because solutions that we don't see yet often come available. There are going to be big changes that may make these family issues less important.

I don't doubt there are changes and at least partial remedies, somewhere out there, that I can't currently see or conceive. But what's particularly interesting, some might say paradoxical, about Judge Peterson's bold speculations is that I know of no jurist who has been more poignantly candid in talking and writing about how immense numbers of missing parents, usually fathers, are hurting children and contributing to crime, as he sees such sadness in his courtroom up close and personal every day. May His Honor be on to something.

The role government is presumed to play in these last seven conceptions of the future varies widely. But generally speaking, how capable is government when it comes to issues we've been talking about as well as others? Three respondents, among others, had severe doubts.

Terry Moe answered the last breath question, in part, by citing "massive environmental problems," including global warming and an overreliance on fossil fuels, plus a whole range of social problems, including health care and pensions, which will be dealt with very poorly by American government. He thought we'll continue having a good economy, "but our society will be troubled by all sorts of increasingly complex and serious problems that our government won't be able to address in a coherent, effective way."

Heather Mac Donald predicted that if marriage among elites remains relatively stable but further deteriorates among others, demands on the welfare state will grow, conjoined with weakened capacity on the part of a large number of workers to earn enough to generate enough tax revenues to support such governmental largesse.

> You can't continue extracting all that you need from the wealthy. Most of the wealthy elite are still pretty liberal. They sort of buy that problems of the poor are systemic, institutional, and caused by racism rather than behavior. So they may be willing to say for some time, "Somehow government has a responsibility to try and resolve these problems." But at some point, you'd think more people are going to realize that there's nothing government can do about them. There just isn't. There's no amount of transfer payments that can compensate for that lack of social capital.

And then there was Abby Thernstrom, who simply said, "I'm very pessimistic about the public sector fixing things. I really am."

Recall, if you will, an excerpt in the introduction from the essay "The Broken Contract: Inequality and American Decline" by the accomplished journalist George Packer.[5] The main point I wanted to make there was that while his 2011 piece was unusually detailed in citing the many harms he saw caused by growing inequality, he never once suggested that huge rates of family fragmentation had anything whatsoever to do with them. Let's return to that *Foreign Affairs* essay, not to critique his omission again, but to see how his fuller litany of bad things (I quoted only about a third of them in the introduction) line up with what respondents have argued in the half-dozen chapters since. "Inequality," Packer wrote,

> will continue to mock the American promise of opportunity for all. Inequality creates a lopsided economy, which leaves the rich with so much money that they can binge on speculation, and leaves the middle class without enough money to buy the things they think they deserve, which leads them to borrow and go in debt. These were among the long-term causes of the financial crisis and the Great Recession. Inequality hardens a society into a class system, imprisoning people in the circumstances of their birth—a rebuke to the very idea of the American dream. Inequality divides us from one another in schools, in neighborhoods, at work, on airplanes, in hospitals, in what we eat, in the condition of our bodies, in what we think, in our children's futures, in how we die. Inequality makes it harder to imagine the lives of others—which is one reason why the fate of over fourteen million more or less permanently unemployed Americans leaves so little impression in the country's political and media capitals. Inequality corrodes trust about fellow citizens, making it seem as if the game is rigged. Inequality provokes a generalized anger that finds targets where it can—immigrants, foreign countries, American elites, government in all forms—and it rewards demagogues while discrediting reformers. Inequality saps the will to conceive of ambitious solutions to large collective problems, because those problems no longer seem very collective.

"Inequality," Packer argued in short, "undermines democracy."

What's fascinating and important about this itemization are the similarities, which is not to say congruence, between Packer's rundown and what many respondents had to say. The substance and tone of the article (which was adapted from an oral presentation of his) suggest that Packer, who's a *New Yorker* staff writer, leans more to the left than do most of the men and women I interviewed, as well as to the left of myself for that matter. It's fair to say, for example, that where he rails against certain governmental policies, business practices, and cultural trends over the last half century, which, he alleges, have made inequality much worse, respondents in the main were of a different mind. They also were less likely to rip the politicians, PAC-meisters, hedge-fund managers, and extraordinarily well-paid business leaders who Packer views as main culprits.

Obviously, my conversations with interviewees would have taken different directions if I had asked Packer-type questions such as, "When it comes to matters of inequality, what does it mean that many CEOs now make hundreds of times more money than what their lowest-paid employees make?" Or, "What impact do you think the weakening of private sector unions has had on growing inequality?" But whatever differences of opinion there may be between Packer and our respondents as to inequality's causes, scope, meaning, and ultimate effects, his framing adds to the good conversations respondents and I had over thirteen months.

We have talked about family fragmentation's extra-large size. Why it's so rampant in the United States of all places. How it's causing us to separate as a people, as if drawn and quartiled (don't bother looking it up). How it's keeping us in our place, which is not a very American-sounding term. How it's changing the ways we govern ourselves and how it might eventually lead to the rise of very un-American radicalisms. And taking everything into account, we've speculated about what our country might come to look like given that so many American babies continue coming into this world outside of marriage and given that so many married couples continue having such tough times keeping things (which is to say their lives) together. So how might we reverse course?

NOTES

1. Abigail Thernstrom and Stephan Thernstrom, *No Excuses: Closing the Racial Gap in Learning* (New York: Simon & Schuster, 2004).
2. *Grutter v. Bollinger*, 539 U.S. 306 (2003).
3. For example, see Betty Hart and Todd R. Risley, *Meaningful Differences in Everyday Experiences of Young American Children* (Baltimore: P. H. Brookes, 1995).
4. Bill Bishop, *The Big Sort: Why the Clustering of Like -Minded America Is Tearing Us Apart* (Boston: Mariner, 2009), 36.
5. George Packer, "The Broken Contract," *Foreign Affairs*, November–December 2011, 20–31.

SEVEN

What to Do?

How to avoid the hostile national landscape many respondents warned about in the last chapter? One where the United States is still the world's leader, but perhaps not. Where we will continue suffering the kinds of troubles we currently have, only more so. Where have-nots have a harder time becoming haves. And where less unity suggests whiffs of unraveling.

To start, and quite obviously, the economic prospects of Americans in the middle and below must improve. This must be done (not that it has much of a populist ring to it) without pursuing policies that make it unproductively harder for upper-income men and women also to do better than they are now. This is the case because "rich" people are precisely the ones who will create most of the jobs that occupants of all quintiles and quartiles will need.

Again, obviously, nonmarital birthrates and divorce rates (especially the former) must fall significantly. The biggest beneficiaries of such a marriage revival will be countless children as they more successfully learn, grow, and eventually pursue lives and careers of their own, with similarly promising and healthier news repeating itself for their own children.

As for commensurate private sector obligations, here's one: Employee "loyalty" has not exactly been the prevailing value in the way in which large numbers of big and smaller businesses have operated ever since (as noted in the introduction) the start of corporate restructurings in the 1970s. I would like to think I'm not naïve about the punishing demands of running a successful enterprise, fully recognizing that political scientist Frederick ("Rick") Hess speaks the truth when he writes about how the "power of the market lurks in the knowledge that even dominant firms may be only one innovation away from being overthrown and that garage inventors may be only one breakthrough away from success."[1]

I also recognize that loyalty can be much more feasible in privately held businesses, as those who run publicly held companies usually have too many bottom-line-fixated shareholders and other stakeholders, and not just in the United States, to keep happy quarterly. Nevertheless, I'm very much of the mind that fierce loyalty to one's employees often can contribute more to profitability than can less-committed interest in the well-being of a company's "people" and their families. I'm of this mind because I've seen it up close and personal.[2]

An essential ingredient in reviving marriage, particularly in inner cities and other low-income neighborhoods, will be assisting millions of men become marriageable, with an emphasis on helping those with criminal records rebuild their lives. Or, as will be the frequent case, build their lives for the first time. Not just rehabilitation, as Peter Bell puts it, but *habilitation*.

Also in regard to low-income communities, one of the important insights coming out of sociologist Kathryn Edin's ethnographic research, or at least reinforced by it, is that low-income men and women tend to put off marriage until they are financially stable—a state of economic affairs that usually never arrives. And hence, neither does marriage. Edin put it this way in a 2002 interview:[3]

> What's interesting and intriguing and complicated . . . [are] the criteria they have for marriage, because the bar we found is very high. Marriage isn't something you do now, and then you and she work together as a couple, or to achieve your dream, the way it maybe was for our parents. Marriage is the finish line. It's the frosting on the cake. It's graduation, once you've achieved financial stability. . . . So it's not that marriage isn't taken seriously. I would say it's taken too seriously in some instances.

Paradoxically, this is another impediment to the revival of marriage in our great and smaller cities.

How do respondents suggest proceeding in reconvincing millions of men and women of the feasibility and benefits of marriage, especially those for children, even if they're not entirely ready to plunge? Let's start, darkly again I'm afraid, by considering not merely the difficulty of reviving marriage in the United States but, as some believe, the impossibility.

A few months after our conversation, a respondent, Joe Selvaggio, sent me an e-mail that ended, "I don't think marriage is coming back." His full note went like this:

> I know you are exposing problems society might face if the disintegration of marriage continues, and it will be a fabulous expose. But if you ever want to write something about the ways in which some people find substitutes for marriage, I have about 20 non-married people for you to interview. They are not sociologists or anthropologists, but ordinary people: rich, poor, and middle class. Since I'm very couples oriented, as well as because I often have a hard time with some of their lifestyles, I've been talking to them about how they get things to work well in their lives. Then there are my three boys. I've seen them mess with marriage and have concluded that none of them should be married. And I've talked to two of my granddaughters who already have babies and have concluded they would make terrible partners, too. In other words, if you ever want to identify substitutes for marriage for those who won't marry or shouldn't marry, I can give you a bunch of people to interview. That may be helpful since I don't think marriage is coming back.

No other respondent expressed doubts this strong. Actually, worse than doubtful, Joe is convinced marriage won't be making the comeback I seek, and, as reflected in other discussions we've had, he isn't particularly worried by its nonreturn. Not incidentally, Selvaggio, who's in his mid-seventies, may be the Twin Cities' most successful and respected entrepreneur in starting and running nonprofit organizations that effectively serve low-income men and women and their children.[4]

Needless to say, I don't share such equanimity. But that's not to say, for example, I believe many of the people I used to run into when my office was in downtown Minneapolis were equipped to participate in healthy or "equal regard" marriages. It's hard not to sound arrogant to the point of bigoted when talking about the mostly male, mostly black, and not exclusively young people who perpetually hung out near liquor and sneakers stores and who seemingly weren't doing much with their lives. As I walked past them on the way to my vehicle almost every weekday, sometimes having to maneuver my way around them, I often asked myself if I could envision them as married men anytime in the foreseeable future. Could I imagine any reasonably self-respecting woman wanting to marry any of them? My answer to myself, accurately or not, fairly or not, was always no. At which point I would challenge myself, wondering if I lacked the kind of fellow-feeling imagination that recognizes that people who are down and out do, in fact, rise above, and do so every day.

Yet it's not hard to react similarly when reading, for instance, about many of the low-income and poorly educated men in Philadelphia profiled in a very good book cited in chapter 2: *Doing the Best I Can: Fatherhood in the Inner City*, by the previously mentioned Kathryn Edin and Timothy J. Nelson. Keep in mind that Edin and Nelson have substantial empathy for the white, black, and Hispanic men they write about, arguing that forces often beyond their control—especially the evaporation of good-paying, low-skilled jobs—have much to do with their severe troubles. Still, they write toward the end of the book: "In sum, declining marriage rates among the less educated, the corresponding rise in nonmarital childbearing, and lower-skilled men's desultory participation in the child-support system all hint that a seismic shift has occurred in lower-skilled men's ability and willingness to shoulder the traditional breadwinning responsibilities of the family. According to our story, at the bottom end of the skills distribution we see not just a withdrawal but a headlong retreat—it is nearly a dead run—from the breadwinning role."[5] In a previous book, written with Maria Kafalis, Edin at one point jarringly talks about "low-quality men."[6]

Earlier in *Doing the Best I Can*, Edin and Nelson write about "Ernest," who "doesn't see his son every day, or even every week, though he has spoken to the boy fairly regularly by phone when he has been sober and not in a lockup. In fact, given his repeated spells of incarceration, heavy drinking, and, more recently, the curfew restrictions imposed by the Salvation Army, months and even years have gone by without any face-to-face interaction." Nevertheless, Edin and Nelson note, "Ernest does not shrink from claiming he plays a vital role" in his son's life.[7]

The notion that some people simply shouldn't marry for whatever reason is not nearly a new one. Neither is it a new thought that people shouldn't be dragged, be it metaphorically or otherwise, to altars against their wishes. Still, one very big problem that has emerged in recent decades is the degree to which vast chunks of American geography and life have become mostly bereft of married mothers and fathers raising their children under one roof. As I began maintaining early in the introduction, this is not good for our country, and it's even worse for our young people. Nevertheless, the main aim of this chapter is not lamenting but rather suggesting ways of benignly blurring class differences, with strengthening marriage as a main means. Precisely how might we do so?

One might be amazed by how few compelling ideas are out there for strengthening marriage and reducing family fragmentation in the United States. Then again, no one should be the least bit amazed by the dearth, since if stunning ideas were to be had, they would have been grabbed by now. There isn't a more hospitable culture to simply "call up," as family scholar Alan Carlson has put it. Granted gratefully, we have made progress in some areas, for example, in reducing teenage pregnancy rates (dramatically, actually)[8] and reducing divorce rates among college-educated men and women.[9] But we have failed miserably in rescuing falling marriage rates among those less educated, leaving immense proportions of children growing up in single-parent households. It's a painfully depleting picture in both economic and human terms.

Despite their collective brilliance (not an overstatement), respondents did much more dissecting than solving. This isn't surprising since I asked many more dissecting than solving questions. In light, the rest of this chapter, more than the others, draws not just on what respondents had to say, and not just on what I have to say, but also on what a variety of scholars and other observers have been saying in recent years, as well as on what a few cities and organizations have been trying.

Economist Isabel Sawhill, who also is one of our forty respondents, in a 2012 op-ed titled "Opportunity in America: The Disadvantages Start at Conception," offered three ideas to "improve the upward mobility chances of less advantaged children."

"First," she wrote, "it would help if more parents were ready to take on the most important responsibility any adult normally assumes, which is the decision to have a child. Unfortunately for far too many teens and young adults, this is not a carefully planned decision." Sawhill noted, for instance, that research has shown that "access to more effective (but expensive and hard-to-get) forms of contraception" could help, with making "Plan B available over the counter" as just one example.

Second, the Brookings scholar, government veteran, and founder of the National Campaign to Prevent Teen and Unplanned Pregnancy suggested education improvements such as "high-quality early-education programs . . . putting better teachers in the classroom, setting higher standards and expecting students and parents to be full partners in this effort."

And third, Sawhill argued that no one should graduate high school without the "specific skills needed by today's employers." Called for, she wrote, is more technical and career education, more community college programs, and more on-the-job training. For a kicker, she asked and answered: "Will we make the needed changes? Not if we remain overly focused on keeping taxes low and fail to restrain spending on the affluent elderly."[10]

A very good blog post titled "Mobility Is a Problem; Now What?" by Ron Haskins, Sawhill's colleague at the Brookings Institution, might leave the impression the two researchers occupy demarcated camps. They don't, as they continue to collaborate closely. But his views in this piece clearly sound as Republican as Sawhill's sound Democratic. "We already spend," Haskins wrote, "something like $650 billion on programs intended to help the poor . . . . A typical child from a poor family enjoys income and housing support for their family, health care, preschool education, public school education, college loans or scholarships, and employment and training programs."

"But unless," Haskins concluded, "adolescents and young adults make wise decisions about their schooling, about marriage before childbearing, and about work . . . all this programmatic spending will do little to boost their chances of moving into the middle class. Federal and state policymakers, program operators and teachers, and parents need to constantly remind themselves and their children that personal responsibility is the key to success and insist that children and adolescents demonstrate more of it." Haskins, as you recall, is also a respondent.

In similar spirit, I might put matters this way: We all need help at times, often a lot. But at the end of days and lifetimes, only individual men and women, strengthened by the love and generosity of others, can break the kinds of cycles we've been talking about. This is the case especially since society may never change as much as many on the Left say is a precondition for all Americans, especially those of color, to overcome and prosper in rightfully greater numbers. Or if you will, "programs" don't overcome; people do. And while urging individuals in harsh situations to pull up their moral socks can be a simplistic suggestion, by no means is it always.

It's not as if progressives don't believe personal responsibility counts, or conservatives are opposed to all governmental interventions, even those that smack of "income redistribution." I'm quite familiar with several successful antipoverty and homeless programs, and each one (more likely led by Democrats than by Republicans) is predicated on clients doing what they're obliged to do. To think otherwise about liberals as a genus is an easy and unfair cliché. As for writers on the Right, the influential Ramesh Ponnuru, in a 2012 *National Review* article subtitled "Conservatives Need Not Surrender Voters of Moderate Income to Democrats,"[11] argues that conservatives need to better accommodate and respond—sometimes via public initiatives that cost money—to the heightened degree middle-income Americans are viewing themselves and their families as economically marginalized. He refers specifically to issues such as energy, health care, and higher education. Ponnuru is right; leaders on the Right need to better engage.

Let's segue here to more marriage-specific matters and do so ecumenically. W. Bradford Wilcox is director of the National Marriage Project at the University of Virginia. Andrew J. Cherlin is a professor of sociology and public policy at Johns Hopkins University. In a 2011 Brookings publication titled "The Marginalization of Marriage in Middle America,"[12] Wilcox is self-identified as conservative and Cherlin as liberal. The piece focuses on one of our major themes, the damaging ways in which moderately educated Americans are increasingly resembling lower-income citizens when it comes to very high out-of-wedlock and divorce rates.

"We come to this brief," the two authors write, "with somewhat different perspectives. Wilcox would emphasize the primacy of promoting and supporting marriage. Cherlin argued in a recent book, *The Marriage-Go-Round*, that stable care arrangements for children, whether achieved through marriage or not, are what matter most. Both of us agree that children are more likely to thrive when they reside in stable, two-parent homes." Out of this combination of views, they jointly propose various efforts to either strengthen marriages, or make them more likely in the first place, among Americans who have high school degrees but not college degrees. There is no room here to flesh them out, but in a few words each, here's some of what the two scholars propose in "The Marginalization of Marriage in Middle America":

Increase training for middle-skill jobs. Cherlin and Wilcox, citing work by economists Harry Holzer and Robert Lerman, argue that demand still exists and may increase for "technicians of various sorts" such as x-ray technicians and respiratory technicians, and crafts workers, such as electricians, in construction and other areas. These are decent-paying jobs that often require some kind of postsecondary education or training but not four-year college degrees.

Start a social marketing campaign to change the culture regarding marriage. One factor, Cherlin and Wilcox write, propelling the weakening of marriage among moderately educated men and women is the "deterioration of a marriage mindset." They cite Haskins and Sawhill, who have suggested such a campaign encouraging young adults to "follow a success sequence characterized by finishing high school, getting a job, and then having children."

Expand the Child Tax Credit to $3,000 and make it fully refundable. This policy, Wilcox and Cherlin contend, likely would improve marriage rates and strengthen marital stability for low-income and moderate-income families, as it would increase their economic security. It also would "signal to them that the nation values the parental investments they are making in the next generation." A generation, not incidentally, which will be obliged to help pay much bigger Social Security and Medicare bills.

Invest in the development of preschool children. Cherlin and Wilcox cite the work of economist James. J. Heckman, who is well-known for saying that investing in early childhood education produces the "largest long-term gains in human capital." This eventually would lead, goes the train, to better educated, better trained, more employable, and more marriageable men and women.

Reform divorce laws. The unintended consequences of no-fault divorce "seem to have been most powerful for couples with fewer emotional and financial resources." One thing to do is take advantage of research by family scholar (and respondent) William J. Doherty and others showing that "at least 10 percent of couples going through a divorce [as reported by Cherlin and Wilcox] are open to efforts to reconcile."

Staying with Wilcox but moving on to matters of faith, the University of Virginia sociologist wrote in 2007, "Churches are bulwarks of marriage in urban America." Drawing on data from the Fragile Families and Child

Wellbeing Study headquartered at Princeton and Columbia Universities, he said indications were that "urban parents who attend church frequently are significantly more likely to marry before the arrival of children or to marry in the wake of a nonmarital pregnancy, and they are more likely to experience higher levels of relationship quality." And in a line that reminded me that Kathryn Edin and Timothy Nelson did not have much, if anything, to say about the church lives of the men they wrote about in *Doing the Best I Can*, Wilcox added, "Religious attendance appears to foster behavior among urban fathers that makes them more attractive mates and better partners."[13] I'll return shortly—or more precisely, respondents will return shortly—to matters of belief.

In the specific matter of reducing teen pregnancies, New York City, in March 2013, took a surprisingly sharp tack, featuring subway and bus posters with cute babies alongside tough texts such as "Dad, you'll be paying to support me for the next 20 years." "Got a good job? I cost thousands of dollars a year." And "Honestly Mom . . . chances are he WON'T stay with you. What happens to ME?"

Extremely not of the mind that this was a proper strategy for city government to pursue, a New York state senator called the campaign "sort of a failed abstinence-only sex-ed curriculum on steroids" which is "laser-focused on shaming already-struggling teen parents." Planned Parenthood said the initiative "stigmatizes teen parents and their children." And the New York Coalition for Reproductive Justice started a campaign of its own by the name of "No Stigma, No Shame."[14] For those who believe that recovering a sense of "stigma" is necessary if out-of-wedlock births, and not just among teenagers, are to adequately fall, these condemnations of the word and idea are not encouraging.

With bite, but not as much as New York's, Milwaukee started a citywide campaign of its own in 2006 led by a broad coalition, which in turn was led by the United Way of Greater Milwaukee. Their aim was to avoid shaming anyone and their statistical goal was to reduce the birthrate of fifteen–seventeen-year-olds in the city by 46 percent by 2015. That audacious number was actually exceeded—hitting 50 percent—two years early in 2013.[15]

I might note that another area in which important progress has been made over the last two decades is in publicly acknowledging that fathers really do matter in the lives of their kids. Granted, this basic fact of life might not have been considered anything approaching "news" anytime before the 1960s and 1970s. But starting around then, significant numbers of observers grew strangely uncomfortable in publicly noting the manifestly obvious: Fathers make unique contributions. Conceding the point somehow came to be seen in many quarters as disrespectful toward single mothers as well as unfeeling toward boys and girls growing up in mother-only homes.[16] Yes, I agree, it made no sense.

Yet, while more leaders now once again readily recognize the contributions of fathers, many persist in stopping short before speaking of marriage and its distinctive and essential contributions. A perfect example of this is an otherwise superb Father's Day message that then–presidential candidate Barack Obama brought to a black church in south Chicago in June 2008, in which he said things such as:

> Of all the rocks upon which we build our lives, we are reminded today that family is the most important. And we are called to recognize and honor how critical every father is to that foundation. They are teachers and coaches. They are mentors and role models. . . . But if we are honest with ourselves, we'll admit that too many fathers are also missing—missing from too many lives and too many homes. They have abandoned their responsibilities, acting like boys instead of men. And the foundations of our families are weaker because of it.

Powerful and beautiful words they are, save for the fact that the president-to-be never once mentioned other key words such as "marriage" or "married." This, even though, he's blessed to be in a wonderful marriage himself.

The last several pages have been but a sketch of research, writing, and other activities focused on aiding mobility, undergirding marriage, and reducing out-of-wedlock births. They haven't included, for instance, anything about marriage education programs aimed at low-income men and women initiated during President George W. Bush's administration.

Likewise, we haven't said anything about ten recommendations for supporting marriage, released in 2013, by David Blankenhorn's Institute for American Values under the heading *The President's Marriage Agenda for the Forgotten Sixty Percent*. A number of the proposals mirror the five Cherlin and Wilcox suggestions above, with new ones including (1) requiring premarital education for people forming stepfamilies and (2) what the report calls "Engaging Hollywood," as in: "Our nation's leaders, including the president, must engage Hollywood in a conversation about . . . marriage and family formation, including critiques and positive ideas for changes in media depictions of marriage and fatherhood." Blankenhorn, too, is a respondent.

In regard to Hollywood, as I was completing this book, the National Bureau of Economic Research released a study that contends that contributing substantially to the previously noted large decline in teenage births were two reality shows on MTV, *16 and Pregnant* and *Teen Mom*, findings which are based on its two authors following the tweets and other social media ways teenagers communicate. Economists Phillip B. Levine and Melissa Schettini calculated that the two shows were responsible for a full one-third of the decline in teen birthrates over an eighteen-month period. Or more specifically, in the year-and-a-half after *16 and Pregnant* debuted in 2009, teen birthrates, as a direct result of the show and its spinoff, *Teen Mom*, fell by 5.7 percentage points. As culture wars go, this is a nice and surprising change of pace.[17]

As abbreviated as this rundown has been, it does provide a decent sense of what's out there, which is to say, nothing of earth-shattering performance or promise. Still, what might respondents and I suggest if our aim, purposefully broad, is smoothing mobility in America, in part by bucking up marriage?

Let's start with the boys, because boys often become the men women don't want to marry and generally for good reasons.

In her 2000 book, *The War against Boys*, Christina Hoff Sommers reported that the U.S. Department of Education had been disseminating more than three hundred pamphlets, books, and working papers on issues of "gender equity," none of which were "aimed at helping boys achieve parity with girls in the nation's schools."[18]

As one might recall from the latter decades of the last century, it often was assumed that American boys and men were doing reasonably fine, or at the very least, better than girls and women were doing. A 1992 report, for example, by the American Association of University Women, which received major play, argued that girls were being demonstrably shortchanged in school.[19] Given the passionate politics of the women's movement, some skewing was to be expected—though a 300-to-0 ratio of pamphlets, books, and working papers left the impression that boys, statistically speaking, were doing *infinitely* better than girls. Empirically speaking, this was not nearly the case and, suffice it to say, reality now is of a different realm, as it has grown to cliché that a great number of boys and young men are doing miserably while a great number of girls and young women are surging. Here are a half-dozen stark comparisons:

- For every 100 girls who repeat kindergarten, 194 boys do so.
- For every 100 tenth-grade girls who play video or computer games one or more hours a day, 322 boys do so.
- For every 100 women who earn a bachelor's degree, 75 men do so.
- For every 100 American women who earn a master's, 66 American men do so.
- For every 100 females, ages 20 to 24, who commit suicide, 624 males do so.
- For every 100 women, ages 18 to 21, in correctional facilities, 1,430 men are so confined.[20]

Very much in this vein, a Finnish economist and his colleagues have found that in every country they studied, girls are more likely than boys to make their way up income ladders—with American boys comparatively *more* disadvantaged than their counterparts elsewhere.[21]

These data are for Americans regardless of race. Though needless to say, socioeconomic and other conditions in regard to African American boys and young men are often orders of magnitude worse. For example, Brian Jacob of Harvard's Kennedy School has found that African American men earn only one-third of all bachelor degrees awarded to African Americans.[22] We already have heard from ethnographer Elijah Anderson, as both a respondent and author, on the sad states of young and not-so-young black males. Here's another bracing excerpt from his opening essay in an anthology he edited, *Against the Wall: Poor, Young, Black, and Male*:

> Many poor black fathers lose touch with their children within a few years after they are born, especially if both parents have moved on to other relationships. They are not raising boys to be men, a situation that has significant consequences for how they turn out. The boys' mothers may be engaged in their lives, but they can only do so much. . . . This dynamic generates profoundly ineffective parenting for young men and, in turn, makes those young men unable to parent their own children."[23]

It's impossible to read Anderson or listen to him and not more acutely recognize how tough all this can be for enormous numbers of African Americans. I almost always avoid terms such as "institutional discrimination" and "systemic discrimination," not because they aren't real phenomena, but because they are regularly construed as near-permanent miasmas and used to explain too much. I also usually avoid such terms because they almost always also suggest a downplaying of personal responsibility, without which progress really does halt for those in greatest need of advancing. Still, Anderson and other scholars such as William Julius Wilson do make it clear what many Americans, disproportionately black and male, often are up against.

Transracially this time, respondents Barbara Dafoe Whitehead and Bill Doherty, in their respective interviews, had complementarily insightful things to say about how boys become men who are socially and emotionally equipped for successful marriages.

Recall how Doherty, in chapter 2, said, "The kind of interpersonal competence now required for couple stability may be at a historic high." He was referring, more specifically, to the "type of competence and habits of mind that men are more likely to achieve in college, since college, at its best, affords people greater flexibility in understanding multiple perspectives." Here's Whitehead's similar take on the matter:

> One reason that non-college men are at a disadvantage and have a harder time forming relationships with women, not to mention getting married, is that men and women in college live by a certain set of rules. Both in and out of classrooms, men have to treat women as equals, as well as be alert to their feelings. It's a social curriculum for upscale kids and some others. Non-college men have nothing like that. Where do they go? They go to bars and hang out with women. There's no pathway for them to understand how to live a life with a woman.

Closing one more circle, boys who grow up in single-parent homes are less likely to graduate high school, never mind attend college, than are boys who grow up with both their mothers and fathers. Hence, they're less privy to marriage-friendly social curricula.

So our starting point is with the boys. Claiming that increasing their chances of getting a good education is ultimately the best strategy for helping millions of men and women wind up in good and healthy marriages might sound elementary to the point of trite. But what more promising route is there? I spent a fair amount of time in *From Family Collapse to America 's Decline*, which was released in 2011, talking about education, and I don't want to make too many similar points now. But a question from that discussion remains central: if millions of boys (and girls) have holes in their hearts where their fathers (and sometimes their mothers) should be, what type of education might work best at filling such gaps?

Other than *rigorous*, adjectives coming quickest to mind are *paternalistic* and *nurturing*, with "paternalistic" suggesting tough-loving charter schools in the "sweat-the-small-stuff" spirit of KIPP schools (Knowledge Is Power Program); and with "nurturing" suggesting places in which religious belief, to one degree or another, animates.

In the specific matter of faith-alert classrooms, in no way am I contending that a religiously rooted private school is the best option for everyone. But might such a school work well, sometimes wonderfully, for large numbers of boys and girls? No question. Which is another way of saying the case for vouchers is a strong one, especially for low-income kids whose family lives are most likely to be complicated and diminished by fragmentation. This is how Harvard's Paul Peterson, who has done extensive work evaluating voucher programs across the country, put it during our conversation: "I find it interesting that we find significant benefits for the African American community if they are given opportunities to go to private schools." (Not all of which are religious or parochial, of course.)

> Most of the students in our studies are living in single-parent families. I think a private school, especially when talking about urban settings, is a quieter place. A more closed space. Students are protected from hostile elements in the larger environment. The street culture is a good example of what's out there especially for boys, but also girls living in single-parent families. This peer group culture is very pernicious to learning and achievement, and it could be beneficial if we could protect kids from that, to some extent, by enabling them to attend private schools. It's not a cure-all. It's not a silver bullet. But it's a positive step.

After I asked Peterson about a study in which he and his colleagues found that kids in a privately funded, low-income voucher program in New York City wound up attending college at much higher rates than a control group, he talked about how the long-term effects of vouchers were the most "meaningful." The key point being that while students in the relatively few low-income voucher programs that have managed to get started over the last generation have not necessarily shown significantly improved achievement test scores, they often have shown measurably better high school graduation rates, which has been a real victory both for them and society.

When I asked about sources of opposition to vouchers and other reforms, including charter schools, Peterson made it clear he wasn't just talking about the National Education Association or American Federation of Teachers. "Everybody wants a monopoly if they can have one. It's not just the teachers unions. School districts are as bad. Local control now means control, or at least an inordinate amount of influence, by the employees of a school system, not just teacher unions. This includes bus drivers here in Boston."

I might not have cited this self-evident comment about teacher unions if another respondent, former Minneapolis mayor and congressman Don Fraser, a progressive icon in Minnesota since his days with Hubert Humphrey in the 1940s, hadn't told me at age eighty-nine, "I look ahead, not backwards, and I see reasons to be hopeful." He was talking about young people making better choices, including frequently choosing to marry. "I do think our educational system will improve, maybe not as quickly as some of us would like to see." But resisting such movement, Fraser continued, will be "folks who find it difficult to change, particularly the unions."

A persistent doubt I can't shake is what I see as the supreme difficulty—to the point of impossibility—of bringing great education programs to sufficient national scale. This, for no other reason than we haven't gotten close in doing so after a half century of trying. But if I were to be as hopeful as Fraser (who, by the way, disagrees with me on vouchers), I might cite journalist Amanda Ripley, who has written about how Finland, South Korea, and Poland each have made remarkable K–12 progress in recent years. If they can do it, one would like to think the United States, of all countries, is likewise equipped.[24]

One more essential point, which doesn't necessarily pertain to family fragmentation, needs to be made about educational achievement and class: It's not just our weakest and most troubled students doing poorly internationally, it's also many of our strongest. Peterson, along with colleagues Eric Hanushek and Ludger Woessmann, compared the math performance of U.S. high school students who had at least one parent with a college degree to *all* high school students regardless of their parents' education in a sample of nations. They had expected these American kids to be among the world leaders, but the percentage performing at the "advanced level" in the class of 2011 was a small 11.6 percent. This meant that "students in sixteen countries, no matter their parents' educational attainment, outrank this more-advantaged segment of the U.S. population."[25] Hard to imagine, though perhaps not.

I had just asked National Public Radio's Krista Tippett how we might take greater advantage of our religious institutions for various purposes—not just fortifying marriage—while also fully respecting the Constitution and American variety. (We agreed that we both preferred "variety" to "diversity.") "We can have robust discussions," she said, "without in any way questioning the wall of separation. The wall between church and state should not be a wall through the integrity of our citizens. It shouldn't be something that decouples how we are in our work places, in our families, and in civil society from the sources of our deepest values. I fault the culture. But I fault the traditions, too."

Of the "traditions," and with marriage in mind, she added: "I really want the traditions to begin fully articulating what they know, what they've known for generations and centuries about what it means to lead a worthy life, about what matters in life, and about who we are to be for each other. They are incredible repositories. We need them. We need them more than we ever have before."

Bob Woodson, who at age seventy-five has spent a lifetime working with and serving poor people, also spoke of the traditions when I asked what he wanted churches to do in regard to family breakdown.

"What I want churches to do is teach the Gospel and live by the principles and not engage in prosperity ministry. We need to get back to the fundamentals. My work helps me to understand what restoration looks like. I deal with people who have been at the very end. They have been drug addicts. They have been prostitutes. They have been thieves. They have been in jail. They have lived at the very far reaches of pathology."

After he noted that most Americans are entirely unfamiliar with the world he just described and couldn't survive a day in it, he went on:

> As I look around the country, what restores people in those situations? I work with grassroots leaders who are able to pull people back from the brink of self-destruction. I've had a chance to learn, to understand restoration and redemption and how it does occur. It really only occurs by adherence to the orthodoxy of the faith. The people I support don't need twelve-step programs. They need just one step. They need to come back and say, "My life is a wreck and I've got to change it. I am an agent of my own restoration, not government, not anyone else." They have freed themselves from blaming anyone, including parents.

> Nothing is more lethal than a good excuse for failure. A lot of what traditional psychology does, and a lot of what religiosity does, is provide people with excuses for failure.

A few moments later Woodson referred to a common principle underlying the different methods used by grassroots leaders who "redeem people everyone else has given up on."

"And what might that principle be?" I asked.

"Loving someone to death. Loving them in spite of themselves. In order to do that, it means emptying the self. It means choosing to be downwardly mobile. When you meet someone you put their interests first. All the people I serve willingly risk their lives." He also spoke of the importance of exercising "revolutionary patience."

But what about marriage in all this? Among all the renewed lives, I asked, are any fathers marrying the mothers of their children? How many mothers are interested in marrying the fathers of their girls and boys? Woodson spoke of a Pastor Shirley Holloway who runs programs for addicts and others in which people do marry and then stay together at high rates. But for the most part, he said, the "face of the marriage movement is that of Ozzie and Harriet." This was not a nostalgic compliment.

If you were to actually hear Lisa Graham Keegan talk about the importance and pain at hand, you would know she also frames matters of marriage and its repair in spiritual and emotional terms, as when she says,

> For me, we can't emphasize enough the beauty of the institution of marriage. And I'm speaking as somebody who has been divorced. I had a starter marriage, and I have to tell you, I'm still close to that man with whom I had children and who I still consider family.
>
> I also keep in close contact with "my" ex-wives: My husband's first wife and my former husband's wife. I'm a little obnoxious on the point, but I insist on it. I don't advocate for divorce. It wasn't a great experience. But if a couple does divorce, the people involved must remember they can never, ever truly separate, particularly if there are children. You just have to figure out how it all will keep looking like a family. You made the commitment. It's always the commitment.

About a half-hour later, when we were talking about our obligations as people, Keegan added:

> My husband and I went to counseling with my ex-husband and his wife to make certain we raised our kids well. My husband and his ex-

> wife went to counseling together a couple of years into our marriage when they realized they were parenting poorly. Do you think any of that was fun? That's not fun! Those are shallow examples of what I'm talking about, but they're essential.

About fifteen or twenty minutes into my conversation with NYU political scientist Lawrence Mead, we agreed that churches and other religious institutions are not doing enough in reinforcing marriage in many communities. Or as he put it, when Irish and Italian immigrants a century and more ago had family problems, "they had the Catholic Church on their back, and it did not relent." This, Mead suggested, is not church practice anymore, for example, when it comes to Hispanic immigrants.

I added that I had long wanted clergy of all denominations to focus more frequently on fragmentation and its resulting ills, but that I had come to better realize in recent years that if preachers did so, it wouldn't take long for pews to thin out. This, for no other reason than many in attendance just about every Sunday might grow offended, given how they weren't the ones in greatest need of hearing or heeding the message. At any rate, Mead concurred when I acknowledged that although I've always been of the mind that family fragmentation is "really complicated and hard," after spending the last five years working intensively on two books on the subject, I had concluded it's even tougher than that.

This, in turn, returned Mead to the importance of work—more specifically, the imperative of low-income men getting and keeping jobs—if we are to have any chance of reviving marriage in urban centers. "Don't forget," he said, "the men are generally worse off than the women. One of the mysteries of poverty is that women, even with children, are more employable than low-income men. That is why welfare reform could succeed. One can only assume that mothers, precisely because they have children, are forced to function at a level that men are not forced to meet."

Several times in our conversation, Mead spoke of the psychological dimensions of nonwork—and, therefore, nonmarriage—as in this pointed passage.

> The basic problem is that the mothers we've been talking about have an easier time in life than men we've been talking about. Mothers are primarily concerned about motherhood. They want to have and raise children. They're usually not in direct competition with other people, whereas men are wired to achieve in the outside world. They're often

> uncompetitive in that world, so they wind up humiliated in ways beyond anything women have to face, leading them to fall apart, as they just can't cope. Although the failures we've been discussing have to do with families, the origin of those failures are actually in the workplace. It's because they can't function at work that they fail to function in families. We have to help them, but we have to require consistent behavior. Enforcement is necessary.

Or, as Mead wrote in *Expanding Work Programs for Poor Men*, "Much of my approach is modeled on welfare reform. Poor fathers, like poor mothers, need both help and hassle. That is, they need more help from government than they are getting. But they must also be expected to help themselves. We need to demand work—and, if necessary, to enforce it." He has proposed doing this by building on the fact that governments already demand child support from absent fathers and they expect men who are leaving prison to work as a condition of parole.[26]

Many other social scientists argue that the real roots of the deficiencies Mead writes about are not psychological, but rather, impediments such as the unavailability of decent-paying jobs for low-skilled men, exacerbated by bigotries of various sorts. But whatever emphasis one favors, Mead's analysis deserves to be judged at least a partial explanation, though I personally believe it's more robust than that.

A quick word fits here about helping ex-offenders, in particular, get on with their lives so that they might be seen as marriageable by reasonably discerning women.

Recall that Mead, in the introduction said, "We have to make it quite clear to any man who comes out of prison, whatever his previous life, we're going to make it possible for him to lead a civilized life going forward." This is not the place for detailing ways of making this happen, as I did so previously, albeit modestly.[27] At bottom, though—in addition to ex-offenders offending no more (not a small point)—is the need to help those who have been imprisoned to eventually cleanse their names by means of pardons and similar routes.

Encouragingly, this increasingly seems to be a goal in some precincts of both Left and Right, as witness, in the latter's camp, the reformist, Texas-based group Right on Crime. For example, the group asserts: "Conservatives understand that reforming offenders is both a moral imperative and requirement of public safety. Breaking the cycle of crime and turning lawbreakers into law-abiding citizens is a conservative priority because it advances public safety, the rule of law, and minimizes the number of future victims." And that while "prisons serve a critical role by incapacitating dangerous offenders and career criminals," they are "not the solution for every type of offender." And in some instances, "they have the unintended consequence of hardening nonviolent, low-risk offenders—making them a greater risk to the public than when they entered."[28]

Similarly heartening is this comment by Senator Mike Lee, a Republican from Utah, at a Heritage Foundation antipoverty conference in November 2013: "The simple fact," he said, "is that in America today, we put too many people in prison for too long with too little benefit to our society. If inmates are violent and threats to our communities, then we have a moral responsibility to keep them locked up." But if they are not violent, pose no such threat, and are ready to return to their communities and families, then "we have just as much moral duty to get them reintegrated into our nation's networks of social and economic mobility."[29] Suffice it to say these are welcomed developments as long as protecting public safety remains job one.

I spent several pages in *From Family Collapse to America 's Decline* considering the effectiveness of state-based marriage-education programs largely initiated by the Healthy Marriage Initiative coming out of George W. Bush's administration.[30] At the risk of misplaced glibness both then and now, I wrote that while I applauded Bush's aim of strengthening marriage among low-income Americans, early evaluations of the state-based programs were not encouraging for no other reason (I concluded) than men don't like sitting through meetings. Actually, given that what we're talking about has to do with the most intimate aspects of a person's life, it's no great surprise that progress has been halting even on good days, meetings or no meetings.

Nonetheless, one state program—the Oklahoma Marriage Initiative (OMI)—is routinely recognized as unusually effective, and to get a better sense as to why, as I was finishing the book I spent two days in Oklahoma City meeting with both staff and the program's impressive Research Advisory Group.[31] I was most appreciative of the invitation, but I must admit I was struck by how the scholars' intellectually rich discussions focused less on finding ways of increasing marriage rates and decreasing divorce rates and focused more on bringing greater stability to romantic relationships more generally. Which, as a practical matter, meant focusing on cohabiting situations to a greater extent than most administration and congressional leaders, almost certainly, envisioned a decade ago. (OMI actually predates passage of Bush's Healthy Marriage Initiative by a few years.)

One reason for the broader emphasis on "relationships" is that the relative absence of marriage affords relatively few opportunities for rescuing faltering ones. What I heard and saw at the two days of meetings, most of all, was keen recognition that it was essential to build as much stability into adult romantic relationships as possible—be those relationships within or without marriage—for the sake of Oklahoma's most vulnerable children. I understand how this has come to be, but the fact remains that cohabiting relationships in the United States are routinely short-lived, meaning that children once again are ill-served.

Let's conclude the chapter with brief notes about two interesting programs, after which we'll hop on an elevator for a very short, albeit not sweet, ride.

For purposes of addressing some of the problems discussed in these pages, family social scientist Bill Doherty has built on an Australian program aimed at meeting another need: providing basic mental-health first-aid training for lay people. "They scaled that puppy and now it has gone international." Doherty's contribution has been to create an akin grassroots project called "Marital First Responders."[32]

"I want to do something similar around marriage and romantic relationships. We're not going to professionalize our way out of our problems. We could quintuple the number of professional marriage counselors, and it won't be sufficient. What I want to do is develop grassroots ways for people who are already confidantes to up their game in terms of how to respond helpfully to people who come to them. That's the group I want to reach."

Doherty noted that we know from a large body of research that people in "relationship struggles" turn to their family and friends long before they turn to any professional, including their clergy. As for the project's prospects, a number of faith communities, he said, are "*very* interested," and he allowed that some people have been using the term "game-changer."

Chris Stewart, who leads the Twin Cities–based African American Leadership Forum, rivets on "mainstreaming," as in keeping boys and men of color on pathways toward the American mainstream and not toward economies outside it. "When we look at wealth gaps between white and black families, the three most important are educational attainment, income, and the 'Big Daddy' of home ownership. If we had those three things right in the black community, differences of all sorts would be much smaller."

I asked what ultimate victory might look like for what sounded like a pretty conventional effort, Stewart's frequently expressed unconventional take on things notwithstanding.

"If you get kids tooled up early so that they have a purpose in the mainstream economy they will do what you have been talking about, which is to say positioned to be marriageable and have a good life. You can't do that without investing in kids and the systems that's producing them." This last point, about what Stewart sees as fundamentally unfair "systems" of various sorts, is central for him.

"Once people figure out they're not tooled up to do anything, they wind up in a totally alternative lifestyle. They now live on some separate planet. I don't know if there's a lot of correcting possible when they wind up on that other planet, because they see the world so differently. At that point either they or you might as well be on Mars."

As for the elevator ride alluded to (I wouldn't say "lift," under the circumstances), how long do you think an effective elevator speech about the heart of what we've been talking about might take? We'll finish off next chapter, the "Conclusion," less abruptly. But for now, I'd argue we could deliver such a speech in no more than a floor or two, as it doesn't take any longer to concede we're just not being fair to our children or our country.

NOTES

1. Frederick M. Hess, *Revolution at the Margins: The Impact of Competition on Urban School Systems* (Washington, DC: Brookings Institution Press, 2002), 8.

2. Several years ago I was commissioned to write a book about an exceedingly successful Minnesota business that had never laid off a single employee for economic reasons—and, not incidentally, never had an unprofitable month, either. This, despite being involved in the up-and-down construction industry. The owner of the business, a brilliantly idiosyncratic older man, lost interest in the book toward the end; so it was never published, and I'm not in a position to identify him or the enterprise he built. But I can say that a clear-cut reason for his success was loyalty to his employees, customers, and others, passionately pursued, regardless of whatever economic condi-

tions were afflicting the nation or his field at any moment. One business consultant I read at the time for intellectual reinforcement was Frederick F. Reichheld, especially his *The Loyalty Effect: The Hidden Force behind Growth , Profits and Lasting Value* (Boston: Harvard Business School Press: 1996).

3. "Interview: Kathryn Edin," *Frontline*, PBS, May 21, 2002.

4. Programs such as Project for Pride in Living, One-Percent Club, and Micro-Grants. I'm a director of MicroGrants.

5. Kathryn Edin and Timothy J. Nelson, *Doing the Best I Can: Fatherhood in the Inner City* (Berkeley: University of California, 2013), 222.

6. Kathryn Edin and Maria Kafalis, *Promises I Can Keep: Why Poor Women Put Motherhood before Marriage* (Berkeley: University of California, 2005), 81.

7. Edin and Kafalis, *Promises I Can Keep*, 138.

8. "The rate of teen births in the United States is at its lowest level in almost seventy years. Yet, the sobering context is that the teen pregnancy rate is far lower in many other countries" (Mike Stobbe, "Even at Lowest, U.S. Teen Birth Rate Far Higher Than W. Europe," *The Huffington Post*, December 30, 2010).

9. "Education and income both play a role in divorce statistics. Data shows that a married couple with a higher education and higher income is less likely to divorce than a couple with lower education and lower income" (*Education Statistics*, National Center for Education Statistics, March 2012).

10. Isabel V. Sawhill, "Opportunity in America: The Disadvantages Start at Conception," *New York Times*, "Room for Debate" online forum, January 8, 2012, http://www.nytimes.com/roomfordebate/2012/01/08.

11. Ramesh Ponnuru, "Right in the Middle: Conservatives Need Not Surrender Voters of Moderate Income to the Democrats," *National Review*, December 17, 2012, 16–18.

12. W. Bradford Wilcox and Andrew J. Cherlin, "The Marginalization of Marriage in Middle America," Center on Children and Families, Brookings Institution, Brief no. 46, August 2011.

13. W. Bradford Wilcox, "Religion, Race, and Relationships in Urban America," Center for Marriage and Families, Institute for American Values, Research Brief No. 5, May 2007.

14. Emily Gogalak, "NYC Anti-teen Pregnancy Campaign Targets Deadbeat Dads with Text Message Games," *Village Voice*, March 13, 2013.

15. Website, Greater Milwaukee United Way, 2013, http://www.unitedwaymilwaukee.org/teenpregnancy; and phone conversation with the GMUW's Lori Holly, December 5, 2013.

16. Mitch Pearlstein, *From Family Collapse to America's Decline: The Educational , Economic , and Social Costs of Family Fragmentation* (Lanham, MD: Rowman & Littlefield. 2011). See especially chapter 1.

17. National Public Radio, *All Things Considered*, "Listen to the Story," January 13, 2014. For an excellent essay based on what teenage girls think about *16 and Pregnant* and its spinoffs, see Rhonda Kruse Nordin, "MTV's 'Teen Mom' Franchise: How Do Young Eyes—and Much Older Eyes—See Teenage Parenthood?," Center of the American Experiment, November 2013.

18. Christina Hoff Sommers, *The War against Boys: How Misguided Feminism Is Harming Our Young Men* (New York: Simon & Schuster, 2000), 38–39. I served in the U.S. Department of Education from 1987 to 1990.

19. American Association of University Women, *The AAUW Report : How Schools Shortchange Girls* (Washington, DC: AAUW, 1992).

20. These six are a small sampling cited in Tom Mortenson, "For every 100 girls . . . ," *Postsecondary Opportunity*, March 28, 2011. A similar, albeit longer list can be found in Pearlstein, *From Family Collapse to America 's Decline*, 130–31.

21. Cited by Kay Hymowitz in "Boy Trouble," *City Journal*, Autumn 2013, 73.

22. The Finnish economist is Markus Jantti, and his colleagues are at the Bonn-based Institute for the Study of Labor. Cited again by Hymowitz in "Boy Trouble."

23. Elijah Anderson, ed., *Against the Wall: Poor, Young, Black, and Male* (Philadelphia: University of Pennsylvania, 2008), 22.

24. Amanda Ripley, *The Smartest Kids in the World and How They Got That Way* (New York: Simon & Shuster, 2013).

25. Eric A. Hanushek, Paul E. Peterson, and Ludger Woessmann, *Endangering Prosperity : A Global View of the American School* (Washington, DC: Brookings, 2013), 52.

26. Lawrence M. Mead, *Expanding Work Programs for Poor Men* (Washington, DC: AEI, 2011), 1–2.

27. Pearlstein, *From Family Collapse to America 's Decline*, 135–42.

28. Right on Crime endorsers include leading conservatives such as Gary Bauer, Bill Bennett, Jeb Bush, Newt Gingrich, David Keene, Ed Meese, Grover Norquist, and J. C. Watts. Right on Crime: A Project of the Texas Public Policy Foundation, www.rightoncrime.com.

29. Senator Mike Lee, "Bring Them In," Remarks to the Heritage Foundation's "Anti-Poverty Forum," Washington, DC, November 13, 2013.

30. Pearlstein, *From Family Collapse to America 's Decline*, 129–30.

31. Members of the research group include the likes of Paul Amato, Philip and Carolyn Cowan, William Doherty, Kathryn Edin, Steven Harris, Ron Haskins, Alan Hawkins, Howard Markman, and Scott Stanley. All except Amato and Doherty attended the 2013 annual meeting, in December.

32. See www.maritalfirstresponders.com. The Australian program is Australian Mental Health First Responders.

EIGHT

Conclusion

I do much of my writing at my neighborhood Caribou Coffee in south Minneapolis, which is under a mile from both my house and Washburn High School, a racially and otherwise diverse public institution with a long history. On a Friday morning, about five months before finishing a first draft of this book, I was parked at one of my favorite spots when I heard two teenage white girls, whom I assumed were Washburn students (I saw a telltale T-shirt), talking about things I didn't care much about and was largely oblivious to. That was until one of them acknowledged that while she was average in most every way—intelligence, athletic ability, looks—the fortunate fact was (as she put it), "I have two parents." Meaning, for all her self-effacing shortcomings, she understood herself as having significant built-in advantages over classmates who didn't have live-in mothers and fathers—which is to say, a big advantage over a great number of her fellow and sister students, disproportionately of color and low-income.

I would argue that an untold number of Americans, not just this young woman, grasp instinctively the fundamentally unequal and unfair ways in which family fragmentation plays out in the lives of children and, when they grow up, adults. It's just that those blessed with the best platforms and loudest megaphones for voicing the issue and expressing concern are routinely least inclined to do so. More than granted, family fragmentation is not the only reason why inequality and mobility are growing American worries. But it's miles from a minor cause, and it would be helpful if more leaders in assorted fields, starting perhaps in entertainment, publicly acknowledged the point.

My not abstract interest throughout these pages has been in affording young and older Americans better chances for good educations, good jobs, and good lives. I haven't spent much time citing reams of scholarly research regarding the ways in which family fragmentation diminishes those chances, as I've pointed to volumes of evidence in the past.[1] But before finishing up, let me tease out what researchers are vitally finding via new disciplinary routes: not just psychology, sociology, and economics but also biology, chemistry, and genetics. This first excerpt is from Paul Tough's celebrated *How Children Succeed: Grit, Curiosity, and the Hidden Power of Character*: "[T]he most profound discovery this new generation of neuroscientists has made," he writes,

> is the powerful connection between infant brain chemistry and adult psychology.
>
> Lying deep between those noble, complex human qualities we call character, these scientists have found, is the mundane, mechanical interaction of specific chemicals in the brains and bodies of developing infants. Chemistry is not destiny, certainly. But these scientists have demonstrated that the most reliable way to produce an adult who is brave and curious and kind and prudent is to ensure that when he is an infant, his hypothalamic-pituitary-adrenal axis functions well.

How to do that? First, Tough writes, is protecting children, to the extent possible, from "serious trauma and chronic stress." Even more important is providing girls and boys with a "secure, nurturing relationship with at least one parent and ideally two. That's not the whole secret of success, but it is a big, big part of it."[2]

The second excerpt comes near the end of Charles Murray's celebrated book *Coming Apart* (albeit not necessarily celebrated by the same crowd that reveres Tough's book).[3]

> I am predicting, that over the next few decades advances in evolutionary psychology are going to be conjoined with advances in genetic understanding, leading to a scientific consensus that goes something like this: There are genetic reasons, rooted in the mechanisms of human evolution, why little boys who grow up in neighborhoods without married fathers tend to reach adolescence not socialized to the norms of behavior that they will need to stay out of prison and to hold jobs. . . . These same reasons explain why society's attempts to compensate for the lack of married biological fathers don't work and will never work.

Do I disagree with Tough when he argues that two biological parents are not inescapably essential for children to succeed? Of course not, especially since he acknowledges that two parents are, in fact, ideal. I would just note that many examples of the kinds of "serious trauma and chronic stress" he warns about are more likely to crop up, both more severely and frequently, in households where lone and hassled parents live. This is another way of saying, as suggested in the introduction, that two-parent families offer no guarantees when it comes to kids doing well—just much better odds.

Given such mixed probabilities, how do our forty respondents envision an America that may lead the industrial world in family fragility? A more optimistic minority saw a nation succeeding because of free markets. Or because of immigration. Or because of religious renewal. Or because of the power of low-income neighborhoods to turn themselves around. Or, while they might not, in fact, have great confidence in the future of the country itself, they were reasonably certain their own well-educated children and their children's well-educated friends would do well.

But outlooks, on distinct balance, were not pleasant ones. No one predicted anything apocalyptic (at least not with certainty). Metaphors had more to do with "wasting diseases" than they did with "heart attacks." Declines were seen as more gradual than as fast acting. Future troubles were seen as similar to current ones—only worse. And future America was seen as a place where problems made worse by fragmentation are managed, not resolved, and where have-nots have tougher times becoming halves.

They imagined a United States that still led the world, but then again, maybe not. An economically successful nation still, but perhaps a less innovative and creative one. A less unified and trusting nation, with demarcations rooted in income, race, ethnicity, culture, values, and behavior—in other words, along familiar lines, but again only more so. A country where enormous numbers of citizens are no better educated than they currently are and, therefore, no better prepared for the kinds of jobs that lead more smoothly to marriage. An America, in sum, where those incapable of cutting it are further cut out.

In light of all this, I'm obliged to ask, can marriage in the United States really make the kind of comeback, especially among low-income and many minority men and women, that I've explicitly argued is necessary and implicitly contended, despite my substantial hesitations, is doable? My guess is a fair number of people would judge me ultimately a hopeless romantic rather than a hardened realist on the question, and there are moments, I'm afraid, when I wouldn't disagree, as it's hard to imagine a tougher job than turning around a ship of state in which marriage has run aground in so many places.

But recall how writer Kay Hymowitz allowed how she has been overly pessimistic on occasion—"I mean *overly*"—when speculating about things such as teenage crime rates. Historian Stephan Thernstrom, who I interviewed along with his political scientist wife Abigail Thernstrom, referred to a 1932 speech by Franklin Delano Roosevelt in which the soon-to-be president talked about how the era of economic expansion was over, as we had as much of everything we needed so long as it was distributed fairly.[4] "That certainly," noted Thernstrom, "was not at all prophetic of what the United States would come to look like." Or, as someone who was certifiably "Smart" in the 1960s frequently put it, "Just missed."[5]

One of the more complexly sanguine (or at least less pessimistic) arguments in recent years in regard to the future of marriage in America is writer Mary Eberstadt's. (I say "complexly" as she fully factors in religion's role. Most social scientists barely make a stab at doing so.) Certainly not alone among observers, Eberstadt can imagine significant numbers of people eventually returning to traditional folds out of necessity if and when welfare states run out of money and are no longer capable of doing for families what families historically have done for their members—be they young, old, ill, or simply struggling.

Might the post–welfare-state West, she asked, "end up imparting economic value to marriage, childbearing, and family ties, as the pre-industrial agricultural state did for many centuries?" One need not conceive a "full-scale crisis," she went on, "to see how the pressures of a shrinking and ageing Western population might make the family look like a grossly undervalued stock."[6] Still, as reasonably promising as her prognosis might be, it's impossible to avoid noting that it's contingent on governmental capabilities nearly collapsing.

Just as I was finishing writing, a respondent sent me an e-mail concerning several articles about marriage that recently had run in the *New Republic*, *New York Times*, and *Wall Street Journal*. One combined conclusion from the pieces might be that while "marriage may in fact be the single issue where the conservative analysis has the most power," that doesn't translate into conservatives actually having anything to contribute in terms of public policy. And as for liberals, they despair about doing anything concerning family fragmentation in the first place and, instead, pragmatically seek adapting to a post–nuclear-family reality. My interviewee saw a different possible course.

His view was that the culture already had shifted among college-educated men and women, with their lower unwed birthrates and lower divorce rates, so that it "can't be impossible" to imagine the rest of America changing, too. A first step, he wrote, is believing it possible.

We have considered many of the prices exacted by family fragmentation, starting with stunted educations. Here's another one, having to do with grandparents.

Rather than leading to a reduction of loving family members, divorce sometimes actually leads to an increase, as is the case in my own family.

My wife and her ex-husband had three sons before divorcing more than thirty years ago. Two of the boys have since married, with my middle stepson and his wife having a young daughter and my youngest stepson and his wife having two young sons. This means that the girl has three sets of committed grandparents: my stepson's father and his wife; my daughter-in-law's mother and father; and my wife and me. And the two boys likewise have three sets of grandparents. In each instance, three sets of grandparents for the regular price of two. Do I believe these three particular grandchildren are well-served by the multitude of doting older family members? Yes.

But then there is a fourth grandchild: our daughter's daughter, who was born outside of marriage, fathered by a man who plays virtually no role in either my daughter or granddaughter's life. Unsurprisingly, his mother (I know nothing about his father) likewise barely plays a part in the little girl's life. In this instance, in other words, instead of having four, never mind six, loving and supportive grandparents, our granddaughter has but two—just us.

Or summing up, when it comes to split families, having a lone engaged grandmother and a lone engaged grandfather is often the best a kid can hope for.

A large reason for telling this story is that it's a perfect setup to what respondent Arvonne Fraser, who's on the cusp of ninety, insightfully said about grandparents.

> I tend to think of generations, but I'm beginning to think—this goes back to the mentor thing—you need more than two generations. Three generations become very important, not that they have to be related. Maybe that's just because I'm old.
>
> But I think back. My grandparents were very important to me. There is this inherent tension between parents and children as they grow up. Children have to separate themselves from their parents, so they need other influences. The word might be role models, mentors, and they don't have to be, as I said, in the same family. They can be external. But it's important for kids to see beyond their parents, to see other age groups to get a sense of what their future is.

Can nonfamily members, as Fraser claims, in addition to grandparents, serve admirably as mentors and role models? Needless to say. But this is where one must ask who's most likely to remain immersed in a boy's or girl's life over longest hauls. Grandparents, usually connected by blood? Or family friends, no matter how good and decent they may be? I'm guessing grandparents.

Speaking of complexities, here's one that definitely isn't your grandfather's or grandmother's: the way in which the drive for same-sex marriage has made talking about family fragmentation and its effects even more difficult. (When Senator Mike Lee, for example, talks about America's "other marriage debate," he's not referring to the same-sex kind of unions.)

I've been of the mind for several years that, so as not to offend advocates of same-sex marriage, be they gay or straight, many opinion leaders are reluctant to talk about men as fathers and women as mothers. Instead, they increasingly talk and write about "parents" generically. Polite as this might be, it fails to recognize that many young people are not faring well precisely because of the absence of a particular parent of a particular gender in their lives.

With all this in mind, I wrote a piece last year for a national think tank in which I purposefully referred to a "mother and father" in a key spot. Just as purposefully, an editor—who's really a very good and sensible writer himself—changed the term to "two parents." Given that I was grateful that he was publishing the piece in the first place, I went along with the change, but I was not surprised when a reader blasted me for the evasive language. The fundamental point here has less to do with whether one believes same-sex marriage is a good, bad, or indifferent idea than it has to do with whether it's at all wise or healthy to further erode the essential roles men play as fathers and women play as mothers.

Nevertheless, whatever one might think of same-sex marriage, the ways in which many gay and lesbian couples have flocked to the institution should be read as illuminating in all communities. When one thinks about it, their aspiring to wedlock shouldn't be surprising—to heck with all the obstacles to marriage cited in chapter after chapter so far—as it's a glorious state when stars align. The fact that so many Americans don't seem to agree is a mystery to me. Or maybe they really do, it's just that their own stars have yet to luckily arrange themselves right.

A final recommendation and hope: may constellations come to do so.

NOTES

1. Mitch Pearlstein, *From Family Collapse to America's Decline: The Educational, Economic, and Social Costs of Family Fragmentation* (Lanham, MD: Rowman & Littlefield, 2011).

2. Paul Tough, *How Children Succeed: Grit, Curiosity, and the Hidden Power of Character* (Boston: Houghton Mifflin Harcourt, 2012), 182.

3. Charles Murray, *Coming Apart: The State of White America, 1960–2010* (New York: Crown Forum, 2012), 299.

4. Here's the key excerpt in Roosevelt's speech to San Francisco's Commonwealth Club on May 23, 1932: "Our task now is not discovery or exploitation of natural resources, or necessarily producing more goods. It is the soberer, less dramatic business of administering resources and plants already in hand, of seeking to reestablish foreign markets for our surplus production, of meeting the need of under consumption, of adjusting production to consumption, of distributing wealth and products more equitably, of adapting existing economic organizations to the service of the people. The day of enlightened administration has come."

5. Maxwell Smart, aka "Agent 86," *Get Smart*, NBC, 1965–1970.

6. Mary Eberstadt, "Faith and Family," *National Review Online*, May 20, 2013, https://www.nationalreview.com/nrd/articles/347192/ . For a fuller explication, see her *How the West Really Lost God* (West Conshohocken, PA: Templeton, 2013).

Appendix 1

Respondents

John Adams. Humphrey School of Public Affairs.
Judith Adams. Community volunteer.
Jason Adkins. Minnesota Catholic Conference.
Paul Allick. Episcopal priest.
Elijah Anderson. Yale University.
Peter Bell. American Refugee Committee.
David Blankenhorn. Institute for American Values.
Stephanie Coontz. Evergreen State College.
William J. Doherty. University of Minnesota.
Chester E. Finn Jr. Thomas B. Fordham Foundation.
Arvonne Fraser. Humphrey School of Public Affairs (Emerita).
Don Fraser. Former Minneapolis mayor.
Eric Hanushek. Stanford University.
Ron Haskins. Brookings Institution.
Kay Hymowitz. Manhattan Institute
Lisa Graham Keegan. Former Arizona superintendent of Public Instruction.
Katherine A. Kersten. Center of the American Experiment.
Glenn Loury. Brown University.
Heather Mac Donald. Manhattan Institute.
C. Peter Magrath. Retired president of four universities.
Elaine Tyler May. University of Minnesota.
Lee McGrath. Institute for Justice.
Lawrence M. Mead. New York University.
Ronald B. Mincy. Columbia University.
Terry Moe. Stanford University.
Alberto Monserrate. Minneapolis School Board.
Bruce Peterson. Hennepin County District Court.
Lissa Peterson. Psychologist.
Paul E. Peterson. Harvard University.

Todd Peterson. Entrepreneur.
Sally Pipes. Pacific Research Institute.
Kristin J. Robbins. Economic Club of Minnesota.
Isabel V. Sawhill. Brookings Institution.
Joe Selvaggio. MicroGrants.
Chris Stewart. African American Leadership Forum.
Abigail Thernstrom. American Enterprise Institute.
Stephan Thernstrom. Harvard University (emeritus).
Krista Tippett. National Public Radio.
Barbara Dafoe Whitehead. Institute for American Values.
Robert Woodson. Center for Neighborhood Enterprise.

Appendix 2

A Brief Note on Method

I conducted thirty-five interviews for *Broken Bonds* with forty respondents in and around Boston, New York, and Washington, D.C., on the East Coast; in and around Seattle and San Francisco on the West Coast; and in the Twin Cities of Minneapolis and St. Paul, all between November 2012 and November 2013. My conversation with Lisa Graham Keegan of Arizona was held in Minneapolis. Five of the sessions had two interviewees each, four of which involved husbands and wives.

A questionnaire, which I used increasingly flexibly over time, drew on sociologist John Lofland's concept of intensive interviewing with an interview guide,[1] which meant sessions, which averaged somewhat more than an hour, often resembled conversations as much as they did interviews.

The respondents—twenty-five men and fifteen women—are a remarkably accomplished and, directly put, very smart group. They were not scientifically selected and do not represent any particular demographic. Rather, I solicited, generally by e-mail, some of the most talented leaders I knew across the country, as well as some I had long wanted to meet. It's an occupationally skewed group with scholars and writers, often quite well-known ones, making up more than half of the forty. But it was exactly scholars and writers I was most intent in interviewing, as they spend more time than do most people thinking about the kinds of difficult and complex topics I wanted to talk about. Average age for the group was fifty-plus (possibly sixty-plus), with several respondents in their seventies and eighties.

The thirty-five interview/conversations resulted in about fourteen hundred double-spaced pages of transcripts as transcribed by my longtime and superb transcriber, Beverly Hermes. How to make sense of so much information? Let's just say the "Find" key is one of the previous century's greatest achievements. It also helped that I had used similar approaches on three other occasions: once for my dissertation, thirty-four years ago (precomputer), and for two more recent books.

The task this time around involved carefully reading hard copies of all thirty-five transcripts and copiously marking them up when respondents talked about pertinent issues. I scribbled additional notes, frequently adding comments such as "terrific" and "great" when respondents said especially insightful, important, or quotable things.

The next chore was turning the thirty-five transcripts into thirty-five new files with the most interesting and quotable things each of the forty respondents said. When it was time to focus on specific chapters, I generally turned those files into additional sets of quote-filled files, as in "John Doe/Chapter 5." Some respondents were so quotable, they wound up with at least a half-dozen chapter files in their name. So as not to miss anything vital that I might have bypassed at the start, I also stayed in close touch with the original fourteen hundred pages of transcripts.

All these hands-on and eyes-on efforts led, as it had in the past, to my gaining (if I do say so) a remarkably familiar grasp of who said what about what. From there the dynamic was not fundamentally different from what's implicit in other kinds of research: reading and rereading, imagining and reimagining, conceiving and reconceiving, connecting and disconnecting, and writing and rewriting, not necessarily in that order.

Before bringing the project to a close, I e-mailed each respondent excerpts of how I had quoted and paraphrased him or her. Needless to say, oral speech is generally not as clean as the written word. Also needless to say, I took great pains in making certain that my adapting was perfectly true to what they said. While a number of respondents made stylistic changes in my revised language (a few, perhaps, to the point of making their thoughts sound more written than spoken), no one made any substantive changes.

NOTE

1. John Lofland, *Analyzing Social Settings : A Guide to Qualitative Observation and Analysis* (Stamford, CT: Cengage Learning, 2006).

Index

About the Author

Mitch Pearlstein is president of Center of the American Experiment, a think tank he founded in Minneapolis in 1990. He previously made his career in journalism, education, and government in Binghamton, New York, and Washington, DC, in addition to the Twin Cities. His previous books include *Close to Home: Celebrations and Critiques of America's Experiment in Freedom* (with Katherine A. Kersten); *Riding into the Sunrise: Al Quie and a Life of Faith, Service, and Civility*; and *From Family Collapse to America's Decline: The Educational, Economic, and Social Costs of Family Fragmentation.* He holds a doctorate in educational administration from the University of Minnesota and is married to the Rev. Diane Darby McGowan, a police chaplain and deacon of an Episcopal parish. They have four adult children, six grandchildren, and two dogs. They non-empty-nest with the latter, Trevor and Bailey, in Minneapolis.

This is the first study in which the principles of generative phonology are applied to French. The book attempts to furnish a description of French phonology and morphology that accounts for the phonological alternations occurring in morphologically related forms. (An example is the morpheme 'want,' which occurs in such phonologically different forms as *veulent, voulons,* and *volonté.*) Professor Schane's emphasis throughout the book is on the interrelationships between the phonological and morphological features of contemporary French. The result is a structural explanation for observable phonological and morphological processes, in which these two aspects of the language emerge as a complete, integrated system rather than as independent phenomena.

Three major areas are treated in detail: elision and liaison, the vowel system, and verbs. Of particular interest is the treatment of the classical problem of elision and liaison, in which the two are shown to be in fact a single phonological phenomenon accompanied by specific morphological and syntactic constraints. The discussion of the vowel system details a set of underlying vowels needed to produce the vocalic alternants observable both within the paradigm and in derivational forms. In the treatment of verbs Professor Schane develops a set of rules for producing the various paradigmatic forms. Furthermore, many "irregular" verbs — including some of the most anomalous forms — can be accounted for under this system.

French Phonology and Morphology will have a wide audience among linguists, in both theory and applications, and among students of French or of Romance languages. In order to make the work accessible to students outside the single field of linguistics, a minimum of linguistic notation is used.

Sanford A. Schane is Assistant Professor of Linguistics at the University of California at San Diego.

MIT Press Research Monograph No. 45

FRENCH PHONOLOGY AND MORPHOLOGY

FRENCH PHONOLOGY AND MORPHOLOGY

SANFORD A. SCHANE

RESEARCH MONOGRAPH NO. 45
THE M.I.T. PRESS, CAMBRIDGE, MASSACHUSETTS

Set in Baskerville Monotype and
printed and bound in the United States of America
by The Riverside Press, Cambridge, Massachusetts

Library of Congress catalog card number: 67-27352

To Marjorie and Sheryl

Foreword

This is the forty-fifth volume in the M.I.T. Research Monograph Series published by The M.I.T. Press. The objective of this series is to contribute to the professional literature a number of significant pieces of research, larger in scope than journal articles but normally less ambitious than finished books. We believe that such studies deserve a wider circulation than can be accomplished by informal channels, and we hope that this form of publication will make them readily accessible to research organizations, libraries, and independent workers.

HOWARD W. JOHNSON

Preface

The purpose of this work is to establish the interrelations between the phonology and morphology of contemporary French. The phonological and morphological aspects of the language are not treated as two separate levels, each functioning independently of the other, but rather they are shown to be integrated into an over-all system. Morphological information is relevant for determining the phonological representation of morphemes, and conversely, phonological considerations are indispensable for establishing the morphological structure of the language.

The description presented here has as its theoretical basis the model of generative phonology as formulated primarily by Morris Halle and Noam Chomsky. To our knowledge, ours is the first attempt to treat French phonology and morphology within this framework. It is therefore our hope that this work will be of general interest to linguists since it is an exemplification of the theory through a well-known language. It is also our desire that specialists in French will find within these pages new insights about the structure of the language. Because French has such an extensive history of linguistic documentation, our analysis is subject to comparison to previous descriptions of French phonology and morphology as well as to the familiar traditional accounts. The reader may then evaluate the validity of our statements and, even more important, of the theoretical orientation which underlies them.

This study does not purport to be an exhaustive treatment of all aspects of French phonology and morphology. We shall treat in detail three major areas. Chapter 1 establishes that words which enter into elision and liaison are represented by a base form which contains final consonants or vowels, and that these final segments are deleted in specific phonological and syntactic environments. Chapter 2 deals with the principal vocalic alternations observable in the morphology. We postulate a single underlying phonological representation for morphemes which exhibit alternation. The various alternating members are then derived from the unique underlying phonological forms by means of phonological rules which state the environments in which the alternations take place. Chapter 3 is concerned with the rules needed for producing the various forms of the verb conjugation and with establishing the network of relationships operating within the paradigm.

We do not present a detailed account of consonant alternation. Such alternations are considered only when they affect the vowel system or the verb conjugation. Nor is there a detailed analysis of the adjective and noun paradigms. Since in French the verb system is much richer morphologically than either the noun or adjective systems, most of the problems to be encountered in adjectives and nouns appear as well in verbs.

As it is our hope that this work will be accessible to French specialists as well as to linguists, we have resorted to a minimum of linguistic notation. Whenever possible, rules are stated in words rather than in the more concise formal notation characteristic of most studies done in generative phonology. Within phonological rules distinctive features are used to characterize classes of sounds but not usually to specify a single phonological segment. For expository purposes we have changed several of the distinctive feature names, replacing them by commonly used articulatory designations. Those familiar with the conventional notation of generative phonology should have no difficulty translating our informal statements into a more formal version.

La Jolla, California
March 22, 1967

SANFORD A. SCHANE

Acknowledgments

I should like to express my gratitude to Morris Halle for the many hours which he devoted to me in the preliminary stages of this study, for his constant encouragement and his clarification of theoretical issues. I am indebted to Edward Klima, David Perlmutter, and Paul Chapin for comments which they made on reading earlier versions of this work. Mary Ellen Crumlish deserves special thanks for her valuable suggestions and for her assistance in the preparation of this manuscript. Completion of this work was facilitated by a Summer Faculty Fellowship granted by the Regents of the University of California.

Contents

List of Symbols

Conventional notation

Italics are used for French orthography: *savant.*

Single quotes are used for English glosses: 'learned, scholar.'

Parallel vertical lines are used for underlying representations: |sAvAnt|.

Parallel diagonal lines are used for phonetic representations: /savã/.

Liaison occurs: *savant‿Anglais.*

Liaison does not occur: *savant/ anglais.*

Parentheses are placed around optional elements.

Braces are placed around disjoint elements.

Square brackets are used to enclose bundles of distinctive features.

→ goes to, becomes.

← comes from, is derived from.

* indicates a nonexistent form.

+ indicates morpheme boundary.

# indicates word boundary.

= indicates presence of a derivational affix.

( ) indicates the domain of the phonological cycle.

~ placed over a vowel indicates that the vowel is nasalized.

ˈ placed before a vowel indicates that the vowel is stressed.

: placed after a vowel indicates that the vowel is long.

Consonant symbols

Standard IPA: p, t, k, b, d, g, f, s, v, z, m, n, r, l, h.

Other: ʃ as in *ch*apeau
ʒ as in *j*our
ɲ as in monta*gn*e
ʎ (palatal l) as in fi*ll*e (dialectal)
j as in *y*acht
w as in *ou*i
ɥ as in h*u*it

Archiphonemes:

S is a dental sibilant unspecified for voicing (i.e., what *s* and *z* have in common)

N is a nasal consonant unspecified for point of articulation (i.e., what *m*, *n*, and *ɲ* have in common)

Vowel symbols

Derived (phonetic) representations

Standard IPA for French: i, e, ɛ, u, o, ɔ, y, ø, œ, a, ɑ, ə, ɛ̃, ɔ̃, œ̃, ã

NOTE: As we are not concerned with fine phonetic detail, we use a broad phonetic transcription, which is essentially equivalent to the phonemic transcription established for orthoepic French.

Underlying (base) representations

Fourteen underlying vowels are postulated; these vowels are either tense or lax. Underlying tense vowels are capitalized:

I, E, Ɛ, A, Ɔ, O, U

Underlying lax vowels are represented by lower-case letters:

i, e, ɛ, a, ɔ, o, u

NOTE: Within the text underlying representations are enclosed in vertical bars and final derived (phonetic) representations are enclosed in diagonal bars. Any intermediate stages between the underlying and the final derived forms are placed within either vertical or diagonal bars; in general, early intermediate forms are enclosed in vertical bars and late intermediate forms in diagonal bars. Similarly, both underlying vowel symbols and derived vowel symbols may occur in intermediate representations. For intermediate forms the choice of symbols (underlying versus derived) has generally been dictated by expository considerations, i.e., our desire to emphasize a particular aspect of a derivation.

Introduction

In French there are groups of words which are morphologically related. For example, the morpheme 'want' occurs as the stem element in the forms: (*ils*) *veulent* '(they) want,' (*nous*) *voulons* '(we) want,' *volonté* 'will (noun).' What is significant about these examples is that the stem constituent exhibits different vowels in its various morphological forms. Within a phonological and morphological description of French we want to be able to account for the phonological alternations that take place in morphologically related forms. Yet the notion "relatedness" needs to be more precisely formulated. To illustrate the types of problems encountered we shall consider the following forms.

1.	(ils) d*oi*vent '(they) must'	(nous) d*e*vons '(we) must'
2.	(ils) m*eu*rent '(they) die'	(nous) m*ou*rons '(we) die'
3.	chev*al* 'horse'	chev*au*x 'horses'
4.	b*on* 'good (masculine)'	b*onn*e 'good (feminine)'
5.	(ils) *ai*ment '(they) love'	*a*mour 'love (noun)'
6.	fl*eu*r 'flower'	fl*o*ral 'floral'
7.	m*e*r 'sea'	m*a*rin 'sailor'
8.	f*ê*te 'holiday'	f*es*tival 'festival'
9.	n*ui*t 'night'	n*oc*turne 'nocturnal'
10.	fr*ê*le 'weak'	fr*ag*ile 'fragile'
11.	r*ais*on 'reason'	r*at*ion 'ration'
12.	n*aï*f 'naive'	n*at*if 'native'

These examples by no means illustrate morphological alternations of the same type. In 1 and 2, the differing forms show up in the verb conjugation (i.e., different persons or tenses of a given verb stem); 3 and 4 exhibit alternations in nouns and adjectives (i.e., singular-plural, masculine-feminine). In any case, the first four examples depict alternations within the same part of speech — alternations between forms which traditionally have been grouped into paradigms — what has generally been referred to as "inflection." Such forms often have a similar syntactic range of occurrence. Examples 5–7 represent vowel alternations between different parts of speech (e.g., verb-noun, noun-adjective), or even sometimes the same part of speech. However, the various forms cannot usually be arranged in convenient paradigms and often occur in very different syntactic environments. These forms illustrate what is generally called "derivation." Examples 8 and 9 are also instances of derivational morphology. However, these forms are phonologically more complicated than the preceding ones since certain consonants, in addition to the vowels, are affected. Examples 10–12 illustrate a third type of alternation — between forms that are "doublets"; etymologically, both forms are derived from the same Latin word but by different routes.

Although alternating forms tend to be closely related both phonologically and semantically, the criteria for what constitutes "phonological" or "semantic" similarity are by no means easy to establish. In the first example (*doivent*, *devons*), the stem elements (*doiv-*, *dev-*) are quite similar phonologically (both forms have the same consonant segments and differ only in the vowel segments); semantically, *dev-* and *doiv-* have the same meaning. In the last example (*naïf*, *natif*) it is seen that both forms share certain phonological segments and one could probably attribute some vague semantic similarity to these forms, vague certainly in comparison to the first example.

It appears that, of the twelve forms cited, those at the top of the list are clearly related, whereas the relatedness of forms near the bottom of the list is less clear. The traditional division of morphological forms into "inflected," "derivational," and "doublet" is of value in that such a classification recognizes the different relationships between each of the categories. Inflected forms (those composing paradigms) comprise tight-knit systems, so that these forms are related in a way in which, say, derivational forms are not. Among the derivational forms, certain ones (for example, *fleur*, *floral*) may have greater phonological similarity than others (*nuit*, *nocturne*). Finally, there are the least clear cases, among which are often doublets. Although doublets invariably exhibit phonological similarities, the semantic relationship may be less apparent.

In determining morphological relatedness, clearly one must resort to some combination of phonological and semantic criteria. Syntactic factors are also significant, particularly for derivational morphology, since many derivational forms can be shown to be transformationally derived from morphologically less complex structures. Nonetheless, even if one takes into consideration all of these factors, there exists no fixed set of principles for determining unequivocally whether or not two or more forms are morphologically related. In a language as morphologically complex as French, there are clear cases of forms which should be related, and clear cases of forms which should not be related, but there is also a significant number of forms where it is difficult to reach a decision concerning relatedness, and accordingly we can expect investigators to handle such cases differently.

We shall try to make use of the following criteria in order to determine whether two or more forms are morphologically related. If the forms can enter into a paradigmatic arrangement, we shall consider this sufficient reason for relating all the included members. In French this will include verbs, which can be inflected for tense, person, and number, adjectives, which are inflected for gender and number, and nouns, which are inflected for number (and sometimes gender). For the other morphological processes (derivation and doublet), we do not generally have recourse to paradigms in order to decide whether the forms are morphologically related. Therefore, we shall determine such cases by the over-all complexity of the description. Can the forms in question be explained by existent rules? If so, there is no reason to exclude them from the analysis. Will additional rules explicate a large class of data which have not yet been accounted for, or will they only explain some isolated forms? If rules will account for a significant body of data, then forms which could be handled by such rules are included as related forms. In general, we have not attempted to relate forms which exhibit quite restricted phonological alternations. For example, we do not give rules for the alternations: *mère*, *maternel* 'mother, maternal'; *père*, *paternel* 'father, paternal'; *frère*, *fraternel* 'brother, fraternal.' Although within each pair the same alternation is exhibited, this alternation is limited exclusively to these three pairs, so that any rule formulated cannot be extended beyond these three instances. However, occasionally we do consider restricted alternations, but we do so only when it can be shown that by including these forms in the analysis a more general rule can be formulated, or else when it is the case that consideration of marginal forms corroborates statements made in other areas of the morphology.

Within each of our problem areas we have generally tried to state briefly the historical developments which are believed to have taken place. We include such information, not because historical considerations are necessarily relevant for a synchronic analysis, but rather because, in a language with such an extensive historical documentation as that found in French, it is interesting to compare the synchronic rules to those which have been attested historically. That the rules needed to account for the phonological alternations occurring in contemporary French may very often recapitulate the historical development of the language should not in itself be too surprising since the alternations observable in the present-day language are the vestiges of historical change.

FRENCH PHONOLOGY AND MORPHOLOGY

1. Elision and Liaison

1.1 Truncation

1.1.1. *Truncation between words**

In French the phonological adjustments made between one word and the next are referred to as "elision" and "liaison." In most grammars and handbooks dealing with pronunciation these have generally been treated as two distinct phenomena.[1] Elision is defined as the suppression or dropping of the final vowel of a word before another word also beginning with a vowel sound:

	l*e* ami	/lami/	'the friend'
but	l*e* camarade	/ləkamarad/	'the comrade'

Liaison, on the other hand, has been defined as the linking of a word final consonant before a word beginning with a vowel sound, the consonant otherwise being mute or dropped:

	le*s* amis	/lezami/	'the friends'
but	le*s* camarades	/lekamarad/	'the comrades'

Such a view implicitly recognizes that the underlying form of those words which can undergo liaison must in all cases terminate in a consonant, and that this consonant is dropped whenever there is absence of liaison, i.e., in utterance final position or before a word beginning

* Notes, indicated by superior figures throughout, appear at the end of the text.

with a consonant sound.[2] Let us suppose that this view concerning the underlying forms and the nature of liaison is the correct one. Then elision for vowels and absence of liaison for consonants can be considered as the same process: deletion of a segment in word final position; that is, a final vowel is deleted or truncated before another word beginning with a vowel, whereas a final consonant is deleted before another word beginning with a consonant. In order to be neutral between the terms "elision" and "absence of liaison," we shall often refer to this one and the same process as "truncation."[3]

In addition to a vowel or a consonant, a word could also terminate or begin with a liquid or a glide. The effects of truncation on these last two classes of sounds have usually been ignored, it being assumed that liquids are simply a type of consonant and glides a subclass of the vowels. This view is not entirely incorrect; nonetheless, it is necessary to treat liquids and glides separately since (as we shall show) in final position liquids do not act like consonants, and glides do not act like vowels.

Since it is possible for a word to terminate in a consonant, vowel, liquid, or glide and for the next word to begin with any one of these four classes of sounds, there is then a total of sixteen possibilities. These sixteen combinations with relevant examples are shown in the accompanying matrix. (Word boundary is indicated by #, and C, V, L, G stand for consonant, vowel, liquid, and glide, respectively. The headings over the vertical columns indicate word initial position and those alongside the horizontal rows indicate word final position.) Truncation has been indicated by a slant line through the appropriate letter.[4]

	#C	#V	#L	#G
C#	peti~~t~~ camarade	petit ami	peti~~t~~ rabbin	petit oiseau
V#	admirable camarade	admirabl~~e~~ ami	admirable rabbin	admirabl~~e~~ oiseau
L#	cher camarade	cher ami	cher rabbin	cher oiseau
G#	pareil camarade	pareil ami	pareil rabbin	pareil oiseau

From the preceding data the following rules can be formulated:

1. In word final position:
   a. Consonants are truncated before consonants and liquids.
   b. Vowels are truncated before vowels and glides.
   c. Liquids and glides are never truncated.

In terms of distinctive features, the four classes of segments referred to can be differentiated one from the other by making maximal use of just two features: "consonantal" and "vocalic," each feature having the value + or −.[5]

Consonant	Liquid	Vowel	Glide
+cons	+cons	−cons	−cons
−voc	+voc	+voc	−voc

From an examination of this distribution of features, it can be seen that consonants and liquids have the feature [+cons] in common, whereas vowels and glides share the feature [−cons].

By making use of distinctive features we can restate 1:

2. In word final position:
   a. Consonants are truncated before [+cons] segments.
   b. Vowels are truncated before [−cons] segments.
   c. Liquids and glides are never truncated.

The segments which undergo truncation can also be represented in distinctive feature notation:

3. In word final position:

a. $\begin{bmatrix} +\text{cons} \\ -\text{voc} \end{bmatrix}$ segments are truncated before [+cons] segments.

b. $\begin{bmatrix} -\text{cons} \\ +\text{voc} \end{bmatrix}$ segments are truncated before [−cons] segments.

Note that no statement is required about the liquids and glides not being truncated; that is, the third statement of 2 is automatically subsumed by the rules of 3. Rules such as 3 — unlike statements such as 1 — express important generalizations to be found in the language. Rule 3 explicitly states in what way consonants and liquids are related and how they form a class of segments which truncates a preceding consonant; that is, word initial consonants and liquids are related in a way in which word final consonants and liquids are not. A similar statement can be made for the vowels and glides.

The two parts of Rule 3 are very similar, and perhaps the rule could be simplified further, revealing a significant generalization. One observes that, wherever we have a + in part *a* of the rule, there is a − in part *b* and vice versa, so that *a* and *b* differ only in the value assigned to each feature but not in the features themselves. It is this complete symmetry in the two rules on which we wish to base the generalization. Therefore, we shall adopt the following notation: the value, i.e., sign of the feature, will be replaced by a variable (the Greek letter α), the convention being that, if α is assigned the value $+$ in one part of the rule, α must accordingly be $+$ wherever else it appears in the rule; similarly, if the initial value of α is $-$, it must be $-$ everywhere.[6] In an alpha rule one may wish to refer to a value opposite to that which is initially assigned to alpha. This is done by using $-\alpha$.

If we employ the alpha notation, the two subrules of 3 can be reduced to a single rule:

4. Rule for truncation:

In word final position:

$$\begin{bmatrix} \alpha \text{ cons} \\ -\alpha \text{ voc} \end{bmatrix} \text{ segments are truncated before } [\alpha \text{ cons}] \text{ segments.}$$

The left side of the rule states that, if α is assigned the value $+$, then $-\alpha$ must be $-$ (i.e., the consonants); on the other hand, if α has the value $-$, then $-\alpha$ is $+$ (i.e., the vowels). In other words, the left side of the rule defines the class of segments which has *opposite* values for the features "consonantal" and "vocalic," i.e., the consonants and vowels. Liquids and glides are excluded by the rule since they have the *same* values, i.e., they are alpha, alpha: liquids are $++$, glides are $--$, for the features "consonantal" and "vocalic." Finally, if α is $+$ on the left side of the rule, then it must be $+$ on the right side (the class of consonants and liquids), and if α is $-$ on the left side, it is $-$ on the right (the class of vowels and glides).

To be sure, 4 is more concise than the two rules of 3 since fewer features are mentioned. To save a few features is not of much interest in itself. Rather, we wish to emphasize that rules such as 4 make important generalizations about the language, which cannot be stated otherwise. Rule 4 asserts that in French vowels and consonants form a class of segments which can be truncated whenever the following segment agrees in consonantality, and that this class is opposed to the class of liquids and glides, which does not undergo truncation. Without the alpha notation it would not be possible to characterize the true vowels and consonants as a natural class opposed to the class of liquids and glides, and instead of a single general rule for truncation, we would have to postulate two distinct rules: one for the deletion of vowels and another for consonants. Two separate deletion rules would be expected if vowel truncation and consonant truncation were two totally unrelated phenomena. However, we have seen that this is certainly not the case for French. In fact, as soon as two separate rules are written, the symmetry of them becomes immediately apparent; that is, the rules are completely identical except for the values (+ or −) assigned to their features. The alpha notation thus provides the formal means for capturing such symmetrical relations.[7]

1.1.2. *Truncation between morphemes*

The sequence adjective plus noun has the following forms in the masculine, depending on the nature of the initial segment of the noun and on whether the noun phrase is singular or plural.

a. petit camarade	/pəti kamarad/	'little comrade'
b. petit ami	/pətit ami/	'little friend'
c. petits camarades	/pəti kamarad/	'little comrades'
d. petits amis	/pətiz ami/	'little friends'

These forms would have the following underlying representations:[8]

a. |pətit# kamaradə#|
b. |pətit# ami#|
c. |pətit+S# kamaradə+S#|
d. |pətit+S# ami+S#|

We have shown that truncation affects the segment which immediately precedes the word boundary so that for the singular forms the final *t* of *petit* is deleted only when the next word begins with a [+cons] segment. If we allow the truncation rule to apply *not only between words but also between morphemes* (thus extending the generality of the rule), we can also account for the plural forms. Furthermore, the rule must apply to *all* segments which meet the required conditions for application of the rule. This means that within a construction two or more segments may be simultaneously deleted. In *petits camarades* the final *t* and the plural *S* will both be truncated since in the underlying form each precedes a juncture which is in turn followed by a consonant. In *petits amis* only the stem final *t* fits the required environment of juncture followed by a [+cons] segment.

An underlying representation exhibits structural regularities which are not necessarily apparent in the derived phonetic forms. Thus, in the above forms the morpheme |pətit| has a consistent underlying representation wherever it occurs; similarly, in the underlying structure the plural morpheme is a constituent of all plural forms, even though it may not always be phonetically realized.[9]

In the feminine the final *t* is not deleted.

a. petite camarade	/pətit kamarad/
b. petite amie	/pətit ami/
c. petites camarades	/pətit kamarad/
d. petites amies	/pətitz ami/

Since the *t* appears throughout the paradigm of the feminine, this segment must be followed by a vowel which protects it from truncation. The vowel in the underlying representation is the morpheme which indicates feminine gender in adjectives and certain nouns. The above feminines would have the following underlying representations:

a. |pətit+ə# kamaradə#| *c.* |pətit+ə+S# kamaradə+S#|
b. |pətit+ə# ami+ə#| *d.* |petit+ə+S# ami+ə+S#|

The truncation rule will delete the final consonant of *petites* in *c* since it is followed by a consonantal segment. The feminine schwa of *petite(s)* will be deleted only in *b*, where it is followed by another vowel. It will be retained in the other forms since it is followed by a consonant. This means that the output of our rules produces forms such as /pətitə kamaradə/, which contain schwas.

The pronunciation of schwa, particularly in word final position, is, of course, not standard colloquial but rather typifies slowed up speech, formal styles such as oratory and declamation, singing and versification, as well as certain dialectal varieties of the south of France. We would derive the more colloquial styles by means of a set of rules which would stipulate the conditions under which schwas are optionally or obligatorily dropped. For rules on the dropping of "e muet," see de Félice (1950), Delattre (1951), Fouché (1956), Grammont (1961), and Pulgram (1961). Such rules are not included within the present study. Therefore, in our phonetic transcriptions we shall indicate a schwa in parentheses whenever one is potentially possible. Postulating final schwas serves a dual purpose: (1) they are structurally imperative if the truncation rule is to operate in the simplest fashion; (2) we are able to account for the appearance of schwa in dialects, more formal styles, songs, and poetry. Such forms containing phonetic schwas are directly related to the corresponding colloquial forms without schwa. In the case of poetry, underlying schwas are of conceptual importance in determining the meter, for schwas in certain positions are counted as syllables.[10]

1.1.3. *Phrase final consonant deletion*

In word final position consonants are deleted whenever the following word begins with a consonant or a liquid. However, word final consonants are also deleted whenever the word occurs in isolation (e.g., *petit* /pəti/), or whenever it is the final word of an utterance or of a phrase (e.g., *il est petit* /il ε pəti/ 'he is small'). Since this phenomenon is not a case of truncation between words, we shall require a rule which deletes consonants in phrase final position, which, of course, includes utterance final position. (Isolated words are also considered to be in phrase final position.)

Rule for final consonant deletion

Delete a word final consonant in phrase final position.

The truncation rule must be applied before the rule for final consonant deletion.[11] This ordering can be determined by noting the derivation of *ils sont petits* /il sɔ̃ pəti/ 'they are small.'

a.	underlying	il+S# sɔ̃t# pətit+S#
	truncation	il # sɔ̃ # pəti +S#
	final cons. deletion	il # sɔ̃ # pəti #
b.	underlying	il+S# sɔ̃t# pətit+S#
	final cons. deletion	il+S# sɔ̃t# pətit #
	truncation	*il # sɔ̃ # pətit #

If the rule for final consonant deletion is applied first (*b*), one obtains the wrong result. The final *S* of |pətit+S| is deleted; however, the truncation rule will not delete the second *t* of |pətit|, as it would no longer be followed by a [+cons] segment.

1.2 Phonological and morphological constraints on truncation

1.2.1. "*H aspiré*"

There are words which, phonetically, have a vowel as the initial segment, but do not permit a preceding word to enter in liaison or elision with them. These are the words which begin with the so-called "h aspiré."[12]

le héros	/lə ero/	'the hero'
les héros	/le ero/	'the heroes'
une honte	/ynə ɔ̃t/	'a shame'

In these examples, the vowel of *le* or *une* is not truncated, whereas the final consonant of *les* is. The nouns of these examples behave precisely like words which begin with a consonantal segment. This fact suggests that in the underlying form the noun must, in fact, begin with a consonant, even though the consonant has no phonetic value. The consonant becomes null only after the truncation rule has been applied.

The orthography would, of course, lead one to postulate that the initial segment should be *h*. Although the orthography may provide insight about the language, such information is of little value in the linguistic description unless one can demonstrate synchronic evidence for it. Is the *h* of more than just orthographic or historical interest?

In the eastern section of France as well as in certain types of "theater pronunciation," a phonetic *h* is actually heard as the initial segment of these words;[13] other speakers will have a glottal stop in this position. This dialectal or idiolectal phonetic evidence, coupled with the previously observed structural pressure for a consonantal segment, that is, failure of these words to undergo liaison and elision, confirms, then, that in the underlying form these words do in effect have an initial nonvowel segment, which we shall set up as |h|.

Another peculiar property of the "h aspiré" words is that a preceding schwa is often pronounced, e.g., *une honte* /ynə ɔ̃t/; that is, the rules for the dropping of "e muet" in final position do not always apply when there is a schwa immediately before one of the words of this special class.[14] Evidently then, there must be some unique initial segment if one is to account for this phenomenon.[15]

1.2.2. *Pronounced final consonants*

In some words the final consonant is pronounced both before a following consonantal segment and in final position.

avec vous	/avɛk/	'with you'
sept camarades	/sɛt/	'seven comrades'
sens	/sɑ̃s/	'sense'
chef	/ʃɛf/	'head'
sec	/sɛk/	'dry'

Therefore, words such as these will have to be marked in the lexicon as exceptions to the deletion rules.[16] However, it is not necessary to mark all such words as being exceptions to both the truncation rule and the final consonant deletion rule. Rather, the forms need to be marked as exceptions only to one rule or the other. This phenomenon can be best illustrated by comparing the behavior of the numerals *trois* 'three,' *six* 'six,' and *sept* 'seven' before a vocalic segment, before a consonantal segment, and in isolation.

trois amis	/trwaz/	trois camarades	/trwa/	trois	/trwa/
six amis	/siz/	six camarades	/si/	six	/sis/
sept amis	/sɛt/	sept camarades	/sɛt/	sept	/sɛt/

Trois is not an exception to either rule; the final segment is deleted before a consonantal segment as well as in final position. *Six*, on the other hand, is truncated before a consonantal segment but not in final position; hence, it is an exception to the rule for final consonant deletion. *Sept* retains its final consonant and accordingly it is an exception to both rules. However, all morphemes which do not undergo truncation (like *sept*) also do not undergo final consonant deletion; therefore, if one knows that a form is an exception to the truncation rule, one can predict that it will also be an exception to the rule for final consonant deletion. The converse, of course, is not true as we showed in the case of *six*. Consequently, in the lexicon *six* will be marked as an exception to the rule for final consonant deletion, whereas *sept* will be marked as an exception to the truncation rule. The fact that *sept* is also an exception to the other deletion rule will be predicted by the following redundancy rule:[17]

Rule for predicting exceptions to final consonant deletion

A morpheme which is an exception to the rule for truncation is also an exception to the rule for final consonant deletion.

The examples cited provide further motivation for two separate deletion rules; otherwise, forms such as *six* and *sept* would be treated identically and one would be unable to account for the differences observed.[18]

Among those words which retain a final consonant the vast majority are nouns so that most of the forms which are exceptions to the truncation rule can be characterized morphologically. If this observation is correct, we have here an interesting example of the relevance of morphological information (in the present case, whether a form is a noun) for the operation of phonological processes. The number of nouns which retain a final consonant is by no means insignificant. Rather than to mark all these forms as exceptions to the truncation rule, a more realistic solution might be to assign all noun stems to one of two phonological classes for purposes of the operation of the truncation rule, that is, those stems which undergo truncation and those which do not.[19] This is analogous to the assignment of all nouns to one of two gender classes for purposes of morphology and syntax. That there should be phonological classes is no more unusual than that there should be morphological classes. (See Note 14.)

1.2.3. *Deletable and nondeletable vowels*

We have shown that certain words have final consonants which are an exception to either the truncation rule, or the rule for final consonant deletion, or else both rules. Similarly, there are final vowels which do not undergo truncation. In a form such as *joli ami* /ʒɔli ami/ 'nice friend,' the final vowel of *joli* is not elided before the following vowel segment. If we assume that every word in French has a stressed vowel, then we can account for the proper instances of elision if we impose the condition that *only unstressed vowels* can be truncated.[20]

Stress at the word level is predictable and the rule for its assignment is well known: *the final syllable bears the stress unless its vowel is schwa, in which case the stress falls on the penultimate.* When the stress rule is applied to the example, the word *joli* will receive stress on the final vowel; and since the vowel bears a stress, it will not undergo deletion. The rules for stress assignment and truncation must apply in this order; otherwise, the final *i* of *joli* would be elided.

Once we revise the truncation rule so that only unstressed segments are deleted, forms such as *joli* cease to be exceptions to truncation. The cost for eliminating these pseudoirregularities is minimal, namely, imposing an additional restriction on the truncation rule. The slight increase of complexity in the truncation rule is insignificant when one considers the number of additional forms which can be handled by this rule.[21]

Rule for truncation (revised)

At a boundary:

$$\begin{bmatrix} \alpha \text{ cons} \\ -\alpha \text{ voc} \\ -\text{stress} \end{bmatrix} \text{ segments are truncated before } [\alpha \text{ cons}] \text{ segments.}$$

1.2.4. *Deletable liquids and glides*

The truncation rule states that at a morpheme or word boundary a preceding consonant or vowel is deleted whenever the following segment agrees in consonantality. Liquids and glides, on the other hand, do not undergo truncation. Yet forms such as *gentil* /ʒãti/ 'nice,' *soûl* /su/ 'drunk,' *étranger* /etrãʒe/ 'foreigner' do not terminate phonetically in a liquid or a glide and appear to be exceptions to the statement that liquids and glides are not truncated. That these forms do, in fact, have a liquid or a glide in their underlying representations is demonstrated by the corresponding feminines, where the stem shows a final liquid or glide before the feminine schwa, e.g., *gentille* /ʒãtij(ə)/, *soûle* /sul(ə)/, *étrangère* /etrãʒɛr(ə)/.

Forms such as these, which appear to be exceptions to the assertion that liquids and glides do not undergo deletion, interestingly enough, can be characterized phonologically. In all cases, the liquid or glide is deleted in phrase final position or else before a morpheme beginning with a consonantal segment, but *only on condition* that a particular vowel precedes the liquid or glide. Thus, |j| is deleted after the high front unrounded vowel |i|, |l| after the high back rounded vowel |u|, and |r| after the low mid front unrounded vowel |ɛ|, the |ɛ| then being raised to /e/.[22] After any vowel other than the one indicated for each liquid or glide, deletion does not take place.

|j|:	pareil	/parɛj/	'same'
	travail	/travaj/	'work'
	fenouil	/fənuj/	'fennel'
	œil	/œj/	'eye'
|l|:	vil	/vil/	'vile'
	sel	/sɛl/	'salt'
	bal	/bal/	'ball'
	bol	/bɔl/	'bowl'
	nul	/nyl/	'none'
	seul	/sœl/	'alone'
|r|:	finir	/finir/	'finish'
	car	/kar/	'since'
	pour	/pur/	'for'
	cor	/kɔr/	'horn'
	sur	/syr/	'on'
	fleur	/flœr/	'flower'

These examples corroborate one of the original assumptions concerning truncation, namely, that liquid and glides are not deleted in final position. For those instances where a final liquid or glide is truncated, it is seen that the forms in question are not just unexplained exceptions to a more or less general tendency. In almost all cases, the deletion of the liquid or glide is attributable to the phonetic character of the preceding vowel. Therefore, no additional constraints need to be imposed on the truncation rule, but, instead, a special set of rules is required which converts |ij| to /i/, |ul| to /u/, and |ɛr| to /e/.

1.3 Syntactic constraints on truncation

Liaison does not occur between just any two contiguous words. There are restrictions which are syntactically determined.[23] For example, liaison is made between an adjective and a following noun but not between a singular noun and a following adjective, so that one can find such minimal pairs as:[24]

Un savant‿Anglais	/œ̃ savãt ãglɛ/	'A wise Englishman'
Un savant/ anglais	/œ̃ savã ãglɛ/	'An English scholar'

Within a generative grammar, the output of the syntactic component becomes the input to the phonological component: syntactic information is then available at the phonological level.[25] This means that information regarding the part of speech membership of words and the constituent structure of higher level units (e.g., phrases, clauses, sentences) can be used — and, in fact, must be used — in determining phonological processes. The presence versus absence of a liaison consonant in the minimal pair we have cited can be easily accounted for, once it is recognized that these two noun phrases have different syntactic analyses:

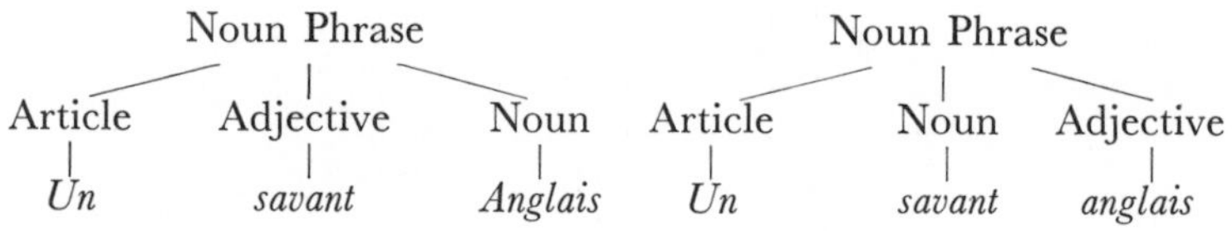

What is important here phonologically is that, when *savant* is a noun, its final consonant is deleted, even though the following word begins with a vowel.

Thus far, we have proposed two deletion rules: the truncation rule and the rule for final consonant deletion. Could either of these rules account for the absence of the final consonant in the case where *savant* is a noun? The truncation rule could not handle the deletion of *t* in *savant anglais* as this rule requires that, in order for a consonant to be deleted, the following segment must be a consonant or a liquid. Since *anglais* begins with a vowel, the appropriate environmental condition is simply not met. The rule for final consonant deletion causes a consonant to be deleted whenever it is found in phrase final or utterance final position. This deletion is not dependent on the phonological nature of any following segment. If we extend the operation of this rule so that it applies to all singular nouns as well as to words in phrase final position, and if we restrict the rule so that it does *not* apply to adjectives, then we can account for the forms we have noted. Thus, when *savant anglais* has the structure noun-adjective, the final consonant of *savant* will be deleted. On the other hand, when this phrase has the structure adjective-noun, the final consonant of *savant* will not be deleted. However, given either constituent structure, the final consonant of *anglais* will be *deleted* — irrespective of whether the word is an adjective or a noun — since in both cases it occurs in phrase final position, and in this environment all final consonants are deleted.[26]

In certain syntactic constructions liaison is optional, its presence or absence generally being a stylistic factor.[27] For example, liaison may or may not occur between a plural noun and a following adjective:

des camarades anglais	/de kamaradəz ãglɛ/ /de kamarad ãglɛ/	'English friends'

Whereas the deletion of a word final consonant is obligatory for a singular noun, it is optional for a plural noun.

Rule for final consonant deletion (revised)[28]

Delete a word final consonant

1. obligatorily,
   a. in phrase final position
   b. in a singular noun;
2. optionally, in a plural noun.

We shall illustrate the rules by deriving both variants of *des camarades anglais*. We shall derive first the variant with liaison, which means that we choose *not* to apply the rule for final consonant deletion to the plural noun, although it will nonetheless still apply in phrase final position where it is obligatory.

underlying form	deS# kamaradə+S# ãglɛz+S#
truncation	de # kamaradə+S# ãglɛ +S#
final cons. deletion	de # kamaradə+S# ãglɛ #

However, if we attempt to derive the variant without liaison, that is, if we choose to apply the rule for final consonant deletion to the plural noun, when the rules are applied in the order which was previously established, namely, truncation, then final consonant deletion, the wrong result is obtained:

underlying form	deS# kamaradə+S# ãglɛz+S#
truncation	de # kamaradə+S# ãglɛ +S#
final cons. deletion	*de # kamaradə # ãglɛ #

The noun *camarades* still has its final schwa. In the type of style where schwas are pronounced, the schwas must either be followed by a consonant or else appear in utterance final position, but under no condition is the schwa pronounced if the following segment is a vowel.

This particular difficulty can be rectified if we change the ordering of our two rules, allowing the rule for final consonant deletion to be applied first:

underlying form	deS#	kamaradə + S#	ãglɛz + S#
final cons. deletion	deS#	kamaradə #	ãglɛz #
truncation	*de #	kamarad #	ãglɛz #

The final *S* and schwa of *camarades* are appropriately deleted. However, in resolving this problem we have created another one, for now the word *anglais* is handled incorrectly; the stem final consonant has been retained, whereas it should not have been.

The difficulty, of course, is that we have certain forms where we require that the rules be applied in the order 1, 2, and other forms where we need the order 2, 1. More specifically, as our example shows, truncation *between morphemes* must precede final consonant deletion. On the other hand, final consonant deletion has to precede truncation *between words*. That is, we need the order: truncation between morphemes, final consonant deletion, truncation between words. Furthermore, we prefer not to have to set up three different rules, for then the first and third rules would be identical except for the juncture and consequently we would destroy the generalization which we previously established.

We are faced, then, with two problems: (1) to find a way to allow the truncation rule to be applied more than once; (2) to apply the truncation rule to morphemes before applying it to words. Both of these problems can be resolved if we capitalize further on the constituent structure provided by the syntactic component of the grammar. We have said that the syntax provides a parsing of each sentence into its various constituents (morphemes, words, phrases, etc.), these constituents being appropriately bracketed and labeled. We have already shown the relevance of part of speech classification for purposes of liaison. The difficulties noted can be resolved if we also take into consideration the higher level syntactic units.

The noun phrase *des camarades anglais* is not ambiguous syntactically. Therefore, it has a single constituent structure, which is shown in the following diagram: *a* and *b* are merely different ways of representing the same structure, *a* being a diagram with labeled branching, whereas *b* is with labeled bracketing.

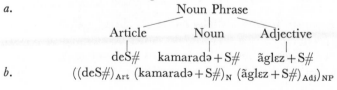

a.

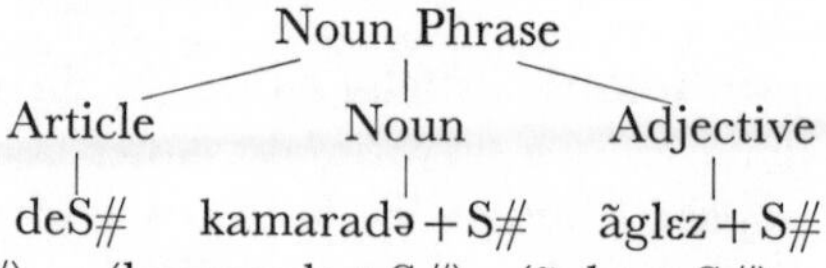

b. ((deS#)$_{\text{Art}}$ (kamaradə + S#)$_{\text{N}}$ (ãglɛz + S#)$_{\text{Adj}}$)$_{\text{NP}}$

So that the phonological rules may be applied more than once, the following convention has been adopted. First, the rules will be applied to the innermost bracketed (or smallest) constituents of a phrase, that is, words comprised of morphemes. Then the same rules will be reapplied to the next larger constituent, e.g., the noun phrase, *des camarades anglais*. This is what is meant by a "cycle," since the set of rules is applied more than once — from smaller to larger units — and the domain of application is determined by the constituent structure.[29] In this way, the truncation rule *can* be applied at two different levels, that is, between morphemes and between words, and furthermore, its application can be initially restricted to the smaller units. Both of these conditions must be met if the problem we have just raised is to be resolved.

The complete cycle is illustrated in the accompanying table. Bracketing has been used to delimit the various constituents. After each application of the complete set of rules the innermost parentheses and their syntactic labeling are erased. The same rules are then reapplied to the constituents within the next set of parentheses. The cycle is terminated after all parentheses have been removed. Making use of the concept of a cycle, we shall show how the nonliaison form, without schwa or *S*, of *des camarades anglais* is derived.

1.	((deS#)$_{\text{Art}}$	(kamaradə+S#)$_{\text{N}}$	(ãglɛz+S#)$_{\text{Adj}}$)$_{\text{NP}}$	underlying form
2.	((deS#)$_{\text{Art}}$	(kamaradə+S#)$_{\text{N}}$	(ãglɛ +S#)$_{\text{Adj}}$)$_{\text{NP}}$	truncation
3.	((deS#)$_{\text{Art}}$	(kamaradə #)$_{\text{N}}$	(ãglɛ +S#)$_{\text{Adj}}$)$_{\text{NP}}$	final consonant deletion
4.	(deS#	kamaradə #	ãglɛ +S#)$_{\text{NP}}$	remove innermost parentheses
5.	(de #	kamarad #	ãglɛ +S#)$_{\text{NP}}$	truncation
6.	(de #	kamarad #	ãglɛ #)$_{\text{NP}}$	final consonant deletion
7.	de #	kamarad #	ãglɛ #	remove final parentheses

Line 1 shows the underlying representation of *des camarades anglais* with the appropriate syntactic bracketing and labeling. Note that the plural morphophoneme *S* is present in all constituents. The rules are applied to the innermost parenthesized constituents, i.e., to the individual words. The truncation rule (line 2) applies only to the stem final |z| of *anglais* since this is the only word which has a segment followed by a + juncture, which is in turn followed by a segment agreeing in consonantality. Final consonant deletion (line 3) deletes the final *S* of *camarades*. The rule may be applied to a plural noun; however, articles and adjectives are not affected by this rule. In line 4 the innermost, i.e., word level, parentheses and their labels have been removed and the set of rules will be reapplied to the whole noun phrase. The truncation rule (line 5) deletes the final *S* of *des* since this segment is followed by a word boundary, which is in turn followed by a consonantal segment. The same rule also deletes the final schwa of *camarades* as this vowel is followed by a word boundary and a vowel. Final consonant deletion (line 6) deletes the plural *S* of *anglais*; this segment is now in phrase final position, i.e., it is the final segment of a noun phrase. In line 7 the parentheses and labeling have been erased.

1.4 Summary

Strings of elements, appropriately bracketed and separated by junctures, constitute the input to the phonological component of the grammar. These strings are then subjected to a sequence of rules, some of which are applied more than once. The cyclic reapplication of a small number of rules simplifies considerably the description of phonological processes. Following this approach, we have shown that the complex system of elision and liaison, which takes place between words in spoken French, can be characterized in a concise manner. The truncation rule and the rule for final consonant deletion, both of which operate within the cycle and delete segments in certain simply statable phonological and syntactic environments, account for the intricate interplay of elision and liaison. The truncation rule also explains some of the morphophonemic processes which take place within the word.

We have represented a given morpheme by a single phonological representation so that throughout the paradigm the same morpheme always has the same phonological shape. The particular morphemic variant is derived from the underlying representation by means of an ordered set of phonological rules. In this way, the underlying representation exhibits a structural regularity which is not always evident from the phonetic form, while the rules serve to explain the particular phonetic form (variant) which occurs.

Interestingly enough, our underlying representations are quite close to the standard orthography, particularly in regard to such features as latent final consonants and occurrences of schwa. This means that French spelling, to a large extent, is highly morphophonemic. To reach this conclusion, one has only to consider the adjective paradigm (e.g., *petit*, *petite*, *petits*, *petites*), where the stem, mark of the feminine, and mark of the plural have a consistent representation. In verbs the same phenomenon may occur, e.g., *vends*, *vendons*. However, to be sure, the standard orthography does not always reflect completely the morphophonemics. Whereas *petite amie* mirrors the underlying phonological representation, *l'amie* does not. Similarly, *vis*, unlike *vends*, does not exhibit the morphophonemic representation for the stem (cf. *vivons*). Yet orthographic *vis* is not a phonemic, or phonetic spelling either, since the person marker *s* has been retained. Rather, the form is representative of a stage of derivation between the morphophonemic and the phonemic or phonetic levels. Within our set of rules, orthographic *vis* characterizes the point at which the truncation rule has been applied, i.e., viv+s → vis, but not the rule for final consonant deletion. In any event, aside from obvious archaisms, French spelling is by and large quite satisfactory for the contemporary language. The orthography often indicates within morphemes those structural regularities which are not necessarily apparent phonetically. It clearly shows relations between the forms of the paradigm, relations which are by no means insignificant for the French speaker. Those who advocate "phonetic spelling" perhaps do not realize that a spelling system based entirely on phonemic principles would completely obliterate the morphological relations and phonological structure presently discernible in the standard orthography of French.

2. The Vowel System

2.1 Oral vowels

In most phonemic analyses of Standard French twelve oral vowels have been recognized:

	front unrounded	front rounded	back rounded
high	i	y	u
high mid	e	ø	o
low mid	ɛ	œ	ɔ
low	a	(ə)	ɑ

Following are examples of these vowels:

/i/	si	/si/	'if'
/e/	thé	/te/	'tea'
/ɛ/	taie	/tɛ/	'pillow case'
/a/	patte	/pat(ə)/	'paw'
/y/	tu	/ty/	'you (familiar)'
/ø/	jeûne	/ʒøn(ə)/	'fast (n.)'
/œ/	jeune	/ʒœn(ə)/	'young'
/ə/	brebis	/brəbi/	'ewe'
/u/	ou	/u/	'or'
/o/	haute	/ot(ə)/	'high (f.)'
/ɔ/	hotte	/ɔt(ə)/	'hood'
/ɑ/	pâte	/pɑt(ə)/	'paste'

This twelve-vowel system is for orthoepic French and appears in many bilingual dictionaries and handbooks for pronunciation.[1]

Many speakers do not have twelve "phonemically distinct" oral vowels. Often no distinction is made between "a antérieur" /a/ and "a postérieur" /ɑ/. Also, the pairs of mid vowels may be in complementary distribution: the high mid vowels /e/, /ø/, /o/ occur in an open syllable, and the low mid vowels /ɛ/, /œ/, /ɔ/ are found in a closed syllable; furthermore, /ø/ and /o/ may occur before /z/. Other speakers retain contrasts only between /o/ and /ɔ/ in a closed syllable but not between the other two pairs.

However, all speakers distinguish the high vowels /i/, /y/, /u/ from all other vowels. Also, an *a*-type vowel is opposed to all other vowels. Thus, although minimal pairs may be found in which /e/ is opposed to /ɛ/, this contrast does not have the same differentiating force as, say, the opposition between /i/ and /e/, so that contrasts of the type /e/:/ɛ/ often may be a matter of individual stylistic variation rather than of essential phonemic opposition.[2] We shall nonetheless represent the high mid and low mid vowels differently in the phonetic (derived) representations as (1), regardless of their "phonemic" status, two types of vowels are phonetically distinguishable for all speakers, and (2), the orthoepists are generally in agreement as to which vowels occur in which words.[3]

The nonphonemic (or perhaps pseudophonemic) character of certain sound types is particularly apparent for "a antérieur" and "a postérieur." Not only do speakers who make the distinction differ widely in which words have which *a*-type vowel, but also the handbooks for pronunciation (cited in Note 1) offer different lists of words illustrating these two vowels. It is this fluctuating and unstable character of the *a*-type vowels which leads us to consider the occurrence of two *a*-vowels definitely as a stylistic phenomenon within modern French and not as a "true" phonemic contrast. Therefore, in our transcriptions we shall employ a single /a/ vowel for the representations of derived forms.[4]

The vowel /ə/ (schwa), variously called "e muet," "e caduc," "e féminin," "e neutre," does not function like the other oral vowels. Unlike the other vowels, /ə/ never is found in tonic position and is the only vowel which may be posttonic.[5] It may also appear in pretonic position, but may not be initial in the syllable. In terms of articulation, /ə/ is somewhat more lax than the other vowels of French. (See Note 19.) Furthermore, it is the schwa vowel which is always elided before other vowels, and which may be deleted in other phonological environments as well.

2.1.1. *Vocalic alternation*

Within the phonological description we want to explain vocalic alternations observable in morphologically related forms. A set of alternating vowels is derived from a *single underlying vowel* through application of the phonological rules. These rules state the environments in which certain underlying vowels are converted to other (derived) vowels. The underlying vowels, ideally, should be set up so as to allow the least complicated set of rules needed for the appropriate conversions.

Some vowel alternations. Following are four sets of alternating pretonic and tonic vowels.[6]

1.	/a/	/'ɛ/		
	cl*a*rté	cl*ai*r	'clearness'	'clear'
	f*a*mine	f*ai*m	'famine'	'hunger'
	form*a*lité	form*e*l	'formality'	'formal'
	popul*a*rité	popul*ai*re	'popularity'	'popular'
	m*a*nuel	m*ai*n	'manual'	'hand'
2.	/ɔ/	/'œ/		
	m*o*rtel	m*eu*rent	'mortal'	'(they) die'
	v*o*lonté	v*eu*lent	'will'	'(they) want'
	s*o*litude	s*eu*l	'solitude'	'alone'
	fl*o*ral	fl*eu*r	'floral'	'flower'
	h*o*raire	h*eu*re	'time table'	'hour'
3.	/e/	/j'ɛ/		
	c*é*leste	c*ie*l	'heavenly'	'sky, heaven'
	b*é*nir	b*ie*n	'bless'	'well'
	p*é*destre	p*ie*d	'pedestrian'	'foot'
	l*é*vrier	l*iè*vre	'greyhound'	'hare'
4.	/e/	/w'a/		
	cr*é*dibilité	cr*oi*re	'belief'	'believe'
	esp*é*rance	esp*oi*r	'expectation'	'hope'
	l*é*gal	l*oi*	'legal'	'law'
	r*é*gal	r*oi*	'regal'	'king'
	s*é*rénade	s*oi*r	'serenade'	'evening'

The forms cited in Column 1 do not exhibit front rounded vowels or diphthongs. A simplification in the vowels will result if we eliminate front rounded vowels and diphthongs from the underlying system and derive them from their vocalic counterparts given in Column 1. Similarly, schwa will not appear in the underlying representations, but will be derived from other vowels. Since the two *a*-type vowels are of stylistic significance rather than of structural importance, the underlying system need only contain a single central /a/. The result is a seven-vowel system for underlying representations.

	front unrounded	central unrounded	back rounded
high	i		u
mid	e		o
low	ɛ	a	ɔ

The following four binary features will be used to specify these vowels: "high," "low," "front," "round." These feature names correspond quite closely to the standard terms used in articulatory phonetics.[7] "High" vowels are defined as [+high, −low]; "low" vowels as [−high, +low]; "mid" vowels as [−high, −low]. Front vowels are specified as [+front], whereas [−front] includes both the "central" and "back" positions. The feature "round" corresponds, of course, to the articulatory term "rounded." The "central" vowel is defined as [−front, −round]. The following chart indicates the feature specifications for the seven underlying vowels:[8]

	i	e	ɛ	a	ɔ	o	u
high	+	−	−	−	−	−	+
low	−	−	+	+	+	−	−
front	+	+	+	−	−	−	−
round	−	−	−	−	+	+	+

Although front rounded vowels do not occur in underlying representations and will be derived from back vowels, it is nonetheless necessary to assign sets of features to the former so that they can be distinguished from all other vowels. Front rounded vowels will be stipulated as [+front, +round].

In the examples cited, it is seen that one alternant occurs in tonic position (Column 2), whereas the other alternant is found in pretonic position (Column 1). Therefore, we shall tentatively establish stress as the conditioning environment, that is, the feature "stress" is needed, and shall derive the stressed vowel, wherever possible, from its unstressed counterpart.[9] In the first set of examples the alternation is between /a/ (unstressed) and /ɛ/ (stressed). If we set up |a| as the underlying vowel, a comparison of the feature chart shows that |a| can be converted to /ɛ/ by changing only one feature, namely, [−front] must become [+front]:[10]

Rule a $\begin{bmatrix} +\text{stress} \\ +\text{low} \\ -\text{front} \\ -\text{round} \end{bmatrix}$ segments become [+front] (stressed |a| → /ɛ/)

Given the two underlying forms:

|kl'ar| |klar+t'e|

(where + indicates morpheme boundary and the stressed vowel is indicated by a preceding diacritic), Rule *a* converts only the |a| of the form on the left to /ɛ/ since this vowel is under stress, yielding:[11]

/kl'ɛr/ /klar+t'e/

In the second set of alternations (/ɔ/:/œ/) we note that /ɔ/ differs from /œ/ only in that /ɔ/ is back rounded, whereas /œ/ is front rounded. Again, we need only change the feature [−front] to [+front].

Rule b $\begin{bmatrix} +\text{stress} \\ +\text{low} \\ -\text{front} \\ +\text{round} \end{bmatrix}$ segments become [+front] (stressed |ɔ| → /œ/)

Rules *a* and *b* are similar, for both change the frontness of an underlying vowel. Since the same type of phonological process is exhibited, it would be desirable to generalize both cases by a single rule. This can be done if one indicates *only those features* which are common to both |a| and |ɔ| in Rules *a* and *b*. As |a| and |ɔ| differ only by the feature "round," the desired generalization can be stated by stipulating all features except rounding. Rule *c* replaces Rules *a* and *b*.

Rule c $\begin{bmatrix} +\text{stress} \\ +\text{low} \\ -\text{front} \end{bmatrix}$ segments become [+front] (stressed low central and back vowels are fronted)

Since it is the feature [−front] which is changed, additional simplification in the rule can be obtained by not indicating frontness in the left half of the rule.

Rule d Rule for vowel fronting

$\begin{bmatrix}+\text{stress}\\+\text{low}\end{bmatrix}$ segments become [+front] (stressed low vowels are fronted)

The feature [+low] specifies the segments |ɛ, a, ɔ|. Since an underlying |ɛ| is inherently [+front], Rule *d* will apply vacuously to it, that is, |ɛ| will be converted to itself. We have already shown that, when |a| and |ɔ| are made [+front], they become /ɛ/ and /œ/ respectively. Rule *d* then replaces Rule *c*. By allowing for vacuous rule application, fewer features need to be indicated in stating rules. This leads to notational simplification as well as to greater generality.[12]

The alternations exhibited in Sets 3 and 4 are between /e/ and /j'ɛ/ on the one hand, and between /e/ and /w'a/ on the other. Although the pretonic vowels of Sets 3 and 4 are identical, the stressed vowels are different. Consequently, the derived vowels for each set do not have the same origin. This means that |e| can occur as the underlying vowel for only one of the sets. The underlying vowel for the other set must be some other vowel. This vowel should be similar to |e| in its feature specification since it will have to be converted to /e/ in pretonic position, and it is desirable for simplicity that the conversion entail the least number of feature changes. The obvious vowel in this case is |ɛ|. A rule is therefore required which raises |ɛ| to /e/ in pretonic position.

Rule for pretonic vowel raising

$\begin{bmatrix}-\text{stress}\\+\text{low}\\+\text{front}\end{bmatrix}$ segments become [−low] (pretonic |ɛ| → /e/)

In stressed position underlying |e| and |ɛ| undergo diphthongization: the former will become /wa/, the latter /jɛ/. We shall consider diphthongization to be the insertion of a glide before the vowel.

Rule for Diphthongization

Insert a glide before a stressed nonhigh front vowel.
The [−low] vowel |e| takes on a /w/ glide, whereas the [+low] vowel |ɛ| takes on a /j/ glide.

According to the diphthongization rule a glide is inserted before a vowel; however, the original quality of the vowel is in no way affected. Therefore, |ɛ| will become /jɛ/ and |e| will become /we/.[13] An additional rule is required which changes /we/ to /wa/.[14]

Rule for wa-adjustment

/we/ becomes /wa/

The diphthongization rule must precede the rule for vowel fronting; otherwise, the /ɛ/ which is derived from |a| would subsequently undergo diphthongization, that is, underlying |ɛ| first becomes /jɛ/, then underlying |a| becomes /ɛ/. Also, the *wa*-adjustment rule must follow vowel fronting; otherwise, the /we/ which becomes /wa/ would be further shifted to /wɛ/.

The following order is then imposed on the rules which we have postulated so far:

1. diphthongization
2. vowel fronting
3. *wa*-adjustment
4. pretonic vowel raising.

The first three rules affect stressed vowels; only these rules must be ordered relative to one another. The rule for pretonic vowel raising could apply at any time since the crucial environment is different.

We have presented four sets of words showing tonic and pretonic vowel alternations. The underlying vowel of each set is represented by a different nonhigh vowel which undergoes change when stressed. The types of changes involved and consideration of appropriate underlying vowels lead to the emergence of a general pattern. The front vowels develop glides; then all low vowels are fronted — this applies vacuously to the front vowel. When pretonic, the low front vowel |ɛ| is raised to mid position.

Additional vowel alternations. The vocalic alternations cited in the preceding section represent a restricted body of data. We established that the vowel |ɔ| shifted, under stress, to /œ/, in order to account for alternations of the type: *volonté*:*veulent*. However, within the verb conjugation tonic /œ/ also alternates with pretonic /u/, as in *veulent*:*voulons*, *meurent*:*mourons*. The unrounded vowels also exhibit an alternate set of variations. In addition to |e| → /wa/ *espérance*:*espoir*, tonic /wa/ alternates with pretonic /ə/, as in *doivent*:*devons*, *reçoivent*:*recevons*. Similarly, whereas |ɛ| → /jɛ/ *bénir*:*bien*, tonic /jɛ/ also is in alternation with pretonic /ə/, as in *viennent*:*venons*, *tiennent*:*tenons*. Finally, in addition to |a| → /ɛ/ *marin*:*mer*, tonic /ɛ/ alternates with pretonic /ə/, as in *parlèrent*:*parleront*.

Examples of these alternations are given in the following chart:

1.	/u/	/'œ/	
	m*ou*rons	m*eu*rent	'(we) die' '(they) die'
	v*ou*lons	v*eu*lent	'(we) want' '(they) want'
	*ou*vrage	*œu*vre	'work' 'work'
	doul*ou*reux	doul*eu*r	'sad' 'sorrow'
2.	/ə/	/'ɛ/	
	parl*e*ront	parl*è*rent	'(they) will speak' '(they) spoke
	m*e*notte	m*ai*n	'little hand' 'hand'
	font*e*nier	font*ai*ne	'fountain-maker' 'fountain'
	gr*e*nu	gr*ai*ne	'grainy' 'seed'
3.	/ə/	/j'ɛ/	
	v*e*nons	v*ie*nnent	'(we) come' '(they) come'
	t*e*nons	t*ie*nnent	'(we) hold' '(they) hold'
	pomm*e*raie	pomm*ie*r	'apple-orchard' 'apple tree'
	cheval*e*rie	cheval*ie*r	'knighthood' 'knight'
4.	/ə/	/w'a/	
	d*e*vons	d*oi*vent	'(we) must' '(they) must'
	rec*e*vons	reç*oi*vent	'(we) receive' '(they) receive'
	s*e*rein	s*oi*r	'calm' 'evening'
	p*e*lu	p*oi*l	'hairy' 'hair'

What is characteristic of the alternations cited in the preceding section of this chapter (hereafter referred to as Type 1 vowels), as well as of those cited in this section (Type 2 vowels), is that both types of alternations exhibit the same set of tonic vowels but different sets of pretonic vowels.

Tonic vowel (both types)	œ	ɛ	jɛ	wa
Pretonic vowel (Type 1)	ɔ	a	e<ɛ	e
Pretonic vowel (Type 2)	u	ə	ə	ə

Since the *tonic* members of both types exhibit the same vowels, i.e., /œ ɛ jɛ wa/, the *underlying vowels* must be the same for both types, namely, |ɔ a ɛ e|, so that the rules for diphthongization (|e| → /we/, |ɛ| → /jɛ/), vowel fronting (|ɔ| → /œ/, |a| → /ɛ/), and *wa*-adjustment (/we/ → /wa/) can be applied in the same way to both groups. However, within each type the underlying vowels |ɔ a ɛ e| undergo different treatment in pretonic position. For Type 1 underlying |ɔ a e| remain unchanged in this environment, whereas underlying |ɛ| is raised to /e/. For Type 2 in pretonic position the underlying rounded vowel |ɔ| is raised to the high vowel /u/, whereas the underlying unrounded vowels |a ɛ e| are converted to schwa /ə/ in this environment.

Rule for pretonic adjustment (Type 2)

Vowels in pretonic position become

a. high (/u/), when the vowel is rounded
b. /ə/ (schwa), when the vowel is unrounded.

Since in pretonic position, for each type, the *same* underlying vowels result in *different* derived vowels, the two types must be formally differentiated. Type 1 alternations are between base forms (e.g., *mer*, *seul*) and derivational forms (e.g., *marin*, *solitude*). Type 2 alternations, on the other hand, are between inflected forms (e.g., *meurs*:*mourons*) as well as between base forms (*main*, *cœur*, etc.) and derivational forms (*menotte*, *courage*, etc.). Therefore, it is necessary to make a formal distinction between *inflectional* and *derivational* morphology as well as between two types of derivational morphology: what we shall call "learned" and "nonlearned." Type 1 alternations exhibit learned derivational morphology, whereas Type 2 alternations are characteristic of inflectional and nonlearned derivational morphology. Learned derivational forms rarely exhibit schwa, the front rounded vowels /ø/ and /œ/, or the high back rounded vowel /u/. These vowels are characteristic of nonlearned forms.[15]

Our examples show that phonological rules do not apply indiscriminately to all forms. Rather, rules have different degrees of generality. Some rules are restricted to particular subsets of the vocabulary (for example, pretonic vowel adjustment), whereas other rules (for example, diphthongization, vowel fronting) have wider applicability. Therefore, within the lexicon forms must be assigned to various morphological classes, which determine the set of rules applicable to a given form. In Note 14 of the preceding chapter we suggested that borrowings, foreign words, and proper names must also be distinguished from the general vocabulary since they often do not undergo particular phonological processes. The distinction between learned and nonlearned is precisely the same type of vocabulary division. Such divisions are arbitrary to the extent that the phonological shape of forms does not in any way determine the particular phonological processes undergone by them; hence, the forms need to be marked in some other way.

A stem may have both nonlearned and learned derivational forms (e.g., *main* 'hand,' *menotte* 'little hand, handcuff,' *manuel* 'manuel') or both inflectional and learned derivational forms (e.g., *veulent* '(they) want,' *voulons* '(we) want,' *volonté* 'will'). Variations of this kind suggest that the learned-nonlearned feature *is not necessarily a property of individual stems*, but rather may depend on the *type of affix with which the stem is concatenated.* Since learned words, for example, often contain characteristic affixes, instead of marking stems as "learned", one could mark the affixes for this feature. Then, if an affix marked "learned" is present in a word, all parts of the word (including the stem) are treated as a learned form. This solution is desirable since it would be more economical to mark affixes than stems (there are fewer of the former). Furthermore, the grammar would show that, in derivation, the phonological variant of the stem vowel is partly a result of the particular affix with which the stem is combined. One would then expect all words containing the same affix to show the same phonological tendencies in their stem constituents.

It is important that the learned-nonlearned distinction within a synchronic description not be confused with the historical events of which this distinction is to a large extent a reflection. Although the historical events may provide an explanation for the alternations attested in the contemporary language, the synchronic description itself does not depend on knowledge of such facts. The grammatical category of gender illustrates this point very well. It is of historical interest to know that French *champ* 'field' is masculine and *table* 'table' is feminine because the Latin words *campus* and *tabula* from which these developed were masculine and feminine respectively. However, this piece of historical information is totally irrelevant for establishing gender classification for contemporary French since the gender distinction in French can be internally motivated morphologically and syntactically. Similarly, that *douleur* 'sorrow' and *endolorir* 'to cause sorrow' are of Latin origin and that *endolorir* came into the language at a later date is not pertinent for determining in modern French that all pretonic |ɔ| do not become /u/. There is sufficient evidence within French to show that pretonic |ɔ| must undergo two different treatments: in some forms |ɔ| becomes /u/; in other forms it remains /ɔ/. If the particular affixes do in fact determine type of phonological process, then, within a synchronic description of French, affixes must be assigned to one of two morphological classes just as nouns must be assigned to one of two gender classes. Since these divisions are established on internal grounds — morphological and phonological evidence within modern French, they may not necessarily correlate with actually attested historical developments within the language. That the effects of such divisions often do coincide with historical facts should not be surprising, however. Within the description of French presented here, the terms "learned" and "nonlearned," although descriptive, are nonetheless arbitrary designations of classes (cf. Type 1 and Type 2 used earlier), and ought to be understood in the same way as other traditionally used terms, such as masculine, first conjugation, inflectional, and so on.

Diphthongized and fronted vowels in pretonic position. According to the rules developed thus far, diphthongization and vowel fronting take place only under stress, so that diphthongs and fronted vowels uniquely appear in tonic position. Yet there are *pretonic* occurrences of fronted vowels and of diphthongs.

1.	/ɛ/	/'ɛ/		
	*ai*mons	*ai*me	'(we) love'	'(he) loves'
	gr*ai*nons	gr*ai*ne	'(we) granulate'	'seed'
	bal*ay*er	bal*ai*	'to sweep'	'broom'
	*ai*mable	*ai*me	'amiable'	'(he) likes'
2.	/œ/	/'œ/		
	pl*eu*rons	pl*eu*re	'(we) cry'	'(he) cries'
	m*eu*blons	m*eu*ble	'(we) furnish'	'furniture'
	fl*eu*rir	fl*eu*r	'to flower'	'flower'
	f*eu*illage	f*eu*ille	'foliage'	'leaf'
3.	/jɛ/	/j'ɛ/		
	acqu*ie*sçons	acqu*ie*sce	'(we) acquiesce'	'(he) acquiesces'
	gr*iè*veté	gr*iè*ve (f.)	'grievousness'	'grievous'
	t*ié*deur	t*iè*de	'tepidity'	'tepid'
	s*ié*ger	s*iè*ge	'to sit'	'seat'
4.	/wa/	/w'a/		
	v*oy*ons	v*oi*s	'(we) see'	'(he) sees'
	s*oi*erie	s*oi*e	'silk goods'	'silk'
	cr*oy*ance	cr*oi*t	'belief'	'(he) believes'
	p*oi*lu	p*oi*l	'hairy'	'hair'

Forms which do not exhibit vocalic alternation in pretonic and tonic positions but rather show the "tonic" vowel throughout are characteristic of verbs of the first conjugation, the so-called "productive" conjugation of French.[16] Verbs which do exhibit alternation in the stem vowel (e.g., *meurent*:*mourons*, *doivent*:*devons*) are the traditional "irregular" verbs, generally considered to be members of the third conjugation. However, some verbs of the third conjugation *do* show the "tonic" vowel throughout, e.g., *vois*:*voyons* 'see,' *crois*:*croyons* 'believe.' Pretonic diphthongized and fronted vowels may occur also in derivational forms, e.g., *aimable* 'amiable,' *fleurir* 'to flower,' *poilu* 'hairy' (alongside *pelu*).

When these forms are included in the corpus, the rules for diphthongization and vowel fronting can no longer be restricted to tonic position but must be applicable to *certain stems* even when these are pretonic. These stems, of course, cannot be subject to the rule for pretonic adjustment, which converts rounded vowels to /u/ and unrounded to /ə/. Therefore, it is necessary to distinguish between stems which undergo pretonic adjustment and stems which do not, the latter instead undergoing diphthongization and fronting. The accompanying diagram depicts those native vocabulary divisions needed so far for the phonology.

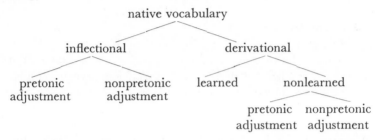

- native vocabulary
  - inflectional
    - pretonic adjustment
    - nonpretonic adjustment
  - derivational
    - learned
    - nonlearned
      - pretonic adjustment
      - nonpretonic adjustment

In tonic position all divisions of the vocabulary undergo the rules for diphthongization and vowel fronting. Only in pretonic position are underlying vowels treated in different ways: the vowels of learned derivational forms remain unchanged, except |ɛ| which is raised to /e/ (e.g., *mortel, clarté, bénir*); inflectional and nonlearned derivational forms which undergo pretonic adjustment have their vowels converted to /ə/ or /u/ (e.g., *venons, menotte, mourons*), whereas inflectional and nonlearned derivational forms which do not undergo pretonic adjustment are subject to diphthongization and vowel fronting (e.g., *aimable, pleurer*).

Forms not subject to pretonic adjustment constitute a special lexical class whose members have to be individually listed *unless the form is a first conjugation verb.*[17] For first conjugation verbs of the type *aimer, pleurer, coiffer*, the lexical marking is of a somewhat different nature. Since first conjugation verbs always exhibit the same stem vowel in all positions (we disregard the minor phonetic adjustments due to open or closed syllable (e.g., *espérer*:*espère*, *mener*:*mène*)), it is *not* necessary to mark the individual stems as exempt from pretonic adjustment for, if a stem is of the first conjugation, one can predict that it will not show vocalic alternation in the paradigm. For these verbs, then, failure to undergo pretonic adjustment is not a property of the individual stem but rather of the conjugation class as a whole. The crucial point here is that for first conjugation verbs the lexical marking is no longer an *ad hoc* device for excluding pretonic adjustment. In the lexicon all verb stems must independently be marked for conjugation class so that the appropriate conjugation vowel can be concatenated with the verb stem (see Chapter 3). Once it is known that a verb stem belongs to the first conjugation, one can then predict that the stem will not undergo pretonic adjustment; that is, the independently motivated conjugation marker allows the specification of stem morphemes which do not undergo pretonic adjustment. Here is another example of the decisive role of morphological class membership in determining phonological processes.

2.1.2. *Tenseness and laxness*

"*E muet*"

We have shown that in pretonic position, in a subset of inflectional and nonlearned derivational morphology, whenever the stem vowel is unrounded, it is converted to /ə/ (schwa), for example, *doivent*:*devons*, *viennent*:*venons*, *parlèrent*:*parleront*. We shall assign French schwa the features of a neutral (lax low central unrounded) vowel.[18] A feature is therefore required to characterize the "lax" (neutral) quality of schwa. This new feature will be called "tense": The neutral or lax vowel will have the value [−tense]; all other vowels will be [+tense].[19] Schwa can be characterized by the following feature complex:

$$\begin{bmatrix} -\text{tense} \\ +\text{low} \\ -\text{front} \\ -\text{round} \end{bmatrix}$$

Except for tenseness, schwa has the same feature specification as /a/:

$$/a/ = \begin{bmatrix} +\text{tense} \\ +\text{low} \\ -\text{front} \\ -\text{round} \end{bmatrix} \qquad /ə/ = \begin{bmatrix} -\text{tense} \\ +\text{low} \\ -\text{front} \\ -\text{round} \end{bmatrix}$$

This feature similarity implies that, structurally, /ə/ is closer to /a/ than to any other French vowel. The structural relationship between /ə/ and /a/ will be significant when the verb conjugation is examined.[20]

The behavior of schwa in syllable initial position is also evidence for the close relationship between /ə/ and /a/. Phonetically, schwa does not occur as a syllable initial vowel. Whenever the rule for pretonic adjustment — which in nonlearned derivational morphology converts an underlying unrounded vowel to schwa — applies to a syllable initial pretonic vowel, the schwa which results is subsequently changed to /a/, the vowel whose feature specification is closest to schwa. That is, /ə/ becomes [+tense] in syllable initial position. Alternations of the type: *aime* /'ɛm(ə)/ '(he) loves': *amour* /am'ur/ 'love,' *amant* /am'ã/ 'lover' illustrate this phenomenon. The underlying representation for the stem is |am|. When the stem vowel bears stress, it is fronted, e.g., |'am+ə| → /'ɛm(ə)/. However, if stress is on the suffix, the stem vowel is converted to schwa and then to /a/ since the vowel is the initial segment, e.g., |am+'ã| → /əm'ã/ → /am'ã/.[21]

At the phonetic level schwa is the only vowel which occurs in posttonic position: *aime* /'ɛm(ə)/ 'like,' *heure* /'œr(ə)/ 'hour.' Since the phonetic features of schwa are identical to those of /a/, except for tenseness, it would be logical to derive posttonic schwa from an underlying |a| since one would only need to make the resultant vowel lax. Actually, however, as we shall demonstrate in subsequent sections, posttonic schwa is derived from any of the low vowels |ɛ a ɔ|. A rule will therefore be needed to convert posttonic low vowels to schwa (the lax low central unrounded vowel).

Rule for schwa conversion

In posttonic position:

$$[+\text{low}] \text{ segments become } \begin{bmatrix} -\text{tense} \\ -\text{front} \\ -\text{round} \end{bmatrix}$$

Not all occurrences of posttonic schwa come from an underlying lax low vowel. In some cases (e.g., *table* /t'ablə/ 'table,' *arbre* /'arbrə/ 'tree,' *possible* /pɔs'iblə/ 'possible'), the schwa is epenthetic. That is, words terminating in a consonant-liquid cluster must have a "supporting" schwa. Since the "supporting" schwa is completely predictable, it does not need to be indicated in the underlying representation and the schwa is instead introduced by a rule.

Rule for schwa insertion

In morpheme final position:

/ə/ is inserted after consonant +liquid

Posttonic schwa has two different sources: it is an epenthetic vowel or it is derived from a low vowel. *Nonlow vowels* in posttonic position are *deleted.* This phenomenon is illustrated by forms such as *visible* /viz'iblə/ 'visible,' *visibilité* /vizibilit'e/ 'visibility.' The former is composed of a stem *vis* plus a suffix *ible.* The latter has the same stem plus the two suffixes *ibili* and *té* (cf. *bon* /b'ɔ̃/ 'good,' *bonté* /bɔ̃t'e/ 'goodness'). However, *ible* and *ibili* are simply variants of the same suffix. The underlying form of this suffix is |ibili|. The representation for *visible* is then |viz + 'ibili| with stress placed on the first vowel of the suffix. The two posttonic nonlow vowels are subsequently deleted: /viz + 'ibl/. A schwa is then inserted after the final consonant-liquid cluster: /viz + 'iblə/. In *visibilité* the suffix *ibili* is not reduced. Since the stress is on the vowel of *té*, the second and third vowels of *ibili* are no longer in posttonic position and are not found in the environment for deletion.

Rule for nonlow vowel deletion

In posttonic position:

[− low] vowels are deleted.

Tense and lax underlying vowels. So far in the analysis we have dealt with four underlying vowels: |e ɛ a ɔ|. We have shown that under stress these vowels diphthongize and are fronted, yielding respectively /we → wa, jɛ, ɛ, œ/. In pretonic position different rules apply to the four underlying vowels, depending on type of morphological process. In learned derivation the vowels remain unchanged in pretonic position, except |ɛ|, which is raised to /e/. In nonlearned derivational morphology some stems undergo pretonic adjustment: |ɔ| becomes /u/; |e ɛ a| merge to /ə/. Other stems do not undergo pretonic adjustment, but instead are subject to the same rules as stressed vowels, i.e., diphthongization, vowel fronting, *wa*-adjustment. We have not yet considered the underlying vowels |i u o|, nor have we examined occurrences of phonetic /ɔ a ɛ e/ in both tonic and pretonic positions, that is, where no vowel alternation takes place. We shall take up the second problem first since the vowels involved correspond to the four underlying vowels already established.

1.	/a/	/'a/		
	pl*a*nons	pl*a*ne	'(we) glide'	'(he) glides'
	décl*a*ration	décl*a*re	'declaration'	'(he) declares'
	esc*a*dron	esc*a*dre	'squadron'	'squadron'
2.	/ɔ/	/'ɔ/		
	c*o*llons	c*o*lle	'(we) adhere'	'glue'
	v*o*leur	v*o*le	'thief'	'(he) steals'
	p*o*mmier	p*o*mme	'apple tree'	'apple'
3.	/e/	/'ɛ/		
	c*é*dons	c*è*de	'(we) cede'	'(he) cedes'
	esp*é*rons	esp*è*re	'(we) hope'	'(he) hopes'
	cr*é*meux	cr*è*me	'creamy'	'cream'

4.	/ə/	/'ɛ/	
	m*e*nons	m*è*ne	'(we) lead' '(he) leads'
	mod*e*lons	mod*è*le	'(we) model' 'model'
	Gen*e*vois	Gen*è*ve	'Genevan' 'Geneva'
5.	/i/	/'i/	
	c*i*tons	c*i*te	'(we) cite' '(he) cites'
	f*i*nesse	f*i*ne	'finesse' 'fine'
	v*i*llage	v*i*lle	'village' 'town'
6.	/y/	/'y/	
	d*u*rons	d*u*re	'(we) last' '(he) lasts'
	c*u*rable	c*u*re	'curable' 'cure'
	déb*u*tant	déb*u*t	'beginner' 'beginning'
7.	/u/	/'u/	
	pr*ou*vons	pr*ou*ve	'(we) prove' '(he) proves'
	tr*ou*vable	tr*ou*ve	'to be found' '(he) finds'
	r*ou*tier	r*ou*te	'of roads' 'roadway'

The vowels /a/ and /ɔ/ of the first two sets of examples — unlike /a/ and /ɔ/ of all previously cited forms — do not undergo fronting in stressed position (cf. |kl'ar| → /kl'ɛr/ *clair*; |s'ɔl| → /s'œl/ *seul*). The vowels /a/, /ɔ/, of the new set of forms also occur in pretonic position even when inflected, i.e., the vowels do not undergo pretonic adjustment (cf. |parlar'ɔ̃| → /parlər'ɔ̃/ *parlerons*, |mɔr'ɔ̃| → /mur'ɔ̃/ *mourons*). Therefore, in the underlying representations it is necessary to distinguish two different |a| vowels as well as two different |ɔ| vowels: those |a| and |ɔ| which undergo fronting and pretonic adjustment and those which do not. A phonological feature is required which will differentiate these two types of vowels.

In the preceding section we showed that at the phonetic level the feature "tense" is needed to distinguish schwa [−tense] from all other vowels [+tense]. This means that, at some point in the phonological derivations, it will be necessary to state for all vowels whether they are tense or lax. Since the tenseness feature is required at the phonetic level, it would be desirable if this particular feature could also be used at the abstract (underlying) level of representation in order to differentiate vowels which undergo vowel alternation from those which do not. Is there a legitimate basis for maintaining that the feature "tense" should appear in underlying forms? If so, is there a nonarbitrary criterion for determining which underlying vowels are tense and which are lax? What is the relation between phonological tenseness and phonetic tenseness?[22]

If most occurrences of the phonetically lax vowel schwa are derived from one class of underlying vowels, whereas most of the phonetically tense vowels are derived from the other class of underlying vowels, it would then be logical to assign the lax feature to those underlying vowels which can yield schwa and to assign the tense feature to those underlying vowels which in general yield phonetically tense vowels. A correlation is then established between the phonological feature "tense" and the phonetic feature "tense" since the tenseness or laxness of the derived vowel is a consequence of the corresponding tenseness or laxness of the underlying vowel. Very few special rules will then be needed to indicate the phonetic correlates of the underlying feature tense. By following this approach, a nonarbitrary basis exists for assigning tenseness or laxness to underlying vowels. Consequently, the feature tense can be motivated at the abstract level of representation.

Once it is established that pretonic /ə/ is derived from an underlying lax vowel, the rule for pretonic adjustment can then apply *only to lax vowels*. Since this rule also converts an underlying |ɔ| to /u/, it follows that |ɔ| in this environment must also be a lax vowel which is later made tense.[23] It is these same underlying vowels which are diphthongized and fronted in stressed position. Therefore, we can establish that lax vowels — not tense ones — exhibit vocalic alternation. Tense vowels, on the other hand, show the same vowel in tonic and pretonic positions.

The vowels cited at the beginning of this section are all tense in their underlying representations (since they do not as a rule exhibit alternation), whereas those cited in previous sections are lax. The rules for diphthongization, vowel fronting, and pretonic adjustment therefore apply only to the lax vowels.[24] As a notational device we shall indicate tense vowels with capital letters and lax vowels with lower-case letters. Underlying lax |a| is the vowel of *main*, *menotte*, tense |A| of *plane*, *planer;* lax |ɔ| is the vowel of *meurent*, *mourons*, tense |Ɔ| of *colle*, *coller;* lax |e| and |ɛ| are the vowels of *doivent*, *devons* and *viennent*, *venons*, respectively. What can be said about tense |E| and |Ɛ|?

Tense |E| is the underlying vowel of forms cited in Set 3 (e.g., *cédons*, *cède*). We have claimed that underlying tense vowels do not exhibit alternation. Yet pretonic /e/ is alternating here with tonic /ɛ/. This /e/:/ɛ/ alternation, however, is not the same type as that exhibited by /a/:/ɛ/ (e.g., *clarté*, *clair*). Although pretonic /a/ alternates with tonic /ɛ/, there are also occurrences of tonic /a/ (e.g., *plane*). It is precisely such contrasts that lead to the tense-lax distinction for underlying vowels. Even though pretonic /e/ alternates with tonic

/ɛ/ (*cédons, cède*), there are *no* occurrences of tonic /e/ plus consonant. It is a phonetic fact of French that /e/ cannot occur in a stressed closed syllable.[25] The original observation that underlying tense vowels do not exhibit alternation must be interpreted to mean *phonological* (contrastive) alternation and not *phonetic* alternation. The lowering of /e/ to /ɛ/ in a stressed closed syllable is handled by a special phonetic rule.

Rule for closed syllable adjustment

In a closed syllable:

$$\begin{bmatrix} +\text{tense} \\ -\text{high} \\ +\text{front} \end{bmatrix} \text{ segments become } [+\text{low}] \quad (|\text{E}| \rightarrow /\varepsilon/)$$

The forms *menons*:*mène*, etc. (Set 4), exhibit alternation between /ə/ and /ɛ/. This alternation, like the preceding one between /e/ and /ɛ/, is phonetically predictable since schwa, like /e/, cannot occur in a stressed closed syllable.[26] If the underlying representation of *menons, mène* is tense |Ɛ|, the stressed vowel is correctly represented. However, in pretonic position |Ɛ| must be converted to /ə/.[27]

Rule for pretonic schwa conversion

$$\begin{bmatrix} -\text{stress} \\ +\text{tense} \\ +\text{low} \\ +\text{front} \end{bmatrix} \text{ segments become } \begin{bmatrix} -\text{tense} \\ -\text{front} \end{bmatrix} \quad (|\mathcal{E}| \rightarrow /\text{ə}/)$$

Phonetic schwa in pretonic position is derived from four different underlying vowels: lax |e| (*devons, doivent*), lax |ɛ| (*venons, viennent*), lax |a| (*menotte, main*), tense |Ɛ| (*menons, mènent*).

The stem vowel of forms such as *cite, citons* (Set 5), does not exhibit pretonic-tonic alternation. The high front unrounded vowel /i/ appears in both environments. Consequently, the underlying vowel must be tense, that is, |I|.

Forms such as *dur, durons* (Set 6), have a high front rounded vowel in both tonic and pretonic positions. The underlying vowel must therefore be tense. In our original seven-vowel system |i e ɛ a ɔ o u|, the front rounded series /y ø œ/ does not occur in underlying forms. We have already shown that /œ/ must be derived from an underlying lax |ɔ|, which is fronted, in order to account for alternations of the type *seul, solitude*. It is of structural interest to entertain the possibility of deriving *all* front rounded vowels from their corresponding back vowels. In this way the underlying representations, i.e., the lexical entries, are considerably simplified. This eliminates the necessity for postulating the front rounded series as part of the basic vowel system and, instead, phonological rules allow these vowels to be derived from the back ones. The high front rounded vowel /y/ would be derived from the corresponding tense back rounded vowel, namely, |U|. This vowel undergoes fronting in all environments. The rule for vowel fronting must accordingly be revised so that it will apply to tense |U| in all environments, as well as to lax low vowels in tonic position and to those lax vowels not subject to pretonic adjustment.

Rule for vowel fronting (revised)

Vowel segments become [+front]:

a. when the vowel is $\begin{bmatrix} -\text{tense} \\ +\text{low} \end{bmatrix}$ and:

i either [+stress]
ii or is not subject to pretonic adjustment

b. when the vowel is $\begin{bmatrix} +\text{tense} \\ +\text{high} \end{bmatrix}$.[28]

Forms such as *prouve*, *prouvons* (Set 7), have a high back rounded vowel in tonic and pretonic environments. The underlying vowel is therefore tense. However, the underlying vowel cannot be tense |U| since it is this vowel from which /y/ is derived. We have already established six underlying tense vowels: |I| (*citer*), |E| (*céder*), |Ɛ| (*mener*), |A| (*planer*), |Ɔ| (*coller*), |U| (*durer*). The only tense vowel which does not yet occur in the analysis is mid back rounded |O|, and it is this vowel which is the source of the /u/ of *prouve*, *prouvons*. A rule is required which raises |O| to /u/.

Rule for back vowel raising

$\begin{bmatrix} +\text{tense} \\ -\text{low} \\ -\text{front} \end{bmatrix}$ segments become [+high]

The rule for back vowel raising must, of course, follow the fronting rule, which converts |U| to /y/. Only after |U| has shifted to /y/ can |O| be raised to /u/.

The rule for back vowel raising converts an underlying |O| to /u/. Postulating an underlying |O| and a conversion rule appears to be an *ad hoc* device for accounting for the vowel of *prouve*, *prouvons*, since the logical vowel would seem to be |U| itself. Yet we are unable to set up |U| as the underlying vowel without destroying the previously established generalization concerning the origin of front rounded vowels. Whereas the |U| to /y/ conversion is motivated — it simplifies the underlying system and allows all front rounded vowels to be derived in the same way, the |O| to /u/ conversion does not really seem justified. We selected |O| by process of elimination: some vowel was needed and it was the only unused one. In fact, so far, the only justification for recognizing tense |O| as the source of /u/ is that only one feature need be changed in the conversion and that the underlying system of tense vowels becomes symmetrical since all seven of them now occur.

In the following section we shall present important morphological evidence to substantiate the claim that tense |O| is the source of the vowel /u/.[29] As a preliminary partial justification, it is instructive to reconsider the other source of pretonic /u/, that is, the /u/ that results from pretonic adjustment (e.g., *meurent*, *mourons*). The rule for pretonic adjustment converts lax unrounded vowels to schwa and lax rounded vowels to /u/. Since /u/ is phonetically tense, the original lax character of the underlying vowel must be changed in addition to its quality. Lax unrounded vowels, on the other hand, remain lax as they become schwa.

The rule for pretonic adjustment as it is presently stated does not bring out any similarity between conversion to /ə/, i.e., [−tense, −round] vowels becoming [+low, −front] and conversion to /u/, i.e., [−tense, +round] vowels becoming [+tense, +high], even though both changes take place in the same environment. In the present rule unrelated features, i.e., frontness for /ə/ and tenseness for /u/, are being changed.

If the feature specifications "front" and "tense" were to be eliminated in the rule, the effect of the rule would be simply to adjust vowel height in pretonic position. Then additional rules would seem to be needed to correct the frontness of unrounded vowels and the tenseness of rounded vowels. However, these features can be handled by rules already established if the various rules are judiciously ordered.

Lax unrounded vowels, that is, |e ɛ a|, in pretonic position become schwa. Lax |a|, of course, is already specified as schwa, i.e., [+low, −front, −round], and need not concern us further. Lax |ɛ| must be made [−front]; its vowel height is correct. Lax |e| must be lowered as well as backed. If pretonic adjustment is simply vowel height adjustment, then it is only necessary to make |e| [+low], i.e., to convert it to lax /ε/. A subsequent change is needed so that all lax /ε/ will become [−front], i.e., schwa. On p. 31 we presented the rule for schwa conversion, which converted *posttonic low* vowels to schwa. If we generalize the rule so that it applies to *all low lax* vowels (posttonic as well as pretonic schwas will be derived from underlying lax vowels), then all pretonic /ε/ will be converted to /ə/. Note that by extending the schwa conversion rule, one can also simplify the rule which converts tense |Ɛ| to schwa in pretonic position (e.g., *mène*, *menons*). Instead of making |Ɛ| both lax and central — it is already low — one need only make it [−tense], so that it becomes lax /ε/. The schwa conversion rule will then take it to schwa.

By generalising the schwa conversion rule, the pretonic adjustment rule is simplified. For unrounded vowels it is only necessary to lower |e| to /ε/. The rounded vowel |ɔ|, on the other hand, must be raised to tense /u/. Vowel height adjustment would be symmetrical for unrounded and rounded vowels if |ɔ| were to be raised to /o/, while |e| is lowered to /ε/. The shift in vowel height for unrounded and rounded vowels would then be inversely proportional: unrounded mid vowels become low; rounded low vowels become mid.

If pretonic lax |ɔ| is raised only to lax /o/, a subsequent rule is required to raise lax /o/ to tense /u/. The rule for back vowel raising already converts tense |O| to /u/ (e.g., *prouve*). This rule can be further generalized by allowing it to apply as well to the new lax /o/ which results from pretonic adjustment. That is, the rule for back vowel raising need no longer be restricted to just tense |O|, but is instead applicable to both (tense and lax) mid back vowels, converting them to tense /u/. The rule for back vowel raising must, of course, apply after the rule for pretonic adjustment.[30] When this analysis is adopted, the rule for pretonic adjustment is considerably simplified and this rule then affects all vowels in a parallel fashion. In addition, the raising of a mid back vowel to high position has greater justification.

Rule for pretonic adjustment

In pretonic position:

a. $\begin{bmatrix} -\text{tense} \\ -\text{round} \end{bmatrix}$ segments become [+low]

b. $\begin{bmatrix} -\text{tense} \\ +\text{round} \end{bmatrix}$ segments become [−low]

The subparts of the rule are identical except for the values of the features "round" and "low"; this inverse symmetry, i.e., lowering of a mid vowel and raising of a low vowel, can be reflected by an alpha rule (see p. 4).

Rule for pretonic adjustment (revised)

In pretonic position:

$$\begin{bmatrix} -\text{tense} \\ \alpha\ \text{round} \end{bmatrix} \text{ segments become } [-\alpha\ \text{low}]$$

Rule for back vowel raising (revised)

$$\begin{bmatrix} -\text{low} \\ -\text{front} \end{bmatrix} \text{ segments become } \begin{bmatrix} +\text{tense} \\ +\text{high} \end{bmatrix}$$

Rule for schwa conversion[31]

$$\begin{bmatrix} -\text{tense} \\ +\text{low} \end{bmatrix} \text{ segments become } \begin{bmatrix} -\text{front} \\ -\text{round} \end{bmatrix}$$

We have so far established eleven underlying vowels: seven tense ones |I E Ɛ A Ɔ O U| and four lax ones |e ɛ a ɔ|. In the following section we shall consider lax |i u o| and discuss further the relation between underlying tense and lax vowels. These eleven underlying vowels have the following phonetic manifestations in tonic and pretonic positions:

Underlying vowel	I	E	Ɛ	A	Ɔ	O	U	e	ɛ	a	ɔ
Derived tonic vowel	i	ɛ	ɛ	a	ɔ	u	y	*wa	*jɛ	*ɛ	*œ
Derived pretonic vowel	i	e	*ə	a	ɔ	u	y	ə	ə	ə	*u

Except for certain phonetic adjustments of vowels derived from |E| and |Ɛ|, underlying tense vowels do not exhibit tonic and pretonic variants; phonological alternation is a function of the lax vowels. The derived vowels are all tense phonetically except schwa, which is lax. An asterisk preceding a derived vowel indicates that the derived vowel does not agree in tenseness with the underlying vowel. For such cases the value of the feature tense will have to be switched. This change applies to only six of the derived vowels. The other sixteen derived vowels do not change the tenseness feature. Since for the majority of derived vowels the feature "tense" correlates precisely with the tenseness feature postulated for the corresponding underlying vowel, justification exists for utilizing this feature at the abstract level to distinguish two types of vowels: those which underlie alternating variants and those which do not.

Following are the ordered rules required so far in the vowel analysis.

1. Diphthongization

$$\begin{bmatrix} +\text{stress} \\ -\text{tense} \\ +\text{front} \end{bmatrix} \text{ segments diphthongize}$$

a. /w/ is inserted before |e|
b. /j/ is inserted before |ɛ|

This rule also applies to forms not subject to pretonic adjustment (e.g., *croyable*). The rule changes |e| to /we/ and |ɛ| to /jɛ/.

2. Vowel fronting

$$\left.\begin{array}{ll} a.\ \begin{bmatrix} +\text{stress} \\ -\text{tense} \end{bmatrix} & \text{segments} \\ b.\ [+\text{high}] & \text{segments} \end{array}\right\} \text{ become } \begin{bmatrix} +\text{front} \\ +\text{tense} \end{bmatrix}$$

This rule also applies to forms not subject to pretonic adjustment (e.g., *aimable*). The rule changes *a*, |a| to tense /ɛ/ (*aime*), |ɔ| to tense /œ/ (*seul*), and *b*, |U| to /y/ (*dur*). Part *a* also applies to /we/ and /jɛ/, making the vowel segment tense; part *b* applies vacuously to |I|. This rule follows diphthongization so that diphthongized lax vowels will become tense.

In an earlier version of the same rule (pp. 23, 36), we specified that the [+stress, −tense] vowel which undergoes fronting had to be also [+low]. This restriction has been relaxed so that, instead, all stressed lax vowels become fronted and tense. In this way, the lax vowel of /we/ (due to the diphthongization of an underlying lax |e|) becomes tense. In the next section we shall show that underlying lax |o| must be fronted to /ø/, which can only take place if fronting is a more general phenomenon.

3. Pretonic adjustment

In pretonic position:

$$a.\ \begin{bmatrix} -\text{tense} \\ \alpha\ \text{round} \end{bmatrix} \text{ segments become } [-\alpha\ \text{low}]$$

$$b.\ \begin{bmatrix} +\text{front} \\ +\text{low} \end{bmatrix} \text{ segments become } [-\text{tense}]$$

Part *a* converts a pretonic lax [−round] segment, i.e., |e|, to a [+low] segment, i.e., /ε/, and a [+round] segment, i.e., |ɔ|, to a [−low] segment, i.e., /o/. Part *b* converts tense |Ɛ| to lax /ε/. Part *a* applies vacuously to lax |ε| and |a|; part *b* applies vacuously to lax /ε/. This rule is not ordered with respect to the first two. Forms with underlying lax vowels which are an exception to pretonic adjustment, instead undergo diphthongization and fronting.

4. Back vowel raising

$\begin{bmatrix}-\text{front}\\-\text{low}\end{bmatrix}$ segments become $\begin{bmatrix}+\text{tense}\\+\text{high}\end{bmatrix}$

This rule converts underlying tense |O| and the lax /o/ (derived from lax |ɔ| by pretonic adjustment) to /u/ (*prouve*, *mourons*). This rule must follow vowel fronting, i.e., underlying |U| is converted to /y/ before |O| can be raised to /u/, and pretonic adjustment, i.e., underlying |ɔ| is raised first to /o/ so that it can subsequently be further raised to /u/.

5. Schwa conversion

$\begin{bmatrix}-\text{tense}\\+\text{low}\end{bmatrix}$ segments become $\begin{bmatrix}-\text{front}\\-\text{round}\end{bmatrix}$

This rule converts all lax low vowels to schwa. It follows 1, fronting, which also makes fronted vowels tense so that fronted low vowels will not subsequently become schwa; 2, pretonic adjustment, which lowers |e| to /ε/ and converts |Ɛ| to /ε/ so that both can subsequently become schwa; 3, vowel raising, which converts lax /o/ to tense /u/.

6. Nonlow vowel deletion

In posttonic position:

[−low] segments are deleted

This rule accounts for forms such as *visible*, *visibilité*; posttonic nonlow vowels are deleted.

7. Schwa insertion

In morpheme final position:

/ə/ is inserted after a consonant-liquid cluster

This rule accounts for final schwa in forms such as *table*.

8. Wa-adjustment

/we/ becomes /wa/

9. Closed syllable adjustment

In a closed syllable:

$$\begin{bmatrix} -\text{high} \\ +\text{front} \end{bmatrix} \text{ segments become } [+\text{low}]$$

This rule converts /e/ to /ε/ in a closed syllable (e.g., *cédons, cède*).

Relation between tense and lax vowels. We have established two types of underlying vowels: tense and lax. The tense vowels do not undergo diphthongization, fronting of vowels, or pretonic adjustment, so that they do not exhibit vocalic alternation (e.g., *colle, collons* with underlying stem |kƆl|). The lax vowels, on the other hand, are subject to the vowel shift rules, and, accordingly, they may show vocalic alternation (e.g., *veulent, voulons*) with underlying stem |vɔl|). Stems with underlying lax vowels may also exhibit a third variant in learned derivation (e.g., *volonté*). The vowel of the learned form does not undergo diphthongization, fronting, or pretonic adjustment, that is, the stem vowel of *volonté* behaves exactly like the corresponding tense vowel. Is it just fortuitous that lax vowels in learned derivation and underlying tense vowels have the same phonological properties, and why should these lax vowels be exceptions to the vowel shift rules?

Although the *underlying vowel* of *volonté* is "lax" (because of *veulent, voulons*), *phonetically* the /ɔ/ of *volonté* is "tense." Special rules are then needed to make the vowels of learned forms tense. However, if we were to claim as a general principle for learned derivation that prior to the application of the phonological rules *all stem vowels* automatically become tense, no special rules would be required to specify the tenseness of the derived vowel. Even more important, there would be an obvious explanation for the nonapplicability of the vowel shift rules to these forms. Learned derivational forms are not affected by the vowel shift rules precisely because, at the point when these rules apply, the original lax vowels have already been changed to the corresponding tense ones. Since the vowels are tense, they behave exactly like other tense vowels.

To illustrate the validity of the tensing principle for learned derivation, we shall consider in detail two examples of this tensing phenomenon. The following forms exhibit nonlearned and learned derivation: *deuil* /d'œj/ 'mourning,' *douleur* /dul'œr/ 'sorrow,' *douloureux* /dulur'ø/

'sorrowful,' *endolorir* /ãdɔlɔr'ir/ 'to become saddened.' The stem |dɔl| is a component of all forms. (We ignore here the conversion of |l| to /j/ in *deuil*; this is discussed in Section 2.4.) *Douleur* is composed of the stem |dɔl| plus the suffix |ɔr|; *douloureux* of stem |dɔl|, suffix |ɔr| and second suffix |ɔz| (cf. *douleureuse* /dulu'røz(ə)/), *endolorir* of prefix |an|, stem |dɔl|, suffix |ɔr|, and infinitival desinence |Ir|. When the stem functions as a word (e.g., *deuil*), the stem vowel receives stress: |d'ɔl|. The lax vowel is therefore fronted (the |l| is converted to /j/): /d'œj/. In the underlying representation for nonlearned *douleur* the stress is on the suffix vowel: |dɔl+'ɔr|. The stressed lax suffix vowel is fronted: /dɔl+'œr/; the pretonic lax stem vowel undergoes pretonic adjustment: /dol+'œr/ and back vowel raising: /dul+'œr/. In nonlearned *douloureux* the final suffix is stressed: |dɔl+ɔr+'ɔz|. The stressed lax suffix vowel is fronted; the two pretonic lax vowels undergo pretonic adjustment and back vowel raising; the final consonant is deleted (see Section 1.1.3): /dul+ur+'ø/. The learned *endolorir* has the following underlying representation: |an+dɔl+ɔr+Ir|. As this is a learned form, vowel tensing occurs before any of the phonological rules are applied: |An+dƆl+Ɔr+Ir|. Stress is placed on the final suffix: |An+dƆl+Ɔr+'Ir|. Since the vowels are all tense, the vowel shift rules will not apply; the first vowel, however, becomes nasalized (see Section 2.2): /ã+dɔl+ɔr+'ir/.

A more dramatic example of the tensing principle is seen in the forms: *aime* /'ɛm(ə)/ 'like,' *aimable* /ɛm'ablə/ 'amiable,' *amabilité* /amabilit'e/ 'amiability.' These forms all contain the stem |am|. In addition, *aimable* has the suffix *able* and *amabilité* has the suffixes *abili* plus *té*. *Able* and *abili* are, of course, variants of an underlying |Abili| (cf. *visible*, *visibilité* cited on p. 31).[32] The representations for *aime*, *aimable*, *amabilité* are respectively |am+a|, |am+Abili|, |am+Abili+tE|. The form |'am+a| is stressed on the stem vowel. Since this vowel is lax, it is fronted; posttonic |a| is equivalent to schwa: /'ɛm(ə)/. In |am+'Abili| the stress is on the tense vowel of the suffix. This word is a derivational form which does not undergo pretonic adjustment; instead, the lax pretonic vowel is fronted. Tense |A|, of course, does not undergo vowel shift. The two posttonic high vowels are deleted as they are lax and nonlow (see p. 31): /ɛm'abl/. A schwa is then inserted after the final consonant-liquid cluster: /ɛm'ablə/. The form |am+Abili+tE| is learned derivational. By the tensing principle all vowels become tense; stress is placed on the final vowel: |Am+AbIlI+t'E|. Once the vowels are tense, no vowel shifts or deletions can take place: since the stem vowel has been made tense, it will not be fronted; the high vowels of *abili* will not be deleted as they are no longer lax or posttonic. Note that suffixes such as |Abili| demonstrate the necessity for underlying lax |i| in representations.

The tensing principle in learned derivation establishes an intimate relation between corresponding tense and lax vowels.[33] Just as in learned derivation underlying lax vowels become tense, conversely, in nonlearned derivation there are instances of underlying tense vowels becoming lax. This phenomenon is peculiar to certain stems and the corresponding nouns derived without suffixation: e.g., *espérons*, *espère* /ɛsper'ɔ̃/, /ɛsp'ɛr(ə)/ 'hope (verb),' versus *espoir* /ɛspw'ar/ 'hope (noun)'; *jouons*, *joue* /ʒu'ɔ̃/, /ʒu/ 'play' versus *jeu* /ʒø/ 'game.' Since the verb paradigm does not show phonological alternation, the underlying stems contain tense vowels. The representation for the stem 'hope' must be |ƐspEr|. When this stem functions as a noun, the final stressed vowel becomes lax |Ɛsp'er|. Stressed lax |e| then shifts to /we/ and subsequently to /wa/. The underlying representation of the stem 'play' is |ʒO| since tense |O| is the source of derived /u/. In the noun the stressed vowel becomes lax: |ʒ'o|. The stressed lax vowel then undergoes fronting: /ʒ'ø/ (see p. 40).

The alternation exhibited by pairs such as *joue*, *jeu* is crucial evidence for deriving /u/ from an underlying mid back vowel, since it is also this vowel which has to be the source of front rounded /ø/.

Other examples of underlying tense vowels becoming lax are: *prouvons*, *prouve* 'prove' versus *preuve* 'proof'; *nouons*, *noue* 'tie' versus *noeud* 'knot'; *labourons*, *laboure* 'toil (verb)' versus *labeur* 'toil (noun)'; *salons*, *sale* 'salt (verb)' versus *sel* 'salt (noun)'; *relevons*, *relève* 'raise, relieve' versus *relief* 'relief.'[34]

We have set up two types of vowels: lax and tense. The lax vowels are diphthongized and fronted in tonic position. Whenever they are pretonic, they undergo pretonic adjustment unless the particular stem is an exception to this phenomenon, in which case the lax vowel in this environment is subject to the same treatment as the stressed vowel. Therefore, in the case of the lax vowels, from a single abstract representation two different derived vowels may result, depending on the location of the stress. Underlying tense vowels, on the other hand, do not exhibit phonological alternation in tonic and pretonic positions. Any difference in tonic and pretonic derived vowels is phonetically conditioned (e.g., the open-closed syllable distinction). This does not mean that underlying tense vowels do not undergo vowel shift — |U| → /y/ and |O| → /u/ — but rather that, whenever vowel shift occurs, it takes place everywhere regardless of stress conditions.

There are seven underlying tense vowels: |I E Ɛ A Ɔ O U|. These all yield phonetically tense vowels except pretonic |Ɛ|, which is one of the sources of schwa. Four of the underlying lax vowels occur in both tonic and atonic positions: |e ɛ a ɔ|. These yield phonetically tense vowels in tonic position; the unrounded ones in pretonic position and the low ones yield schwa. Lax |i| only occurs posttonically (e.g., the suffix *abili*) and in this environment it is obligatorily deleted; lax |o| results from the laxing of tense |O| in noun stems; in Chapter 3 we shall show that underlying lax |u| is needed in order to account for the morphology of the verb. Therefore, fourteen underlying vowels are required (or thirteen if lax |o| is not counted) within the phonological system of French. Front rounded vowels do not appear as underlying vowels and are always derived from the corresponding back vowels. The underlying tense and lax vowels do not function as two completely unrelated systems. Between nonlearned and learned, and between inflectional and derivational forms, there are interesting interrelations among the corresponding pairs of tense and lax vowels. The accompanying chart illustrates some of these "families" of related words:

Vowel	*Tense*	*Lax Tonic*	*Lax Atonic*
|I i|	vis*i*b*i*l*i*té		visib*ili* → visible
|E e|	s*é*rénade	so*i*r	s*e*rein
|Ɛ ɛ|	av*è*nement	v*ie*nnent	v*e*nons
|A a|	m*a*nuel	m*ai*n	m*e*notte
|Ɔ ɔ|	c*o*l*o*ré	coul*eur*	c*ou*leur
|O o|	pr*ou*ve	pr*eu*ve	
|U |	d*u*re		

2.2 Nasalized vowels

In French four nasalized vowels occur in the phonetic output: /ɛ̃/, /ã/, /ɔ̃/, /œ̃/. In addition to their being nasalized, we shall assume that these four vowels are all low (as indicated in the IPA transcription) and are differentiated from each other by the following features:

	ɛ̃	ã	ɔ̃	œ̃
front	+	−	−	+
round	−	−	+	+

That is, /ɛ̃/ is front unrounded, /ã/ is central, /ɔ̃/ is back rounded, and /œ̃/ is front rounded.[35]

Is nasalization an inherent feature of these vowels or is it predictable? The charts on pp. 46 and 47 show that an oral vowel plus nasal consonant alternates with a nasalized vowel.

Alternation of Oral Vowel plus Nasal Consonant with Nasalized Vowel

	Pretonic Oral Vowel	Tonic Oral Vowel	Nasal Vowel			
1.	/i/	/ˈi/	/ˈɛ̃/			
	div*i*nité	div*i*ne	div*in*	'divinity'	'divine (f.)'	'divine (m.)'
	f*i*nesse	f*i*ne	f*in*	'finesse'	'fine (f.)'	'fine (m.)'
	jard*i*nier	jard*i*ne	jard*in*	'gardener'	'garden (v.)'	'garden (n.)'
2.	/e/	/ˈɛ/	/ˈɛ̃/			
	pl*é*nitude	pl*ei*ne	pl*ein*	'fullness'	'full (f.)'	'full (m.)'
	refr*é*ner	refr*è*ne	fr*ein*	'to restrain'	'(he) restrains'	'brake'
	sér*é*nade	ser*ei*ne	ser*ein*	'serenade'	'serene (f.)'	'serene (m.)'
3.	/a/ (learned)					
	/ə/ (nonlearned)	/ˈɛ/	/ˈɛ̃/			
	hum*a*nité	hum*ai*ne	hum*ain*	'humanity'	'human (f.)'	'human (m.)'
	f*a*mine		f*aim*	'famine'		'hunger'
	m*e*notte		m*ain*	'little hand'		'hand'
	v*a*nité	v*ai*ne	v*ain*	'vanity'	'vain (f.)'	'vain (m.)'
	gr*e*nu	gr*ai*ne	gr*ain*	'grainy'	'seed'	'grain'
4.	/ɛ/ (learned)					
	/ə/ (nonlearned)	/jˈɛ/	/jˈɛ̃/			
	av*è*nement, v*e*nons	v*ie*nne	v*ien*t	'advent' '(we) come'	'(that he) come'	'(he) comes'
	ch*e*nil	ch*ie*nne	ch*ien*	'kennel'	'dog (f.)'	'dog (m.)'
		m*ie*nne	m*ien*		'mine (f.)'	'mine (m.)'

5.	/ə/	/w'a/	/w'ɛ̃/			
		so*i*gne	so*in*		'(he) cares for'	'care'
		él*oi*gne	l*oin*		'(he) removes'	'far'
	f*e*nil		f*oin*	'hayloft'		'hay'
6.	/a/	/'a/	/'ã/			
	pl*a*ner	pl*a*ne	pl*an*	'to glide'	'level' (f.)'	'level (m.)'
	rom*a*niste	rom*a*ne	rom*an*	'Romanist'	'Romance (f.)'	'Romance (m.)'
	print*a*nier		print*em*ps	'spring (adj.)'		'spring (noun)'
7.	/e/ (learned) /ə/ (nonlearned)	/'ɛ/	/'ã/			
	pr*e*nons	pr*e*nnent	pr*en*d	'(we) take'	'(they) take'	'(he) takes'
	g*é*nérique		g*en*re	'generic'		'kind'
8.	/ɔ/	/'ɔ/	/'ɔ̃/			
	b*o*nheur	b*o*nne	b*on*	'happiness'	'good (f.)'	'good (m.)'
	t*o*nalité	at*o*ne	t*on*	'tonality'	'atonic'	'tone'
9.	/y/	/'y/	/'œ̃/			
	*u*nique	*u*ne	*un*	'unique'	'one (f.)'	'one (m.)'
	parf*u*merie	parf*u*me	parf*um*	'perfumery'	'(he) perfumes'	'perfume'
	br*u*nir	br*u*ne	br*un*	'to turn brown'	'brown (f.)'	'brown (m.)'
10.		/'ø/	/'œ̃/			
		j*eû*ne	j*eun*		'fast'	'fasting'

If the underlying representations contain a vowel plus nasal consonant, the following rule allows one to predict a nasalized vowel for the forms cited in Column 3:

Rule for vowel nasalization

Before nasal consonants:

Vowels become [+nasal] whenever the nasal consonant is

a. in word final position

b. followed by a consonantal segment.

A nasal consonant is subsequently deleted if the preceding vowel has been nasalized.

Rule for nasal consonant deletion

After nasalized vowels:

Nasal consonants are deleted.

Nasalization does not take place whenever the nasal consonant is followed by a vowel. Therefore, the forms cited in Column 2 will always require a vowel after the nasal consonant; words such as *fine*, *brune* must therefore terminate in a lax central vowel in their underlying forms.[36]

Nonparadigmatic evidence can be brought forth to show that nasalized vowels must be derived from underlying oral vowel-nasal consonant sequences. In forms such as *persister* /pεrsist'e/ 'persist,' *insister* /ε̃sist'e/ 'insist,' *résister* /rezist'e/ 'resist,' which contain the morpheme *sist* |sIst|, the initial sibilant |s| is voiced intervocalically: *persister* versus *résister*. Although, phonetically, the initial |s| of *sist* is intervocalic in *insister* /ε̃sist'e/, the sibilant is not voiced. If *insister* is derived from underlying |In+sIst+Er|, and if sibilant voicing precedes nasalization, then, when sibilant voicing occurs, the |s| is not intervocalic but is still preceded by the nasal consonant.

Once it has been demonstrated that nasalized vowels do not appear in the underlying representations, but rather are derived from oral vowel plus nasal consonant, this assumption then holds for all nasalized vowels in the language, even where there are no pairs exhibiting alternation.[37]

The table below lists for each of the ten sets previously given the "underlying vowel," the "derived oral vowel (stressed)," and the corresponding "derived nasalized vowel."

Underlying vowel	I	E	a	ε	e	A	Ɛ	Ɔ	U	o
Derived oral vowel	i	e	ε	jε	wa	a	ε	ɔ	y	ø
Derived nasalized vowel	ε̃	ε̃	ε̃	jε̃	wε̃	ã	ã	ɔ̃	œ̃	œ̃

As there are only four nasalized vowels, a single nasalized vowel may be paired with two or more oral vowels. The rules for nasalization cause the "underlying vowels" to become nasalized whenever the appropriate environmental conditions are met; these nasalized vowels then undergo whatever vowel shift rules are applicable to them. Therefore, nasalized /ĩ/, /ẽ/, /ɛ̃/, /jɛ̃/, /ỹ/, etc., result from application of the nasalization and various vowel shift rules. However, not all of these nasalized vowels occur phonetically; two or more of them may coalesce in a single derived nasalized vowel.

An examination of the last two rows of the chart reveals that — except for /wa/, which is paired with /wɛ̃/, and except for the /ɛ/, where the derived nasal counterpart is /ã/ — a derived oral vowel agrees *in frontness and roundness* with its corresponding derived nasalized vowel. That is, front unrounded oral vowels are paired with /ɛ̃/ (including /jɛ̃/), central oral vowels with /ã/, back rounded oral vowels with /ɔ̃/, and front rounded oral vowels with /œ̃/. Although a derived oral vowel and the corresponding nasalized vowel share the same values for the features "front" and "round," they do not necessarily agree in vowel height. The derived nasalized vowel is *always low.*

Rule for nasal quality adjustment

[+nasal] vowels become [+low]

After application of this rule the intermediate derived vowels /ĩ/, /ẽ/, /ɛ̃/, merge to /ɛ̃/ and the intermediate /ỹ/, /ø̃/ merge to /œ̃/. It is the rule for nasal quality adjustment which explains the occurrence of only four phonetic nasalized vowels, all of which are [+low].

The rule for nasal quality adjustment is relatively simple as it affects only the vowel height of the nasalized vowels without changing the frontness or roundness. Yet the vowel segments of derived /wa/ and /wɛ̃/ do not agree in frontness, i.e., /a/ is [−front]; /ɛ̃/ is [+front]. (One would expect the nasalized counterpart of /wa/ to be /wã/.) However, /wa/ is derived from an underlying |e| via an intermediate /we/, i.e., the rule for diphthongization. The vowel of /we/ is [+front], and it is the nasalized vowel from this intermediate stage which is lowered to /wɛ̃/. Therefore, the rule for nasal quality adjustment occurs before /we/ is converted to /wa/. Only after nasalized /wẽ/ has been lowered to /wɛ̃/ is oral /we/ shifted to /wa/. Nasalization provides compelling evidence for having the diphthongization of |e| take place in two steps.[38]

In Set 7 derived nasalized /ã/ alternates with derived oral /ə/ or /e/ (nonlearned versus learned). The underlying vowel is tense |Ɛ|, since *prenons*, *prennent* exhibits the same vocalic alternation as *menons*, *mènent* (and not that of *venons*, *viennent* or *devons*, *doivent*). In nonlearned forms underlying |Ɛ| becomes /ə/, i.e., a central vowel, in pretonic position; when |Ɛ| underlies a derived nasalized vowel, it also becomes central: /ã/, the vowel of *prends*. Therefore, a rule is required which centralizes underlying |Ɛ| after it has been nasalized.

Rule for nasal centralizing

$$\begin{bmatrix} +\text{nasal} \\ +\text{tense} \\ +\text{low} \end{bmatrix} \text{ vowels become } [-\text{front}]$$

This rule applies vacuously to |Ã| and |Ɔ̃|. It must follow the rules for nasalization, but must precede the vowel shift rules.

The accompanying chart shows the derivation of nasalized vowels from the various underlying vowels.[39] Only those rules which are relevant for nasalized vowels are given.

	I	E	a	ε	e	A	Ɛ	Ɔ	U	o
Nasalization	Ĩ	Ẽ	ã	ε̃	ẽ	Ã	Ɛ̃	Ɔ̃	Ũ	õ
Centralizing	–	–	–	–	–	–	Ã	–	–	–
Diphthongization	–	–	–	jε̃	wẽ	–	–	–	–	–
Fronting	–	–	ε̃	–	–	–	–	–	ỹ	ø̃
Nasal adjustment	ε̃	ε̃	–	–	wε̃	ã	ã	ɔ̃	œ̃	œ̃
	/ε̃/	/ε̃/	/ε̃/	/jε̃/	/wε̃/	/ã/	/ã/	/ɔ̃/	/œ̃/	/œ̃/

2.3 Long vowels

2.3.1. *The vowel /o/*

So far in the analysis we have established that underlying lax |ɔ| and |o| are fronted to /œ/ and /ø/ respectively, e.g., |fl'ɔr| → /fl'œr/ *fleur*; |ʒ'O| (cf. *joue*) → |ʒ'o| (laxing of stressed stem vowel) → /ʒ'ø/ *jeu*. Underlying tense |O| is raised to /u/, e.g., |pr'Ov+a| → /pr'uv(ə)/ *prouve*. Tense |Ɔ| underlies the /ɔ/ of *col* /k'ɔl/ 'collar,' *sotte* /s'ɔt(ə)/ 'stupid(f),' *hotte* /'ɔt(ə)/ 'hood,' etc. What is the source of /o/ in such words as *sot* /s'o/ 'stupid (m),' *chose* /ʃ'o:z(ə)/ 'thing,' *haute* /'o:t(ə)/ 'high (f),' *côte* /k'o:t(ə)/ 'coast,' *atome* /at'o:m(ə)/ 'atom'? (In a stressed closed syllable /o/ is always long. This lengthening will be dealt with in the next section.)

One must distinguish between those /o/ which occur in final position and those which are found in a closed syllable. Phonetically, /ɔ/ never occurs finally; one only finds /o/ in this environment. This phonetic adjustment accounts for the alternations: *sotte* /s'ɔt(ə)/ (closed syllable): *sot* /s'o/ (open syllable); *idiote*: *idiot* 'idiot,' etc. Forms such as *métro* /metr'o/ 'subway,' *auto* /ɔt'o/ 'auto,' *moto* /mɔt'o/ 'motor scooter,' will have their final vowel represented as |Ɔ|: |mEtrƆ|, and so on (cf. *métropolitain* /metrɔpɔlit'ɛ̃/, *automobile* /ɔtɔmɔb'il(ə)/, *motocycle* /mɔtɔs'ikl(ə)/).

It also happens that /ɔ/ becomes /o/ before /z/: *chose* /ʃ'o:z(ə)/ 'thing,' *pose* /po:z(ə)/ 'pose.' This phenomenon is similarly a case of phonetic adjustment.[40]

Rule for rounded vowel adjustment

In word final position or before /z/:
[+round] vowels become [−low].

In order to handle those cases where there is an /o/ before a consonant other than /z/, it is necessary to consider paradigmatic forms in which /al/ frequently alternates with /o/.

cheval	/ʃəv'al/	chevaux	/ʃəv'o/	'horse(s)'
journal	/ʒurn'al/	journaux	/ʒurn'o/	'newspaper(s)'
amical	/amik'al/	amicaux	/amik'o/	'friendly'
valent	/v'al(ə)/	vaut	/v'o/	'be worthy'
falloir	/falw'ar/	faut	/f'o/	'be necessary'

The first three forms of Column 2 are plurals; the last two forms are third person singular verbs. Let us assume that the forms of Column 2 are equivalent to the corresponding forms of Column 1 (they contain |Al| in the underlying representation) with the addition of the plural morpheme |S| or the third person singular morpheme |t|.[41]

|ʃƐvAl+S#| |AmIkAl+S#| |fAl+t#|

Then |Al| becomes /o/ when followed by a consonant. (The rule for final consonant deletion (Section 1.1.3) will drop the final consonant under particular conditions.)

Rule for o-conversion

Before a consonantal segment:
|Al| becomes /o/.

The /al/ : /o/ alternation is also found among derivational forms: *altitude* /altit'yd(ə)/ 'altitude': *haut* /'o/ 'high,' *falsifier* /falsifj'e/ 'to falsify': *fausse* /f'o:s(ə)/ 'false(f),' etc. Here, too, the forms exhibiting /o/ can be represented as containing an underlying |Al| (e.g., |hAlt|, |fAls|).[42] The rule which converts |Al| to /o/ must, of course, occur after the vowel raising rule, which converts |O| to /u/.

Pairs such as *côte* /k'o:t(ə)/ 'coast, rib': *costal*/ kɔst'al/ 'coastal,' *hôpital* /ɔpit'al/ 'hospital': *hospitaliser* /ɔspitaliz'e/ 'to hospitalize,' where stressed /o/ (or pretonic /ɔ/) alternates with /ɔs/, demonstrate the need for an underlying |Ɔs| (e.g., |kƆst|), which in nonlearned forms is converted to /o/ (tonic) or /ɔ/ (pretonic).[43]

Rule for o-conversion (part 2)

In nonlearned forms before a consonantal segment:

|Ɔs| becomes: { /o/ when stressed; /ɔ/ when unstressed }

This rule accounts for the possessive pronouns *nôtre*, *vôtre* /n'o:tr(ə)/, /v'o:tr(ə)/, 'ours,' 'yours,' (which are always stressed), in contrast to the possessive determiners *notre*, *votre* /nɔtr(ə)/, /vɔtr(ə)/ 'our,' 'your' (which are unstressed) — from underlying |nƆstr|, |vƆstr|.

Finally, there is a group of words which exhibit either stressed /ɔ/ or /o/. Often, the vowel appears before nasal plus schwa:

économe	/ekɔn'ɔm(ə)/	'economical'
polygone	/pɔlig'ɔn(ə)/	'polygon'
téléphone	/telef'ɔn(ə)/	'telephone'
atome	/at'o:m(ə)/	'atom'
axiome	/aksj'o:m(ə)/	'axiom'
pôle	/p'o:l(ə)/	'pole'

Those forms which contain stressed /ɔ/ raise no problem since they are derived from underlying tense |Ɔ|. Forms with stressed /o/ cannot have underlying |O|, as this vowel is the source of /u/ (e.g., |pr'Ov+a| → /pr'uv(ə)/ *prouve*). Within the present framework this problem has three possible solutions: (1) the forms with stressed /o/ are derived from an underlying |Al| or |Ɔs|; (2) the forms have a tense |O| as the underlying vowel, but are exceptions to the rule which raises |O| to /u/ so that /o/ remains as the vowel; (3) the forms have tense |Ɔ| as the underlying vowel and constitute a special morphological class where |Ɔ| is raised to /o/.

The first solution is the least desirable one since there is no nonarbitrary procedure for deciding between underlying |Al| or |Ɔs|, precisely because there is no morphological evidence even to suggest an underlying |Al| or |Ɔs|. Also, the conversion of |Al| and |Ɔs| to /o/ applies to the nonlearned division of the vocabulary, and the pretonic vowels of the forms under consideration do not exhibit the characteristics of nonlearned forms (e.g., schwa, front rounded vowels, /u/).

The second solution, that is, postulating underlying |O|, is preferable to the first. The price for this solution is that the forms in question must be marked as exceptions to the rule which raises |O| to /u/. This procedure is quite feasible since the number of words involved is relatively small.

The third solution, postulating underlying |Ɔ|, like the second, requires marking the particular forms as exceptions. Only, here, the marked forms undergo a special rule which raises |Ɔ| to /o/. We prefer this solution for two reasons. First, in pretonic position /ɔ/, and not /o/, occurs: *atomique* /atɔm'ik(ə)/ 'atomic,' *axiomatique* /aksjɔmat'ik(ə)/ 'axiomatic,' *polaire* /pɔl'ɛr(ə)/ 'polar'; (contrast these with forms derived from |Al| where /o/ occurs pretonically, e.g., *hauteur* /ot'œr/ 'height'). Therefore, by adopting the third solution, only tonic |Ɔ| needs to be raised to /o/. Also, many of these stressed /o/ are in free variation with /ɔ/, so that, for several of the forms, there is fluctuation from speaker to speaker and from dictionary to dictionary. To cite just a few examples: *icone*, *ozone*, *amazone*, *hippodrome* may show either vowel. (These fluctuations are reminiscent of the "*a* antérieur"–"*a* postérieur" problem.) For fluctuating forms the third solution has merit over the second. With the second proposal *icone*, for example, may have either |IkƆna| or |IkOna| as its underlying representation. In the third solution there is a *single* underlying representation |IkƆna|, with the proviso that the morpheme may be *optionally* marked to undergo the special vowel raising rule. The third solution is particularly attractive in that it distinguishes stylistic variation from phonemic contrast. Alternant forms (e.g., /iko:n(ə)/, /ikɔn(ə)/) have the same underlying representation and are marked as to whether they have stylistic variants.[44]

2.3.2. *Vowel duration*

Fouché (1956) gives the following rules for phonetic vowel length in French:

1. Unaccented vowels are always short.
2. Accented vowels are:

a. long:

i before single /r z ʒ v/: *rire*, *rase*, *neige*, *neuve*;

ii /o ø ɑ ã ɛ̃ ɔ̃ œ̃/ before all consonants: *haute*, *jeûne*, *pâte*, *danse*, *mince*, *montre*, *humble;*

b. short otherwise: *robe*, *sud*, *bague*, *tasse*, *riche*, *dame*, *fine*, *coule*, *feuille*, *gagne*, *haut*, *mais*, *rue*.

For all stressed vowels in a closed syllable the following consonant or consonants determine the duration of the vowel, except for those vowels in 2.*a*.ii, which are inherently long. Let us for the moment exclude these "inherently" long vowels. Then we can set up the underlying vowel as *basically short* in length. The following phonetic adjustment rule will lengthen those stressed vowels which precede voiced continuants (2.*a*.i).

Rule for preconsonantal vowel lengthening

In a closed syllable:

A stressed vowel becomes long if followed by a voiced continuant.

Why should the nasalized vowels and /o/ always be lengthened in a closed syllable under stress? We showed that nasalized vowels do not occur in the underlying representations, but are always derived from an oral vowel plus a nasal consonant; the vowel is nasalized and the nasal consonant is deleted. Similarly, /o/ in a closed syllable (except before /z/) is often derived from either |Al| or |Ɔs|. The vowel is shifted to /o/ and the following consonantal segment is deleted. What is common to both /o/ and the nasalized vowels is the shift in vowel quality and deletion of the following segment with compensatory lengthening in the vowel.

Rule for vowel lengthening

Within the word, whenever a nonfinal consonantal segment is deleted the preceding vowel becomes lengthened if it is stressed.

Finally, a phonetic adjustment rule is required which shortens vowels in final position (for those vowels which have become long by the preceding rules and which eventually occur as final).

Rule for final vowel shortening

In final position a vowel becomes short.

According to the vowel lengthening rule, all nasalized vowels and /o/ are made long in a stressed closed syllable. In orthoepic French one finds other oral vowels which are long. Minimal pairs such as the following are often cited:

/ɛ/	/ɛ:/		
faite	fête	'done'	'holiday'
bette	bête	'beet'	'animal'
mettre	maître	'to put'	'master'
/a/	/a:/		
patte	pâte	'paw'	'paste'
mal	mâle	'badly'	'male'
dame	âme	'lady'	'soul'
/œ/	/ø:/		
jeune	jeûne	'young'	'fast (noun)'

There is considerable fluctuation among speakers as to which pairs of this type are differentiated. Many speakers make no distinction in length for any of these. Nonetheless, it is of interest to see how these forms fit in the overall description. One would suspect that these long vowels are perhaps also due to the deletion of a consonant. For some of the forms this assumption is borne out, e.g., *bestial*, *bête* 'beastly,' 'beast'; *festin*, *fête* 'feast,' 'holiday'; *pastel*, *pâte* 'pastel,' 'paste.' If the underlying representations for Column 2 are: |bEst|, |fEst|, |pAst|, long vowels would result from the vowel lengthening rule. The same type of alternation is found in the verb conjugation, e.g., *connaissent* /kɔnɛs(ə)/ 'know'; *connaître* /kɔnɛ:tr(ə)/ 'to know.' In the section on verbs we shall show that the underlying form of the stem is |kƆnEss|, that the infinitive is |kƆnEstr|. The vowel lengthening rule, of course, will lengthen the stressed stem vowel and delete the following |s|. This observation for vowel lengthening suggests the possibility of representing even words like *maître*, *mâle*, *âme*, *jeûne* (which are not paired with easily relatable forms) with an underlying consonant which becomes deleted and causes the preceding vowel to be lengthened.[45]

The derivations in the accompanying chart illustrate the vowel lengthening rules developed in this section.

	haut	*haute*	*fête*	*chose*
Underlying form	hAlt#	hAlt+a#	fEsta#	ʃƆza#
Vowel lengthening and Al → o	o:t#	o:t+a#	fɛ:ta#	——
Final consonant deletion	o: #	——	——	——
ɔ → o	——	——	——	ʃo za#
Precons. vowel lengthening	——	——	——	ʃo:za#
Final vowel shortening	o #	——	——	——
Schwa deletion (optional)	——	o:t #	fɛ:t #	ʃo:z #
	/o/	/o:t/	/fɛ:t/	/ʃo:z/

2.4 Semivowels (glides)

In French there are three semivowels or glides: /j w ɥ/.

/j/	
id*i*ot	'idiot'
d*i*able	'devil'
v*i*ande	'meat'
act*i*on	'action'

/w/	
*ou*i	'yes'
*ou*est	'west'
L*ou*is	'Louis'

/ɥ/	
s*u*ivre	'to follow'
l*u*i	'him'
pers*u*ader	'to persuade'

These glides correspond in point of articulation to the high vowels /i u y/, so that /j/ is front unrounded, /w/ is back rounded, and /ɥ/ is front rounded.

	/j/	/w/	/ɥ/
front	+	−	+
round	−	+	+

We have already shown that one source of /j/ and /w/ is the diphthongization of a lax front unrounded vowel, that is, |ɛ| → /jɛ/, |e| → /we/ → /wa/. This accounted for the glide in such words as: *ciel*, *bien*, *pied*, *croire*, *espoir*, *loi*, etc. What are the sources of the glide before other vowels? Within the verb paradigm a high vowel often alternates with its corresponding glide.[46]

/i/	/j/				
scie	scier	/s'i/	/sj'e/	'saw'	'to saw'
étudie	étudier	/etyd'i/	/etydj'e/	'study'	'to study'
/u/	/w/				
joue	jouer	/ʒ'u/	/ʒw'e/	'play'	'to play'
loue	louer	/l'u/	/lw'e/	'praise'	'to praise'
/y/	/ɥ/				
tue	tuer	/t'y/	/tɥ'e/	'kill'	'to kill'
pue	puer	/p'y/	/pɥ'e/	'smell'	'to smell'

A rule is required which states that, whenever an unstressed high vowel is followed by another vowel, the high vowel becomes a glide. In distinctive feature notation a vowel is defined as [−cons, +voc], whereas a glide is [−cons, −voc]. (Consonants are [+cons, −voc]; liquids are [+cons, +voc].) Vowels then differ from glides by the feature "vocality."

Rule for glide formation

Before $\begin{bmatrix}-\text{cons}\\+\text{voc}\end{bmatrix}$ segments, i.e., vowels:

$$\begin{bmatrix}-\text{cons}\\+\text{voc}\\-\text{stress}\\+\text{high}\end{bmatrix} \text{ segments become } [-\text{voc}]$$

This rule changes the feature [+voc] of an underlying unstressed high vowel to [−voc], converting the vowel to a glide. The glide formation rule must, of course, follow the rule which fronts |U| to /y/ and raises |O| to /u/. The latter phenomenon presupposes that the underlying "glide" vowels must be tense, which they are unquestionably in the paradigmatic forms we have given.

Deriving glides from vowels leads to a considerable simplification in underlying representations. If glides are eliminated from the system, only vowels remain to contrast with the consonants and the liquids (which are both [+cons]). Therefore, vowels need be marked only for the feature [−cons], and the feature [+voc] can be introduced by a redundancy rule which must occur before the glide formation rule.

Rule for vocalic redundancy

[−cons] segments are also [+voc]

In the examples we have given, the high vowel which becomes a glide precedes the other vowel. There are also instances of postvocalic glides. It is precisely examples of this type which are adduced for establishing "phonemic" contrast, at least between /i/ and /j/.

oui	houille	/w'i/	/'uj/	'yes'	'coal'
pays	paye	/pe'i/	/p'ɛj/	'country'	'pay (subj.)'
naïf	travail	/na'if/	/trav'aj/	'naive'	'work'

The problem is, of course, that if the postvocalic glide is also derived from a vowel, then, for example, *oui* and *houille* would be indistinguishable since both would be represented as |OI| (the |O| is raised to /u/).

One must conclude either that *i* and *j* are distinct underlying segments, or that postvocalic /j/ has a different origin from prevocalic /j/. A similar problem does not arise with the glides /w/ and /ɥ/ since they only occur prevocalically. The fact that all glides occur prevocalically, but only /j/ is found postvocalically leads one to suspect that the origin of postvocalic /j/ is quite different from that of its prevocalic confrere.

Since phonological alternation is of such prime importance for determining the underlying representations, to find paradigmatic alternations with postvocalic /j/ would be of interest. One notes that /l/ alternates with /j/ in the subjunctive of certain verb forms.

veulent	veuillent	/v'œl(ə)/	/v'œj(ə)/	'want'
valent	vaillent	/v'al(ə)/	/v'aj(ə)/	'be worthy'
falloir	faille	/falw'ar/	/f'aj(ə)/	'be necessary'
aller	aille	/al'e/	/'aj(ə)/	'go'

The /l/ : /j/ alternation is also found in derivation: *feuille*:*foliation* 'leaf, foliation'; *fille*:*filial* 'daughter, filial,' etc.

Furthermore, in certain nouns /aj/ becomes /o/ in the plural.

travail	travaux	/trav'aj/	/trav'o/	'work'
vitrail	vitraux	/vitr'aj/	/vitr'o/	'window'
bail	baux	/b'aj/	/b'o/	'lease'

The alternation /aj/ : /o/ is parallel to that of /al/ : /o/. The similarity of behavior between /l/ and /j/ when after /a/, and the fact that /l/ and /j/ alternate in certain verb forms and in derivation suggests that postvocalic /j/ is a type of *l*. (Let us call it l_2 for the moment to distinguish if from l_1, regular /l/.) The rule which converts |Al| to /o/, when followed by a consonant, can then be generalized to apply to either type *l*. Any l_2 which have not been subjected to this rule will ultimately become /j/.

What kind of *l* is l_2? While l_1 is dental in articulation, l_2, of course, must be kept distinct from the dental *l*. We know that l_2 will eventually become /j/, which is a palatal glide (high front semivowel). It is therefore desirable that l_2 should have as many of the features of /j/ as possible, yet still retain its *l*-like identity. This requirement leads us to deduce that l_2 is a palatal *l* (ʎ).

If postvocalic /j/ is derived from palatal *l*, do these palatal *l* occur in the underlying representations? The alternation which takes place between dental *l* and palatal *l* (which becomes /j/) in certain subunctive and in derivational forms suggests that palatal *l* is derived from dental *l*. A comparison of pairs such as *feuille*, *foliation* reveals the relevant environment for the conversion of dental *l* to palatal *l*. The stem element common to this pair must have |fɔlia| as its underlying representation. The |l| is followed by the lax front unrounded vowel |i|, and it is this particular vowel then which causes the preceding |l| to become palatalized. A subsequent rule converts /ʎ/ to /j/.[47]

Rule for l-palatalization

|li| becomes /ʎ/

Rule for palatal glide conversion

/ʎ/ becomes /j/

To illustrate these rules we contrast the derivation of *feuille* with that of *foliation. Feuille* has the following underlying representation: |f'ɔlia#|. (1) Since the |l| is followed by the lax high front vowel |i|, it becomes palatalized (rule for l-palatalization): /f'ɔʎa#/. (2) Stressed lax |ɔ| is shifted to /œ/ (Rule for vowel fronting, see p. 40): /f'œʎa/. (3) /ʎ/ becomes /j/ (rule for palatal glide conversion): /f'œja/. Posttonic lax /a/ is equivalent to schwa, which may be deleted in this environment: /f'œj(ə)/.

The form *foliation* /fɔljasjɔ̃/ also has |fɔlia| as one of its underlying morpheme constituents. However, when this morpheme is combined with the "learned" suffix (*-tion*), all the vowels become tense: |fƆlIA+sIƆn|. (See p. 42.) Due to the tense vowels, certain phonological processes can not take place. The |l| will not be palatalized since the rule for palatalization requires that the following high front vowel be lax. Similarly, vowel fronting will not take place. However, both occurrences of prevocalic |I| will be converted to /j/ by the rule for glide formation (cited earlier in this section) and, of course, the vowel |Ɔ| of the suffix will become nasalized (see Section 2.2).

Once it is established that postvocalic /j/ is derived from an intervocalic |l| before a lax |i|, whereas prevocalic /j/ is derived from a tense |I| preceding a vowel, forms such as *houille* and *oui* can be unambiguously represented: the underlying forms are |hOlia#| and |OI#|, respectively.

In summary, glides do not occur in the underlying morphemic representations. What appears phonetically as a prevocalic glide has as its origin either a lax front vowel which diphthongizes (|e| → /we/, |ɛ| → /jɛ/), or else a high vowel (|I| in the case of /j/, |O| in the case of /w/, and |U| in the case of /ɥ/) which precedes another vowel. Glide formation takes place after the rules for vowel fronting and vowel raising (|U| → /y/, |O| → /u/). Postvocalic /j/ results from an underlying /l/ which is followed by a lax |i|. The |l| is palatalized (/ʎ/) and then changed to /j/.

The derivations of several forms are shown in the accompanying table.

	animal	*travail*	*animaux*	*travaux*
	AnIm'Al	trAv'Ali	AnIm'Al+S	trAv'Ali+S
1. l-palatalization	——	trAv'Aʎ	——	trAv'Aʎ+S
2. o-conversion	——	——	AnIm'o +S	trAv'o +S
3. palatal glide conversion	——	trAv'Aj	——	——
4. final consonant deletion	——	——	AnIm'o	trAv'o
	/anim'al/	/trav'aj/	/anim'o/	/trav'o/

2.5 Stress

For French it has been maintained that within the word stress is predictable, being placed in all cases on the last pronounced vowel, e.g., *petit* /pət'i/, *petite* /pət'it/, *naturel* /natyr'ɛl/, *naturelle* /natyr'ɛl/.[48] This observation is valid only for the type of French where final schwas are not pronounced, and only if the rule is formulated in terms of the final output as has always been done traditionally.

For those dialects or styles in which final schwas are pronounced, a slightly more complex rule is required: within the word the final syllable bears the stress unless its vowel is schwa, in which case the stress falls on the penultimate, e.g., /pət'i/, /pət'itə/, /natyr'ɛl/, /natyr'ɛlə/. Since, *phonetically*, schwa is the only lax vowel of French (all other vowels are tense), the above stress rule can be restated in terms of vowel tenseness: within the word, place stress on the rightmost tense vowel.[49]

We have been talking about stress as though it were a phenomenon uniquely associated with the phonetic level, where all vowels are tense except schwa. However, in our analysis we have been representing morphemes in a more "abstract" manner, the phonetic output being derived from an underlying representation through application of the ordered phonological rules. It has been shown that *many of the phonological changes are a consequence of stress*. Therefore, stress placement has to be a relatively high-ordered rule (in fact, one of the early rules). Can the stress rule as it is stated apply to underlying vowels?

The words we have cited in this section have the following underlying representations: |pƐtIt#|, |pƐtIt+a#|, |nAtUrEl#|, |nAtUrEl+a#|.

The stress rule places stress on the rightmost tense vowel. When this rule is applied to these underlying representations, the appropriate vowel receives stress. These forms exhibit a one-to-one correspondence between underlying vowels and derived vowels, that is, a finally stressed underlying vowel corresponds to a finally stressed derived vowel (e.g., |pƐt'It#| /pət'i/), and similarly, a penultimately stressed underlying vowel corresponds to a penultimately stressed derived vowel, assuming here the retention of final schwas at the phonetic level (e.g., |pƐt'It+a#| /pət'it(ə)/).

There need not be a one-to-one correspondence between underlying segments and derived segments since underlying segments are frequently deleted.[50] Thus, *travail*, which is phonetically /trav'aj/ has |trAvAli#| as its underlying representation; stress must be placed on the second |A|: |trAv'Ali#|. The underlying form has penultimate stress, whereas the derived form has final stress. (The final lax |i| is no longer present after it has caused the preceding |l| to become palatalized.) The rule for stress will nonetheless place stress on the second |A| of |trAvAli#| as this is the rightmost tense vowel. Whereas in derived forms only one lax vowel, i.e., schwa, is recognized, in underlying forms there are several lax vowels, some of which are later deleted. In any event, even for this underlying form |trAvAli#|, stress still occurs on the penultimate vowel, one of the traditionally permitted stress positions. However, this is not the case for *visible* /viz'iblə/, where the underlying representation is |vIzIbili#| (cf. *visibilité*; see Section 2.1.2.); stress must be placed on the antepenultimate vowel — the tense |I|. The crucial point here is that for underlying forms stress is not restricted to the final or penultimate vowels. The reason stress uniquely appears in these two environments phonetically is because, whenever in the underlying representation there are two or more posttonic lax vowels, all of them, or all of them save one, are deleted. Yet the stress rule, when stated in terms of vowel tenseness, still applies correctly to |vIzIbili#|; it is the rightmost tense vowel which bears stress.

Although *phonetically* there is at least *one tense* vowel in a word, *underlying forms* may contain *only lax* vowels (one or more of which subsequently become phonetically tense), e.g., *fleur* /fl'œr/ < |flɔr#| (cf. *floral*); *vaine* /v'ɛn(ə)/ < |van+a#| (cf. *vanité*); *feuille* /f'œ j(ə)/ < |fɔlia#| (cf. *foliation*). For such forms — where the underlying vowels are all lax — it is the initial vowel which receives the stress. Once stressed, the vowel is fronted and becomes tense. The rule for stress placement must be revised so that an underlying form containing no tense vowel is stressed on the leftmost (lax) vowel.

Rule for stress placement

Within the word, place stress on the first vowel in a sequence so that no tense vowel follows.

According to the stress rule, in polysyllabic forms *noninitial underlying lax vowels* could not be stressed. Yet the following forms, which all show diphthongization or vowel fronting, must have had a noninitial underlying stressed vowel which was lax.

chanteur	/ʃãt'œr/	'singer'
pâtissier	/patisj'e/	'baker'
danoise	/danw'az(ə)/	'Danish (f.)'
devient	/dəvj'ɛ̃/	'(he) becomes'

These are all derivational forms and are therefore composed of more than one morpheme. In the first three examples the derivational suffix bears the stress, in the fourth the stem. Derivational suffixes, unlike inflectional endings, can receive stress. (In a form such as *petite* |pƐtIt+a#| the inflectional ending, "e féminin," would never be stressed.) This fact about word stress provides additional evidence for formally distinguishing between inflectional and derivational morphology. This formal difference will be indicated by the type of juncture by which the affix is separated from neighboring constituents. Inflectional endings will be separated from other elements by a + juncture, while the derivational affixes will be separated from other constituents by a different juncture =. The words we have cited are then represented as follows:

ʃAnt=ɔr#
pAtIs=ɛr#
dAn=ez+a#
dƐ=vɛn+t#

The stress rule must be restated so that in derivation the vowel of the stem is stressed if there are prefixes but no suffixes (e.g., *devient*); or, if there are suffixes, the vowel of the last suffix bears the stress (e.g., *danoise*). In other words, a vowel cannot receive stress if it is followed by any morpheme other than an inflectional ending.

Rule for stress placement (revised)

Within the word, place stress on the first vowel in a sequence so that no tense vowel or = juncture follows.

The rule states that stress occurs somewhere within the last morpheme which is not an inflectional ending. Thus, in a form such as *danoise* |dAn=ez+a#|, even though the tense |A| is followed by lax vowels, it will not be stressed since there is an intervening = juncture. Only the lax |e| meets the required environment of first vowel in a sequence with no following tense vowel or = juncture; |e| is followed, however, by + and lax |a|, but the rule allows this. In a form such as *devient* |dƐ=vɛn+t#|, the prefix vowel will not receive stress as there is a following = juncture; instead, stress will fall on the lax stem vowel.

The following forms also are instances of polysyllabic words which exhibit stressed diphthongized or fronted vowels:

framboise	/frãbw'az(ə)/	'raspberry'
balai	/bal'ɛ/	'broom'
neveu	/nəv'ø/	'nephew'
couleuvre	/kul'œvr(ə)/	'snake'

The underlying representations must contain noninitial lax vowels, which will have to receive stress. However, these words — unlike forms such as *danoise* — are not derivational; they are all composed of a single morpheme. The stress on the underlying lax vowel cannot therefore be attributed to the presence of a derivational affix.

If the underlying representation of *framboise,* for example, is |frAmbeza#|, according to the stress rule, stress should be placed on the leftmost vowel, i.e., the first vowel in a sequence such that no tense vowel or = juncture follows, cf. *feuille* |fɔlia#|. However, for *framboise* it is the second vowel which must be stressed. If this vowel were tense, then the correct vowel would receive stress — |frAmb'Eza#|, but then the vowel would not undergo diphthongization unless the tense stressed vowel subsequently were made lax in some way so that, when the rule for diphthongization applies, the vowel would no longer be tense. Is the laxing of a stressed tense vowel simply an *ad hoc* maneuver for handling apparent exceptions to the stress rule, or can such a laxing phenomenon be independently justified?

On p. 44 we showed that verbs such as *espère*:*espérer*; *prouve*:*prouver*, which do not exhibit diphthongization or fronting, must have stems with underlying tense vowels: |ƐspEr|, |prOv|. However, the related nouns *espoir*, *preuve* show diphthongized or fronted vowels. When the stem functions as a noun, the tense stem vowel becomes lax so that the appropriate vowel shifts will take place. If *espère*:*espoir*, *prouve*:*preuve* are to be related, then within the grammar there must be recognized a class of nouns with underlying tense vowels which receive stress and subsequently become lax. So long as this class is required in the grammar in any event, nouns such as *framboise* can be assigned to this special group. No additional rules are then needed to explain the occurrence of stress on a noninitial lax vowel in nonderivational forms.

The price paid for underlying tense vowels which become lax is minimal: assignment of certain nouns to a particular morphological class. Any other treatment of such nouns can be shown to be costlier. If these nouns are treated as exceptions to the stress rule, then an additional stress rule must be postulated. Adopting this alternative proposal, one must mark morphemes as exceptions to the general stress rule and furthermore set up another stress rule, the only purpose of which is to handle the exceptions. In the original proposal one need only mark morphemes, that is, indicate that they belong to a particular morphological class. The original stress rule and the independently motivated laxing principle automatically apply to these forms. Furthermore, the generality of the stress rule is in no way weakened and any *ad hoc* subsidiary stress rule is entirely dispensed with.

We have shown that stress is predictable. Unlike traditional rules for stress placement, which are formulated in terms of the phonetic sequence of segments, within our analysis stress must be assigned to underlying forms as stress is an important conditioning environment for many phonological processes. Stress placement is correlated with the tenseness feature of vowels, provided that a formal distinction is made between inflectional and derivational affixes. This distinction is signaled by the type of juncture accompanying the affix: inflectional endings being concatenated with a + juncture; derivational affixes being concatenated with a = juncture. Stress is placed on the first vowel in a sequence such that no tense vowel or = juncture follows. There is a special class of polysyllabic forms with noninitial stressed diphthongized or fronted vowels. These words start out with underlying tense vowels, which receive stress, then subsequently become lax.

2.6 Summary

In the morphemic (abstract phonologic) representation we have employed a seven-vowel system. Each of the seven vowels may be tense or lax, which is equivalent to recognizing a total of fourteen distinctive vowel segments. The feature "tense" is not simply an arbitrary marker for distinguishing two types of vowels. We have chosen this particular feature — and not some other one — since, ultimately, at the phonetic level we will have to state whether the vowels are tense or lax. In most instances, the underlying specification of tenseness corresponds to that of the derived vowel: underlying atonic lax vowels become lax schwa if they are not deleted; tonic or pretonic tense vowels remain tense. However, the underlying tense vowel |ɛ| in pretonic position and the lax vowels in tonic position change their tenseness at the phonetic level. The lax vowels undergo diphthongization and vowel fronting. That the lax rather than the tense vowels must undergo diphthongization and fronting can be verified by examining "learned" words, which do not usually exhibit diphthongized or fronted vowels or schwas.

Pairs of corresponding tense and lax vowels account for phonological alternations observable in related forms. Underlying lax vowels become tense whenever the stem is combined with certain ("learned") derivational affixes. Once the vowels have become tense, they will not undergo the various rules which affect only lax vowels. This phenomenon compels us to make a formal distinction between "learned" and "nonlearned" derivational affixes. There are also instances of underlying tense vowels which become lax, particularly for verb stems functioning as nouns, as well as for a class of nouns which exhibit noninitial stressed diphthongized or fronted vowels.

Nasalized vowels are not found in the underlying representations, but rather are derived from an oral vowel followed by a nasal consonant, the latter being either in word final position or followed by another consonant. The quality of the nasalized vowel results from a rule which makes all nasalized vowels low. That this rule is relatively uncomplicated is attributed to the fact that the nasalized vowels first undergo all of the previously established rules for vowel shift. The "inherent" length of nasalized vowels when in a stressed closed syllable is due to the deletion of the nasal consonant. In an analogous manner we have established that the "inherent" nonnasalized long vowels — the so-called "phonemic" long vowels — also are due to consonant deletion. This fact coupled with observed paradigm alternations led us to derive /o/ from an underlying |Al| or |Ɔs|, except for those instances where /o/ comes from |Ɔ|.

We have been able to eliminate semivowels or glides from the underlying representation. This permits us to mark vowels only for the feature [−cons], this feature alone serving to differentiate vowels from true consonants and liquids, both of which are marked [+cons]. The fact that vowels are also [+voc] is then completely predictable. Prevocalic glides are derived from high vowels, whereas the unique postvocalic glide /j/ results from palatalization of an underlying intervocalic |l|; the palatalization is due to a following lax |i|.

Since many of the vocalic changes are conditioned by the relation of a particular vowel to the tonic syllable, stress must be assigned to one of the vowel segments. The location of the stress depends on the tenseness feature of the underlying vowels as well as on the presence or absence of various junctures, so that stress is placed on the first vowel in a sequence such that no tense vowel or = juncture follows.

3. The Verb System

3.1 The verb conjugation

Verbs in French are conjugated for six persons (first, second, and third; singular and plural) and seven tenses (present, imperfect, present subjunctive, future, conditional, preterite, past subjunctive). In addition, there are three nonfinite forms (infinitive, present participle, past participle). This yields a total of 45 possible forms for a given verb stem.[1] The tenses, participles, and infinitive are often divided into three subgroups, the forms within each subgroup exhibiting morphological and phonological similarities. For convenient reference, we shall refer to these three subgroups as the "unmarked aspect," the "future aspect," and the "past aspect."[2]

Unmarked Aspect	Future Aspect	Past Aspect
Present	Future	Preterite
dor-s	dorm-i-ra-s	dorm-i-s
Imperfect	Conditional	——
dorm-ai-s	dorm-i-r-ai-s	
Present subjunctive	——	Past subjunctive
dorm-e-s		dorm-i-ss-e-s
Present participle	Infinitive	Past participle
dorm-ant	dorm-i-r	dorm-i

A verb such as *dormir* 'sleep' clearly illustrates these similarities. In the second singular of the unmarked aspect the stem is directly followed by the person ending or the tense marker; in the future aspect the stem is followed by the conjugation vowel *i* plus *r*; in the past aspect the conjugation vowel is also present. Within each aspect there is one non-finite form (present participle, infinitive, past participle). Furthermore, there are certain morphological similarities between some of the tenses of the unmarked and marked aspects. Thus, the conditional (after the *r*) exhibits the morphological characteristics of the imperfect tense. The past subjunctive (after the *ss*) shows the features of the present subjunctive. The marked aspects — unlike the unmarked aspect — contain only two finite tenses: there are no tenses corresponding to a future subjunctive or a past imperfect.

Traditionally, there are three principal verb conjugations based on the infinitive endings: the first, or "productive," conjugation (*arriver* 'arrive'); the second conjugation with two subclasses: those forms which insert *-iss* in certain persons and tenses (*finir* 'finish') and those which do not (*dormir* 'sleep'); the third conjugation with two subclasses: those forms which have infinitives in *-re* (*perdre* 'lose') and those with infinitives in *-oir* (*vouloir* 'want'). We shall demonstrate that the partitioning of verbs into three principal conjugations and the subgrouping of tenses that we have noted are the correct classifications for the verbal forms of modern French.[3]

We shall present an analysis of all persons and tenses of "regular" verbs as well as of those "irregular" verbs, where the stems exhibit phonological alternation. We shall not be concerned with "irregular" verbs with suppletive stems.[4]

3.2 Verb tenses

3.2.1. *Unmarked aspect*

Present. The second conjugation verb *dormir* 'sleep' is conjugated as follows in the present tense:

je dors	/d'ɔr/	nous dormons	/dɔrm'ɔ̃/
tu dors	/d'ɔr/	vous dormez	/dɔrm'e/
il dort	/d'ɔr/	ils dorment	/d'ɔrm(ə)/

Phonetically, the third plural may or may not have a final schwa, depending on the particular dialect or style under consideration. Therefore, in the phonetic transcriptions we shall continue to indicate a schwa in parentheses, whenever one is potentially possible.

Throughout the plural, the verb stem manifests itself phonetically as /dɔrm/ (with a stem final consonant), whereas in the singular the stem is /dɔr/ without the stem final consonant. One could, of course, postulate two allomorphs for the morpheme 'sleep,' namely, |dɔr| and |dɔrm|, these two allomorphs being distributed in the singular and in the plural respectively. However, this solution is of limited interest since it merely restates the already observable facts and in no way explains why the verb stem should exhibit this difference at all. Instead, we shall represent a given morpheme by a single phonological representation so that, throughout the paradigm, the same morpheme will always have the same phonological shape. The particular morphemic variant which occurs is derived from the underlying representation by means of the phonological rules. The rules state the environments in which the alternations occur. Therefore, for the forms we have cited, we shall postulate |dɔrm| as the underlying phonological representation for the morpheme 'sleep.' What is needed, then, is a rule which deletes the stem final consonant in the singular.

The deletion of final consonants is a common phenomenon in French. In Chapter 1 we showed that, in order to account for elision and liaison between words as well as for adjective inflection, certain morpheme final or word final consonants and vowels are deleted, depending on the nature of the initial segment of the following morpheme or word. The truncation rule which effects these deletions is stated again as follows:

Rule for truncation

At a boundary:

$$\begin{bmatrix} \alpha \text{ cons} \\ -\alpha \text{ voc} \\ -\text{stress} \end{bmatrix} \text{ segments are truncated before } [\alpha \text{ cons}] \text{ segments.}$$

The truncation rule states that segments which have opposite values for the features "consonantal" and "vocalic," i.e., consonants and vowels, are deleted before a boundary and a segment which agrees in consonantality. Liquids and glides are not truncated, nor are stressed vowels (e.g., *joli ami*).

Since the truncation rule deletes a consonant whenever it is followed by a boundary and a consonantal segment, there is a natural explanation for the absence of a stem final consonant in the present singular if it can be shown that this consonant is followed by another consonantal segment. Such is the case if one takes into consideration those styles which exhibit liaison forms of verbs.

Je vis en France	/ʒə viz ã frãs(ə)/	'I live in France'
Il vit en France	/il vit ã frãs(ə)/	'He lives in France'

The full liaison form of the paradigm is:

/v'iz/	/viv'ɔ̃z/
/v'iz/	/viv'ez/
/v'it/	/v'iv(ə)t/

Therefore, we shall postulate the following person endings for all verb forms:[5]

1st singular	|S|	1st plural	|ONS|
2nd singular	|S|	2nd plural	|ES|
3rd singular	|t|	3rd plural	|at|

The underlying vowels of the first and second persons plural must be tense since these vowels receive stress. Recall that stress is placed on the rightmost tense vowel.

The members of the paradigm can then each be represented in the underlying form as a sequence of two morphemes: the stem (which has the same phonological shape throughout the paradigm) plus a person ending.

|dɔrm+S#|	|dɔrm+ONS#|
|dɔrm+S#|	|dɔrm+ES#|
|dɔrm+t#|	|dɔrm+at#|

For the singular forms, the stem final consonant is in all cases followed by a + boundary and a consonantal segment. The truncation rule will therefore apply to these forms. The plural person markers, however, all begin with a vowel and it is this vowel which prevents the preceding stem consonant from being deleted. We have noted that, phonetically, the final schwa of the third plural may or may not be present according to style. However, at the more abstract level of representation, that is, for the underlying forms before any of the phonological rules are applied, the schwa is not optional but is in all cases a structural necessity if the behavior of the stem in the plural is to be at all generalized. It is the schwa which prevents deletion of the stem final consonant in the third plural. Following are derivations of the third singular and plural. (In all derivations the following format will be adopted. The ordered list of rules applicable in the derivations is first given. The forms to be derived are then identified by the standard orthography. Beneath the standard spelling appears the underlying representation. The numbers to the left of intermediate forms indicate the particular rule (from the preceding list) which has been applied.

The form given between diagonal bars is the final derived form after all rules have been applied and all junctures have been eliminated.)

1. stress placement
2. truncation
3. final consonant deletion

	dort	*dorment*
	d ɔrm+t#	d ɔrm+at#
1.	d'ɔrm+t#	d'ɔrm+at#
2.	d'ɔr +t#	——
3.	d'ɔr #	d'ɔrm+a #
	/d'ɔr/	/d'ɔrm(ə)/

In this derivation the last rule deletes final consonants in utterance final position (see Section 1.1.3). In Chapter 1 we showed that truncation must precede final consonant deletion: such is the case here, too. For the singular |dɔrm+t#|, if the final |t| were deleted first, the final stem consonant |m| would no longer be followed by a consonantal segment and could not undergo truncation.

In first conjugation verbs such as *arriver* 'arrive,' the stem final consonant is retained throughout the singular.

j'arrive	/ar'iv(ə)/	nous arrivons	/ariv'ɔ̃(z)/
tu arrives	/ar'iv(ə)/	vous arrivez	/ariv'e(z)/
il arrive	/ar'iv(ə)/	ils arrivent	/ar'iv(ə)(t)/

The plural forms appear to have the same person endings as those exhibited by second conjugation verbs. Since the stem final consonant is retained throughout the singular, it is the presence of an underlying lax vowel (schwa) — whether or not phonetically realized — which protects the stem consonant from deletion. However, what is the status of this schwa which appears in the singular? If the schwa represented the singular person endings, there would be a different set of endings for first conjugation and for second conjugation verbs. But, in fact, the person endings for first conjugation are the same as those for second, and the schwa which potentially appears in the first conjugation is a part of the stem. More correctly, it is the conjugation marker — hereafter called "thematic vowel" — for first conjugation verbs. This is corroborated by the interrogative form of the third singular and certain imperative forms of the second singular.

Arrive-t-il?	/ariv(ə)til/	'Does he arrive?'
Arrives-y.	/ariv(ə)zi/	'Arrive there.'

In these forms the schwa of the stem and the consonant of the singular person marker occur together.

On p. 30 we assigned schwa the features of a lax low central vowel, i.e., [−tense, +low, −front, −round]. Except for tenseness, schwa has the same feature specification as /a/. Schwa and /a/ should therefore be closely related structurally. First conjugation verbs illustrate this intimate relation: both /ə/ and /a/ occur as variant thematic vowels, e.g., *inviterons* /ɛ̃vitər'ɔ̃/ 'invite (future),' *invitassions* /ɛ̃vitasj'ɔ̃/ 'invite (past subjunctive).' (The environmental conditions for alternation are dealt with in Section 3.3.1.) This /ə/:/a/ alternation is also observable in derivation, *inviterons* /ɛ̃vitər'ɔ̃/ 'invite (future),' *invitation* /ɛ̃vitasj'ɔ̃/ 'invitation.'

The underlying structural similarity between /a/ and schwa not only accounts for these vowel alternations but also explains another phenomenon observable within the verb paradigm — the absence of a linking consonant in certain of the liaison forms of the verb.

Il vit en France.	/il vit ã frãs(ə)/	'He lives in France.'
Il arrive en France.	/il ariv ã frãs(ə)/	'He arrives in France.'

but not:

*Il arrive-t-en France. /il ariv(ə)t ã frãs(ə)/

Whereas in the third conjugation it is stylistically possible for the singular person marker — /t/ in the examples we have given — to function as a liaison consonant, a liaison consonant is not possible with a first conjugation singular form. If the liaison forms of these two verbs are compared, the nonoccurrence of a linking consonant becomes apparent.

present	il vit	/vit/	il arrive	/ariv(ə)/
imperfect	vivait	/vivɛt/	arrivait	/arivɛt/
subjunctive	vive	/viv(ə)/	arrive	/ariv(ə)/
future	vivra	/vivra/	arrivera	/ariv(ə)ra/
conditional	vivrait	/vivrɛt/	arriverait	/ariv(ə)rɛt/
preterite	vécut	/vekyt/	arriva	/ariva/
past subjunctive	je vécusse	/vekys(ə)/	j'arrivasse	/arivas(ə)/

il va	/va/	'he goes'
il a	/a/	'he has'
il est	/ɛt/	'he is'

A liaison consonant is not found whenever the final vowel is either an /a/ or a schwa. Treating schwa in its underlying phonological representation as a low central vowel, then, provides a structural explanation for the nonoccurrence of a linking consonant in the forms we have cited. There is an obligatory deletion of the final consonant which indicates singular person whenever this consonant follows a central vowel.[6]

Rule for singular person deletion

In word final position (in the environment +——#):

Delete a consonant preceded by a central vowel.

This rule, of course, applies only to verbs. Thus, the +S, which is the mark of the plural in adjectives and nouns, is not deleted after central vowels. Although the final *t* of the third plural |at| is preceded by a central vowel, this *t* is not deleted as there is no intervening + juncture.

The sequence of constituents for first conjugation singular forms is: stem + thematic vowel + person ending, |ArIv + a + S#| *arrive*. However, at the phonetic level the plural forms do not exhibit any conjugation marker, and it would appear that a form such as *arrivons* should simply have as its underlying representation: stem + person ending, |ArIv + ONS#| *arrivons*. The disadvantage of such a representation is that, although *arrive* and *arrivons* are both first conjugation present forms, their underlying structure is quite different and it becomes necessary to impose a restriction on permitted morpheme sequences, namely, that the thematic vowel occurs with singular but not with plural forms. A more general distributional statement would result if we could show that in the underlying forms a thematic vowel is present everywhere. Then, the plural of *arrivons* would be represented not as |ArIv + ONS#| but rather as |ArIv + a + ONS#|. If the latter is accepted as the underlying representation, a rule is required which deletes the thematic vowel in the plural. Such a rule already exists since the truncation rule deletes a vowel whenever it is followed by a boundary and another vowel or glide. (All plural person markers begin with a vowel segment.) Hence, no additional rules are needed to convert |ArIv + a + ONS#| to its appropriate phonetic form, and this particular underlying representation becomes well motivated. All first conjugation present forms are then composed of three morphemes: stem + thematic vowel + person ending, and consequently, the underlying representation exhibits a structural regularity which is not evident from the phonetic transcription exclusively.

We illustrate the rules so far formulated by deriving the first persons singular and plural of a first conjugation verb.

1. stress placement
2. truncation
3. singular person deletion

	arrive	*arrivons*
	Ar Iv+a+S#	ArIv+a+ ONS#
1.	Ar'Iv+a+S#	ArIv+a+ 'ONS#
2.	——	ArIV + 'ONS#
3.	Ar'Iv+a #	——
	/ar'iv(ə)/	/ariv'ɔ̃(z)/

Imperfect

j'arrivais	/ariv'ɛ(z)/	nous arrivions	/arivj'ɔ̃(z)/
tu arrivais	/ariv'ɛ(z)/	vous arriviez	/arivj'e(z)/
il arrivait	/ariv'ɛ(t)/	ils arrivaient	/ariv'ɛ(t)/

While the present tense is unmarked phonologically, the imperfect tense (at the phonetic level) has /ɛ/ as the tense marker throughout the singular and in the third plural. The mark of the imperfect in the first and second plural is /j/. The distribution of these two morphemic variants is straightforward: /ɛ/ appears whenever the stress is on the tense marker, whereas /j/ occurs when the following person ending bears the stress. In the underlying representation the mark of the imperfect must be a tense vowel if the imperfect marker is to be stressed throughout the singular and in the third plural. Since we wish to have the same morphemic representation throughout the imperfect, we shall represent this marker everywhere by tense |Ɛ|. In order to account for the first and second plural forms where it is the person ending which bears the stress and the imperfect is represented by a yod, we shall need a rule which converts |Ɛ| to /j/ whenever |Ɛ| is followed by a stressed vowel.

Rule for yod formation

Before a stressed vowel (in the environment +___+):

|Ɛ| becomes /j/.

This rule must, of course, follow the rule which assigns stress to the individual word.

Following are derivations of the first persons singular and plural in the imperfect. The sequence of constituents is: stem + thematic vowel + tense marker + person ending.

1. stress placement
2. yod formation
3. truncation

	arrivais	*arrivions*
	ArIv+a+ Ɛ+S#	ArIv+a+Ɛ+ ONS#
1.	ArIv+a+'Ɛ+S#	ArIv+a+Ɛ+'ONS#
2.	——	ArIv+a+j +'ONS#
3.	ArIv +'Ɛ+S#	ArIv +j +'ONS#
	/ariv'ɛ(z)/	/arivj'ɔ̃(z)/

The truncation rule must follow the rule for yod formation; otherwise, in the first plural both the lax |a| — which is the thematic vowel — and the tense |Ɛ| — which is the imperfect marker — would be deleted before the vowel of the person ending since vowels are truncated before vowels. That is, in the third line of the derivation of *arrivions*, the |Ɛ| of the imperfect is first converted to /j/. The /j/ is not deleted by the truncation rule since it is a glide, and we have shown that glides do not undergo truncation. However, the lax /a/, which indicates first conjugation, *is* deleted since vowels are truncated before both vowels and glides. The behavior of yod within the paradigm provides additional evidence for the truncation rule as it was originally formulated, namely, that vowels are deleted before nonconsonantal segments, whereas glides are not deleted.

Another interesting aspect of the truncation rule is observed in the derivation of the third person plural of the imperfect: *arrivaient* |ArIv+a+Ɛ+at#|. The imperfect marker is not converted to yod since it is not followed by a stressed vowel. Rather the imperfect marker itself is stressed as it is the rightmost tense vowel. Although the imperfect marker is followed by another vowel, the imperfect marker is *not* subsequently deleted by the truncation rule since stressed vowels do not undergo truncation. Only the thematic vowel is deleted: |ArIv+'Ɛ+at#|. Finally, a rule would be needed which deletes the lax vowel of the third plural whenever it follows another vowel: |ArIv+'Ɛ+t#|. Moreover, this deletion is not restricted to the verb paradigm, for it is a general phonological phenomenon of French that a postvocalic schwa is deleted.

Present subjunctive

je dorme	/d'ɔrm(ə)/	nous dormions	/dɔrmj'ɔ̃(z)/
tu dormes	/d'ɔrm(ə)/	vous dormiez	/dɔrmj'e(z)/
il dorme	/d'ɔrm(ə)/	ils dorment	/d'ɔrm(ə)(t)/

It is of particular interest to note that (1) the first and second plural forms are homophonous with the corresponding forms of the imperfect, that is, the subjunctive of these forms is represented by a yod at the phonetic level; (2) the stem final consonant appears throughout the singular, unlike the present tense, where the stem consonant is deleted. Thus, in the present tense /dɔr/ is found in the singular and /dɔrm/ in the plural, whereas in the subjunctive /dɔrm/ occurs throughout both the singular and the plural.[7] In the underlying representation for the subjunctive forms, then, the stem must be followed by a vocalic segment, i.e., the subjunctive marker, and it is this vowel which prevents deletion of the stem final consonant. Furthermore, the subjunctive marker has to be a lax vowel since, throughout the singular and in the third plural, the stress is on the vowel of the stem. If the vowel which indicates the subjunctive were tense, it would receive stress according to the stress rule, exactly as was the case in the imperfect (where the tense marker is |Ɛ|).

It would appear that the subjunctive marker should be schwa or lax |a|. However, this representation is not possible since, in the first and second persons plural of the subjunctive, the subjunctive marker is ultimately represented by a yod. Therefore, we would need a rule — analagous to the rule in the imperfect — which converts a lax |a| to /j/ whenever it is followed by a stressed vowel. However, such a rule would produce incorrect forms in the present tense of the first conjugation where the thematic vowel has already been established as lax |a|. Consider the following forms, where we contrast a first conjugation present tense form with a second conjugation subjunctive form.

|ArIv + a + 'ONS#|	*arrivons*	(present)
|dɔrm + a + 'ONS#|	*dormions*	(subjunctive)

In the present tense (*arrivons*) the lax vowel, which is the thematic vowel, must be deleted by the truncation rule; in the subjunctive (*dormions*) the lax vowel indicating the subjunctive must be converted to yod. If the same vowel indicates both first conjugation and subjunctive, there would be no way to differentiate these two cases. Therefore, the vowel for the subjunctive must have a different underlying representation, even though it appears at the phonetic level as a schwa. This means, then, that what is a schwa at the phonetic level may have different representations in the underlying phonological forms. On pp. 30–31 we showed that the source of phonetic schwa is a low vowel. (Nonlow vowels, on the other hand, are deleted in post-tonic position, for example, the suffix |'Abili| → /'abl/.) Since lax |a| is needed as the first conjugation thematic vowel, the subjunctive vowel must be either lax |ε| or |ɔ|.

If the subjunctive has |ε| as its representation, we can then account for the homophony of the first and second persons plural of the subjunctive with the corresponding forms of the imperfect. The rule for yod formation converts the imperfect marker |Ɛ| to /j/ whenever it precedes a stressed vowel. An analogous rule is required to convert the subjunctive marker to /j/ under the same conditions. If the subjunctive marker is |ε|, then the vowels which indicate respectively the imperfect and the subjunctive have the same features except for tenseness. In both instances, it is a low front unrounded vowel which becomes yod before a stressed vowel. Hence, yod formation in the imperfect and subjunctive can be generalized to a single rule.

Rule for yod formation (revised)

Before a stressed vowel (in the environment +____+):

$\begin{bmatrix} +\text{front} \\ +\text{low} \end{bmatrix}$ vowels become /j/.

Given the rule for yod formation and the underlying phonological representations for the imperfect and subjunctive, we then have a structural explanation for the homophony exhibited in these two tenses.

On pp. 71–72 we noted that in liaison, singular forms do not exhibit a linking consonant whenever the final vowel is phonetically an /a/ or a schwa. We accounted for this phenomenon by treating phonetic /a/ structurally as an underlying (tense) |A| and phonetic /ə/ as (lax) |a|. The rule for singular person deletion was generalized to handle either low central vowel. The present subjunctive is one of the tenses which does not have a linking consonant for singular forms. Moreover, we have established that the mark of the subjunctive is |ε|, which, of course, is not a central vowel. It appears that the rule for singular person deletion would need modification in order to include singular subjunctives. However, no new rules or modification of existent rules is in fact required providing that the rules already established are properly ordered. Since different underlying lax vowels ultimately become schwa, the rule for schwa conversion was needed, which converts all lax low vowels to lax |a|. We then allow the rule for

Arrive, Arrive, Arrivions, Arrivions

1. stress placement
2. yod formation
3. truncation
4. schwa conversion
5. singular person deletion

	arrive (present)	*arrive* (subjunctive)	*arrivions* (subjunctive)	*arrivions* (imperfect)
	Ar Iv+a+S#	Ar Iv+a+ε+S#	ArIv+a+ε+ ONS#	ArIv+a+Ɛ+ ONS#
1.	Ar'Iv+a+S#	Ar'Iv+a+ε+S#	ArIv+a+ε+ 'ONS#	ArIv+a+Ɛ+ 'ONS#
2.	——	——	ArIv+a+j + 'ONS#	ArIv+a+j + 'ONS#
3.	——	Ar'Iv +ε+S#	ArIv +j + 'ONS#	ArIv +j + 'ONS#
4.	——	Ar'Iv +a+S#	——	——
5.	Ar'Iv+a #	Ar'Iv +a #	——	——
	/ar'iv(ə)/	/ar'iv(ə)/	/arivj'ɔ̃(z)/	/arivj'ɔ̃(z)/

singular person deletion — which deletes a singular person marker whenever it follows a central vowel — to apply after the schwa conversion rule, which will have already converted |ε| to |a|. Early application of the schwa conversion rule allows us to treat different lax vowels alike at a subsequent point in the derivation.

To illustrate the rules, we cite on page 77 derivations in the first conjugation of the first person singular of the present and of the subjunctive (which are homophonous), and of the first person plural of the subjunctive and of the imperfect (which are also homophonous). In all cases, the homophonous forms have different underlying representations, and the required ambiguity results automatically when the ordered phonological rules are applied to these underlying forms.

Present participle

dormant /dɔrm'ã(t)/ arrivant /ariv'ã(t)/

The present participle is stressed on the vowel of the participle ending. This vowel must be tense if it is to receive stress. We shall therefore set up |Ant| as the underlying representation of the present participle.[8]

1. stress placement
2. truncation
3. nasalization

arrivant

ArIv+a+ Ant#
1. ArIv+a+ 'Ant#
2. ArIv + 'Ant#
3. ArIv + 'Ã t#

/ariv'ã(t)/

3.2.2. *Future aspect*

Future

je dormirai	/dɔrmir'e/	nous dormirons	/dɔrmir'ɔ̃(z)/
tu dormiras	/dɔrmir'a/	vous dormirez	/dɔrmir'e(z)/
il dormira	/dɔrmir'a/	ils dormiront	/dɔrmir'ɔ̃(t)/

In all forms a vowel appears before /r/. This is the thematic vowel for second conjugation verbs. As the vowel is phonetically /i/, it is derived from an underlying tense |I|. Although all the forms we have cited have the same vowel before /r/, they exhibit different vowels after the /r/. The first and second plurals show the characteristic vowel of their person markers. However, what is the origin of the vowels found in the other forms? The second and third singulars suggest that the future marker is |rA|; the vowel must be tense since it is stressed in these forms and does not undergo vowel shift. The underlying representation for the third singular then is |dɔrm+I+rA+t#|. Stress is placed on the last tense vowel: |dɔrm+I+r'A+t#|. The absence of the final consonant in liaison is due to the preceding central vowel (Rule for singular person deletion; see p. 72): /dɔrmir'a/. The second singular is similarly derived from an underlying: |dɔrm+I+rA+S#|.

The underlying representation for the first plural is |dɔrm+I+rA+ONS#|. Stress is placed on the last tense vowel, that is, the person marker: |dɔrm+I+rA+'ONS#|. The truncation rule deletes the |A|: |dɔrm+I+r+'ONS#|. The second plural is similarly derived.

The third person plural is unique in that the future is the only tense which exhibits a stressed nasalized vowel /dɔrmir'ɔ̃(t)/. The nasalization of the vowel can only be due to a following nasal consonant, which must be one of the segments of the person marker; this means that the third plural ending is composed of three segments: some vowel followed by a nasal consonant followed by *t*. (The |at| ending which appeared in previous derivations was a temporary expedient.) We can therefore represent the future as |dorm+I+rA+Vnt#|, where V signifies the yet unspecified vowel. This vowel has to be lax since, elsewhere in the paradigm, it does not receive stress. Furthermore, it must convert preceding |A| to a back rounded vowel, which is then nasalized; that is, the sequence |A| plus some vowel becomes /o/. As there is no obvious morphological evidence to aid us in deciding which particular vowel should appear in the third plural (other than the fact that it is lax and ultimately becomes schwa for all tenses except the future), we will need to resort to a criterion other than morphological alternation for determining the nature of this vowel. As we prefer not to pick just any arbitrary vowel, we could initially select the vowel entirely on general phonological grounds and then bring forth evidence from within French to justify the choice. In terms of general phonological considerations, the ideal vowel is, of course, one which frequently combines with /a/ to yield /o/. The preferred vowel in this case is /u/ since the conversion of /au/ to /o/ is an attested phonological change in a wide variety of languages. Therefore, we could set up the third plural ending as |unt|. We would then need a rule to convert tense |A| plus lax |u| to |O|.

Rule for o-conversion

|Au| becomes |O|.

Dormiront, then, has the following underlying representation: |dɔrm+I+rA+unt#|. Stress is placed on the rightmost tense vowel: |dɔrm+I+r'A+unt#|. O-conversion occurs: /dɔrm+I+r'O+nt#/; then nasalization and lowering /dɔrmir'ɔ̃(t)/.

Setting up the third plural ending as |unt| requires a rule which converts |Au| to |O|. Can this conversion rule be internally motivated within French morphology? If so, then further justification exists for underlying |unt| as the third plural marker. On pp. 51 and 58 we showed the necessity for a rule, which before consonants, converts |AL| (|L| indicates both dental *l* and palatal *l*) to |O| (e.g., *cheval, chevaux; travail, travaux*). The conversion of |AL| to |O| and of |Au| to |O| are similar processes. This similarity can be brought out by dispensing with the |AL| to |O| rule and, in its place, setting up a rule which only converts preconsonantal |L| to |u|.

Rule for L-vocalization

In nonlearned forms:

|L| becomes |u| before a consonant.

This rule converts |AL| to |Au|. All |Au| (both original and those derived from |AL|) are then converted to |O|. Although the conversion of preconsonantal |L| to |u| may be less complex than a direct conversion of preconsonantal |AL| to |O|, nonetheless this recourse to simplicity is not a strong argument since the rule for L-vocalization presupposes the existence of the rule which converts |Au| to |O|, and it is precisely the latter's existence that we wish to justify. Therefore, L-vocalization has to be established independently of o-conversion. Is there any evidence other than an appeal to rule simplicity to indicate that the |L| to |u| conversion is in fact required?

We have shown that liquids do not undergo truncation, so that, for example, the third singular present *meurt* /m'œr(t)/ 'die,' derived from an underlying |mɔr+t#| (the lax |ɔ| becomes /œ/ under stress), retains the stem final /r/, even though it is followed by a consonantal segment. (Cf. *dort* /d'ɔr(t)/ derived from |dɔrm+t#|.) The form *veut* /v'ø(t)/ 'want' is derived from an underlying |vɔl+t#| (cf. *veulent* /v'œl(ə)(t)/). Although the underlying final stem segment of *veut* also terminates in a liquid, |l|, this segment has been deleted. It might be, of course, that the absence of a stem final liquid is simply an inexplicable fact about the singular present forms of the verb 'want.'

However, the rule for L-vocalization allows a natural explanation for this curious phenomenon. Since the form |v'ɔl+t#| contains an |l| followed by a consonantal segment, the |l| would become vocalized if the grammar contains a rule which converts preconsonantal |L| to |u|: |v'ɔu+t#|. The stressed lax vowel is fronted: |v'œu+t#|. As lax |u| is not preceded by tense |A|, the |u| does not combine with the preceding vowel. Instead, the |u| is deleted since it is a posttonic nonlow vowel: /v'œ+t/. (The /œ/ is raised to /ø/ in an open syllable; a vowel followed by a + juncture and a single consonant (liaison consonant) counts as an open syllable.)

The deletion of a posttonic nonlow vowel is a common phenomenon within French phonology. If the stem final |l| of |vɔl+t#| can be converted to a nonlow vowel, then the absence at the phonetic level of a final stem segment can be explained by a vowel deletion rule which is required in any event within the grammar. Furthermore, in the case of *veut*, the vocalization of |l| is totally independent of a preceding tense |A|. Once the need for L-vocalization has been independently established, the conversion of |Au| to /o/ is an automatic consequence. Just as |vɔl+t#| becomes |v'ɔu+t#|, similarly |fAl+t#| must become |fAu+t#|, as the environmental conditions are identical. The latter form is subsequently converted to /f'o(t)/ *faut* 'is necessary.' Note that the rules for L-vocalization, o-conversion, and nonlow vowel deletion must be applied in this order.

Since a rule is needed which converts |Au| to /o/, the third plural future has a natural explanation if the person ending is |unt|. In this way, the lax |u| of the ending will combine with the preceding tense |A| of the future marker |rA| to yield /o/, which is subsequently nasalized. However, in all other tenses the third plural becomes /ət/, e.g., *arrivent* /ar'iv(ə)(t)/. The derivation of /ət/ from an underlying |unt| results from rules previously established. The underlying representation for *arrivent* is now |ArIv+a+unt#|. Stress is placed on the rightmost tense vowel: |Ar'Iv+a+unt#|. Since the |u| is not preceded by tense |A|, it does not combine with the preceding vowel. The |u| subsequently becomes nasalized and is lowered: /Ar'Iv+a+ɔ̃t#/. The unstressed thematic vowel is then truncated as it precedes another vowel: /Ar'Iv+ɔ̃t#/. The posttonic lax low vowel is converted to schwa: /ar'iv(ə)(t)/. What eventually becomes schwa in the third plural starts out as a high back vowel |u|. Normally, high vowels are deleted in posttonic position (for example, the suffix |'Abili| → /abl/, |v'ɔut| → /v'œt/). However, when nonlow vowel deletion takes place, |u| has already been lowered, the lowering being a consequence of nasalization, that is, all nasalized vowels become [+low]. The low back vowel then becomes schwa. Schwa conversion affects all lax low vowels, whether or not they are nasalized, since there is only one phonetically lax vowel in French.

The first person singular of the future terminates in a stressed mid front vowel, /dɔrmir'e/. The mark of the future is |rA| here, just as it is for all other persons. Thus, |rA| must combine with some following segment (the person marker) to yield /e/. The obvious segment for this conversion would be |i|; just as |Au| becomes /o/, one would expect |Ai| analogously to become /e/. It would seem, then, that the first person singular marker should be |i|. However, a vowel cannot be the person marker for nonfuture forms (e.g., *dors* |dɔrm+S#|). For these forms the first person singular marker has to be a consonant; a consonant is imperative if the preceding stem consonant is to be truncated, and if liaison is to take place. Therefore, |S| must be set up as the underlying first singular marker and a special rule is needed to convert |S| to |i|. This conversion entails changing only two features: "consonantal" and "vocalic." Within the distinctive feature framework, |S| has the features [+cons, −voc, +cont, +diffuse, −grave, −round] ([−round] is redundant), whereas |i| has the feature complex [−cons, +voc, +cont, +diffuse, −grave, −round] ([+cont] is redundant). Recall that our features [+high] and [+front] are mnemonic labels for articulatory positions and actually correspond respectively to the Jakobsonian features [+diffuse] and [−grave] (see Chapter 2, Note 7). Therefore, to convert |S| to |i|, it is only necessary to switch the values of the "consonantal" and "vocalic" features.

The conversion of |S| to |i| takes place provided two conditions are met: (1) |S| is the first person singular marker, and (2), |S| is preceded by tense |A|. The first condition is imposed so that the second person singular ending |S| will not also be converted to |i|: *dormiras* |dɔrm+I+rA+S#|. The second condition assures that the singular |S| is not converted to |i| in the other tenses, where the person marker is not preceded by |A|. If both conditions are met, |A+S#| becomes |A+i#|, which is subsequently converted to /e#/.[9]

Rule for first singular vocalization

In word final position:

the first singular marker |S| becomes |i| when preceded by |A|.

Rule for e-conversion

|Ai| becomes /e/.

Although we have found no actual phonetic alternations between a dental sibilant and a high front unrounded vowel, we believe we have

Dormira, Dormirai, Dormiront, Dormirons

1. stress placement
2. truncation
3. first person vocalization
4. o-conversion and e-conversion
5. nasalization and lowering
6. singular person deletion

	dormira	*dormirai*	*dormiront*	*dormirons*
	dcrm+I+r A+t#	dɔrm+I+r A+S#	dɔrm+I+r A+unt#	dɔrm+I+rA+ ONS#
1.	dɔrm+I+r'A+t#	dɔrm+I+r'A+S#	dɔrm+I+r'A+unt#	dɔrm+I+rA+ 'ONS#
2.	——	——	——	dɔrm+I+r + 'ONS#
3.	——	dɔrm+I+r'A+i #	——	——
4.	——	dɔrm+I+r'E #	dɔrm+I+r'O+ nt#	——
5.	——	——	dɔrm+I+r'ɔ̃ t#	dɔrm+I+r + 'ɔ̃ S#
6.	dɔrm+I+r'A #	——	——	——
	/dɔrmir'a/	/dɔrmir'e/	/dɔrmir'ɔ̃(t)/	/dɔrmir'ɔ̃(z)/

presented adequate indirect evidence in support of the present analysis for the first person singular, and for rules which convert |A+S#| to |A+i#| and then to /e#/, rather than a single rule which directly converts |A+S#| to /e#/: (1) the conversion of |Ai| to /e/ is supported by the independently required symmetrical conversion of |Au| to /o/;[10] (2) that the vowel which converts |A| to /e/ is |i| and not some other vowel receives support from the simplicity criterion: |i| is the vowel whose feature specifications are most similar to those of a dental sibilant; (3) as phonological phenomena, the conversions of |S| to /i/ (or /j/) and of |Ai| to /e/ are more general, that is, likely to occur both synchronically and diachronically, than a direct conversion of |AS| to /e/.[11]

We illustrate on page 83 derivations of the various future forms.

Conditional

je dormirais	/dɔrmir'ɛ(z)/	nous dormirions	/dɔrmirj'ɔ̃(z)/
tu dormirais	/dɔrmir'ɛ(z)/	vous dormiriez	/dɔrmirj'e(z)/
il dormirait	/dɔrmir'ɛ(t)/	ils dormiraient	/dɔrmir'ɛ(t)/

Morphologically, the conditional resembles the future up to the /r/ and the imperfect after the /r/. To show this resemblance, we shall represent the conditional by a sequence of two morphemes: the future aspect followed by the imperfect tense.[12] The derivations are straightforward and require little explanation: |Ɛ| becomes /j/ when followed by a stressed vowel and the |A| of |rA| in all cases is truncated by the following [−cons] segment.

1. stress placement
2. yod formation
3. truncation
4. nasalization and lowering

	dormirait	*dormirions*
	dɔrm+I+rA+ Ɛ+t#	dɔrm+I+rA+Ɛ+ ONS#
1.	dɔrm+I+rA+'Ɛ+t#	dɔrm+I+rA+Ɛ+'ONS#
2.	——	dɔrm+I+rA+ j+'ONS#
3.	dɔrm+I+r +'Ɛ+t#	dɔrm+I+r + j+'ONS#
4.	——	dɔrm+I+r +j+'ɔ̃ S#
	/dɔrmir'ɛ(t)/	/dɔrmirj'ɔ̃(z)/

Infinitive

dormir /dɔrm'ir/

The underlying representation for the infinitive marker is |r|: |dɔrm+I+r#|. Stress is placed on the tense thematic vowel. The final |r| is never deleted as liquids are not truncated.

3.2.3. *Past Aspect*
Preterite (*passé simple*)

je dormis	/dɔrm'i(z)/	nous dormîmes	/dɔrm'im(ə)(z)/
tu dormis	/dɔrm'i(z)/	vous dormîtes	/dɔrm'it(ə)(z)/
il dormit	/dɔrm'i(t)/	ils dormirent	/dɔrm'ir(ə)(t)/

The preterite forms are characteristically stressed on the thematic vowel, and show special person markers for the first and second plurals.[13] The only output form which has an overt tense marker is the third plural *dormirent*, where /r/ appears to be the marker of the preterite. If this marker were to appear in the underlying representations of the other five forms, it would have to be deleted at some point in the derivation. One notes further that all the person endings, except the third plural, begin with a consonant, *-s*, *-s*, *-t*, *-mes*, *-tes*, and it must be this consonant which causes the preceding tense marker to be truncated. Yet we have shown (Section 1.1.1) that liquids are never truncated. Hence, the underlying representation of the tense marker for the preterite must not be |r| but rather a true consonant, i.e., a segment which is [+cons, −voc]; this consonant becomes /r/ only in the third plural (where it is intervocalic).

Since the preterite is overtly marked only in the third plural — and it is /r/ here — but is not overtly indicated in any of the other persons, the paradigmatic forms are of no help in determining which consonant must be present in underlying representations. However, elsewhere within French morphology can be found occurrences of alternations between /r/ and a true consonant, namely, a dental sibilant: *acquérir*, *acquisition*, /aker'ir/, /akizisj'ɔ̃/, 'acquire,' 'acquisition,' *chanteur*, *chanteuse* /ʃãt'œr/, /ʃãt'øz(ə)/ 'singer (m), singer (f).' Further evidence that the underlying representation for the preterite is a dental sibilant is found in the past subjunctive, a tense morphologically related to the preterite, where a voiceless dental sibilant occurs phonetically as the tense marker, e.g., *dormisse* /dɔrm'is(ə)/. (See p. 89.) We shall represent the preterite morpheme as |+S| — a dental sibilant unspecified for voicing — which is converted to /r/ whenever it is intervocalic.[14]

Rule for rhotacism

|+S| becomes /+r/ when intervocalic.

Although the person markers for the first and second persons singular are also |+S|, they are not converted to /r/ as the person markers occur word finally and not intervocalically.

With the preterite represented as |S|, the underlying representations for the third singular *dormit* and the third plural *dormirent* are respectively |dɔrm+I+S+t#| and |dɔrm+I+S+unt#|. In the singular the preterite |S| is truncated by the following consonantal segment; in the plural the |S| is intervocalic and becomes /r/.

Another characteristic of the preterite is the "special" set of person endings in the first and second plurals, i.e., *-mes*, *-tes*. Are these endings at all related to those which are found in the other tenses, i.e., *-ons*, *-ez*? The underlying representation for the first plural ending is |ONS|, where |N| is an unspecified nasal consonant. If this underlying form is compared to the preterite variant *-mes* /məz/, it is seen that, whereas the former is composed of three segments — vowel+nasal+sibilant, the latter also contains these three general segment types but in a different order: nasal+vowel+sibilant. Therefore, if the first two segments of the underlying form were to undergo metathesis in the preterite, the appropriate sequence of segments would appear for the derived ending: /NOS/. However, the initial nasal and following vowel segments need to be further specified. In the underlying form the nasal was originally unspecified since either /m/ or /n/ could cause a preceding vowel to become nasalized. In the preterite the nasal consonant must be /m/. If the underlying form is |OmS|, that is, the nasal consonant is not an archiphoneme but is specified as the bilabial nasal, the preceding vowel would still become nasalized; whenever |OmS| undergoes metathesis, the appropriate initial nasal would be obtained for the preterite: |mOs|. The underlying vowel segment, i.e., tense |O|, must be changed to schwa for the preterite variant. If |O| were to be made lax and low, i.e., |ɔ|, the rule for schwa conversion would then convert |ɔ| to /ə/ since posttonic lax low vowels always become schwa. The metathesis rule must therefore perform two functions: (1) it interchanges the first two segments of underlying |OmS| and (2) it lowers and laxes the vowel segment.

The second plural preterite ending *-tes* is similar to the first plural ending *-mes*, so that the former would also seem to result from metathesis. The underlying form for the second plural would then have to contain three segments, the second of which is |t|: |EtS|. The metathesis rule would accordingly interchange the first and second segments and would lower and lax the vowel segment: /tɛS/. The lax low vowel would be converted to schwa.

The special first and second person plural endings found in the preterite are derivable from the underlying endings |OmS| and |EtS|.[15] To relate the underlying forms to the derived ones, a rule is required which interchanges the first two segments and adjusts the vowel quality. These changes occur whenever the person endings follow the preterite marker |+S|.

Rule for metathesis

After |+S| the endings |+OmS|, |+EtS|

1. undergo metathesis of the first two segments
2. the vowel becomes [−tense, +low].

The preterite marker is the only tense marker represented as a single consonant. All other tense markers have been vowels or have terminated in a vowel: |Ɛ| imperfect, |ε|, subjunctive, |rA| future. Therefore, the metathesis rule need only state that a preceding single consonant causes metathesis in the first and second plural person endings.

Rule for metathesis (revised)

After a single consonant morpheme, |+OmS|, |+EtS|:

1. undergo metathesis of the first two segments.
2. the vowels becomes [−tense, +low].

Having established that the underlying forms for the first and second plural are |OmS| and |EtS|, we must reconsider the occurrence of these morphemes in the nonpreterite tenses. The representations for the present forms *dormons* /dɔrm'ɔ̃(z)/ and *dormez* /dɔrm'e(z)/ become respectively |dɔrm+OmS#| and |dɔrm+EtS#|. Stress is placed on the tense vowel of the person ending. In the first plural the |O| is nasalized by the following nasal consonant. The nasal consonant is deleted and the nasalized vowel is lowered. In the second plural the |t| needs to be deleted. Since there is not an intervening juncture between the |t| and following |S|, the |t| will not be deleted by the truncation rule. Therefore, a rule is required which, within the word, deletes a prefinal consonant.

Rule for prefinal consonant deletion

Before consonant plus word boundary (____C#) a consonant, that is, [+cons, −voc] segment, is deleted.

The rule for prefinal consonant deletion is not an *ad hoc* device for converting |EtS| to /e(z)/. This rule is independently required elsewhere in the phonology to account for forms such as *respect* /rεsp'ε/ 'respect.' The derivational form *respectable* /rεspεkt'abl(ə)/ 'respectable' shows that the underlying representation for *respect* is |rEspEkt#|. The |k| is deleted by the rule for prefinal consonant deletion and the |t|

by the rule for final consonant deletion. In |rEspEkt=Abl#| the |k| is not in the environment before C# and, hence, is not deleted. The plural *respects* is represented as |rEspEkt+S#|. The |t| is deleted by the truncation rule: |rEspEk+S#|. The |k| is now in prefinal position and will be deleted by the prefinal consonant deletion rule. The |S|, of course, is deleted by the rule for final consonant deletion. The example establishes the relative order of the three types of deletion rules.

One might maintain that the rule for prefinal consonant deletion is not really needed and that the rule for final consonant deletion should be reformulated to delete final consonant sequences as well as single final consonants. In this way, the final |tS| of |dɔrm+'EtS#| would be deleted by a single rule. This treatment of final clusters is not valid, however, for cases of liaison. In liaison forms the final consonant is retained (e.g., /dɔrm'ez/); however, the underlying prefinal |t| of |EtS| still has to be deleted. Prefinal consonant deletion must therefore be independent of final consonant deletion. This independence of prefinal consonant deletion is corroborated by the forms *sept* /s'ɛt/ 'seven,' *septante* /sɛpt'ãt(ə)/ 'seventy (Belgian, also Swiss),' *septimo* /sɛptim'o/ 'in seventh place.' The underlying representation for *sept* must be |sEpt#|. The prefinal consonant is deleted but not the final one.[16]

Derivations of the third and second plural preterites are shown in the accompanying table; the latter is contrasted with the present tense.

1. metathesis
2. stress placement
3. truncation
4. rhotacism
5. nasalization and lowering
6. schwa conversion
7. prefinal consonant deletion

	dormirent	*dormîtes*	*dormez*
	dɔrm+ I+S+unt#	dɔrm+ I+S+EtS#	dɔrm+ EtS#
1.	——	dɔrm+ I+S+tɛS#	——
2.	dɔrm+'I+S+unt#	dɔrm+'I+S+tɛS#	dɔrm+'EtS#
3.	——	dɔrm+'I +tɛS#	——
4.	dɔrm+'I+r +unt#	——	——
5.	dɔrm+'I+r +ɔ̃ t#	——	——
6.	dɔrm+'I+r +ə t#	dɔrm+'I +təS#	——
7.	——	——	dɔrm+'E S#
	/dɔrm'ir(ə)(t)/	/dɔrm'it(ə)(z)/	/dɔrm'e(z)/

Metathesis must precede stress placement since metathesis also causes the underlying vowel of the person marker to become lax; stress is then placed on the rightmost tense vowel (the thematic vowel). Rhotacism follows metathesis. In the second plural, *dormîtes*, the preterite |S| is initially intervocalic. This |S| cannot undergo rhotacism: metathesis destroys the intervocalic environment and the preterite |S| is subsequently deleted. Whereas in the underlying representation of the second plural the preterite |S| is followed by a vowel (an environment where consonant truncation does not take place), after metathesis has occurred the preterite marker is followed by a consonant and will therefore be truncated. Thus, there is mutual influence between the tense marker and the person ending; in the derived form the metathesized person ending is the overt remnant of this interaction.

Past subjunctive

je dormisse	/dɔrm'is(ə)/	nous dormissions	/dɔrmisj'ɔ̃(z)/
tu dormisses	/dɔrm'is(ə)/	vous dormissiez	/dɔrmisj'e(z)/
il dormît	/dɔrm'i(t)/	ils dormissent	/dɔrm'is(ə)(t)

Just as the conditional shows morphological features of the future and the imperfect, the past subjunctive resembles both the preterite and the subjunctive. Except for the third singular *dormît*, all other forms exhibit an /s/ (the past morpheme), followed by either /ə/ or /j/ (variants of the subjunctive). We shall therefore represent the past subjunctive in its underlying structure as a sequence of two morphemes: past aspect + subjunctive. The subjunctive morpheme is identical to that which is found in the present subjunctive, that is, lax |ɛ|. The past aspect marker overtly appears as a voiceless dental sibilant and one might suppose that the underlying marker is |s|.

The morpheme which indicates the preterite has also been represented as a dental sibilant, |S|, a segment unmarked for voicing, as we had no reason there to choose |s| or |z| since the segment is always deleted or rhotacized. In the past subjunctive the past marker is phonetically voiceless. Since the past subjunctive morphologically resembles the preterite, it would be attractive to set up a single morpheme for both, which would appear on the basis of the past subjunctive to be |s|. If |s| then becomes the past aspect marker occurring in both the preterite and past subjunctive, one would expect this morpheme to undergo the same treatment in identical environments, which, however, is not the case. In the third plural preterite rhotacism occurs (e.g., *dormirent*); in the past subjunctive forms intervocalic |s| is not rhotacized: *dormissent* /dɔrm'is(ə)(t)/. It is true that preterite and past subjunctive forms would have different underlying representations

(|dɔrm + I + s + unt# |and |dɔrm + I + s + ɛ + unt#| — the latter contains also the subjunctive morpheme) and one could maintain that rhotacism does not take place before | + ɛ| or occurs only before | + u|. However, any such restriction is completely *ad hoc* (note also that the choice of constraint is totally arbitrary), particularly since rhotacism is not a phenomenon uniquely associated with the verb paradigm.

To obviate this difficulty one might set up two variants of the past aspect morpheme — |z| and |s| — the latter occurring before the subjunctive marker. Then, only |z| would become rhotacized. This solution receives superficial support from other occurrences of rhotacism where /z/ alternates with /r/, e.g., *acquisition, acquérir* /akizisj'ɔ̃/, /aker'ir/, *chanteuse, chanteur* /ʃɑ̃t'øz(ə)/, /ʃɑ̃t'œr/. However, it cannot be shown conclusively that /z/ must actually occur here in the underlying representations since at a morpheme boundary intervocalic |s| always becomes /z/, e.g., *persister* /pɛrsist'e/ 'persist': *résister* /rezist'e/ 'resist.' Hence, if |s| is the mark of the past subjunctive, rhotacism is still not totally excluded, but even if it were, there is the further problem of |s| becoming voiced intervocalically at a morpheme boundary, which, of course, does not happen in the past subjunctive.

Using the voicing feature to distinguish the two variants of the past aspect morpheme does not receive support from within the phonological system of French. Yet the two variants need to be formally distinguished, and it is furthermore clear that sibilants must underlie both of them. Since voicing cannot be motivated as the distinguishing feature, another possible type of differentiation would be a single sibilant |s|, as against a geminate sibilant |ss|, the former occurring in the preterite, the latter in the past subjunctive: |dɔrm + I + s + unt#|, |dɔrm + I + ss + ɛ + unt#|. The single intervocalic | + s| would, of course, become rhotacized, whereas | + ss| would not be affected by the rhotacism rule or the rule which voices intervocalic sibilants. After these two rules had applied, the geminate cluster would be simplified.

Rule for degemination

C_1C_2 becomes C_1, where $C_1 = C_2$.

Setting up geminate consonants requires a rule which later degeminates them. However, the rule for degemination is independently required and is not formulated solely as a mechanism for undoing underlying gemination. Forms such as *illégal* /ileg'al/ 'illegal,' *irresponsable* /irɛspɔ̃s'abl(ə)/ 'irresponsible,' contain the underlying prefix *in-* (cf. *inoubliable* /inubli'abl(ə)/ 'unforgettable'): |In = lEg = Al#| |In = rEspOns = Abili#|. The |n| of *in-* is assimilated to the following consonantal segment; the resulting geminate is then simplified.

Is |+ss| as the past aspect marker in the past subjunctive simply an appeal to French spelling? In Section 3.3.2 we shall present additional supporting evidence for geminate clusters when we consider second conjugation verbs of the type *finir*, which contain the infix *-iss* in many of their forms. In order to account for the paradigmatic forms, |ss| must be recognized as the infix. In 3.3.1 we shall also show that in the first conjugation the difference between *arriva* (preterite) and *arrivât* (past subjunctive) depends on the presence or absence of a geminate. Forms such as *connaître* /kɔn'ε:tr(ə)/ 'know,' with a stressed long vowel (Section 2.3.2), can only be accounted for if the stem terminates in a geminate: |kɔn'Ɛss+r#|, where |+r| is the infinitival desinence. Dentals before |r| become stops: |kɔn'Ɛst+r#|. The stressed vowel becomes long (rule for vowel lengthening), due to the deletion of the postvocalic consonant (Section 2.3.2): /kɔn'ε:tr#/.

Derivations of imperfect subjunctives of the third singular and second plural, which are contrasted with the third plural preterite, are shown in the accompanying table. The past aspect marker is |s| for the preterite and |ss| for the past subjunctive. The latter is followed by the subjunctive marker |ε|. However, the third singular is defective; it does not exhibit in its underlying representation the subjunctive marker, that is to say, the expected *dormisse* does not occur.[17]

1. stress placement
2. yod formation
3. truncation
4. rhotacism
5. nasalization and lowering
6. schwa conversion
7. prefinal consonant deletion
8. degemination

	dormît	*dormissiez*	*dormirent*
	dɔrm+ I+ss+t#	dɔrm+I+ss+ε+ EtS#	dɔrm+ I+s+unt#
1.	dɔrm+'I+ss+t#	dɔrm+I+ss+ε+'EtS#	dɔrm+'I+s+unt#
2.	——	dɔrm+I+ss+j+'EtS#	——
3.	dɔrm+'I+s +t#	——	——
4.	——	——	dɔrm+'I+r+unt#
5.	——	——	dɔrm+'I+r+ɔ̃ t#
6.	——	——	dɔrm+'I+r+ə t#
7.	dɔrm+'I +t#	dɔrm+I+ss+j+'E S#	——
8.	——	dɔrm+I+s +j+'E S#	——
	/dɔrm'i(t)/	/dɔrmisj'e(z)/	/dɔrm'ir(ə)(t)/

Past participle

dormi /dɔrm'i/

The underlying representation for the past participle morpheme will be dealt with on pp. 105–110, as the choice of an ending is contingent on the analysis of irregular verbs. For the present, it suffices to note that the past participles of regular verbs are stressed on the thematic vowel.

3.2.4. *Summary*

The underlying representations for the person endings and the aspect markers are listed as follows:

Person endings	
first singular	|S|
second singular	|S|
third singular	|t|
first plural	|OmS|
second plural	|EtS|
third plural	|unt|
Aspect and tense markers	
Unmarked aspect	
present	unmarked
imperfect	|Ɛ|
subjunctive	|ε|
present participle	|Ant|
Future aspect	
future	|rA|
conditional	|rA + Ɛ|
infinitive	|r|
Past aspect	
preterite	|s|
past subjunctive	|ss + ε|

The singular person endings are represented as single consonants; the plural person endings have vowels as the initial segment. The tenses belonging to the unmarked aspect also have vowels as the initial segment except the present tense, which is unmarked. The three tenses of the future aspect begin with |r|; the two tenses of the past aspect with |s|.

The singular person markers are deleted whenever they follow a central vowel (/a/ or /ə/), so that in derived forms they do not appear in the present tense of first conjugation verbs (*arrive*), all subjunctive forms (*dorme*, *dormisse*), and third person singular future forms (*dormira*). In the first singular future the person ending |S| becomes |i| after the tense |A| of the future marker: |rA+i#|. Subsequently, |A+i| becomes /e/. Analogously, in the third plural future |rA+unt#| becomes |rO+nt#|. The |A| of the future aspect marker is truncated before the vowel of the first and second plural endings and throughout the conditional. The first and second plural endings undergo metathesis in the preterite, the only tense where they are preceded by a single consonant. The preterite |s| is subsequently truncated everywhere except in the third plural, where it is intervocalic and undergoes rhotacism. In the past subjunctive the past aspect marker |ss| is degeminated after rhotacism has taken place.

3.3 Thematic vowels

3.3.1. *First conjugation*

In 3.2.1 we showed that first conjugation present forms have a thematic vowel, which prevents truncation of the final stem consonant in the singular: |Ar'Iv+a+t#| → /ar'iv(ə)/. The second conjugation verb *dormir*, on the other hand, did not contain a thematic vowel; therefore, the stem final consonant was truncated before the consonant of the singular person ending: |d'ɔrm+t#| → /d'ɔr(t)/. However, throughout the future and past aspects, second conjugation forms have a thematic vowel, |I|: *dormiras*, *dormirais*, *dormir*, *dormis*, *dormisses*, *dormi*.

First conjugation verbs of the type *arriver* also exhibit a thematic vowel throughout the future and past aspects, although, unlike the second conjugation, the same vowel does not occur all through the paradigm.

future (second singular)	arriv*e*ras	/arivər'a/
conditional (second singular)	arriv*e*rais	/arivər'ɛ(z)/
infinitive	arriv*e*r	/ariv'e/
preterite (first singular)	arriv*ai*	/ariv'e/
preterite (second singular)	arriv*a*s	/ariv'a/
preterite (third plural)	arriv*è*rent	/ariv'ɛr(ə)(t)/
past subjunctive (second singular)	arriv*a*sses	/ariv'as(ə)/
past participle	arriv*é*	/ariv'e/

In these forms /a/, /ə/, /e/, /ɛ/ all occur as variants. In the infinitive, preterite, and some forms of the past subjunctive, stress falls on the thematic vowel, which means that for these forms the thematic vowel must be tense when the stress rule applies. If the first conjugation vowel is tense |A|, we can then account for all forms of the past subjunctive and all forms of the preterite, except the first singular and third plural.

1. stress placement
2. yod formation
3. truncation
4. nasalization and lowering
5. singular person deletion
6. degemination

	arrivas (preterite)	*arrivassions* (past subjunctive)
	ArIv+ A+s+S#	ArIv+A+ss+ɛ+ OmS#
1.	ArIv+ 'A+s+S#	ArIv+A+ss+ɛ+ 'OmS#
2.	——	ArIv+A+ss+j+ 'OmS#
3.	ArIv+ 'A +S#	——
4.	——	ArIv+A+ss+j+ 'ɔ̃ S#
5.	ArIv+ 'A #	——
6.	——	ArIv+A+s +j+ 'ɔ̃ S#
	/ariv'a/	/arivasj'ɔ̃(z)/

The first singular preterite *arrivai* /ariv'e/ terminates in a stressed mid front unrounded vowel. We have already noted this same ending for the first singular future, *dormirai,* where the underlying representation was |dɔrm+I+rA+S#|. The singular marker becomes |i| after tense |A|; the combination |A+i| subsequently is converted to /e/. Since the first conjugation thematic vowel is tense |A|, this vowel would be converted to /e/ in the first singular preterite if it, too, were immediately followed by the person ending. Yet in the preterite the thematic vowel and person ending are separated by the preterite marker |s| so that the underlying representation for *arrivai* is |ArIv+A+s+S#|. However, if the rule for first singular vocalization, which converts |A+S#| to |A+i#|, follows truncation, the appropriate environmental conditions will be met for the subsequent operation of the rule for first singular vocalization: |ArIv+ 'A+s+S#| → |ArIv+ 'A+S#| (truncation) → |ArIv+ 'A+i#| (first singular vocalization) → /ArIv+ 'e/ (e-conversion). The preterite *arrivai* provides, then, further motivation for the first singular vocalization rule. This rule was originally formulated to handle just the future. The same rule explains as well first person singular preterite forms of the first conjugation.

The third plural preterite, *arrivèrent* /ariv'ɛr(ə)(t)/, exhibits a stressed low front unrounded vowel. Whereas /a/ is phonetically the thematic vowel for most preterite forms (*arrivas*), /ɛ/ is the phonetic manifestation of the thematic vowel only in the third plural. Stressed /ɛ/, as we have shown, alternates with /a/ (e.g., *clair*, *clarté*). In order for a vowel to be fronted, it must be lax at the time the rule for vowel fronting is applied. If the thematic vowel were lax in the third plural, this would be the only preterite form with a lax thematic vowel since elsewhere in the preterite the thematic vowel must be tense |A|. Some statement is then required to account for this irregular behavior of the thematic vowel, that is, its being lax only in the third plural. But, in fact, this "irregularity" is only superficial since it can be demonstrated that in the underlying representation the thematic vowel for the third plural preterite must, in fact, be a tense vowel, just as it is a tense vowel for all other preterite forms. In the underlying representation of *arrivèrent*, a lax |a| is not even possible, that is, the underlying form cannot be |ArIv+a+s+unt#|: stress would not be placed on the thematic vowel as the stress rule assigns stress to the rightmost tense vowel (which would here be the |I| of the stem). Since the thematic vowel is stressed in the third plural preterite, the *underlying representation* of *arrivèrent* can only contain a tense vowel: |ArIv+A+s+unt#|, and only after the stress rule has applied does this vowel become lax so that it will subsequently be fronted. What is the environment which causes an underlying tense thematic vowel to become lax?

The third plural is the only preterite form where the tense marker |s| is followed by a vowel. In the other forms of the preterite the |s| is followed by a consonant, i.e., the person endings *-s*, *-s*, *-t*, *-mes*, *-tes*, the last two due to metathesis. Stating these facts somewhat differently, we can say that in the third plural the thematic |A| is followed by a single consonant — the preterite |s|; elsewhere, thematic |A| is followed by two consonants — preterite |s| plus the consonant of the person ending. The thematic vowel, then, becomes lax whenever it is followed by a single consonant.

Rule for thematic laxing

Before a single consonantal segment ([+cons]):
a [−high] thematic vowel becomes [−tense].

The rule must be restricted to nonhigh thematic vowels since the thematic vowel |I| of the second conjugation remains tense everywhere throughout the future and past aspects. We contrast the derivation of the third singular *arriva* with the third plural *arrivèrent.*

1. stress placement
2. thematic laxing
3. truncation
4. rhotacism
5. nasalization and lowering
6. vowel fronting
7. schwa conversion
8. singular person deletion

	arriva	*arrivèrent*
	ArIv+ A+s+t#	ArIv+ A+s+unt#
1.	ArIv+ 'A+s+t#	ArIv+ 'A+s+unt#
2.	——	ArIv+ 'a +s+unt#
3.	ArIv+ 'A +t#	——
4.	——	ArIv+ 'a +r+unt#
5.	——	ArIv+ 'a +r+ɔ̃ t#
6.	——	ArIv+ 'ɛ +r+ɔ̃ t#
7.	——	ArIv+ 'ɛ +r+ə t#
8.	ArIv+ 'A #	——
	/ariv'a/	/ariv'ɛr(ə)(t)/

Note that thematic laxing must *precede* truncation; otherwise, the thematic vowel in the third singular would be followed by a single consonant and would become lax.

The rule for thematic laxing also accounts for the phonetic manifestations of the thematic vowel in the future aspect forms. The infinitive *arriver* has the following underlying form: |ArIv+A+r#|. Stress is placed on the rightmost tense vowel: |ArIv+ 'A+r#|. The thematic vowel becomes lax as it precedes a single [+cons] segment: |ArIv+ 'a+r#|. The stressed lax vowel is fronted: ArIv+ 'ɛ+r#|. Final /ɛr/ is then converted to /e/: /ariv'e/ (cf. *étrangère*, *étranger;* see 1.2.4).

Since the underlying form of the first conjugation thematic vowel must be tense in the infinitive, if stress is to be correctly placed on the thematic vowel, one would expect that the thematic vowel in its underlying form should be tense everywhere throughout the future aspect. Although the future and conditional forms all show a schwa as the thematic vowel (*arriveras*), the schwa in these forms is attributable to the pretonic position of the laxed thematic vowel. The underlying representation for *arriveras* is |ArIv+A+rA+S#|. Stress is placed on the rightmost tense vowel: |ArIv+A+r'A+S#|. The thematic vowel becomes lax before the single consonantal segment: |ArIv+a+r'A+S#|. The lax thematic vowel is not fronted as it is not under stress; lax |a| in pretonic position is equivalent to schwa. The singular person marker is then deleted after the central vowel: /arivər'a/.

Thematic vowel laxing provides additional evidence for |ss| as the aspect marker of the past subjunctive. It is the double consonant which prevents the preceding thematic vowel from becoming lax and shifting to /ɛ/; hence, stressed /a/ appears throughout the past subjunctive: *arrivasse.* The geminate cluster also accounts for the presence or absence of a linking consonant in the third singulars past subjunctive and preterite.

1. stress placement
2. truncation
3. singular person deletion
4. prefinal consonant deletion

	arriva (preterite)	arrivât (past subjunctive)
	ArIv+ A+s+t#	ArIv+ A+ss+t#
1.	ArIv+'A+s+t#	ArIv+'A+ss+t#
2.	ArIv+'A +t#	ArIv+'A+s +t#
3.	ArIv+'A #	——
4.	——	ArIv+'A +t#
	/ariv'a/	/ariv'a(t)/

When the rule for singular person deletion applies, the person marker for *arrivât* is not immediately preceded by a central vowel. The |s| of the past aspect intervenes between the vowel and person marker, and it protects the person marker from deletion.[18]

For the first two conjugations the thematic vowel is tense |A| or |I| throughout the future and past aspects. The vowel must be tense as stress falls on the thematic vowel in many of the forms. After the stress rule has applied, the low vowel |A| of the first conjugation becomes lax whenever it is followed by a single consonantal segment. If stressed, the vowel is fronted to /ɛ/, otherwise it remains lax, that is, schwa. Whereas an originally tense thematic vowel appears throughout the future and past aspects, the unmarked aspect, that is, present, imperfect, subjunctive tenses and present participle, exhibits no thematic vowel for second conjugation forms but exhibits lax |a| as the first conjugation thematic vowel. It is the absence of a thematic vowel in the second conjugation which accounts for the truncation of the stem final consonant in the present singular, |d'ɔrm+t#| → /d'ɔr+t#/, and it is the presence of a thematic vowel in the first conjugation which protects the stem consonant from deletion (|Ar'Iv+a+t#|). The thematic vowel must be initially lax if stress is to fall on the stem vowel. To sum up, we can say that, for forms of the unmarked aspect, the thematic vowel is either lax or absent; for the future and past aspects, the thematic vowel is always initially tense.[19]

3.3.2. *Second conjugation, type -iss*

There are two types of second conjugation verbs: those like *dormir* 'sleep' and those like *finir* 'finish.'

dormir	*finir*	
dors	finis	/fin'i(z)/
dormons	finissons	/finis'ɔ̃(z)/
dormais	finissais	/finis'ɛ(z)/
dormes	finisses	/fin'is(ə)/
dormant	finissant	/finis'ã(t)/
dormiras	finiras	/finir'a/
dormirais	finirais	/finir'ɛ(z)/
dormir	finir	/fin'ir/
dormis	finis	/fin'i(z)/
dormisses	finisses	/fin'is(ə)/
dormi	fini	/fin'i/

The *finir* type verb is conjugated exactly like *dormir* throughout the future and past aspects; that is, the thematic vowel is tense |I|. In the tenses which comprise the unmarked aspect, the *finir* type verbs — unlike the *dormir* type — also have the thematic vowel. In addition, there is an infix marker |ss| which appears between the thematic vowel and the following tense marker or person ending. Derivations of the second singular of the present and imperfect tenses are shown in the accompanying table.

1. stress placement
2. truncation
3. prefinal consonant deletion
4. degemination

	finis	*finissais*
	fIn+ I+ss+S#	fIn+I+ss+ Ɛ+S#
1.	fIn+'I+ss+S#	fIn+I+ss+'Ɛ+S#
2.	fIn+'I+s +S#	——
3.	fIn+'I +S#	——
4.	——	fIn+I+s +'Ɛ+S#
	/fin'i(z)/	/finis'ɛ(z)/

The infix marker must be |ss| since rhotacism does not take place when the marker is intervocalic: *finissais*. Additional justification for an infix |ss|, as well as for geminates in general within the verb paradigm, can be shown by contrasting the second plural present and preterite.

1. metathesis
2. stress placement
3. truncation
4. schwa conversion
5. prefinal consonant deletion
6. degemination

	finissez	*finîtes*
	fIn+I+ss+ EtS#	fIn+ I+s+EtS#
1.	——	fIn+ I+s+ tɛS#
2.	fIn+I+ss+ 'EtS#	fIn+ 'I+s+ tɛS#
3.	——	fIn+ 'I + tɛS#
4.	——	fIn+ 'I + təS#
5.	fIn+I+ss+ 'E S#	——
6.	fIn+I+s + 'E S#	——
	/finis'e(z)/	/fin'it(ə)(z)/

In the present (*finissez*) the person marker |EtS| is preceded by the infix |ss|; in the preterite (*finîtes*) the person marker is preceded by preterite |s|. Metathesis takes place after the preterite marker but not after the infix. In other words, metathesis occurs only when the person ending follows a single consonant morpheme.

3.3.3. *Third conjugation*

Third conjugation, type -oir

devoir

dois	/dw'a(z)/
devez	/dəv'e(z)/
devais	/dəv'ɛ(z)/
doives	/dw'av(ə)/
deviez	/dəvj'e(z)/
devras	/dəvr'a/
devrais	/dəvr'ɛ(z)/
devoir	/dəvw'ar/
dus	/d'y(z)/
dusses	/d'ys(ə)/
dû	/d'y/

The past aspect forms are irregular and will be considered elsewhere. The forms of the unmarked aspect are conjugated like *dormir* type verbs, that is, there is no thematic vowel. The underlying stem |dev| contains a lax vowel, which becomes /wa/ when stressed (*dois, doives*); in pretonic position it undergoes pretonic adjustment (pp. 24–27) and is converted to schwa (*devais*).

The infinitive *devoir* /dəvw'ar/ terminates in stressed /wa/, which can only be the manifestation of a thematic vowel. In general, stressed /wa/ is derived from an underlying lax |e|. However, if stress is to be placed on the thematic vowel, it must be tense, that is |E|, when the stress rule applies; only subsequently does the thematic vowel become lax. In the first conjugation the same phenomenon occurred: |ArIv+ 'A+r#| → |ArIv+ 'a+r#| (thematic vowel laxing) → |ArIv+ 'ε+r#| (vowel fronting) → /ariv'e/. The rule for thematic vowel laxing causes a nonhigh thematic vowel to become *lax* when it precedes a single consonantal segment. Therefore, if tense |E| is the underlying thematic vowel, existent rules will automatically account for the appropriate form of the infinitive. Stress will be correctly assigned to the underlying tense thematic vowel: |dev+ 'E+r#|. The rule for thematic laxing then applies: |dev+ 'e+r#|. The vowel shift rules subsequently convert stressed |e| to /we/, then /wa/, and pretonic |e| to schwa: /dəvw'ar/.

The future and conditional forms, *devras* /dəvr'a/ — unlike the infinitive *devoir* — do not exhibit any phonetic manifestation of a thematic vowel. Since a thematic vowel is present in the future and conditional of first and second conjugation verbs (*arriveras*, *dormiras*), structural parallelism would lead us to suspect that a thematic vowel should also occur *in underlying forms* of the third conjugation as well. In fact, a thematic vowel is indispensable if one is to account for these future and conditional forms. If no thematic vowel were present, that is, if the underlying representation for *devras* were |dev+rA+S#|, the truncation rule would delete the stem final consonant |v| since this consonant is followed by a juncture and a consonantal segment. Therefore, when the truncation rule applies, a vowel must intervene between the stem and the future marker. This vowel could only be the thematic vowel, which is then deleted after the truncation rule has been applied. As we have established that the thematic vowel is |E| for *-oir* type verbs, the underlying representation for *devras* must be |dev+E+rA+S#|. Stress is placed on the rightmost tense vowel — the vowel of the future marker: |dev+E+r'A+S#|. A nonhigh thematic vowel becomes lax before a single consonantal segment /dev+e+r'A+S#/. Truncation does not apply. A rule is needed to delete the lax pretonic thematic vowel. On pp. 31–32 we showed that posttonic nonlow vowels are obligatorily deleted (e.g., the suffix |'Abili| → /'Abl/). Lax low vowels, on the other hand, are converted to schwa. If we allow the rule for nonlow vowel deletion to apply to pretonic vowels as well to posttonic ones — thus extending the rule to all atonic vowels — the lax nonlow thematic |e| would be deleted. Nonlow vowel deletion takes place after the rule for pretonic adjustment, which converts the *lax stem vowel* to lax |ε| which subsequently becomes schwa since it is a low vowel: |dev+e+r'A+S#| → |dεv+e+r'A+S#| (pretonic adjustment) → |dεv+r'A+S#| (nonlow vowel deletion) → /dəv+r'A+

S#/ (schwa conversion). Note that pretonic adjustment applies to stem vowels but not to the thematic vowel.

In 2.1.1 we showed that lax |e| and |ɛ| underlie the diphthongs /wa/ and /jɛ/. That |e| was the source of /wa/ and |ɛ| of /jɛ/ — rather than the converse — was taken primarily on faith. Third conjugation verbs in *-oir* corroborate this original assumption. If the source of /wa/ were the lax low vowel |ɛ|, then this vowel would not be deleted in pretonic position as low vowels are always converted to schwa. Since the thematic vowel for *-oir* verbs is deleted in the future and conditional, where it is atonic, the vowel could only be a nonlow vowel: |e|.

Third conjugation, type -re

perdre 'lose'

perds	/p'ɛr(z)/
perdez	/pɛrd'e(z)/
perdais	/pɛrd'ɛ(z)/
perdes	/p'ɛrd(ə)/
perdant	/pɛrd'ã(t)/
perdras	/pɛrdr'a/
perdrais	/pɛrdr'ɛ(z)/
perdre	/p'ɛrdr(ə)/
perdis	/pɛrd'i(z)/
perdisses	/pɛrd'is(ə)/
perdu	/pɛrd'y/

The forms of the unmarked aspect have no thematic vowel. The absence of a thematic vowel accounts for the deletion of the stem final consonant throughout the present singular: |pɛrd+S#| → /pɛr+S#/.

The infinitive *perdre* /p'ɛrdr(ə)/ differs from the infinitives of the other conjugation classes (*arriver*, *dormir*, *finir*, *devoir*) in several important respects: (1) there is no phonetic manifestation of an underlying thematic vowel; (2) the stress falls on the vowel of the stem; (3) the infinitive /r/ is followed by a schwa. The final schwa is due to the rule for schwa insertion which adds an epenthetic schwa after a consonant-liquid cluster. If the underlying representation of *perdre* were |pɛrd+r#|, the stem final |d| would be truncated before the following consonantal segment. Therefore, there must be an intervening thematic vowel to protect the stem final consonant from deletion. Furthermore, this vowel has to be lax so that stress is placed on the vowel of the

Devoir, *Perdre*, *Devra*, *Perdra*

1. stress placement
2. thematic laxing
3. vowel shifts
4. nonlow vowel deletion
5. singular person deletion
6. schwa insertion

	devoir	*perdre*	*devra*	*perdra*
	dev+ E+r#	p ɛrd+e+r#	dev+E+r A+t#	pɛrd+e+r A+t#
1.	dev+ 'E+r#	p'ɛrd+e+r#	dev+E+r'A+t#	pɛrd+e+r'A+t#
2.	dev+ 'e+r#	——	dev+e+r'A+t#	——
3.	dəv+w'a+r#	——	dəv+e+r'A+t#	——
4.	——	p'ɛrd +r#	dəv +r'A+t#	pɛrd +r'A+t#
5.	——	——	dəv +r'A #	pɛrd +r'A #
6.	——	p'ɛrd +rə#	——	——
	/dəvw'ar/	/p'ɛrdr(ə)/	/dəvr'a/	/pɛrdr'a/

stem. Finally, the thematic vowel must also be nonlow so that it will be deleted by the rule for nonlow vowel deletion.

Third conjugation verbs in *-oir* and *-re* are morphologically similar in many respects. Since the underlying thematic vowel for the *-oir* forms is tense |E|, the logical vowel for the related *-re* forms would be lax |e|. The vowels would differ only in tenseness. The morphological similarity existing between *-oir* and *-re* verbs is then reflected in the phonological similarity of the thematic vowels. To illustrate these resemblances we give on page 102 derivations of the infinitives and third singular future of *-oir* and *-re* type third conjugation verbs.

The thematic vowel of *-re* type verbs appears as /i/ throughout the preterite and past subjunctive (*perdis*, *perdisses*) and as /y/ in the past participle (*perdu*). The raising of the mid thematic vowel is discussed on pp. 108–109.

All verbs of the three principal conjugations have thematic vowels in at least some of their forms. The accompanying table summarizes the occurrence of thematic vowels.

Conjugation		*Unmarked Aspect*	*Marked Aspects*
I	*-er* type (arriver)	|a|	|A|
II	*-ir* type (dormir)	——	|I|
	-ir type with *-iss* (finir)	|I+ss|	|I|
III	*-oir* type (devoir)	——	|E|
	-re type (perdre)	——	|e|

Weak and strong verbs. Within the past aspect of the third conjugation it is necessary to distinguish between weak and strong stems. Weak verbs are stressed on the thematic vowel, whereas strong verbs exhibit no thematic vowel and are instead stressed on the vowel of the stem. Therefore, what will characterize strong forms is that they never have a thematic vowel in their underlying representations. The first and second conjugations contain only weak stems.

Conjugation		*Preterite (second singular)*	*Past participle*
I	(weak)	arriv*as*	arriv*é*
II	(weak)	dorm*is*	dorm*i*
II	-*iss* (weak)	fin*is*	fin*i*
III	-*re*	perd*is* (weak)	perd*u* (weak)
		peign*is* (weak)	p*ei*nt (strong)
		écriv*is* (weak)	écr*i*t (strong)
		f*is* (strong)	f*ai*t (strong)
		m*is* (strong)	m*is* (strong)
		l*us* (strong)	l*u* (strong)
III	-*oir*	voul*us* (weak)	voul*u* (weak)
		ass*is* (strong)	ass*is* (strong)
		d*us* (strong)	d*û* (strong)

In the finite forms (preterite and past subjunctive) of strong verbs the stressed vowel is always /i/ or /y/. Therefore, no matter what the original quality of the stem vowel is, in strong forms the stem vowel is raised to one of these two high vowels. For stems that terminate in /v/ one can predict that the strong vowel will be /y/: *devoir*, *dus; savoir*, *sus; pouvoir*, *pus; mouvoir*, *mus; pleuvoir*, *plut; boire*, *boivent*, *bus; recevoir*, *reçus; avoir*, *eus*. For the remaining dozen or so strong preterites there do not appear to be any obvious phonological criteria for determining which verbs have /i/ and which have /y/. For these stems it is necessary to mark in the lexicon which high vowel a given stem vowel is converted to.[20]

Rule for high vowel raising

In the past aspect:

the vowel of a strong stem becomes $\begin{bmatrix} +\text{tense} \\ +\text{high} \end{bmatrix}$ and

a. [+front] for stems marked [+front]

b. [−front] for stems marked [−front] and for stems which terminate in |v|.

This rule converts the stem vowel to either |I| or |U|; |U| is subsequently fronted to /y/. (See pp. 35–36.)

Derivations of *fis* and *dus* are shown in the accompanying table. The verb *faire* is marked as taking the [+front] strong vowel; *devoir*, on the other hand, takes the [−front] strong vowel, since the stem terminates in |v|. The underlying form of the stem for *faire* is |faz| (cf. *faire*, *fais*, which result from vowel fronting); the underlying stem for *devoir* is, of course, |dev|.

1. high vowel raising
2. stress placement
3. truncation
4. vowel fronting

	fis	*dus*
	faz+s+S#	dev+s+S#
1.	f Iz+s+S#	d Uv+s+S#
2.	f'Iz+s+S#	d'Uv+s+S#
3.	f'I +S#	d'U +S#
4.	——	d'y +S#
	/f'i(z)/	/d'y(z)/

In underlying representations strong stems *never* are followed by a thematic vowel; the stem is followed directly by the preterite marker |s| and the second singular ending |S|. It is the absence of a thematic vowel which allows stress to be placed on the raised stem vowel and which explains the truncation of the stem final consonant — there is no intervening thematic vowel between this consonant and the consonant of the following preterite marker.

The strong forms of the past participle have much in common with the strong preterites and past subjunctives. There are nonetheless certain characteristics peculiar to strong past participles. Whereas strong preterites only have /i/ or /y/ as the stressed vowel (*pris*, *dus*, *fis*), strong past participles, on the other hand, may show some other vowel (*pris*, *dû*, *fait*). There are additional phonological phenomena associated with the particular past participle vowel. If the strong vowel is /i/, there is generally a following sibilant (*pris*, *mis;* cf. the feminine *prise* /priz(ə)/, *mise* /m'iz(ə)/); if the strong vowel is /y/, there is no following consonant (*dû*, *lu*); whenever the strong vowel is neither /i/ nor /y/, the participle terminates in /t/ (*fait*, *peint;* cf. the feminine *faite* /f'ɛt(ə)/, *peinte* /p'ɛ̃t(ə)/).[21]

If the underlying form of the past participle were |t|, we could easily account for those strong past participles which are like *fait*. The underlying representation would be |faz+t#|. As this is a strong past participle, there is no thematic vowel. Stress is placed on the stem vowel: |f'az+t#|. The final stem consonant is truncated before the past participle |t|: /f'a+t#/. The stressed lax vowel is fronted: /f'ɛ(t)/. Other past participles like *fait* are: *dit* 'said,' *cuit* 'cooked,' *écrit* 'written,' *confit* 'preserved,' *peint* 'painted,' *joint* 'joined,' *frit* 'fried.'

For those strong past participles which terminate in a sibilant (*pris*, *mis*), if the underlying marker of the past participle is |t|, then a rule is required to convert |t| to /s/. However, such a rule is independently needed in the grammar in order to account for alternations such as *diplomate*, *diplomatie* /diplɔm'at(ə)/, /diplɔmas'i/ 'diplomatic, diplomacy'; *aviateur*, *aviation* /avjat'œr/ /avjasj'õ/ 'aviator,' 'aviation.' That is, |t| becomes /s/ whenever it is followed by /i/ (or /j/ which is derived from |i|).[22]

Rule for assibilation

Before a $\begin{bmatrix} +\text{high} \\ +\text{front} \end{bmatrix}$ vowel

|t| becomes /s/

If the assibilation rule is to account for the past participles in *s* by converting the underlying past participle marker |t| to a sibilant, then the |t| must be followed by a high front vowel since this is the crucial environment for assibilation. That is, the underlying form of the past participle should be |ti|; after assibilation has taken place, the lax |i| is deleted by the rule for nonlow vowel deletion.

1. high vowel raising
2. stress placement
3. truncation
4. assibilation
5. nonlow vowel deletion

pris (past participle)
pr Ɛn + ti#

1. pr In + ti#
2. pr 'In + ti#
3. pr 'I + ti#
4. pr 'I + si#
5. pr 'I + s #

/pr 'i(z)/

If the past participle ending is |ti| for all verbs, assibilation would also occur for forms such as *fait*, *écrit*, etc. Therefore, some constraint needs to be imposed on assibilation. However, if the past participle vowel were not |i|, but some other vowel — say, a mid vowel — then the |t| would, of course, not be converted to /s/. The mid vowel would still be deleted since it is a nonlow vowel. But then, if it is a mid vowel which follows the past participle |t|, assibilation should not occur either in forms such as *pris*, unless there were a means for converting the mid vowel of the past participle to |i| for forms like *pris* but not for other strong past participles.

Strong past participles which terminate in *s* have a high front stem vowel — the stems belong to the class marked for the [+front] variant when the rule for high vowel raising applies, e.g., |prƐn| → |prIn|. If the rule for raising and fronting the stem vowel also raises and fronts the past participle vowel whenever the past participle is concatenated with a stem which undergoes vowel raising, then, in the past participle ending the high front vowel |i| will appear only in those forms where it is needed for assibilation, that is, |i| occurs only when there is a preceding raised front stem vowel. One can think of this as a type of vowel harmony; except for tenseness, the past participle vowel agrees in quality with the preceding raised stem vowel.

Strong past participles in *u* (for example, *dû*) do not exhibit a final consonant segment. The /y/ which appears in strong past participles is due to high vowel raising (|dev| → |dUv|). Although a past participle consonant does not appear in the output, nonetheless the past participle |t| must be present in the underlying representation since it is this consonant which is responsible for the truncation of the stem final consonant; that is, there is no way to account for |dUv| becoming |dU| unless the stem final |v| is followed by a juncture and consonantal segment. For past participles in *u*, then, both the |t| and following vowel of the underlying past participle ending must be deleted at the phonetic level, but only after the truncation rule has applied. For those strong participles (like *pris*) where the stem vowel is raised to |I|, we also raised the past participle vowel to |i| so that the preceding |t| would undergo assibilation. If we were to treat the *u* participles analogously, that is, harmonize the past participle vowel to the preceding raised stem vowel, then the past participle vowel would become |u| whenever the preceding stem vowel is raised to |U|: |d'Uv+tu#|. The truncation rule is then applied: |d'U+tu#|. A rule is still needed to delete the |t|. Let us say that |t| is deleted whenever it precedes the lax vowel |u|: |d'U+u#|. Tense |U| then undergoes vowel fronting and posttonic lax |u| is deleted: /d'y/.

Rule for t-deletion

In past participles:

|t| is deleted before lax |u|.

In strong verbs the past participle morpheme undergoes different treatment depending on the type of phonological process affecting the underlying vowel of the stem. Whenever this vowel is raised to |I|, the |t| of the past participle marker is converted to /s/. If the stem vowel, however, is raised to |U|, then the past participle |t| is deleted. Only when the stem vowel remains unchanged is the |t| of the past participle retained. An underlying |t| is indispensable in all cases, since a consonantal segment is needed in order to delete the preceding stem final consonant. The conversion of |t| to /s/, when followed by |i|, is independently motivated by instances of assibilation which are to be found elsewhere in the language. However, the deletion of |t|, when followed by |u|, does not gain any general support from within French phonology. Hence, the rule for t-deletion is to a large extent an *ad hoc* means to account for the shape of particular past participles.

Note that it would not resolve the problem if one were to postulate a zero allomorph for those past participles, which, like *dû*, do not terminate in a consonant, since one would then need some *ad hoc* rule to account for the deletion of the stem final consonant (|dUv → |dU|). This particular proposal, then, requires one to set up a zero allomorph of the past participle for certain stems and to formulate a special rule for deleting stem final consonants. On the other hand, by postulating a consistent underlying representation for the past participle morpheme, the deletion of the stem final consonant is an automatic consequence of a general rule — the truncation rule — provided, of course, that this rule precedes the rule for t-deletion. Although a special deletion rule, i.e., the rule for t-deletion, is needed, it is not necessary in addition to postulate different representations for the past participle morpheme. This solution is therefore preferable to the other alternative suggested. Although the rule for t-deletion is to a large extent arbitrary, nonetheless it is not totally *ad hoc* since a rule which deletes a consonant before |u| serves to explain two marginal forms — the third plural presents *ont* 'have' and *font* 'do.'[23]

Whereas strong past participles are stressed on the stem vowel, weak past participles, on the other hand, are stressed on the thematic vowel (*arrivé*, *dormi*, *perdu*). For these participles the final vowel is not followed by a consonant; if in the underlying forms the past participle vowel is also raised to |u| whenever there is a preceding thematic vowel, then the underlying |t| of the past participle would be appropriately deleted by the rule for t-deletion: |dɔrm + 'I + tu#| → |d'ɔrm + 'I + u#| (rule for t-deletion) → /dɔrm'i/ (nonlow vowel deletion).

In all cases, the underlying form of the past participle morpheme is |t| followed by a mid vowel, that is, either |te| or |to| is a possible representation. For strong verbs, if the stem vowel has been raised, then the mid vowel of the past participle is also raised, and furthermore agrees in frontness with the stem vowel so that |ti| results whenever the stem vowel has been raised to |I| and |tu| occurs whenever the stem vowel has been raised to |U|. Since, for *weak* verbs, the underlying mid vowel of the past participle ending *does not harmonize* with the preceding vowel, but is *always* raised to |u|, this phenomenon in weak verbs permits us to choose lax |o| rather than |e| as the underlying mid vowel for the past participle. That is, if the underlying form of the past participle is |to|, it is necessary to change only one feature, i.e., [−high] becomes [+high], to convert |to| to |tu| whenever there is a preceding thematic vowel.[24]

First conjugation past participles have derivations analogous to those of second conjugation forms: |ArIv+ 'A+to#| → |ArIv+ 'A+tu#| (raising of past participle vowel after a thematic vowel). Note that the thematic vowel must be tense in order for stress to be placed correctly. Nonhigh thematic vowels become lax before a single consonantal segment: |ArIv+ 'a+tu#|. The |t| and |u| are subsequently deleted and the stressed lax |a| is shifted to /ɛ/: /arIv+ 'ɛ#/. Stressed |ɛ| in a final open syllable is raised to /e/: /ariv'e/. First conjugation forms in fact corroborate an underlying past participle |t| for weak verbs as well as strong ones. In the first conjugation the thematic vowel initially has to be a tense vowel for proper stress placement. In order for vowel fronting to take place, however, the stressed thematic vowel *must be made lax* and we have presented sufficient evidence showing that thematic laxing only takes place before a single consonantal segment.

In the third conjugation the phonetic manifestation of the thematic vowel is /i/ in the preterite and past subjunctive and /y/ in the past participle (*perdis*, *perdisses*, *perdu*). On pp. 99 through 103, we showed that the underlying form of the thematic vowel is |e| for *-re* verbs and |E| for *-oir* verbs. Therefore, in the past aspect the thematic vowel must be raised and made tense. In fact, in the past aspect the thematic vowel of third conjugation weak verbs behaves precisely like the stem vowel of many third conjugation strong verbs since in both cases the stressed vowel is /i/ or /y/. In order to reflect this similarity the rule for high vowel raising can be generalized to apply to weak verbs as well as to strong verbs, to thematic vowels as well as to stem vowels.

The rule for high vowel raising will then account for diverse phenomena observable in past aspect forms. In the finite forms (preterite and past subjunctive) the stem vowel of strong verbs is raised to either |I| or |U|. The particular raised vowel which occurs must be indicated for each strong stem, unless the stem terminates in |v|, in which case the raised vowel must be |U|. The thematic vowels of third conjugation weak verbs — |e| and |E| — are raised to |I|. In the past participle the stem vowel of *strong* verbs may also be raised to either |I| or |U|. However, for third conjugation *weak* verbs the thematic vowel is always raised to |U|. For *weak* verbs of *all* conjugations the final mid vowel of the past participle ending is raised to |u| after any thematic vowel; for strong verbs the past participle vowel harmonizes with a preceding raised stem vowel. If the past participle vowel has been raised to |i|, the preceding |t| becomes /s/ (e.g., *pris*), whereas, if the participle vowel has been raised to |u|, the preceding |t| is deleted (e.g., *dû*). Whenever the past participle vowel is not raised, the |t| is retained (e.g., *fait*). For all verbs the atonic nonlow participle vowel is ultimately deleted.

Rule for high vowel raising (revised)

In the past aspect a vowel becomes [+high] and :

a. [+tense] if it is:
  i a mid thematic vowel
  ii a stem vowel marked for raising

b. [+front] if it is:
  i a mid thematic vowel in finite forms
  ii a stem vowel marked [+front]
  iii a past participle vowel and the stem vowel is marked [+front]

c. [−front] if it is:
  i a mid thematic vowel in the past participle
  ii a stem vowel marked [−front] or the stem terminates in |v|
  iii a past participle vowel and:
    (a) the stem is marked [−front]
    (b) any thematic vowel precedes.

Examples of vowel raising follow:

*b*i |pɛrd+e+s+S#| → |pɛrd+I+s+S#| (*perdis*)
*b*ii |faz+s+S#| → |fIz+s+S#| (*fis*)
*b*iii |prƐn+to#| → |prIn+ti#| (*pris*)
*c*i |pɛrd+e+to#| → |pɛrd+U+to#| (*perdu*)
*c*ii |dev+s+S#| → |dUv+s+S#| (*dus*)
*c*iii (a) |dev+to#| → |dUv+tu#| (*dû*)
*c*iii (b) |ArIv+A+to#| → |ArIv+A+tu#| (*arrivé*), |pɛrd+U+to#| (see *c*i) → |pɛrd+U+tu#| (*perdu*).

Derivations of various past participles are shown in the accompanying table.

1. high vowel raising
2. stress placement
3. truncation
4. assibilation
5. t-deletion
6. vowel fronting
7. nonlow vowel deletion

	fini	*perdu*	*fait*	*pris*	*dû*
	fIn+ I+to#	pɛrd+ e +to#	f az+to#	pr Ɛn+to#	d ev+to#
1.	fIn+ I+tu#	pɛrd+ U+tu#	——	pr In+ti#	d Uv+tu#
2.	fIn+'I+tu#	pɛrd+'U+tu#	f'az+to#	pr'In+ti#	d'Uv+tu#
3.	——	——	f'a +to#	pr'I +ti#	d'U +tu#
4.	——	——	——	pr'I +si#	——
5.	fIn+'I+ u#	pɛrd+'U+ u#	——	——	d'U + u#
6.	——	pɛrd+'y + u#	f'ɛ +to#	——	d'y + u#
7.	fIn+'I #	pɛrd+'y #	f'ɛ +t #	pr'I +s #	d'y #
	/fin'i/	/pɛrd'y/	/f'ɛ(t)/	/pr'i(z)/	/d'y/

Once it is recognized that the underlying form of the past participle is |to|, a phonological explanation becomes possible for the similarities observed in past aspect forms (*dus, dusses, dû*). All past aspect morphemes begin with a dental consonant: preterite |s|, past subjunctive |ss+ɛ|, past participle |to|. The particularly intimate relationship between the finite forms (preterite and past subjunctive) is due to the initial sibilant of the tense marker.

It is the phonological shape of the tense markers which also explains similarities observable within the future aspect and within the unmarked aspect. The tense markers of the future aspect (*devras, devrais, dévoir*) all begin with the liquid |r|: future |rA|, conditional |rA+Ɛ|, infinitive |r|. Similar phonological processes which take place in the finite forms (future and conditional) result from the fact that these forms all contain an underlying |rA|. Whereas past aspect markers begin with a consonant and future aspect markers begin with a liquid, the tenses of the unmarked aspect (*dois, devais, doives, devant*) begin with a vowel or, in the case of the present, the tense is unmarked: |Ɛ| imperfect, |ɛ| subjunctive, |Ant| present participle.

3.4 Some irregular verbs[25]

3.4.1. *Vivre versus écrire*

We have shown that strong verbs in the past aspect do not contain a thematic vowel in their underlying representations. In this way, the past participle forms of *fini* and *écrit* can be explained.

1. high vowel raising
2. stress placement
3. truncation
4. t-deletion
5. nonlow vowel deletion

	fini	*écrit*
	fIn+ I+to#	Ekr Iv+to#
1.	fIn+ I+tu#	——
2.	fIn+ 'I+tu#	Ekr'Iv+to#
3.	——	Ekr'I +to#
4.	fIn+ 'I+ u#	——
5.	fIn+ 'I #	Ekr'I +t #
	/fin'i/	/ekr'i(t)/

The vowel of the past participle is raised to |u| after a thematic vowel. Since no thematic vowel is present in the underlying representation of *écrit* (nor is the stem vowel raised; it is originally a high vowel), the past participle vowel is not raised. As there is no thematic vowel, the underlying stem final consonant |v| is truncated before the past participle |t|. Since the past participle vowel has not been raised in *écrit*, the |t| will not be deleted; t-deletion takes place only before |u|.

Irregularities in other verb tenses can also often be explained as absence of the thematic vowel. The verbs *vivre* 'live' and *écrire* 'write' are conjugated identically in the tenses of the unmarked aspect: *vivons*, *écrivons*, etc. The underlying stems must therefore be |vIv| and |EkrIv|.[26] However, in the future aspect the conjugations differ.

vivras	écriras
vivrais	écrirais
vivre	écrire

Ecrire has lost its stem final consonant. Since both verbs belong to the third conjugation (type *-re*), the thematic vowel is |e|. If the thematic vowel, however, is absent for *écrire*, we can account for the difference in the forms.[27]

1. stress placement
2. truncation
3. nonlow vowel deletion

	vivre	*écrire*
	v Iv+e+r#	Ekr Iv+r#
1.	v'Iv+e+r#	Ekr'Iv+r#
2.	——	Ekr'I +r#
3.	v'Iv +r#	——
	/v'ivr(ə)/	/ekr'ir(ə)/

The infinitives *vivre* and *écrire* both terminate in schwa. In the case of *vivre*, the schwa is inserted as a supporting vowel after the consonant-liquid cluster (cf. *table*). Schwa insertion must occur after the nonlow thematic vowel has been deleted; before vowel deletion the consonant and liquid are not contiguous. If schwa insertion takes place after all the other rules have applied, there is no way to account for the final schwa of *écrire*, where the infinitive *r* is not preceded by a consonant. However, in the underlying form of écrire |EkrIv+r#|, the |r| is preceded by the stem consonant. This suggests that perhaps schwa insertion is an early rule, but then |vIv+e+r#| would no longer receive a supporting schwa since the |r| here is preceded by a vowel. No matter which order is adopted, we can only explain one of the forms to the exclusion of the other. This cul-de-sac is reached only if one goes on the assumption that all the phonological rules must be strictly ordered relative to one another. Our example indicates that this may not necessarily be so, and that some rules perhaps are not rigidly ordered, but instead apply at any point in the derivation providing the appropriate environmental conditions are met. Setting this problem in the context of our French example, we claim that there is a phonological constraint in French which does not permit final consonant-liquid clusters and that, whenever this combination occurs — whether as an underlying form or as a subsequently derived form, a supporting vowel must be inserted at the moment the cluster first appears. Therefore, *écrire* receives its final schwa before truncation takes place, when the representation is still /EkrIv+r#/, whereas *vivre* from underlying /vIv+e+r#/ receives its schwa relatively late, after the nonlow thematic vowel has dropped.[28]

3.4.2. *Croire versus voir*

Since *croire* 'believe' terminates in /r(ə)/, the supporting schwa must be due to a consonant-liquid cluster. If the stem terminated in a consonant, there would be a logical explanation for a consonant-liquid cluster, but nowhere, throughout the conjugation of *croire*, does a stem final consonant appear phonetically, for example, *croit*, *croyons*, *cru.*[29] In learned derivation, however, a stem final consonant is found —

crédibilité /kredibilit'e/ 'credibility'—so that the underlying stem would seem to be |kred| and the infinitive would be |kr'ed+r#| after stress had been applied. A schwa is then inserted after the consonant-liquid cluster: /kr'ed+rə#/. The truncation rule deletes the final stem consonant /kr'e+rə#/. The stressed lax stem vowel is diphthongized: /krw'ar(ə)/. If the underlying stem is |kred|, one would expect the |d| to show up phonetically whenever the stem is followed by a vowel, but *croidez* or *credez* do not exist; one finds instead *croyez* /krwaj'e(z)/. In the paradigm the |d| is always deleted, even when intervocalic. If one examines third conjugation verbs, one notes that, phonetically, stems do not terminate in a stop preceded by a vowel, only in consonant clusters or a single liquid, nasal, or continuant.[30] There is no obvious phonological reason why single stops ought to be excluded from underlying representations. Their phonetic nonoccurrence is rather a special fact about the third conjugation (and nonlearned derivational forms like *croyable* based on verbs of this conjugation), namely, that in the third conjugation intervocalic stops are always deleted. Other third conjugation verbs with stems which must terminate in |d| include: *voir* 'see,' *asseoir* 'sit,' *surseoir* 'delay,' *conclure* 'conclude,' *rire* 'laugh,' *traire* 'milk,' *frire* 'fry.'

Voir, unlike *croire*, does not terminate in schwa. Therefore, the /wa/ which appears is not the stem vowel but the thematic vowel. The underlying representation for *voir* is |ved+'E+r#| with stress placed on the tense thematic vowel. Nonhigh thematic vowels become lax before a single consonantal segment: /ved+'e+r#/. Intervocalic stops are deleted in the third conjugation: /ve+'e+r#/. The pretonic lax vowel is converted to schwa; the stressed lax vowel diphthongizes: /və+w'a+r#/. Within the word, a schwa before a vowel or a glide, i.e., a [−cons] segment, must be deleted: /vw'ar/. In the past aspect *vis*, *visses*, *vu*, the stressed vowels are also thematic vowels (cf. *perdis*, *perdisses*, *perdu*) with stem vowel deletion as in the infinitive. In the unmarked aspect the stem vowel does not undergo pretonic adjustment and become schwa; instead, the underlying vowel is diphthongized (*voyez*); hence, it is not deleted.

3.4.3. *Vouloir versus mourir*

Vouloir 'want' is a third conjugation verb where the thematic vowel is tense |E|. *Mourir* 'die,' on the other hand, appears to be a second conjugation verb since its infinitive terminates in *-ir*. Except for the infinitive, *mourir* as well as *courir* 'run' and *acquérir* 'acquire' exhibits none of the characteristics of second conjugation verbs, but all of the characteristics of third conjugation forms. Thus, whereas second conjugation verbs do not have alternant stem vowels (e.g., *dorment, dormons*), *mourir* and *acquérir* show vocalic alternation: *meurent, mourons; acquièrent, acquérons* (compare third conjugation *veulent, voulons; doivent, devons*). Second conjugation futures and conditionals have thematic /i/ before the /r/: *dormiras, dormirais; mourir, courir,* and *acquérir* do not have /i/ before the finite forms of the future aspect *mourras, courras, acquerras* (compare third conjugation *devras, devrais*). Second conjugation forms have past participles in /i/: *dormi;* although *mourir* has an irregular past participle (*mort*),[31] the past participle of *courir* terminates in /y/: *couru* (compare third conjugation *voulu*). *Acquérir* has strong forms in the past aspect: *acquis, acquisses, acquis;* strong stems are limited to the third conjugation. The verbs *mourir, courir,* and *acquérir,* then, are unquestionably third conjugation verbs with anomalous infinitives. Since the infinitives have a stressed thematic vowel and do not terminate in *re,* we must conclude that *mourir,* etc., are to be classed with *-oir* type verbs, that is, the thematic vowel is |E|: e.g., |mɔr+E+r#|. Therefore, *vouloir* and *mourir* both exhibit the same underlying thematic vowel. *The anomalous infinitives,* in fact, have a phonological explanation. In the third conjugation *-oir* does not occur after an *r* so that the expected — but nonexistent — *mouroir, couroir,* and *acquéroir* appear instead as *mourir, courir,* and *acquérir;* that is, whenever thematic |E| is stressed, which happens only in the infinitive, it is raised to |I| if it is preceded by |r|.

3.4.4. *Tenir and venir*

Tenir 'hold' and *venir* 'come,' like *mourir* 'die' and *acquérir* 'acquire' (Section 3.4.3), have forms exhibiting vocalic alternation (*tient*), even though the infinitive terminates in *-ir.* This fact suggests that *tenir* and *venir* should also be included in the third conjugation, that analogous to *mourir,* etc., the underlying thematic vowel is |E|. Whenever this vowel is stressed, as it is in the infinitive, it is raised to |I|. Within the class of third conjugation verbs with thematic vowel |E|, *tenir* and *venir* are the only verb stems which terminate in a nasal. Therefore, we can restate the rule for the raising of |E| to |I| to include verbs with stems terminating in |n|, as well as those with stems terminating in |r|.

Prendre 'take,' where the stem is |prƐn|, is a third conjugation verb with a stem final nasal. However, since its infinitive terminates in *-re,* it is not in the same class as *venir;* whereas the thematic vowel for the latter is tense |E|, the thematic vowel for the former must be lax |e| so that stress will fall on the vowel of the stem. (The /d/ in *prendre* is inserted by a subsequent rule; Section 3.4.9.)

In the past aspect finite forms (preterite and past subjunctive) *tenir* and *prendre* have strong forms: *tins*, /t'ɛ̃(z)/ and *pris* /pr'i(z)/, respectively. In *tins* the underlying stem vowel of |tɛn+S#| is raised |tIn+S#|, nasalized and then lowered (all nasalized vowels become [+low]). In *pris* the underlying stem vowel is also raised |prIn+S#|. In the past aspect this stem is an exception to the vowel nasalization rule. Since the raised vowel is not nasalized, it will not be lowered. The stem final consonant is truncated before the following consonantal segment.[32]

3.4.5. *The preterites: voulus, fallut, valus, moulus, mourus, courus.*

The thematic vowel for third conjugation forms is either mid |e| for *-re* verbs or |E| for *-oir* verbs. In the past aspect the thematic vowel is raised to /i/ in the finite forms (preterite and past subjunctive) and it is raised to /y/ in the past participle (as in *perdis*, *perdisses*, *perdu*). However, forms such as *voulus*, *volusses*, *voulu* 'wanted' exhibit /y/ throughout the past aspect. Although these forms may seem to be exceptions to the general statement that /i/ appears as the vowel of finite forms, the aberrant behavior of *voulus*, etc., can be explained entirely on phonological grounds: /y/ appears whenever the preceding segment is a liquid. This observation is corroborated by a comparison of the verbs *coudre* 'sew' and *moudre* 'mill.' These verbs have identical conjugations everywhere except in the preterite and past subjunctive where the former is *cousis*, *cousisses*, while the latter has the forms *moulus*, *moulusses*. This behavior of third conjugation stems which terminate in liquids provides further evidence that *mourir* and *courir* are third conjugation verbs in spite of their infinitives.

3.4.6. *Ouvrir*, *couvrir*, *offrir*, *souffrir*

The verbs *ouvrir* 'open,' *couvrir* 'cover,' *offrir* 'offer,' and *souffrir* 'suffer' with stems terminating in a labial continuant plus /r/ are second conjugation verbs conjugated on the model of *dormir*, except for the present singular and past participle: *ouvres*, *ouvrais*, *ouvres*, *ouvrant*, *ouvriras*, *ouvrirais*, *ouvrir*, *ouvris*, *ouvrisses*, *ouvert*. Although the present singular forms *ouvre*, *ouvres*, *ouvre* /'uvr(ə)/ resemble the first conjugation and not the second, these forms are only superficially anomalous since the final schwa is not the thematic vowel — as it is in the first conjugation — but rather the epenthetic schwa inserted after a consonant-liquid cluster. The underlying representation is completely regular as far as second conjugation verbs are concerned. Just as the underlying representation for *dors* is |dɔrm+S#|, the underlying form of *couvres* is |kOvr+S#|. A schwa is inserted after the consonant-liquid cluster: |kOvrə + S#|. The singular person marker is then deleted after a central vowel: |kOvrə#|. Tense |O| is raised to /u/: /k'uvr(ə)/.

The past participle *couvert* /kuv'ɛr(t)/ is irregular; a stressed vowel appears between the original consonant-liquid cluster. The expected *couvri* does not occur. It appears that the irregularity is again due to the absence of a thematic vowel with other associated phonological processes which are not entirely clear. Without a thematic vowel the underlying representation is |kOvr + to#|. Schwa is inserted: |kOvrə + to#|. Perhaps some such processes as the following subsequently take place. The schwa and preceding liquid are metathesized: |kOvər + to#|. Stress is placed on the schwa (probably because of the following strong cluster): |kOv'ər + to#|. Schwa — which is equivalent to lax |a| — under stress is fronted: |kOv'ɛr + to#|. Tense |O| is raised to /u/ and the posttonic nonlow vowel is deleted: /kuv'ɛr(t)/.

3.4.7. *The subjunctives: veuille, vaille, faille, aille*

The subjunctives *veuille* 'want,' *vaille* 'be worth,' *faille* 'be necessary,' *aille* 'go' exhibit /j/ before the subjunctive vowel: /v'œj(ə)/, and so on. Elsewhere in the paradigm, the stem terminates in /l/: *voulons* /vul'ɔ̃(z)/. In Section 2.4 we showed that postvocalic yod results from a palatalized *l*, which in turn is derived from an |li| sequence. Since, for the above verbs, there is no reason to assume that the stems terminate in |li| (palatalization does not normally occur in the paradigm), the palatalization in the subjunctive is a special fact about these forms, that is, a stem final |l| is palatalized whenever it is followed by the subjunctive marker |ɛ|. Palatalization must occur only after the subjunctive |ɛ| has been converted to /j/ in the first and second plural since the stem |l| of these forms is not palatalized (e.g., *voulions* /vulj'ɔ̃(z)/). Palatalization must take place before truncation since first conjugation verbs — which have a thematic vowel — do not exhibit palatalized *l* in the subjunctive (e.g., *cale* /k'al(ə)/ 'wedge'). The subjunctive forms in the table illustrate the required rule ordering. Note that the subjunctives with forms in palatalized *l* do not contain a thematic vowel in their underlying representations.

1. stress placement
2. yod formation
3. palatalization before | + ɛ|
4. truncation
5. schwa conversion
6. singular person deletion

	cale	*vaille*	*calions*	*valions*
	k Al+a+ε+t#	v Al+ε+t#	kAl+a+ε+ OmS#	vAl+ε+ Oms #
1.	k'Al+a+ε+t#	v'Al+ε+t#	kAl+a+ε+'OmS#	vAl+ε+'OmS#
2.	——	——	kAl+a+j+'OmS#	vAl+j+'OmS#
3.	——	v'Aj+ε+t#	——	——
4.	k'Al +ε+t#	——	kAl +j+'OmS#	——
5.	k'Al +ə+t#	v'Aj+ə+t#	——	——
6.	k'Al +ə #	v'Aj+ə #	——	——
	/k'al(ə)/	/v'aj(ə)/	/kalj'ɔ̃(z)/	/valj'ɔ̃(z)/

In the first conjugation (*cale*) the thematic vowel intervenes between the stem final |l| and the subjunctive |ε|, thus protecting the former from palatalization. Here, as for other forms already noted, the presence or absence of a thematic vowel plays a decisive role in the phonological processes subsequently undergone by forms.

3.4.8. *Bout versus cueille, assaille*

Verbs such as *bouillir* 'boil,' *cueillir* 'gather,' *assaillir* 'assail' are of the second conjugation. In the present singular *bout* /b'u(t)/ is regular: the underlying representation is |bOli+t#|; |li| becomes palatalized: |bOʎ+t#|. The palatalized *l* is then vocalized before a consonantal segment (see pp. 58–60): |b'Ou+t#|. The tense |O| is raised to /u/ and the posttonic lax nonlow vowel is deleted: /b'u(t)/. The present tense of *cueillir* and *assaillir* is irregular; these forms are conjugated like first conjugation verbs, that is, they take thematic |a|: |kɔli+a+t#|, |AsAli+a+t#|. Palatalization takes place: |k'ɔʎ+a+t#|. The palatalized *l* is not vocalized as it is not followed by a consonant. Instead, it will ultimately become /j/. The stressed stem vowel is fronted; the person marker is deleted after a central vowel: /k'œj(ə)/.

In the future and conditional *assaillir* is regular; it takes the second conjugation thematic vowel |I|: *assailliras*, *assaillirais*. The verb *cueillir*, on the other hand, takes the first conjugation thematic vowel in the future and conditional: *cueilleras*, *cueillerais*.

What characterizes verbs such as *cueillir* and *assaillir* is that, for certain tenses, they must be assigned to a different conjugation class other than the one which accounts for most of their forms. Several other verbs have this peculiarity: *vêtir* 'dress' is a second conjugation verb with a third conjugation past participle: *vêtu; suivre* 'follow' is a third conjugation verb with a second conjugation past participle: *suivi; être* 'be' has a first conjugation past participle: *été*. We have already seen that *mourir*, *courir*, *acquérir*, *venir* and *tenir* are third conjugation verbs with infinitives that show the second conjugation thematic vowel.

3.4.9. *Vaudra, faudra, tiendra, coudre, connaître*

These forms exhibit a /t/ or /d/ before the future aspect /r/. The stems however do not terminate in a dental stop (cf. *valait* 'was worthy,' *fallait* 'was necessary,' *tenait* 'held,' *cousait* 'sewed,' *connaissait* 'knew'). The /t/ or /d/ is an epenthetic consonant inserted between a stem final dental segment and a following /r/: |vAl+rA+t#| → |vAld+rA+t#|, |tɛn+rA+t#| → |tɛnd+rA+t#|, |kOz+r#| → |kOzd+r#|, |kƆnEss+r#| → |kƆnEsst+r#|. Note that /t/ is inserted after voiceless segments and /d/ after voiced ones. When the segment preceding the epenthetic dental stop is an obstruent — only |s| or |z| in the above examples — the obstruent is deleted: |kOzd+r#| → |kOd+r#| → /k'ud+r#/ (back vowel raising) → /k'udr(ə)/ (schwa insertion); |kƆnEsst+r#| → |kƆnEst+r#| → /kƆn'E:t+r#| (vowel lengthening; p. 54) → /kɔn'ɛ:tr(ə)/ (schwa insertion). Verbs like *connaître* must have stems which terminate in geminate |ss| if one is to account for the stressed long stem vowel of the infinitive. The second |s| is deleted before the epenthetic /t/. The other |s| — now before /t/ — is subsequently deleted by the rule for vowel lengthening, causing the preceding stressed vowel to become long.

Note incidentally that the rule for dental stop insertion in its most general sense would apply to all dental consonants before |r|. Thus, a form such as *perdre*, where /d/ appears to be the stem consonant, would not be specifically excluded from epenthesis since the rule as it is stated would convert |pɛrd+r#| to |pɛrdd+r#| with subsequent deletion of the original stem final obstruent.

Whenever the segment preceding the epenthetic dental stop is not an obstruent, it is retained but is then subjected to other phonological rules: |vAld+r'A+t#| → |vAud+r'A+t#| (vocalization of *l* before a consonantal segment) → |vod+r'A+t#| (conversion of |Au| to /o/) → /vodr'a/ (singular person deletion); |tɛnd+r'A+t#| → |tɛ̃d+r'A+t#| (nasalization) → /tjɛ̃dr'a/ (diphthongization of stem vowel and singular person deletion).

Palatal consonant segments also receive an epenthetic dental stop: *peindre* /p'ɛ̃dr(ə)/ 'paint' (cf. *peignait* /pɛɲ'ɛ(t)/); *faudra* /fodr'a/ 'will fail' (cf. *faillir* /faj'ir/, homophonous with *faudra*, future of *falloir* 'be necessary'). The verb *faillir* is particularly interesting since there are two variants for finite forms of the future aspect: *faillira* /fajir'a/ and *faudra* /fodr'a/. The difference is due entirely to presence or absence of the second conjugation thematic vowel.

1. stress placement
2. l-palatalization
3. dental insertion before |r|
4. l-vocalization (before consonant)
5. o-conversion
6. singular person deletion
7. palatal glide conversion

	faillira	*faudra*
	fAli+I+r A+t#	fAli +r A+t#
1.	fAli+I+r'A+t#	fAli +r'A+t#
2.	faʎ +I+r'A+t#	fAʎ +r'A+t#
3.	——	fAʎd+r'A+t#
4.	——	fAud+r'A+t#
5.	——	fo d+r'A+t#
6.	fAʎ +I+r'A #	fo d+r'A#
7.	fAj +I+r'A #	——
	/fajir'a/	/fodr'a/

The derivation of *faudra* provides further evidence that |li| must go through an intermediate |ʎ| before becoming /j/. It is the |ʎ| (palatal consonantal segment) preceding the |r| which provides the environment for the epenthetic /d/.

Other verbs which take an epenthetic dental stop include: *vouloir* 'want,' cf. *voudra*, *absoudre* 'absolve' (like *valoir*); *venir* 'come,' cf. *viendra* (like *tenir*); *craindre* 'fear,' *joindre* 'join' (like *peindre*); *naître* 'be born,' *paître* 'graze,' *croître* 'grow' (like *connaître*).

The rule for dental insertion, like the rule for schwa insertion, is not ordered with respect to the other rules, but applies whenever the environmental conditions are met, if there are not to be inconsistencies in ordering. The rule which converts |A| plus lax |u| to tense |O| must, of course, precede the rule for nonlow vowel deletion; otherwise, lax |u| would be deleted. To explain *vaudra*, /d/ insertion must occur *before* the *au* to *o* and nonlow vowel deletion rules, while the dental |l| of the stem is still present: |vAl+r'A+t#|. For *coudre*, however, /d/ insertion must take place *after* the rule for nonlow vowel deletion has applied since the latter rule is needed to delete the mid thematic vowel which intervenes between the stem and future aspect marker: |kOz+e+r#|. A thematic vowel is required in the underlying form, otherwise the truncation rule would delete the final stem consonant as it would be followed by |r|. (Although |vAl+r'A+t#| contains no thematic vowel, the stem final |l| is not deleted since liquids are never truncated.) Only after nonlow vowel deletion does |k'Oz+e+r#| become |k'Oz+r#|. Hence, /d/ insertion must be an early rule for some forms like *vaudra* and a late rule for others like *coudre*. So far, the only other rule which could not be ordered was the rule for schwa insertion. Interestingly enough, both of these rules are concerned with epenthesis.

Rules cannot be ordered whenever in the language there are overriding phonological constraints which simply do not allow certain sequences to occur within the course of a derivation. Thus, in French final consonant-liquid clusters must always have a supporting vowel, whether as underlying forms or as subsequently derived forms. Similarly, at a morpheme boundary the sequence dental or palatal consonantal segment plus /r/ is not permitted and whenever this sequence occurs, it is always broken by an epenthetic dental stop.

3.4.10. *Dites, faites, êtes*

These irregular second plurals of the verbs *dire* 'say,' *faire* 'do,' and *être* 'be' are the only present forms that do not terminate in *-ez*. Instead, they have the variant of the person ending which is found in the preterite (e.g., *dormîtes* /dɔrm'it(ə)(z)/). These forms are irregular, then, to the extent that the first two segments of the person ending |EtS| are metathesized whenever the ending is directly preceded by one of these three verb stems. We contrast the derivation of *lisez* 'read' with that of *dites*. The stem for the latter is |dIz| (cf. *disons* /diz'ɔ̃(z)/).[33]

1. metathesis
2. stress placement
3. truncation
4. schwa conversion
5. prefinal consonant deletion

	lisez	*dites*
	lIz + EtS#	d Iz + EtS#
1.	——	d Iz + tɛ S#
2.	lIz + 'EtS#	d'Iz + tɛ S#
3.	——	d'I + tɛ S#
4.	——	d'I + tə S#
5.	lIz + 'E S#	——
	/liz'e(z)/	/d'it(ə)(z)/

3.4.11. *Ont, vont, sont, font*

These third plural present forms of the verbs *avoir* 'have,' *aller* 'go,' *être* 'be,' and *faire* 'do' are the only ones which terminate in *-ont* /ɔ̃(t)/, the characteristic ending found in the future. In the future the third plural *-ront* /rɔ̃(t)/ is derived from an underlying |rA + unt#|, where |A + u| becomes /o/ and is subsequently nasalized. The derivation of *vont* raises no special problems. The underlying stem for *vont* must be |vA| (cf. *vas, va* /v'a/). This stem combined with the third plural ending gives |vA+unt#|; o-conversion and nasalization then apply as expected.

The underlying stem for *ont* is |Av| (cf. *avons, avez*). The third plural should be |Av+unt#|. If it were |A+unt#|, the correct derived form could be obtained. The irregularity then hinges on the deletion of the intervocalic |v|. In the past participle we showed that the |t| of the past participle ending is deleted whenever it is followed by lax |u|: |dɔrm+'I+tu#| → |dɔrm+'I+u#| → /dɔrm'i/ (nonlow vowel deletion). For |Av+unt#| the |v| is also followed by a lax |u|. Although it is by no means clear to us what the precise conditions are for the deletion of the stem final |v|, nonetheless it appears that the lax |u| of the third plural must in some way be the contributing factor. Similarly, *font* is derived from an underlying |fAz+unt#| with deletion of |z|.[34] *Sont* has a suppletive stem and is derived from an underlying |s+unt#|. Stress falls on the vowel of the ending; the stressed vowel is then nasalized, lowered, and made tense.

The other persons of the present of *avoir* are completely regular. Third singular *a* is derived from an underlying |Av+t#|. The truncation rule deletes the final stem consonant as it precedes a consonantal segment: |'A+t#|. The singular person marker is deleted after a central vowel: /'a/. The first singular *ai* is derived from an underlying |Av+S#|. The stem consonant is truncated: |'A+S#|. The first person singular ending is vocalized after tense |A| (cf. the future *dormirai*, page 82): |'A+i#|. The sequence |'A+i#| is then converted to /'e/.

3.5 Conclusion

Finite verbs exhibit the structure: stem(+thematic vowel)(+aspect)(+tense)+person. The stem and person marker are obligatory throughout the paradigm. One or more of the other constituents may also be present. Examples of the various combinations include: stem+person|dɔrm+S#| *dors;* stem+thematic+person|ArIv+a+S#| *arrives;* stem+aspect+person|EkrIv+rA+S#| *écriras*; stem+tense+person |dɔrm+Ɛ+S#| *dormais;* stem+thematic+aspect+person|dɔrm+I+rA+S#| *dormiras*; stem+thematic+tense+person|ArIv+a+Ɛ+S#| *arrivais;* stem+aspect+tense+person|EkrIv+rA+Ɛ+S#| *écrirais;* stem+thematic+aspect+tense+person|dɔrm+I+rA+Ɛ+S#| *dormirais.* Nonfinite forms of the verb (infinitive and participles) have the structure: stem(+thematic vowel)+nonfinite ending: |dɔrm+Ant#| *dormant;* |dɔrm+I+r#| *dormir;* |dɔrm+I+to#| *dormi.*

The underlying form of the singular person endings is a single consonant: |S|, |S|, |t|; while the plural endings begin with a vowel: |OmS|, |EtS|, |unt|. It is the consonantality of the singular person endings which is responsible for the deletion of stem final consonants throughout the present singular of verbs of the second and third conjugations: |dɔrm+S#| → /d'ɔr(z)/ *dors*. The first singular |S| is vocalized after tense |A|: |dɔrm+I+rA+S#| → |dɔrm+I+rA+i#| → /dɔrmir'e/ *dormirai;* |ArIv+A+s+S#| → |ArIv+A+S#| (truncation) → |ArIv+A+i#| → /ariv'e /*arrivai*. The singular person marker is deleted after central vowels (/a/and/ə/): |ArIv+a+t#| → /ar'iv(ə)/ *arrive;* |dɔrm+I+rA+t#| → /dɔrmir'a/*dormira*. The first and second plural markers undergo metathesis of the first two segments in the preterite: |dɔrm+I+s+Ets#| → |dɔrm+I+s+tεS#| → /dɔrm'it(ə)(z)/ *dormîtes*. The initial vowel of the third plural |unt| combines with a preceding tense |A|: |dɔrm+I+rA+unt#| → |dɔrm+I+rO+nt#| → /dɔrmir'ɔ̃(t)/ *dormiront*. When |unt| is not preceded by |A|, it is nasalized, lowered, and converted to schwa: |d'ɔrm+unt#| → |d'ɔrm+ũt| → |d'ɔrm+ɔ̃t| → /d'ɔrm(ə)(t)/ *dorment*.

There are two tense markers: imperfect |Ɛ| and subjunctive |ε|, and two aspect markers: future |rA| and past |s| (or |ss|). The present tense is unmarked; |dɔrm+S#| *dors;* the imperfect and the present subjunctive are unmarked for aspect but marked for tense: |dɔrm+Ɛ+S#| *dormais* and |dɔrm+ε+S#| *dormes*. Within the future aspect, the future tense is marked for (future) aspect but unmarked for tense: |dɔrm+I+rA+S#| *dormiras*, whereas the conditional is marked for both (future) aspect and (imperfect) tense: |dɔrm+I+rA+Ɛ+S#| *dormirais*. Within the past aspect, the preterite is marked for (past) aspect but not tense: |dɔrm+I+s+S#| *dormis*, whereas the past subjunctive is marked for both (past) aspect and (subjunctive) tense: |dɔrm+I+ss+ε+S#| *dormisses*. The past aspect marker has two variants: |s| for the preterite and |ss| for the past subjunctive. Within the marked aspects the subjunctive tense marker does not cooccur with the future aspect marker and the imperfect tense marker does not cooccur with the past aspect marker. Within each aspect there is a nonfinite form: the present participle |Ant| for the unmarked aspect, the infinitive |r| for the future aspect, and the past participle |to| for the past aspect. The tenses and nonfinite forms within each aspect can be characterized phonologically. Forms of the unmarked aspect are either unmarked or begin with a vowel: present (unmarked), imperfect |Ɛ|, present subjunctive |ε|, present participle |Ant|; future aspect forms have a liquid — specifically |r| — as the initial segment: future |rA|, conditional |rA+Ɛ|, infinitive |r|; past aspect forms begin with a consonant — specifically, a dental obstruent — preterite |s|, past subjunctive |ss+ε|, past participle |to|.

There are three verb conjugations, distinguishable by the thematic vowel. First conjugation verbs have |A| as the thematic vowel. The second conjugation thematic vowel is |I|. The third conjugation thematic vowel has two variants: tense |E| for *-oir* verbs and lax |e| for *-re* verbs. The thematic vowels can be characterized phonologically according to vowel height (all are unrounded): first conjugation |A| is a low vowel; second conjugation |I| a high vowel, and third conjugation |E| or |e| a mid vowel. Morphological similarities in *-oir* and *-re* verbs are attributable to the common feature of a mid thematic vowel; differences are due to the tenseness of the thematic vowel. For regular verbs a thematic vowel appears throughout the future and past aspects. Whenever a nonhigh thematic vowel (|e|, |E|, or |A|) is followed by a single consonantal segment, it becomes lax: |ArIv+ 'A+r#| → |ArIv+ 'a+r#| → |ArIv+ 'ɛ+r#| → /ariv'e/*arriver*. In the unmarked aspect only first conjugation verbs and second conjugation verbs in *-iss* exhibit a thematic vowel. The first conjugation thematic vowel is lax |a| for these forms. The vowel is lax so that stress can fall on the vowel of the stem in certain present and subjunctive forms: |ArIv+a+t#| → /ar'iv(ə)/*arrive*. Furthermore, it is the thematic vowel which protects the stem final consonant from deletion in the singular and which accounts for the potential phonetic schwa of these forms.

Our division into three conjugations according to type of thematic vowel parallels closely the traditional classification based on the infinitive ending since *-er* verbs have |A| or |a| as the thematic vowel, *-ir* have |I|, *-oir* have |E| and *-re* have |e|. There are only a few discrepancies between the two types of classification. For example, verbs of the type *venir*, *mourir*, are not second conjugation forms but third conjugation with thematic |E|; the thematic vowel is raised to /i/ in the infinitive where it is stressed. In this way it is seen that phonological processes such as vocalic alternation of the stem vowel or vowel raising for tenses of the past aspect are restricted to the third conjugation. Otherwise, our conjugation classes reflect the traditional division, and we believe that there is sufficient internal structural evidence to justify the traditional classification.

A number of "irregularities" can be characterized by the absence of a thematic vowel. In fact, for strong verbs of the past aspect of the third conjugation the absence of a thematic vowel is a consistent characteristic of these forms. Characterizing certain irregular verbs as absence of a thematic vowel is particularly attractive since often no new rules have to be added to the grammar to produce the anomalous forms. Of even greater interest, for a substantial number of verbs this notion permits an explanation of the concept "irregular verb."

Notes

Notes to Chapter 1

1. Grevisse gives the following definitions of elision and liaison: "L'élision est l'amuïssement d'une des voyelles finales *a*, *e*, *i*, devant une initiale vocalique. L'élision n'est pas toujours marquée dans l'écriture; quand elle l'est, la voyelle qui s'élide est remplacée par une apostrophe." (p. 60) "Une consonne finale, muette dans un mot isolé, se prononce dans certains cas, devant la voyelle ou l'*h* muet initial du mot suivant et s'appuie même si intimement sur ce mot que pour la division en syllabes, elle lui appartient: c'est ce qui s'appelle faire une *liaison*." (Grevisse (1964), *Le bon usage*, Gembloux, Duculot, p. 56.)
2. "La liaison consiste par conséquent à prononcer devant un mot commençant par une voyelle une consonne finale, muette *en dehors de cette condition*." [My italics.] (Fouché (1956), *Traité de prononciation française*, Paris, Klincksieck, p. 434.)
3. Meigret (sixteenth century) recognized the similarity between elision and absence of liaison: "Si une voyelle se retranche devant une autre voyelle, une consonne qui ne se prononce pas devra se supprimer devant une autre consonne." (Livet (1859), *La grammaire française et les grammariens du XVIe siècle*, Paris, Didier, p. 62.) Meigret's statement is in reference to a spelling reform which he was proposing.
4. Forms such as *petit ami* /pətit ami/ 'little friend,' *petit oiseau* /pətit wazo/ 'little bird' establish the necessity for representing the morpheme *petit* with a stem final consonant, i.e., |pətit|. However, this consonant is deleted whenever the following word begins with a consonant or a liquid: *petit camarade* /pəti kamarad/ 'little comrade,' *petit rabbin* /pəti rabɛ̃/ 'little

rabbi.' A word final vowel, on the other hand, is deleted, not when the following word begins with a consonant or a liquid, but when it begins with a vowel or a glide: *admirable camarade* /admirablə kamarad/ 'admirable comrade,' *admirable rabbin* /admirablə rabɛ̃/, *admirable ami* /admirabl ami/, *admirable oiseau* /admirabl wazo/. However, word final liquids and glides are not deleted: *cher camarade* /ʃɛr kamarad/ 'dear comrade,' *cher rabbin* /ʃɛr rabɛ̃/, *cher ami* /ʃɛr ami/, *cher oiseau* /ʃɛr wazo/; *pareil camarade* /parɛj kamarad/ 'such a comrade,' *pareil rabbin* /parɛj rabɛ̃/, *pareil ami* /parɛj ami/, *pareil oiseau* /parɛj wazo/.

5. Jakobson, Fant, Halle (1961), *Preliminaries to Speech Analysis*, Cambridge, Mass., M.I.T. Press, pp. 18–20.
6. The alpha rule can perhaps be best illustrated by considering a case of simple assimilation. In English the "plural" morphophoneme *S* is implemented as voiceless after voiceless segments and as voiced after voiced segments, e.g., "backs" /bæks/, "bags" /bægz/. A possible set of rules (much simplified) would be the following:

   The morphophoneme *S* becomes:

   a. [+voiced] after [+voiced] segments

   b. [−voiced] after [−voiced] segments

   Rather than to make two separate statements, one would prefer to say that *S* has the same voicing as the preceding segment, i.e., to state this fact by a single rule. Since these two rules are very similar and differ only in the value of the signs, they can be collapsed to a single rule if the individual values are replaced by a variable.

   The morphophoneme *S* becomes:

   [α voiced] after [α voiced] segments

   where α is either + or −, observing the convention that if α is assigned the value + on one side of the rule, it must also be + on the other side and likewise for −.

   For the use of the alpha notation in phonological statements, see Halle (1962), "A Descriptive Convention for Treating Assimilation and Dissimilation," *Quarterly Progress Report*, No. 66, M.I.T., pp. 295–296.
7. If the following two rules were to appear in a language:

   a. $\begin{bmatrix} +\text{cons} \\ -\text{voc} \end{bmatrix}$ segments are truncated before [+nasal] segments

   b. $\begin{bmatrix} +\text{cons} \\ +\text{voc} \end{bmatrix}$ segments are truncated before [+voc] segments

   these would simply be two unrelated instances of truncation. When this hypothetical case is contrasted with the situation which is actually found in French:

   a. $\begin{bmatrix} +\text{cons} \\ -\text{voc} \end{bmatrix}$ segments are truncated before [+cons] segments

   b. $\begin{bmatrix} -\text{cons} \\ +\text{voc} \end{bmatrix}$ segments are truncated before [−cons] segments the symmetrical relation between the latter two truncation rules — as against the former two — becomes apparent. It is symmetry of this type that we want the rules of the grammar to reflect.

8. In the underlying forms + indicates morpheme boundary and # indicates word boundary. We represent the "plural" morpheme by *S* (an archiphoneme which is not marked for voicing), since in liaison the voicing is predictable.

Rule for voicing in liaison

The morphophoneme *S* becomes [+voiced] before [−cons] segments. In some styles all the liaison continuants are voiced whereas the liaison stops (noncontinuants) are voiceless, e.g., *neuf heures* /nœv œr/, *grand ami* /grãt ami/, 'big friend,' *long été* /lɔ̃k ete/. These cases would be accounted for by an alpha rule:

In word final position:

$$\begin{bmatrix} +\text{cons} \\ -\text{voc} \\ \alpha\ \text{cont} \end{bmatrix} \text{ segments become } [\alpha \text{ voiced}] \text{ before } [-\text{cons}] \text{ segments.}$$

9. A single underlying phonological representation for each morpheme obviates the necessity of listing allomorphs. The particular variants result from the phonological rules. Furthermore, there is not necessarily a one-to-one correspondence between morphophonemes and phonetic segments. In fact, as our examples show, the former may have no phonetic manifestation at all since they may be deleted in certain environments.

10. "Ce qui oppose aujourd'hui la langue de la poésie française à celle de la prose, c'est beaucoup moins le recours à un vocabulaire spécial que le maintien d'un phonétisme archaïque." (Bourciez (1958), *Précis de phonétique française*, 9th ed., Paris, Klincksieck, p. 26.)

In our analysis the underlying stem of an adjective such as *petit(e)(s)* terminates in a consonant, e.g., |pətit|. Whether or not the consonant remains depends on the nature of the following segment. The underlying base form gives priority to neither the masculine nor the feminine; that is, we do not derive one gender from the other. (The feminine is derived from the masculine in traditional grammar, the masculine from the feminine in Bloomfieldian linguistics.) Thus, Bloomfield says: ". . . if we take the feminine form as our basis [meaning the feminine as it is phonemically, e.g., /pətit/], we can describe [the formation of the masculine] by the simple statement that the masculine form is derived from the feminine by means of a minus feature, namely, loss of the final consonant . . ." (Bloomfield, 1933, *Language*, New York, Holt, p. 217.) Harris remarks: "The interchange may be between any phoneme in a given position and zero in that position; i.e., it may consist of omitting a phoneme." (Harris (1960), *Structural Linguistics*, Chicago, Univ. of Chicago Press, p. 168.) However, Harris notes the difficulties encountered in this type of description for French: "This analysis ceases to be applicable if we take into consideration forms in which the 'mute *e*' is pronounced, as in poetry; if we consider forms in which the final consonant is pronounced, as in liaison, it is the masculine pre-consonantal form which is derived from the masculine prevocalic form . . ." (p. 168, Note 28.) By having abstract underlying representations, these difficulties do not arise.

11. From a historical point of view, truncation between words and phrase final consonant deletion were two separate developments with phrase final consonant deletion occurring later. It appears that phrase final consonants were pronounced in the sixteenth century. "[Dubois] ajoute cette double règle: 'A la fin des mots, on ne prononce aucune consonne, à moins qu'une voyelle ne suive, ou que la phrase ne soit terminée.' . . . la dernière partie de la règle posée par Dubois . . . peut se formuler ainsi: les consonnes finales se prononcent à la fin des phrases: Dans: *le*(*s*) *femme*(*s*) *son*(*t*) *bones*, la consonne finale se prononce seulement dans *bones*." (Livet, *La Grammaire française et les grammariens du XVI*[e] *siècle*, pp. 8–9.)
12. Fouché (1956) cites about 700 words which begin with "h aspiré." This list does not include proper names or foreign borrowings.
13. "Ce n'est que dans le français régional (en Gascogne, en Saintonge, en Bretagne et surtout en Lorraine dans la Wallonie Orientale) que l'*h* aspiré se prononce avec un souffle, comme l'h allemand ou anglais par exemple. Exceptionnellement, même en français correct, l'h aspiré se prononce avec un souffle dans le cas d'exclamations poussées avec force (cf. *han! hola! hep! hop! hue! halte!*, etc.), dans le cas de sentiments violents (cf. *je te hais*, *c'est une honte*, etc.), et, comme moyen expressif, lorsqu'on veut donner de l'accent à tel ou tel mot, par exemple dans le cas des verbes *halter*, *se hisser*, *hurler*, etc." (Fouché, *Traité de prononciation française*, p. 252.) See also Martinet (1945), *La prononciation du français contemporain*, Paris, E. Droz, pp. 185–187.
14. ". . . [l'h aspiré] ne permet pas, comme le fait n'importe quelle consonne simple, la chute d'un *e* final devant lui: tandis que l'on dit 'un(e) tache' sans *e*, on prononce l'*e* de *une* dans 'un*e* hache.'" (Grammont (1961), *Traité pratique de prononciation française*, Paris, Delagrave, p. 124.) This observation concerning schwa before "h aspiré" also provides further justification for having schwas in the underlying representations (particularly in final position where they are practically always deleted). Forms such as *le onze*, *le yacht* could reasonably be regarded as "h aspiré" words. The latter form might be best considered a borrowing. Foreign words, proper names, dialectal loans, etc., will need to be noted as such in the lexicon as they invariably do not obey the same phonological constraints as the mass of words which form the native stock. Since particular phonological rules will not necessarily be applicable to all morphemes in the language, morphemes must be assigned to different classes. This is analogous to the situation in morphology where verb stems, for example, are assigned to different classes for the purpose of conjugation.
15. Within the present theory of distinctive features *h* and glottal stop are defined as glides, i.e., they are represented by the features [$-$cons, $-$voc].

However, in French it is not possible to consider the "h aspiré" as a glide since we have seen that vowel elision takes place before glides as well as before vowels (cf. *l'oiseau*). This means that "h aspiré" must be specified as a true consonant ([+cons, −voc]). In the underlying forms one could, of course, set up "h aspiré" as the velar spirant *x*, since this spirant does not occur elsewhere within the French phonological system. A later phonological rule (after the truncation rule had been applied) would then convert the consonant *x* to the glide *h*. In fact, it is precisely in this way that Chomsky and Halle (*Sound Pattern of English*) handle English *h*, which for structural reasons must also be classed as a true consonant. However, this solution is not too satisfying since it requires setting up an abstract consonant, the phonetic interpretation of which is dependent on a prior rule which first converts it to a glide. The only motivation for the underlying spirant and the conversion rule is that they provide a means for circumventing the difficulty that in French and in English *h* is simply *not* a glide structurally. Furthermore, this analysis of *h* is dependent on the nonexistence of velar spirants for the languages in question. It does not seem entirely unlikely that a language would have both a velar spirant and an *h* which functions structurally as a consonant. A case of this type would *a fortiori* preclude the possibility of assigning to *h* the features of a velar spirant.

This is not to say that *h* never functions as a glide structurally. Indeed, there are languages requiring that in the underlying representations *h* have the features of a glide, and for these languages the present distinctive feature characterization of *h* is entirely adequate. It seems to us that what is manifested as an *h* phonetically may have two different sources phonologically, i.e., phonetic *h* may be derived from either a laryngeal spirant or a laryngeal glide, the particular choice of segment for any language being dependent on the structure of the phonological system. See Postal, *Aspects of Phonological Theory*, New York, Harper & Row, where a similar situation arises in Mohawk; there, it is necessary to derive *j* and *w* from consonantal segments. Postal also argues for the possibility of deriving phonetic glides from either phonological (underlying) glides or consonantal type segments. James McCawley (personal communication) has suggested that among the consonants *h* be considered as the unmarked spirant. Any of the preceding proposals would, of course, entail a revision in the Jakobsonian features.

16. To say that a word is an exception to a rule implies that there is no structural reason for its erratic behavior; rather, its failure to undergo a rule is just an idiosyncratic fact about the word, and this observation must be noted in the lexicon. That words with pronounced final consonants are indeed exceptions to the deletion rules, rather than, say, instances of some undiscovered rule, can be ascertained by looking at those words with fluctuating forms, i.e., where the final consonant may or may not be pronounced. Grammont cites: *sens, donc, soit!, granit, but, fat, fait, accessit, vivat, aconit, exact, porc, cerf, mœurs, ours*. He also lists quite a large number of words where the treatment of final consonants by southern speakers differs

from the standard norm. (Grammont, *Traité pratique de prononciation française*, pp. 93–95.) Hence, speakers will have different sets of words which are exceptions to the deletion rules, so that what is an exception for one speaker is not necessarily an exception for some other.

17. Forms which are an exception to the truncation rule are also an exception to the rule which voices word final sibilants before a vowel, e.g., *sens* /sãs/ 'sense, direction,' *sens unique* /sãs ynik/ 'one way'; compare this with a form which undergoes truncation, e.g., *sans* /sã/ 'without,' *sans amour* /sãz amur/ 'without love.'

18. The deletion rules permit us to explain the few "irregular" nouns where the stem final consonant is pronounced in the singular but not in the plural.

bœuf	/bœf/	bœufs	/bø/	'steer(s)'
œuf	/œf/	œufs	/ø/	'egg(s)'
nerf	/nɛrf/	nerfs	/nɛr/	'nerve(s)'
os	/ɔs/	os	/o/	'bone(s)'

These morphemes are exceptions to the truncation rule whenever they are *not* combined with some following morpheme (for example, the plural marker). Therefore, in the singular, where the final consonant of the noun stem is in word final position, the consonant is not deleted. In the plural the final consonant of the stem is no longer in word final position, i.e., it is followed by the morphophoneme *S*. Since in this environment the above forms are not exceptions to the truncation rule, the stem consonant will be accordingly deleted; the *S* is subsequently deleted since it is in final position, where this morpheme is always deleted. Similarly, in compound nouns of the type *bœuf gras* /bø gra/ 'fatted ox,' *cerf-volant* /sɛr vɔlã/ 'kite' the stem final consonant of the first word of the compound is truncated; here, as in the plural, the forms in question are combined with a following morpheme.

19. In addition to marking forms as exceptions to the truncation rule or assigning them to different phonological classes, there is a further alternative for handling forms with pronounced final consonants. In their underlying representations these forms could terminate in some arbitrary vocalic segment, i.e., some vowel which otherwise does not occur in final position. The presence of a final vowel would then prevent the preceding consonant from being deleted since this consonant would no longer be immediately followed by a consonantal segment or be in final position. A subsequent rule (after the deletion rules had been applied) would be needed to delete this abstract vowel since it never has any phonetic manifestation. Postulating an underlying vowel in final position is parallel to the "h aspiré" situation, where it was necessary to set up an initial consonantal segment so as to prevent the preceding vowel from being truncated. However, it should be noted that the singular-plural forms of the nouns cited in Note 18 or the three phonological variants for certain numerals cannot be accounted for on the basis of a final vowel in the underlying representation. To be sure, these particular examples are quite marginal. Nonetheless, we

prefer either of the solutions discussed in the text since they in fact account for all the data. In any event, whichever solution one opts for, one must indicate those forms which do not undergo truncation — either overtly by means of a vowel in the phonological representation, or else indirectly by marking in the lexicon whether the form is an exception to a rule or by indicating the phonological class to which it is assigned.

20. ". . . la première condition pour qu'une voyelle puisse être élidée est d'ètre inaccentuée . . ." (Grammont (1962), *Petit traité de versification française*, 19th ed., Paris, Colin, p. 25.) This means that forms such as *je*, *me*, *te*, *se*, *le*, *la*, *ne*, *que*, *de* must not receive word stress since the vowels of these forms do in fact undergo elision. Except for *que* and *de* these forms are either articles or elements of the verb group, i.e., the personal pronouns and *ne*, so that, by and large, the forms which are not affected by the stress rule can be characterized morphologically. For a detailed treatment of the phonological processes which take place within the verb group, as well as an analysis of *que* and *de*, see Schane, "La phonologie du groupe verbal français, Langages VII."

21. The added condition that a segment must be unstressed in order to be truncated would apply vacuously to consonants since they are inherently unstressed. It should be noted that, at the word level, stress is not postulated simply as a device for preventing vowel truncation; stress may also condition the choice of morphemic alternants (e.g., *devons* '(we) must,' *doivent* '(they) must,' *voulons* '(we) want,' *veulent* '(they) want'), where the stem vowel exhibits stressed and unstressed variants. Therefore, although stress is a conditioning environment for vowel elision, its presence is not uniquely associated with this one phenomenon. Thus, at the word level, stress has two important functions: (1) it prevents truncation of vowels, and (2) it conditions certain vowel shifts. However, it has been noted for French that, at the phrase level, the individual words are not necessarily stressed, that all words generally have the same degree of stress except for the last word, the final or penultimate vowel of which is spoken with slightly greater intensity. "Toute suite de mots qui exprime une idée simple et unique constitue un seul élément rhythmique et n'a d'accent que sur sa dernière syllable . . . L'accent n'appartient donc pas au mot, mais au groupe, et un mot donné le porte ou ne le porte pas, selon la place qu'il occupe dans le groupe et le rôle qu'il y joue." (Grammont, *Traité pratique de prononciation française*, pp. 105–106.) Although stress is significant at the word level, where it is needed to account for elision and vowel alternation, it does not play a relevant role within the phonetics of larger syntactic units. (We are not considering here contrastive stress or "l'accent d'insistance.") We shall therefore require a rule which, within the phrase, deletes all word stresses except for the stress on the final word.

Rule for phrase stress

Within a phrase, delete all word stresses except the final one.

22. The observation that /j/ does not occur after /i/, nor /l/ after /u/, nor /r/ after /ɛ/ is borne out with very few exceptions. Words such as *drill* /drij/

'kind of baboon,' *mandrill* /mãdrij/ 'mandrill,' are clearly borrowings; *capitoul* /kapitul/ 'Toulouse magistrate' is dialectal, *tamoul* /tamul/ 'Tamil,' is a borrowing, *maboul* /mabul/ 'crazy' (slang) is argot, while *redoul* /rədul/ 'a type of plant' also has a regular form without l: *redou.* An exception of a different type is *cul* /ky/ 'rear' (cf. *culotte* /kylɔt(ə)/ 'breeches'); here, the /l/ has been dropped after /y/, an environment where it should be retained. Similarly, the pronoun *il(s)* /i/ 'he,' 'they' in colloquial speech may show a deleted liquid. The interesting exceptions are those in /ɛr/: *air* /ɛr/ 'air,' *ber* /bɛr/ 'launching cradle,' *fer* /fɛr/ 'iron,' *enfer* /ãfɛr/ 'hell,' *hier* /jɛr/ 'yesterday,' *cuiller* /kɥijɛr/ (but also *cuillère*) 'spoon,' *clair* /klɛr/ 'clear,' *mer* /mɛr/ 'sea,' *amer* /amɛr/ 'bitter,' *pair* /pɛr/ 'even,' *chair* /ʃɛr/ 'flesh,' *cher* /ʃɛr/ 'dear,' *ter* /tɛr/ 'thrice,' *ver* /vɛr/ 'worm,' *vair* /vɛr/ 'Vair,' *hiver* /ivɛr/ 'winter.' Many of these are monosyllabic words. For these cases, the final /r/ can be explained since monosyllabic /ɛr/ does not become /e/. The actual number of exceptions therefore turns out to be quite minimal. Forms such as *frater* /fratɛr/ 'frater,' *poker* /pɔkɛr/ 'poker,' are of course borrowings. The /ɛr/ → /e/ change is productive and accounts for first conjugation infinitives of the type *parler* /parle/ 'speak.' That first conjugation verbs have an |r| as the mark of the infinitive in the underlying representation can be seen by considering the other verb classes where infinitive |r| is always present, e.g., *finir* /finir/ 'finish,' *vouloir* /vulwar/ 'want,' *vendre* /vãdre(ə)/ 'sell.' (See Chapter 3.)

23. "Words which have preserved a liaison form are generally words which occur in close grammatical relationship with the following word, or words, for which liaison performs a special function, e.g., indicates the plural, expresses a change of meaning. Thus, it is not surprising to find that many of them are adjectives which can precede nouns, pronouns, adverbs of degree, prepositions, verbs of very common use, plural nouns." (Armstrong (1959), *The Phonetics of French*, London, G. Bell, p. 161.)

24. "La liaison ne se fait jamais après la consonne finale d'un nom au singulier. . . ." (Grevisse, *Le bon usage*, p. 60.) "Des expressions comme 'le sang‿humain, le respec(t)‿humain' sont livresques." (Grammont, *Traité pratique de prononciation française*, p. 132). Forms such as *Champs‿Elysées*, *accent‿aigu* are probably best regarded as compound words analogous to *pied-à-terre*, *cerf-volant*, etc. (See Note 18.)

25. Post-Bloomfieldian American linguistics — with its insistence on the strict separation of levels — did not permit recourse to syntactic information at the phonological level. Traditional grammarians, on the other hand, have relied on syntactic information in describing phonological processes (for example, the treatment of liaison in French). In fact, the interplay of elision and liaison in French is unquestionably one of the clearest examples of the impracticability of describing certain phonological phenomena without taking into consideration the syntactic analysis of the constituents involved. (Concerning the relation between the syntactic and phonological components of a generative grammar, see Chomsky (1962), "The

Logical Basis of Linguistic Theory," *Proceedings of the IX International Congress of Linguists*, The Hague, Mouton, and (1965), *Aspects of the Theory of Syntax*, Cambridge, Mass, M.I.T. Press, and Postal, *Aspects of Phonological Theory*.)

26. All consonants are deleted in phrase final position unless the form has been marked as an exception to the rule for final consonant deletion (see Note 19). That *anglais* must in fact terminate in a consonant in its underlying representation can be ascertained by considering the feminine form *anglaise* /ãglɛz(ə)/.

27. There are grammatical environments where liaison is obligatory, others where it is not permitted, and still others where it is optional. Optional liaison is often a question of style. "La liaison dépend du style. Elle se fait d'autant moins que le style est plus familier. On peut distinguer au moins quatre styles:

    1. la conversation familière
    2. la conversation soignée
    3. la conférence
    4. la récitation des vers

    Dans la conversation familière, on ne fait pas ou prèsque pas de liaisons facultatives: Des‿hommes/illustres/ont/attendu. Dans la conversation soignée, on en fait une petite proportion: Des‿hommes/illustres/ont‿attendu. Dans la conférence, on en fait la majorité: Des‿hommes‿illustres/ont‿attendu. Dans la récitation des vers, on les fait toutes: Des‿hommes‿illustres‿ont‿attendu." (Delattre (1951), *Principes de phonétique française*, Middlebury, Vermont, Middlebury College, pp. 26–27.)

28. The rule for final consonant deletion must, of course, be further extended to handle all other cases where in particular syntactic environments liaison is either not permitted or else optional. Since it is not the purpose of this study to investigate fully the cases of obligatory, optional, or non-permitted liaison, our examples serve rather to illustrate the way in which syntactic constraints on liaison would be handled within the framework of generative phonology. The problem of syntactic conditions within liaison is by no means a simple one. One has only to consult works such as Fouché or Grammont to realize the complexity of the situation. Furthermore, the mass of data presented is not always consistent from author to author. Not only is there an intricate array of phonological, morphological, and syntactic factors at play, but the problem is further complicated due to stylistic, dialectal, and euphonic considerations.

29. For cyclic rules in phonology, see Chomsky, "The Logical Basis of Linguistic Theory"; Chomsky and Miller (1963), "Introduction to the Formal Analysis of Natural Languages," *Handbook of Mathematical Psychology*, New York, Wiley; Chomsky and Halle, *The Sound Pattern of English*.

Notes to Chapter 2

1. The symmetric twelve-vowel system shown at the beginning of this chapter is the one set up by Hall (1948). We have placed schwa in parentheses as we do not agree with his classification of schwa as a low front rounded vowel. (See p. 30.) Togeby (1965) has these twelve oral vowels in his analysis; so do Jakobson and Lotz (1949). Trager (1944) has eleven as he does not recognize /œ/ as a phoneme. Grevisse (1964) recognizes twelve oral vowels in the phonology section of his grammar, and so do Delattre (1951), Fouché (1956), and Grammont (1961) in their handbooks for pronunciation.
2. "In describing French in general, it cannot be said that *près* differs from *prés* in the same way as *pris* differs from *prés*, although physically the three vowels are close to cardinal [i e ɛ], because *all* French speakers distinguish *prés* from *pris*, but millions identify *prés* and *près*." (Martinet (1962), *A Functional View of Language*, Oxford, Clarendon, p. 107.) "D'un point de vue purement phonétique la différence entre *i* et *e* français n'est pas plus grande que la différence entre *e* et *ɛ*. Mais malgré cela pour tout français l'intimité de la parenté entre *e* et *ɛ* est évidente, tandis qu'entre *i* et *e* il ne peut pas être question d'une intimité particulière: cela vient naturellement de ce que l'opposition *e–ɛ* est neutralisable, alors que l'opposition *i–e* est constante." (Troubetzkoy (1957), *Principes de Phonologie*, Paris, Klincksieck, p. 81.)
3. All French phoneticians recognize at least *two phonetic variants* for the mid vowels, regardless of whether they are in complementary distribution or in a contrastive environment. It is this gross level of phonetic distinguishability which is indicated in our phonetic transcriptions. In our analysis underlying representations are enclosed in vertical bars, whereas the derived phonetic representations are enclosed in diagonal bars. The latter convention has been used for traditional phonemic transcriptions. Therefore, although we also employ diagonal bars, our difference in usage should be kept in mind. Since we are not concerned with fine phonetic detail, we have settled for a broad phonetic transcription. Our phonetic transcription is practically identical to the traditional IPA representation for French, which is essentially the same as an orthoepic phonemic transcription.
4. "Le timbre de l'*a* est moins fixe que celui des autres voyelles fermes. 'C'est pour l'*a* que les divergences individuelles de prononciation ou les flottements sont les plus fréquents', dit M. Grammont. Dans ces conditions, toute classification des *a* en plusieurs timbres distincts est vouée à ne concorder qu'avec la prononciation de bien peu de gens. Il est préférable de considérer toutes ces variations comme les nuances acceptables d'une seule couleur, celle d'un *a* bien central. Cet *a* est acceptable dans tous les mots." (Delattre, *Principes de Phonétique Française*, p. 22.)

   Although, within modern French, there is only a single /a/ vowel which is of structural significance, it is nonetheless necessary to indicate in some way the stylistic occurrence of two phonetically distinguishable *a*-

type vowels (for those speakers who in fact have two different vowels). That is, some feature is required to differentiate "a antérieur" from "a postérieur." However, this feature would not be one of the binary phonological features (in the sense of Jakobsonian features) since it is these features which characterize the *relevant phonological oppositions* within a language. Since the "a antérieur: a postérieur" distinction is not a relevant phonological opposition within contemporary French, the particular feature utilized for this distinction would be drawn from a different set of features — perhaps from a set of affective, i.e., stylistic, features, features which Troubetzkoy referred to as *expressive*.

5. It is often noted that there is an exception to the observation that schwa does not occur as the stressed vowel of a word, namely in imperatives of the type *dites-le* /dit(ə) l'ə/ 'say so,' where the schwa of *le* bears stress. However, this particular example is not an instance of stress within the word (which we are discussing here) but is due to the position of *le* within the phrase.
6. We have restricted the body of data. To be sure, other alternations occur which we have not cited here. We shall consider some of these later in the chapter. This initial small set suffices to delimit the problem. For the present, we ignore the nasal "coloring" on some of the vowels. (For additional examples of alternations, see Nyrop (1903), *Grammaire historique de la langue francaise*, Vol. II, Copenhagen, E. Bojesen, pp. 18–24.)
7. As there is a single central /a/, the low mid vowels /ɛ/ and /ɔ/ have been relabeled as low vowels since they are now the lowest vowels in their respective series. This does not mean that *phonetically* /ɛ/ or /ɔ/ is as low as /a/. We shall show, however, that structurally /ɛ/ and /ɔ/ do function as low vowels and must be indicated as such in underlying representations. It is the structural properties of the vowel which we are characterizing by binary features.

   Our features "high," "low," "front," "round" correspond respectively to the Jakobsonian features "diffuse," "compact," "acute" (as opposed to "grave"), "flat." We have changed the terminology in order to facilitate presentation since terms such as "high," "low," etc., correlate more closely with familiar articulatory designations for vowels. Within the Jakobsonian framework the features diffuse, compact, grave, flat characterize consonants as well as vowels. Our corresponding terms, on the other hand, are uniquely used for classifying vowels. However, this should cause little difficulty since this study is almost exclusively restricted to the vowel system and vocalic alternations and it will rarely be necessary for us to designate consonants by complexes of features.

   For representing phonological segments in terms of binary features, see Jakobson, Fant, and Halle, *Preliminaries to Speech Analysis;* Halle (1957), "In Defense of the Number Two," *Studies Presented to J. Whatmough*, The Hague, Mouton, pp. 65–72; Halle (1959), *Sound Pattern of Russian*, The Hague, Mouton; Halle (1962), "Phonology in Generative Grammar," *Word*, XVIII, pp. 54–72. For a representation in distinctive features of the orthoepic twelve-vowel system of French, see Jakobson and Lotz, "Notes on the French Phonetic Pattern."

8. One can eliminate redundant features so as to obtain the minimal set of features needed to distinguish a segment from all other segments.

	i	e	ɛ	a	ɔ	o	u
high	+	−				−	+
low		−	+	+	+	−	
front	+	+	+	−	−	−	−
round				−	+		

   The redundant features are then introduced by the following rules:
   a. [+high] segments must be [−low], i.e., high vowels are nonlow.
   b. [+low] segments must be [−high], i.e., low vowels are nonhigh.
   c. [+front] segments must be [−round], i.e., front vowels are unrounded.
   d. $\begin{bmatrix} -\text{low} \\ -\text{front} \end{bmatrix}$ segments must be [+round], i.e., high and mid nonfront vowels are rounded.

   See Stanley, "Redundancy Rules in Phonology" (forthcoming) for a discussion of redundancy rules.

9. One can legitimately ask why the forms in Column I are taken as basic. Could one not consider the stressed vowels as the underlying ones and derive the unstressed counterparts from them? Actually, there is no *a priori* reason for preferring either set of forms as basic, since a more "abstract" representation is indeed required in many cases. The rationale behind our choice for an underlying vowel can be appreciated only after the entire vowel system has been exposed and the details of vowel fronting, schwa formation, vowel nasalization, and stress placement have been set forth.

10. In Rule *a* it is unnecessary to state that |a| is [−high] since one knows that if it is [+low] it must be [−high] (see redundancy rules, Note 8). One need only indicate the minimum subset of features which is sufficient to distinguish a vowel from all other vowels of the system. Unless stated otherwise, it will be assumed that all rules developed in this chapter apply only to segments which are vowels, i.e., which contain the feature specification [−cons, +voc].

11. Phonetically, /a/ occurs under stress, e.g., *car* /k'ar/ 'since.' We shall show (p. 34) that phonetically stressed /a/ has a different underlying origin from those phonetically stressed /ɛ/ which are derived from an underlying |a|. The same observation holds for phonetically stressed /ɔ/ and /e/, which are not the same as the |ɔ| and |e| discussed elsewhere in this section.

12. Halle ("Phonology in Generative Grammar") has suggested as an evaluation measure that the notation used for stating rules should reflect the complexity of the rules. Given the two rules, (1) all low vowels are fronted; (2) /a/ is fronted, the first rule is obviously more general. One

crucial motivation for distinctive features in phonological rules is that they provide a basis for evaluating relevant generalizations; fewer features are required to characterize the more general statement. Translating the above rules into feature notation: 1, [+low] segments become [+front]; 2, [+low, −front, −round] segments become [+front], one can readily see that the general statement has a simpler feature specification.

13. It appears that two different rules would be needed to account for diphthongization: one rule for |ɛ| → /jɛ/, the other for |e| → /wa/. To show the parallelism, i.e., glide insertion, of the two forms, we have stated the glide formation rule in such a way that the particular glide depends on the lowness feature of the stressed vowel. The justification for |e| → /we/, |ɛ| → /jɛ/, rather than the converse, will be found elsewhere in this chapter where we discuss families of related words and will be dealt with again in Chapter 3 where we consider the verbs. The choice is by no means arbitrary.

14. The rule for *wa*- adjustment could be eliminated if there were two separate diphthongization rules: |ɛ| → /jɛ/ and |e| → /wa/ (without the intermediate /we/ as presented here). However, the |e| → /we/ → /wa/ stages not only allow the generalization of the diphthongization rule (see Note 13) but become imperative for describing the nasalized counterpart of /wa/ which is /wɛ̃/. This point is discussed further in Section 2.2. Historically, /wa/ is derived from an earlier /we/ or /wɛ/. (Bourciez, *Précis de phonétique francaise*, pp. 55–56.) Canadian French, interestingly enough, has /we/ where standard French has /wa/.

    Not all occurrences of /wa/ in the contemporary language necessarily come from an underlying |e|. Alternations of the type *gloire* /glw'ar(ə)/ 'glory': *glorieux* /glɔrj'ø/ 'glorious'; victoire /viktw'ar(ə)/ 'victory': *victorieux*/viktɔrj'ø/ 'victorious'; *histoire* /istw'ar(ə)/ 'history': *historien* /istɔrj'ɛ̃/ 'historian' suggest that some /wa/ are to be derived from an |ɔ| followed by a consonant and a high front vowel or glide.

15. Historically, the derivational forms which interest us here are of Latin origin and represent the two sources of Latinisms in French. ". . . on distingue les suffixes *populaires*, c'est à dire ceux qui dans leur passage du latin au français ont subi tous les changements que leur imposaient certaines lois dites phonétiques, et les suffixes *savants* — ceux qui ont été pris au latin plus tard, et qui n'ont pas ressenti l'influence des lois phonétiques." (Thomav (1960), *Morphologie du français moderne*, Sophia, Science et Art, pp. 12–13.)

16. In Middle French alternations took place in first conjugation verbs, e.g., *je treuve*:*nous trouvons* 'find'; *je pleure*:*nous plourons* 'cry.' (Pope (1961), *From Latin to Modern French*, Manchester, Manchester University Press, p. 351.) In Modern French the first conjugation has been regularized. Some verbs have generalized the pretonic form (*je trouve* : *nous trouvons*), others the tonic form (*je pleure* : *nous pleurons*).

17. Just as the learned-nonlearned dichotomy may be a consequence of the particular affix with which the stem is combined, it may equally be the

case that those stems which do not undergo pretonic adjustment in derivation could also be recognized by their particular affixes.

18. The precise phonetic quality of "e muet" is one of the most disputed problems within French phonetics. "Les orthoépistes sont loin de tomber d'accord sur la façon dont on doit prononcer *e* caduc." (Martinet, *La prononciation du français contemporain*, p. 64.) Some phoneticians assign it to the front rounded series; others consider it a central vowel. There is the further problem of lip-rounding and the problem of vowel height: is it low, mid, or somewhere intermediate? The conflicting views are summed up by Martinet:

> "Ces différentes opinions se ramènent, en fait, aux possibilités suivantes: 1° *e* caduc se prononce comme [œ] ouvert (Grammont et, en partie, Gougenheim); 2° *e* caduc ne se confond pas tout à fait dans ses réalisations avec celles de l'archiphonème Œ, ceci, sans doute, du fait de l'absence d'arrondissement des lèvres dans le cas de *e*, le degré d'ouverture étant sensiblement le même que pour [œ] ouvert (Bruneau), ou un peu moins considérable (Martinon). Il existe une troisième possibilité que M. Gougenheim suggère pour l'*e* de *prends-le*, qui est la confusion avec [œ] fermé." (Martinet, *La prononciation du francais contemporain*, p. 65.)

Our description of schwa is similar to that of Bruneau. This characterization of schwa accords with Pleasants' study of "e muet." She concludes that "e muet" is a low central vowel which is generally unrounded: "Articulatoirement, *e* muet parait se distinguer des voyelles de la zone du type *eu* de la façon suivante: Il a son point d'articulation en arrière de celui de *eu* fermé et même de *eu* ouvert; la langue est moins élevée que pour *eu* ouvert et à plus forte raison que pour *eu* fermé; . . . Les caractéristiques de l'articulation de [ə] décrites ci-dessus sembleraient indiquer que [ə] *est une voyelle centrale* [my italics]. . . Si on ne remarque pas de mouvement lingual sensible vers l'antériorisation, on doit observer, par contre, une tendance dans le sens de la labialisation; en fait, chez nos sujets, cette tendance se manifeste par une moyenne de 25% à la tonique, de 11,5% à l'atone. . . . *E* muet est bien, la plupart du temps, la 'voyelle neutre du français.'" (Pleasants (1956), *Etudes sur l'e muet*, Paris, Klincksieck, pp. 247–248.)

Considering schwa in its historical perspective, one notes that phoneticians in the eighteenth century were basically in agreement in specifying schwa as a lax central unrounded vowel: ". . . pour beaucoup de grammariens du XVIIIe siècle . . . l'*e* muet est une voyelle neutre, faible et probablement non labiale." (Pleasants, *Etudes sur l'e muet*, p. 259.)

19. ". . . a tense vowel compared to its lax counterpart is produced with a greater deviation from the *neutral position* [my italics] of the vocal tract . . ." (Jakobson and Halle, "Tenseness and Laxness," p. 57.) Perceptually lax vowels are more obscure than corresponding tense vowels. Pleasants notes

the "muffled" quality of French schwa: "[E muet] paraît garder son timbre propre dont le caractère essential serait un léger assourdissement. Il est certain que, même en tonique, même quand il est long et spécialement intense, *e* muet ne produit sur l'oreille ni l'impression d'une voyelle *claire*, ni l'impression d'une voyelle *éclatante*." (Pleasants, *Etudes sur l'e muet*, p. 37.)

20. We claim that, for structural reasons, schwa must be classified as a lax low central unrounded vowel. We have then argued that this description of schwa is also phonetically correct. If the phonetic characterization of schwa is not that of a central unrounded vowel, this fact would in no way affect the structural basis for schwa which we have established. A phonetic rule would be required which would convert the lax low central unrounded vowel to its "precise" phonetic specification.

21. One might maintain that the rule for pretonic adjustment does not apply to initial vowels. Then an underlying |a| in initial pretonic position would not be affected by this rule and would remain unchanged, yielding the correct final vowel. However, the rule for pretonic adjustment also converts an underlying rounded vowel to /u/, which *does* occur in syllable initial position: e.g., *œuvre*, *ouvrage*. Allowing pretonic adjustment to apply to initial rounded vowels but not to initial unrounded vowels unduly complicates the rule and obscures the generality of the original statement. The generalization pertaining to *all* pretonic vowels can be maintained once it is recognized that the absence of initial /ə/ is a subsequent development.

22. We have shown that two types of |a| and |ɔ| vowels are needed in the underlying representations. Any *ad hoc* feature could suffice to differentiate these two types of vowels. However, we claim that the choice of a feature is by no means arbitrary, but rather that the tenseness feature, which will be utilized to characterize the distinction, is well motivated. I am indebted to Theodore Lightner, who first pointed out to me the necessity for justifying the feature "tense" at the abstract level of representation.

23. It is not the case that all underlying lax vowels yield phonetically lax vowels or even that all underlying tense vowels have a tense phonetic manifestation. Some of the underlying vowels require that their original tenseness or laxness be changed in the course of derivation. We shall show that very few derived vowels actually require switching of the underlying feature tense so that, for the majority of vowels, phonetic tenseness is *completely determined* by the tenseness of the underlying vowel.

24. James Foley (1965) has shown for Spanish that underlying tense and lax vowels are required and that only the latter are diphthongized. Mario Saltarelli (personal communication) has found that the tense-lax distinction is also needed for Italian and again it is the lax vowels which diphthongize. Underlying tense and lax vowels are probably required for the other Romance languages as well. There is, no doubt, a correlation between the long and short vowels of Latin and the tense and lax vowels of the daughter languages. Although this correlation is somewhat obscured for French, it is nonetheless discernible in the verb conjugation (Chapter 3).

25. ". . . [e] n'apparaît que dans une syllabe *phonétiquement ouverte* [my italics], [ɛ] aussi bien dans les syllabes fermées que dans les syllabes ouvertes, d'où un changement de voyelle dans différentes formes flexionnelles du verbe (*céder/cède*): un *e* féminin présuppose l'existence de [ɛ] à l'exclusion de [e] dans la syllabe précédente." (Togeby (1965), *Structure immanente de la langue francaise*, Paris, Larousse, pp. 58–59.) The derived front rounded vowel /ø/ undergoes the same phenomenon and is lowered to /œ/. The rule which effects these changes has been generalized to lower both mid front vowels (/e/ and /ø/).
26. "Si l'accent vient à tomber sur une syllabe dont la voyelle est -e- ou -ə-, suivie d'au moins une consonne tenace [une consonne qui, dans le mot considéré, ne disparaît pas, même hors liaison], cet -e- ou cet -ə- se change en -ɛ-." (de Félice (1950), *Eléments de grammaire morphologique*, Paris, Didier, p. 12.)
27. In learned derivations underlying |Ɛ| is raised to /e/ (e.g., *bien*, *bénir*). Only in nonlearned forms does underlying |Ɛ| become /ə/. This different treatment of |Ɛ| accounts for such phenomena as the distribution of the prefix *re-*, *ré*; compare *reclus* /rəkl'y/ 'recluse' with the derived *réclusion* /reklyzj'ɔ̃/ 'reclusion.' In pretonic position |Ɛ| is not converted to /ə/ if the following syllable contains a vowel which becomes schwa: e.g., *hôtel* /ot'ɛl/ 'hotel,' *hôtelier* /otəlj'e/ 'inn keeper,' but *hôtellerie* /otɛlər'i/ 'inn keeping'; *mène* /m'ɛn(ə)/ '(he) leads,' *menons* /mən'ɔ̃/ '(we) lead,' but *mènerons* /mɛnər'ɔ̃/ '(we) shall lead.' Similarly, |E| becomes /ɛ/ in the same environment: e.g., *cède* /s'ɛd(ə)/ '(he) cedes,' *cédons* /sed'ɔ̃/ '(we) cede,' but *céderons* /sɛdər'ɔ̃/ '(we) shall cede.' In pretonic position |Ɛ| is not converted to /e/ or /ə/ if a consonant cluster follows, e.g., *septembre* /sɛpt'ãbr(ə)/ 'September.' Occurrences of pretonic /ɛ/ before a single consonant (e.g., *aimons* /ɛm'ɔ̃/ '(we) love') are derived from a lax |a| which has undergone vowel fronting.
28. The rule for vowel fronting, in its most general form, converts all tense high vowels to front vowels. It therefore applies vacuously to |I| since this vowel is inherently front.
29. Historically, /y/ is derived from an earlier /u/ and /u/ from an earlier /o/, the changes occurring in this order. "*U* (late Latin and Germanic) palatalized to *y*. . . . The sound *u* thus disappeared for a while out of the francien sound system but was brought in again by the raising of *o* to *u*." (Pope, *From Latin to Modern French*, p. 90.) From a historical point of view an /o/ to /u/ conversion is completely justified. However, we believe that synchronic rules must be internally motivated and that their sole justification can not be the corresponding diachronic rules, although, to be sure, the latter certainly help to corroborate the validity of the former. In working out an analysis, it is unquestionably an advantage to know the historical developments of the langauge just as it is advantageous to have access to the standard orthography (for a written language) and to have information on related dialects and languages. To ignore completely historical developments in a language so extensively documented as French would be

foolish indeed. Knowing the history of the language allows one to formulate hypotheses concerning the nature of underlying forms and the types of phonological changes still operative in the contemporary language. The confirmation of these hypotheses must then be demonstrated uniquely within the synchronic description. Such internal synchronic justification is indispensable if linguistic descriptions are to have psycholinguistic import and are to characterize what speakers know about their language.

30. Historically, pretonic /u/ derived from /ɔ/ went through an intermediate /o/: "The strengthening of the stress on the tonic syllable in Gallo-Roman was accompanied by a lessening of the secondary stress sufficient to cause a modification of the pronunciation of the mid open vowels ɛ and ɔ; . . . ɔ *countertonic closing to o*. . . . In the course of Early Old French . . . *o* countertonic [was] further modified: *o* moved up to *u*, *in this syllable as elsewhere*." [My italics.] (Pope. *From Latin to Modern French*, p. 107.) Thus, the rule which raised /o/ to /u/ was applicable to pretonic /o/ ← /ɔ/ as well as to original /o/ and would have to apply after pretonic adjustment.

31. The rule for schwa conversion changes low lax vowels to schwa. We have shown that lax |ɛ| becomes schwa in pretonic position. Lax |ɔ| would become schwa also; however, in pretonic position earlier rules convert |ɔ| to /o/ and then /u/. Yet there are examples of pretonic schwa coming from underlying |ɔ| (cf. *enchanteur* /ãʃãt'œr/ 'enchanter,' *enchanteresse* /ãʃãtər'ɛs(ə)/ 'enchantress.' Both forms contain stem plus agentive suffix |ɔr|. The feminine in addition has the suffix |Ɛsa| (cf. *prince* /pr'ɛ̃s(ə)/ 'prince,' *princesse* /prɛ̃s'ɛs(ə)/ 'princess'). In the masculine *enchanteur* stress falls on the suffix |ɔr|; the vowel then undergoes fronting. For the feminine *enchanteresse* the stress is on the feminine suffix and the suffix |ɔr| is in pretonic position. However, this form is an exception to the rule for pretonic adjustment so that the pretonic vowel is not raised to /o/ and then to /u/. The form is also an exception to vowel fronting; the vowel is not shifted to /œ/. Therefore, pretonic |ɔ| remains as such. Since |ɔ| is a lax low vowel, the schwa conversion rule will subsequently take it to /ə/. The forms *valeureux* /valørø/ 'valorous' and *chaleureux* /ʃalørø/ 'warm' are exceptions to pretonic adjustment but unlike *enchanteresse* undergo fronting in pretonic position (cf. *pleurons*). Note, incidently, that in *docteur* /dɔkt'œr/ 'doctor' *doctoresse* /dɔktɔr'ɛs(ə)/ 'woman doctor' the feminine form is treated as a learned word; hence, the agentive |ɔr| does not undergo any vowel change.

32. The derivational endings |Abili|, |Ibili| are themselves variants of a single suffix. Jeanne Halgren has shown that, with very few exceptions, the vowel (|A| or |I|) can be predicted either from the phonological form of the stem or from the morphological class membership of the stem, particularly where the stem also occurs as a verb.

33. In learned derivation, when underlying lax low |ɛ| becomes tense, it is automatically raised to mid |E| (cf. *bien*, *bénir* with underlying stem |bɛn|). In nonlearned forms pretonic tense |Ɛ| yields schwa; e.g., *mène*, *menons*. Schwas do not generally occur in learned derivation.

34. *Preuve* /pr'œv(ə)/, phonetically, has a stressed low front rounded vowel. Underlying |prOva| becomes lax |o| which under stress is fronted: /pr'øvə/. The rule for closed syllable adjustment automatically lowers mid front vowels (cf. *cédons*, *cède* /sed'ɔ̃/, /s'ɛd(ə)/). (See Note 25.)
35. These features indicate the minimal set of binary oppositions needed for nasalized vowels and do not necessarily reflect fine phonetic detail: /ɛ̃/ is considered to be slightly more open than /ɛ/; for /ã/, the tongue is more retracted and the mouth more closed than for the central /a/; the articulatory position of /ɔ̃/ is between /ɔ/ and /o/, but nearer to the latter; while /œ̃/ is quite close to /œ/. (Delattre, *Principes de phonétique française*, p. 23.) These phonetic details would be indicated in a narrow phonetic transcription but are not relevant for defining the structural oppositions with which we are concerned.
36. These forms terminate in the so-called "e féminin." *Fine* is represented as |fIn+a#|, *brune* as |brUn+a#|, etc. (where |+a| is the morpheme which indicates feminine gender). Postulating final schwa is not only imperative in order to prevent nasalization, but final schwas are also necessary to account for the retention of final consonants in feminine adjectives (Chapter 1), as well as the retention of stem final consonants for present singular verb forms of the first conjugation (Chapter 3). Final schwas appear phonetically before "h aspiré" (e.g., *une honte* /ynə ɔ̃t(ə)/, Section 1.2.1). Finally, only by postulating underlying schwas can one explain stylistic and dialectal differences in the treatment of presence versus absence of "e muet" (Section 1.1.2).

    Nasalization takes place whenever the nasal consonant is followed by a word boundary. A more refined statement is actually required since this rule holds only when the nasal consonant is in phrase final (which includes utterance final) position, e.g., *C'est bon* /bɔ̃/ 'It's good,' but not always within the phrase if the next word begins with a vowel, e.g., *bon ami* /bɔn ami/ 'good friend.' In addition, there are forms (determiners, some adverbs, etc.) where the vowel is nasalized and the nasal consonant is also retained, e.g., *un ami* /œ̃nami/ 'a friend.' As we are considering words in isolation, the simplified rules which we have given will suffice.

    Historically, of course, nasalized vowels developed from oral vowels plus nasal consonant. *All* vowels were nasalized with subsequent denasalization in the case of a nasalized vowel followed by nasal consonant plus vowel.
37. Once there has been established the necessity for having underlying oral vowels plus nasal consonants instead of underlying nasalized vowels, a simpler description results if all nasalized vowels have as their origin vowel plus nasal consonant. Words such as *sombre* /sɔ̃brə/ 'dark,' *vendre* /vãdrə/ 'sell' must also contain in the underlying representation an oral vowel and nasal consonant, even though these forms do not exhibit vocalic alternation as do *fine*, *fin*. Suppose one were to postulate underlying nasalized vowels only for those words which do not exhibit alternation. Then nasalization would be a contrastive feature of vowels and it would be necessary to mark

every vowel (except those occurring before a nasal consonant) of every morpheme + or − nasalization, which would add a considerable number of features to the lexicon. The independently motivated rule for nasalization is required in any event and it costs nothing, i.e., the rule becomes no more complex, if the rule applies to all sequences of vowel plus nasal consonant so that all nasalized vowels are derived in the same way, whereas it can be shown that, by recognizing in underlying representations both nasalized vowels and oral vowel plus nasal consonant sequences, the grammar increases in complexity.

38. It was shown on p. 23 that an intermediate /we/ simplifies the formulation of the diphthongization rule: diphthongization is the insertion of a glide before a vowel: |e| → /we/, |ɛ| → /jɛ/. Diphthongization of underlying |e| and |ɛ| is therefore a parallel process.

39. Tense |O| underlies no derived nasalized vowel; that is, there are no alternations in French between /un/ and a nasalized vowel. Our rules predict, however, that, if such alternations existed, the nasalized vowel would be /ɔ̃/.

40. For southern speakers, /ɔ/ may actually occur before /z/, e.g., *chose* /ʃ'ɔz(ə)/; for eastern speakers, /ɔ/ may occur finally, e.g., *idiot* /idj'ɔ/. (Grammont, *Traité pratique de prononciation francaise*, p. 19.) Just as /ɔ/ becomes /o/ in word final position or before /z/, similarly /œ/ becomes /ø/ in the same environment. The rule applies then to all rounded vowels, i.e., it states that low rounded vowels do not occur in certain environments. The rule applies vacuously to /u/ and /y/ as they are [−low] vowels to begin with.

41. Phonetic evidence for a "plural" or "person" morpheme is found in the style of speech where liaison is made between plural noun and following adjective, or between finite verb and following word: *chevaux espagnols* /ʃəvoz ɛspaɲɔl/ 'Spanish horses,' *il faut être ici* /fot ɛtr/ 'you must be here.'

42. The conversion of |Al| to /o/ applies only to the nonlearned division of the lexicon. Learned derivational forms such as *altitude*, *falsifier* exhibit /al/ followed by a consonantal segment. The /al/:/o/ alternation provides another bit of evidence for the necessity of the learned-nonlearned dichotomy within French; the applicability or nonapplicability of numerous rules is contingent on this morphological distinction. The /o/ which comes from |Al| is represented by *au* in the standard orthography. Historically, the change was /al/ → /au/ → /o/. When we consider verbs, we shall see that synchronic evidence can be found for the intermediate /au/.

Just as |Al| becomes /o/ in nonlearned morphology, similarly |El| becomes /o/ and |Ɔl| becomes /u/, e.g., *belle* /b'ɛl(ə)/ 'beautiful (f),' *beau* /b'o/ 'beautiful (m),' *collier* /kɔlj'e/ 'necklace,' *cou* /k'u/ 'neck.' That is, underlying unrounded vowels plus |l| become /o/, whereas underlying rounded vowels plus |l| become /u/ (cf. *soûle* /s'ul (ə)/ 'drunk (f),' *soûl* /s'u/ 'drunk (m),' cited in Section 1.2.4).

43. Grammont notes that there is hesitation between pretonic /o/ and /ɔ/ for the words: *côté, côtelette, hôtel, hôtelier, hôpital, rôtir*. "Mais la tendance générale à ouvrir les *o* inaccentués triomphe de plus en plus . . .; la prononciation avec ɔ ouvert est plus fréquente et plus spontanée; ceux qui mettent dans ces mots un *o* fermé, bien que nombreux, sont visiblement influencés par l'accent circonflexe." (Grammont, *Traité pratique de prononciation française*, p. 22.)

Historically, of course, words such as *côte, hôte* did at one time have an *s*. The loss of *s* is generally indicated in the current orthography by means of a circumflex accent over the *o*, the accent mark serving also to indicate the long close vowel.

44. These words with either stressed /o/ or /ɔ/ belong to the Greek element of the lexicon, and there is strong phonological evidence — in addition to the /o/:/ɔ/ problem — for the third solution: that of having these forms constitute a special morphological class. For example, the prefix *pneum(at)o-* /pnøm(at)ɔ/ begins with a consonant sequence which violates the normal phonotactic constraints of French; the form also exhibits a mid front rounded vowel in pretonic position. Such forms must, therefore, constitute a special class of items which undergo certain phonological processes foreign to the majority of morphemes listed in the lexicon. Once the necessity for a special morphological class is recognized, the stressed /o/:/ɔ/ problem can be viewed in its proper perspective: a phenomenon peculiar to a specific subset of the lexicon.

45. Historically, forms like *maître, mâle, âme* had postvocalic consonants which were deleted. Pairs of the type *maître:magistrat*, 'master, magistrate'; *mâle:masculin*, 'male, masculine'; *âme:animer*, 'soul, animate' can be brought forth as marginal evidence for deleted underlying consonants (and vowels). It is dubious, however, whether in modern French such pairs should be derived from a common underlying stem. We have not done so as the required rules would be relatively complicated and *ad hoc;* they would not readily lend themselves to generalizations beyond these marginal forms.

46. In verbs the replacement of a high vowel by its corresponding glide is optional so that either /si'e/ or /sj'e/ *scier*, /ʒu'e/ or /ʒw'e/ *jouer*, /ty'e/ or /tɥ'e/ *tuer* may occur. If the high vowel is preceded by a consonant-liquid cluster, only the dissyllabic form occurs, e.g., *crier* /kri'e/ 'cry,' but not */krj'e/.

47. The conversion of |l| to /ʎ/ before a front vowel and the subsequent change of /ʎ/ to /j/ are attested historically. Prior to the seventeenth century postvocalic /ʎ/ occurred in words such as *fille*; /ʎ/ still appears in certain dialects: "Le mouillement de *l* . . . date de la période romane primitive. La réduction de ʎ à *j* . . . est au contraire d'origine toute moderne. On la rencontre d'abord, vers le milieu du XVIIe siècle . . . mais au Midi (sauf en Provence), on retrouve encore un peu partout ʎ mouillé, ainsi en Languedoc, en Gascogne, de même qu'à l'Ouest en Saintonge et à l'Est en Suisse." (Bourciez, *Précis de phonétique française*, p. 185.)

48. "Dans les mots français prononcés isolément et sans mouvement affectif, l'accent d'intensité frappe la dernière syllabe à voyelle prononcée." (Grevisse, *Le Bon Usage*, p. 54.)
49. Dans un plurisyllabe français, c'est toujours la dernière voyelle "ferme" qui est accentuée. Ainsi l'accent est sur l'*i* de *gentil*, sur l'*é* de *bonté*, sur l'*a* de *Montmartre*, sur l'o de *vignoble*, etc." (Fouché, *Traité de prononciation française*, p. L, Introduction.)
50. Derived segments may also be added by phonological rules (e.g., the insertion of schwa after consonant-liquid clusters) so that a derived segment need not correspond to any underlying segment. Thus, |t'Abl#| has final stress as an underlying form, although phonetically the stressed vowel is the penultimate one: /t'ablə/.

Notes to Chapter 3

1. Theoretically, there are 45 possible forms. However, certain verbs are *defective* and do not occur in particular tenses or persons. This defectiveness is a peculiarity of individual stems and one therefore has to note in the lexicon those persons or tenses for which the stem does not exhibit forms.

   Most verbs also have three imperative forms: second person singular and first and second persons plural. In almost all cases, these are identical to the corresponding present tense forms, except for *être* 'be,' *avoir* 'have,' *savoir* 'know,' and *vouloir* 'want' where the stems are those of the present subjunctive: *sois*, *aie*, *sache*, *veuille*. Therefore, we shall omit the imperatives from the analysis since they do not demonstrate characteristics not found elsewhere in the paradigm. Also, we shall not be concerned with the compound tenses (auxiliary *avoir* or *être* plus past participle) as the component parts can be described in terms of the simple tenses and nonfinite forms.
2. The term *aspect* is not intended to imply any particular syntactic or semantic analysis of the French verb system. It is used here simply as a convenient cover term for a group of morphologically related tenses. *Tense*, on the other hand, has its traditional signification. This terminology permits us to distinguish, for example, between future forms, i.e., future tense: *dormiras*, and future-like forms, i.e., future aspect: *dormiras*, *dormirais*, *dormir*.
3. Verbs like *partir* are sometimes included in the third conjugation, the reason generally being that these *-ir* types are not productive (Grevisse, Grammaire Larousse). The third conjugation, then, becomes a pot-pourri of various subtypes; all the "irregular" verbs are included here. In Bloomfield's analysis (1945) there is one "regular" conjugation, i.e., the first. All other verbs are considered "irregular"; these include about a dozen classes plus some odd stems which do not conveniently fit into any class. Trager (1944) has three conjugations with two subclasses in the second and third. Thus, our classification is the same as his. Hall (1948) also has three conjugations: the first is, of course, composed of verbs with infinitives in *-er*; the second conjugation includes forms with an infinitive in *-ir* but

not those which insert *-iss*; the third conjugation contains everything else. Within each of these major divisions there is also an intricate system of minor groupings based on cross classification in order to account for the similarities in different conjugations. De Félice (1950) classifies the verbs according to two criteria: (1) the past participle ending; (2) whether or not the past participle has the same number of syllables as the stem. He has a total of nine groups, some of these in turn having subclasses. He is unable to show any interrelation among the groups and is forced to repeat similar statements in his rules.

4. The suppletive stems of a morpheme and the tenses where they occur must be noted in the lexicon since no general phonological rules exist for deriving the morphological alternants from a common underlying stem. Thus, given the present singular *vas* /v'a/ '(you) go' and the plural *allez* /al'e/ '(you) go,' short of a completely *ad hoc* formulation, there is no general phonological rule for deriving the stem alternant |vA| from an underlying |Al|. Note that an *ad hoc* rule, such as |Al| becomes |vA| in the present when stressed, is equivalent to listing in the lexicon the stem alternants and their distribution.

5. It is immaterial whether the final consonant segments for the first and second person markers are represented by |s| or |z| since liaison continuants are always voiced. Therefore, we shall represent this segment by |S|, an archiphoneme (|S| has only the features which |s| and |z| share); hence, it is not marked for voicing. Recall that nasalized vowels are derived from an oral vowel plus nasal consonant (Section 2.2). For the first person plural marker we represent the nasal consonant as an archiphoneme since it is not relevant at this point whether it is actually |m| or |n|. Also, the vowel of the first plural marker may be either |Ɔ| or |O| as nasalized vowels are always lowered. The lax |a| of the third plural marker is, of course, equivalent to schwa.

   Note that in the underlying representations we have represented the stem *dorm-* with a lax vowel: |dɔrm|. When stressed, a lax vowel is normally fronted. However, in morphemes such as *dorm-* it is really immaterial whether the underlying vowel is tense or lax since, within a morpheme, vowel fronting takes place only when the vowel is followed by, at most, a single consonantal segment. Words such as *meuble* /m'œbl(ə)/ 'piece of furniture,' which appear to have a fronted vowel preceding two consonants actually do not contain two contiguous consonantal segments in the underlying form: |mɔbili| (cf. *mobilier* /mɔbilj'e/ 'furniture').

6. The singular person marker is not deleted in interrogative and imperative forms when a pronoun follows the verb, e.g., *arrive-t-il* /ariv(ə)t'il/ 'does he arrive,' *arrives-en* /ariv(ə)z'ã/ 'arrive from there.' The retention of the person marker is due to a syntactic constraint: the verb group (verb and preceding or following pronouns) constitutes a close-knit syntactic construct with special phonological properties. (S. A. Schane, "La Phonologie du Groupe Verbal Français.")

7. In the first conjugation the stem final consonant is retained throughout both the present tense and the subjunctive. Therefore, for first conjugation verbs, the singulars and the third plural of the present are homophonous with the corresponding forms of the subjunctive: *j'arrive, tu arrives, il arrive, ils arrivent.* In the second conjugation only the third plural forms are homophonous: *ils dorment.*
8. Whenever the present participle functions as an adjective, it agrees with the noun which it modifies, and accordingly the morpheme or morphemes which indicate feminine gender and/or plural number are attached to the present participle morpheme.
9. Condition (1) could be dispensed with if |i| were set up as the underlying first singular marker and were converted to |S| everywhere except after |A|. However, we shall show (p. 94) that, if we are to account for first conjugation preterites (e.g., *arrivai*), the underlying marker has to be |S|, which is converted subsequently to |i|.
10. We will consider the change of |Ai| to /e/ and of |Au| to /o/ as being a raising and concomitant fronting or rounding of tense |A| with simultaneous deletion of the lax vowel. The rules for e-conversion and o-conversion can be replaced by a single alpha rule:

$$\begin{bmatrix} +\text{tense} \\ -\text{front} \\ -\text{round} \end{bmatrix} \begin{bmatrix} -\text{tense} \\ +\text{high} \\ \alpha\,\text{front} \end{bmatrix} \text{ becomes } \begin{bmatrix} -\text{low} \\ \alpha\,\text{front} \\ -\alpha\,\text{round} \end{bmatrix} \text{ null}$$

where null indicates that the second segment on the left has been deleted.

11. The change of a continuant consonant to a lax high vowel (or glide) appears to have taken place in Italian: Latin *vadis*, French *vas*, Spanish *vas*, Italian *vai;* Latin *nos*, French *nous*, Spanish *nos*, Italian *noi.* (Meyer-Lübke (1890), *Grammaire des langues romanes, Tome I: Phonétique*, Paris, H. Wetter, pp. 495–496; Elcock (1960) *The Romance Languages*, New York, Macmillan, p. 52.) For Diegueño, a Yuman language, Margaret Langdon has found cases of word final *s, z,* and *j* occurring in free variation. (*A Grammar of Diegueño* (1966), Doctoral Dissertation, University of California, Berkeley, p. 49.)
12. Historically, the future and conditional were originally periphrastic tenses based on the infinitive plus the auxiliary verb *avoir*, e.g., *arriver + ai, dormir + as, vendr + a,* with absence of *av-* in the dissyllabic forms of the auxiliary, e.g., *finir + ez, finir + ait.* (Elcock, *The Romance Languages*, pp. 106–107.)
13. The preterite (as well as the past subjunctive) does not generally occur in spoken French, except in certain oratorical styles or in the recitation of text. However, since the forms can be spoken, they ought to be included in the morphological description. Furthermore, the phonological processes exhibited in the preterite and past subjunctive provide additional evidence and motivation for particular phonological rules.
14. As we have not investigated the conditions under which rhotacism takes place, we are not able to give a general rule which will account for both

preterite rhotacism and other instances of rhotacism. Rhotacism is not a widespread phenomenon in modern French and is probably restricted to a limited number of morphemes.

15. Historically, *-oms* and *-ets* were both stages in the development of the first and second plural endings. (Brunot (1887), *Précis de grammaire historique de la langue française*, Paris, Masson, p. 80; Grevisse, *Le bon usage*, p. 572.)
16. *Sept* is an exception to final consonant deletion but not to prefinal consonant deletion. On the other hand, if a form is an exception to prefinal consonant deletion, one can predict that it is also an exception to final consonant deletion — that is, if the prefinal consonant is retained then so is the final one, e.g., *exact* /ɛgz'akt/ 'exact.'
17. The anomalous third singular is due to the absence of the subjunctive marker |ɛ| after the past subjunctive marker |ss|. One could alternatively postulate both markers and then have a special rule which would delete |ɛ| in the environment + ss + ____ + t#. However, this rule is just another way of stating that |ɛ| does not occur in the third singular of the past subjunctive. Furthermore, this rule would not yield correct results without extensive modification since |ss| is also the infix morpheme of certain second conjugation verbs where the |ɛ| of the present subjunctive is retained in the above environment, e.g., *il finisse* |fIn + I + ss + ɛ + t#| 'he finishes.'
18. Since *arriva* and *arrivât* are literary forms, the presence or absence of a linking consonant may well be an artificial device based on spelling. If, in fact, the final *t* of *arrivât* does not enter in liaison we can account for its absence by adopting a different rule order. The rule for singular person deletion would apply after (instead of before) the rule for prefinal consonant deletion.
19. Alternatively, we could say that the thematic vowel in its underlying form is always tense and that, prior to the application of the stress rule, the thematic vowel becomes lax before another vowel or before a single true consonant, the environments where the thematic vowel occurs in the unmarked aspect: |ArIv + A + unt#| → |ArIv + a + unt#| → |Ar'Iv + a + unt#| *arrivent*; |ArIv + A + t#| → |ArIv + a + t#| → |Ar'Iv + a + t#| *arrive.*
20. The stems which undergo high vowel raising have to be so indicated in the lexicon since there is no way to predict consistently this phenomenon simply by examining the phonological segments of the stem. In actuality, very few stems will have to be marked for high vowel raising. This phenomenon affects only third conjugation (*-re* and *-oir*) verbs. Therefore, first and second conjugation stems will be automatically excluded from high vowel raising. Within the third conjugation of *-re* verbs many stems terminate in a nasal consonant plus stop (e.g., *vendre* 'sell') and these stems never undergo vowel raising either. We are left then with those *-re* verbs, the stems of which generally terminate in a single consonant (about 25 verbs) and it is this group in which some of the forms show a raised stem vowel. The members of the group must accordingly be marked as to

whether or not their stem vowels are raised and, if so, whether the vowel is front or back. The *-oir* verbs also show high vowel raising. Within this group, however, we can predict that, if the stem ends in |v| (e.g., *sav-* 'know,' *pouv-* 'be able'), the form has a raised vowel and that this vowel is always /y/.

21. There is one strong past participle which terminates in a sibilant not preceded by /i/: *clos, close* /kl'o(z)/, /kl'o:z(ə)/ 'closed,' and one with vowel /i/ not followed by a sibilant: *fui(e)* /fɥ'i/ 'fled.' These forms are irregular in that the bare stem (cf. *ils closent, ils fuient*) — without any suffix added — functions as the past participle.
22. The assibilation rule has to be further constrained so as to exclude assibilation in forms such as *sympathie* /sɛ̃pat'i/ 'sympathy,' *idiotique* /idjɔt'ik(ə)/ 'idiotic.' As we have not thoroughly investigated consonant alternation, we shall not go into details here. What we wish to show here is that, since there are alternations in French between /t/ and /s/, some rule (with appropriate restrictions) will unquestionably be needed to account for such alternations and it seems likely that the appearance of a sibilant in past participles could also be handled by the same rule.
23. The deletion of a consonant before lax |u| accounts for irregular forms such as *ont* /'ɔ̃(t)/, the third plural present of *avoir* 'have.' The underlying representation for *ont* is |Av+unt#|. The stem final consonant is deleted before the lax |u| of the third plural ending: |'A+unt#|. Then |A+u| become /o/ (Section 3.4.11).
24. *-to* from Latin *-tu(m)* or *-tu(s)* occurs as the past participle ending in Italian: *amato* 'loved'; in Spanish *to* → *do* through lenition: *amado*. Historically, the past participle ending in French was also *-to*. The *t*, as in Spanish, underwent lenition; the posttonic nonlow vowel was deleted with subsequent deletion of the lenited consonant. (Luquiens (1909), *An Introduction to Old French Phonology and Morphology*, New Haven, Conn., Yale University Press, p. 105.)
25. The Bescherelle (1959) lists about 80 "irregular" verbs. An "irregular" verb is one which cannot be conjugated on the models of the three regular conjugations. In this section we do not intend to treat every "irregular" verb of French. We are primarily interested in those verbs where the irregularities give information regarding the underlying phonological system and we shall examine in particular those instances where the rules which were originally formulated for problems encountered elsewhere in the phonology serve to explain an "irregular" form. For irregular forms one would need to note in the lexicon which persons or tenses are irregular. If a complete tense or group of tenses is irregular in the same way, one would then note this generalization and there would be no need to indicate separately that every person of the tense was irregular. Note that the vowel shifts (apophony) are not irregularities. These vowel shifts are a consequence of the tense-lax distinction established in 2.1.2.
26. In the past aspect *écrire* has weak forms for the finite tenses: *écrivis, écrivisses* (cf. *perdis, perdisses*); it is only the past participle *écrit* which is

strong. *Vivre*, on the other hand, has only weak forms throughout the past aspect: *vécus*, *vécusses*, *vécu*. In these forms a suppletive stem is found and the thematic vowel has been raised to /y/ everywhere.

27. One does not need to state that |EkrIv| has no thematic vowel throughout the future, conditional, and infinitive. Since a general statement is preferred, one need only state that |EkrIv| has no thematic vowel when the following tense marker begins with a [+cons, +voc] segment. Hence, the environments in which a thematic vowel does not appear can often be phonologically defined.

28. There are two types of phonological rules: (1) those which apply at only one point in a derivation (or within a given cycle) and (2) those, like the schwa insertion rule, which must apply at any point in the derivation provided, of course, that the appropriate environmental conditions are met. The first type actually exhibits ordering only with respect to blocs of rules. Thus, there may be rules A, B, C, such that the order ABC or BAC produces the same results; that is, whereas it can be demonstrated that A and B taken together must precede C, there is no evidence for ordering A and B relative to each other. Rules of the second type are ordered neither with respect to each other nor with respect to the blocs of ordered rules.

29. The /j/ which appears in forms such as *croyez* /krwaj'e(z)/ '(you) believe' is not an inherent part of the stem but is a predictable transitional glide inserted between vowels.

30. *Mettre* 'put' appears to be an exception since it is a third conjugation verb where the stem phonetically terminates in a single stop: e.g., *mettons* /mɛt'ɔ̃(z)/ '(we) put.' However, if *mettons* has a single |t| in its underlying form, it is difficult to account for the stem vowel /ɛ/ since, before single consonants, /e/ or /ə/—instead of /ɛ/—is the usual vowel. However, if the stem *mett-* terminates in a geminate, the /ɛ/ can be explained since the vowel is found before a consonant cluster; but then *mettre* is no longer an exception to the nonoccurrence in the third conjugation of a stem terminating in a vowel plus single stop. The nonoccurrence of single stops in the third conjugation is probably in some way tied up with the nonoccurrence of /t/ in most past participle forms.

31. *Mort*, the past participle of *mourir*, like *écrit*, *fait*, has no thematic vowel. In addition, the underlying stem vowel has been made tense: |mɔr+to#| → |mƆr+to#|. The tense vowel will not undergo vowel fronting (cf. the third singular present *meurt* /m'œr(t)/ derived from |mɔr+t#|).

32. The past participle of *prendre*, like the other past aspect forms, has a raised stem vowel: *pris*/pr'i(z)/. *Venir*, on the other hand, has a weak past participle: *venu* /vən'y/ (cf. *voulu* /vul'y/ 'wanted').

33. *Redites* '(you) say again' also occurs without the thematic vowel, although other compounds with *dire* retain the thematic vowel: *vous contredisez* 'you contradict,' *vous médisez* 'you slander,' etc. Children often can be heard to say *disez* and *faisez*, thus regularizing the forms. The "regularized" forms also occur in substandard speech. (Bauche (1951), *Le langage populaire*, Paris, Payot, pp. 114–115.)

34. Another irregular feature of the third plural present *font* is the tense |A| of the stem vowel: |fAz + unt#|. Note that the vowel must be tense if it is to combine with |u| after the stem final consonant has been deleted. However, elsewhere in the paradigm, the stem must be |faz| — with a lax vowel — since the vowel is fronted to /ɛ/ when stressed, but remains as schwa in pretonic position, e.g., *fais* /f'ɛ(z)/, *faisons* /fəz'ɔ̃(z)/.

Bibliography

Included herein are the references cited in the text as well as some additional works pertaining to French phonology and morphology.

Armstrong, L. F. (1959), *The Phonetics of French*, London, G. Bell.

Ayer, C. (1885), *Grammaire comparée de la langue française*, 4th ed., Geneva, Georg.

Bauche, H. (1951), *Le langage populaire*, Paris, Payot.

Bescherelle (1959), *L'art de conjuguer: Dictionnaire des 8000 verbes usuels*, Paris, Hatier.

Bloomfield, L. (1933), *Language*, New York, Holt.

——— (1945), "On Describing Inflection," Festschrift für M. Blakemore Evans, *Monatshefte für deutschen Unterricht*, XXXVII: Nos. 4–5, pp. 8–13, Madison, Wisconsin, University of Wisconsin Press.

Bourciez, E. (1958), *Précis de phonétique française*, 9th ed., Paris, Klincksieck.

Brunot, F. (1887), *Précis de grammaire historique de la langue française*, Paris, Masson.

Chomsky, N. (1962), "The Logical Basis of Linguistic Theory," *Proceedings of the IX International Congress of Linguists*, The Hague, Mouton; a later version, "Current Issues in Linguistic Theory," appears in *The Structure of Language: Readings in the Philosophy of Language*, ed. Fodor and Katz, Englewood Cliffs, N.J., Prentice-Hall, 1964.

——— (1965), *Aspects of the Theory of Syntax*, Cambridge, Mass., M.I.T. Press.

Chomsky, N., and M. Halle (forthcoming), *Sound Pattern of English*, New York, Harper & Row.

Chomsky, N., and G. A. Miller (1963), "Introduction to the Formal Analysis of Natural Languages," *Handbook of Mathematical Psychology*, ed. Luce, Bush, and Galanter, New York, Wiley.

Clédat, L. (1912), *Dictionnaire étymologique de la langue française*, Paris, Hachette.

Delattre, P. (1951), *Principes de phonétique française*, 2nd ed., Middlebury, Vermont, Middlebury College.

de Félice, Th. (1950), *Eléments de grammaire morphologique*, Paris, Didier.

Dubois, J. (1965), *Grammaire structurale du français*, Paris, Larousse.

——— (1965), "Grammaire transformationnelle et morphologie: structure des bases verbales," *Français Moderne*, No. 2, pp. 81–96; 178–187.

——— (1966), "Essai d'analyse distributionnelle du verbe: les paradigmes de conjugaison," *Français Moderne*, No. 3, pp. 185–209.

Elcock, W. D. (1960), *The Romance Languages*, New York, Macmillan.

Foley, J. (1965), *Spanish Morphology*, M.I.T. Ph.D. thesis, Cambridge, Mass.

Fouché, P. (1956), *Traité de prononciation française*, Paris, Klincksieck.

Grammaire Larousse du XXe siècle (1936), Paris, Larousse.

Grammont, M. (1960), *Traité de phonétique*, 6th ed., Paris, Delagrave.

——— (1961), *Traité pratique de prononciation française*, Paris, Delagrave.

——— (1962), *Petit traité de versification française*, 19th ed., Paris, Colin.

Grevisse, M. (1964), *Le bon usage*, 8th ed., Gembloux, Duculot.

Haden, E. F. (1956), "Mute e in French," *Lingua* XIII, pp. 166–176.

Hall, R. A., Jr. (1948), "French," Language Monograph No. 24, Structural Sketches 1, *Language* XXIV: 3.

Halle, M. (1957), "In Defense of the Number Two," *Studies Presented to J. Whatmough*, The Hague, Mouton, pp. 65–72.

——— (1959), *Sound Pattern of Russian*, The Hague, Mouton.

——— (1961), "On the Role of Simplicity in Linguistic Descriptions," Structure of Language and its Mathematical Aspects, *Proceedings of Symposia in Applied Mathematics*, Vol. XII, Providence, R.I., Mathematical Society of America, pp. 89–94.

——— (1962), "Phonology in Generative Grammar," *Word*, XVIII: 1–2, pp. 54–72; reprinted in *The Structure of Language: Readings in the Philosophy Language*, ed. Fodor and Katz, Englewood Cliffs, N.J., Prentice-Hall, 1964.

——— (1962), "A Descriptive Convention for Treating Assimilation and Dissimilation," *Quarterly Progress Report*, No. 66, M.I.T., pp. 295–296.

Harris, Z. S. (1960), *Structural Linguistics*, Chicago, University of Chicago Press.

Jakobson, R., C. G. M. Fant, and M. Halle (1961), *Preliminaries to Speech Analysis*, Cambridge, Mass., M.I.T. Press.

Jakobson, R., and M. Halle (1956), *Fundamentals of Language, I: Phonology and Phonetics*, The Hague, Mouton.

——— (1965), "Tenseness and Laxness," in *Preliminaries to Speech Analysis*, 6th printing, R. Jakobson, C. G. M. Fant, and M. Halle, Cambridge, Mass., M.I.T. Press, 1965, pp. 57–61.

Jakobson, R., and J. Lotz (1949), "Notes on the French Phonetic Pattern," *Word* V, pp. 151–158; reprinted in *Selected Writings, I: Phonological Studies*, R. Jakobson, The Hague, Mouton, 1962, pp. 426–434.

Juilland, A. (1965), *Dictionnaire inverse de la langue française*, The Hague, Mouton.

Klein, H. W. (1963), *Praktische Phonetik und Phonologie des heutigen Französich*, Munich, M. Hueber.

Körting, G. (1893), *Formenlehre der französischen Sprache, I: Der Formenbau des französichen Verbums in seiner geschichtlichen Entwicklung*, Paderborn, F. Schöningh.

Lebrun, L. and J. Toisoul (1937), *Dictionnaire étymologique de la langue française basé sur le groupement des mots en tableaux synoptiques*, Paris, Nathan.

Livet, Ch. L. (1859), *La grammaire française et les grammariens du XVI*[e] *siècle*, Paris, Didier.

Luquiens, F. B. (1909), *Introduction to Old French Phonology and Morphology*. New Haven, Conn., Yale University Press.

Marchand, H. (1951), "Esquisse d'une description des principales alternances dérivatives dans le français d'aujourd'hui," *Studia Linguistica*, V, 2, pp. 95–112.

Marouzeau, J. (1957), *Du latin au français*, Paris, Société d'édition Les Belles Lettres.

Martinet, A. (1945). *La prononciation du français contemporain*, Paris, E. Droz.

——— (1958), "De l'économie des formes du verbe en français parlé," *Studia Philologica et Litteraria in Honorem L. Spitzer*, ed. Hatcher, Berne, Francke, pp. 309–326.

——— (1962), *A Functional View of Language*, Oxford, Clarendon.

Meyer-Lübke, W. (1890), *Grammaire des langues romanes, I: Phonétique*, Paris, H. Welter.

Millet, A. (1933), *Les grammariens et la phonétique*, Paris, J. Monier.

Nyrop, Kr. (1903), *Grammaire historique de la langue française*, Vol. I, II, Copenhagen, E. Bojesen.

Pleasants, J. V. (1956), *Etudes sur l'e muet*, Paris, Klincksieck.

Pope, M. K. (1961), *From Latin to Modern French*, Manchester, Manchester University Press.

Postal, P. (forthcoming), *Aspects of Phonological Theory*, New York, Harper & Row.

Pulgram, E. (1961), "French /ə/: Statics and Dynamics of Linguistic Subcodes," *Lingua* X, pp. 305–325.

——— (1965), "Prosodic Systems: French," *Lingua* XIII, pp. 125–144.

Schane, S. A. "La phonologie du groupe verbal français ," *Langages*, VII.

Sholes, G. N. (1958), *Transformations in French Grammar*, Indiana University doctoral thesis, Bloomington, Ind.

Stanley, R. (forthcoming), "Redundancy Rules in Phonology," *Language*.

Thomav, Th. (1960). *Morphologie du français moderne*, Sophia, Science et Art.

Togeby, K. (1965), *Structure immanente de la langue française*, Paris, Larousse.

Trager, G. L. (1944), "The Verb Morphology of Spoken French," *Language* XX: 3, pp. 131–141.

Troubetzkoy, N. S. (1957), *Principes de phonologie*, Paris, Klincksieck.

List of Rules

Included herein is an alphabetic listing of most of the rules developed in the text; not included are special rules which apply to only a few items (for example, some of the rules for irregular verbs). More than one page entry for a rule signifies that the original formulation of the rule (first entry) has undergone modification (subsequent entries).

Index